Create Rapid Web Applications Using Oracle Application Express

(Second Edition)

A hands-on resource for those passionate to rapidly develop data-centric web applications for desktop and mobile platforms.

RIAZ AHMED

Create Rapid Web Applications Using Oracle Application Express

Second Edition

Copyright © 2013 Riaz Ahmed

All rights reserved.

ISBN-13: 978-1-492-31418-9
ISBN-10: 1492314188

No part of this publication may be reproduced, stored in a retrieval system or transmitted in any form or by any means, electronic, mechanical, photocopying, recording, scanning or otherwise, except as permitted under Sections 107 or 108 of the 1976 United States Copyright Act, without the prior written permission of the Author.

Limit of Liability/Disclaimer of Warranty: The author make no representations or warranties with respect to the accuracy or completeness of the contents of this work and specifically disclaim all warranties, including without limitation warranties of fitness for a particular purpose. No warranty may be created or extended by sales or promotional materials. The advice and strategies contained herein may not be suitable for every situation. This work is sold with the understanding that the author is not engaged in rendering legal, accounting, or other professional services. If professional assistance is required, the services of a competent professional person should be sought. The author shall not be liable for damages arising here from. The fact that an organization or Web site is referred to in this work as a citation and/or a potential source of further information does not mean that the author endorses the information the organization or Web site may provide or recommendations it may make. Further, readers should be aware that Internet Web sites listed in this work may have changed or disappeared between when this work was written and when it is read.

Trademarks: Oracle is a registered trademark of Oracle Corporation. All other trademarks are the property of their respective owners. The author is not associated with any product or vendor mentioned in this book.

DEDICATION

To Saad, Sameer, Sarim and my beloved TR.
I am fortunate to be surrounded by such beautiful people.

TABLE OF CONTENTS

1. Develop Applications for Desktop & Smartphone Platforms
   What are you going to create? 2
   Understanding the Application 3
   The Home Page 4
   Manage Customers 6
   Setup Products 8
   Place Orders 10
   Generate Graphical Reports 12
   Advanced Reporting 13
   Users Management 14
   Mobile Application 15
   Summary 20

2. Introduction to Oracle Application Express
   What is APEX? 22
   Migrating to APEX 24
   Application Express Engine 25
   Application Express Environments 25
   Browser Requirements 25
   APEX Application Types 26
   What is a Page? 27
   Global Page 28
   Tree and Component Views 28
   The Page Definition 28
   Understanding Applications and Processes 29
   How the Application Express Engine Renders and Processes Pages 29
   Page Rendering 29
   Page Processing 32
   Shared Components 33
   Reports in APEX 37
   APEX URL Syntax 40
   Session State Management 43
   Referencing Strings 48
   Database Application Components and Controls 49
   Controlling Access 52
   Incorporating JavaScript 52
   Declarative Support for Building Mobile Web Applications 52
   Sending E-mail from an Application 52
   Finding Objects 53
   Packaged Applications 53
   Oracle Application Express Architecture 54

Supported Databases 57
APEX Development Environment 58
Application Deployment 59
What you need to develop the Sales Web Application? 59
Download and Install Oracle XE Database 60
Upgrade APEX 61
Create Workspace for Application 62
Start Building the Application 63
The Underlying Database Objects 68
Add Database Functions 68
Create DEMO_USERS Table 70
Summary 72

3. Construct The Building Blocks

The Shared Components 74
Tabs 75
Lists 77
Breadcrumbs 81
Navigation Bar Entries 81
Authentication Schemes 82
Authorization Schemes 84
List of Values (LOV) 87
Plug-Ins 90
Images 91
Summary 92

4. The Home Page

About the Application Home Page 94
Modify the Home Page 95
Create Regions 96
    This Month's Sales 96
    Sales by Product 98
    Sales by Category 99
    Top Customers 100
    Top Products 102
    Top Orders by Date 104
Create Buttons 106
    View Orders for this Month 106
    View Customers 107
    Add Customer 108
    View Products 109
    Add Product 109
    View Orders 110
    Add Order 110
Create Hidden Item 111
Test Your Work 112
Summary 112

5. Manage Customers
Customers' Management   114
Create Pages to Manage Customers   115
Modify Customers Main Page   118
Modify Customer Details Page   120
    Create Region - Orders for this Customer   121
    Modify Item Attributes   124
    Change Item Type and Attach LOV   125
    Apply Input Mask to Items   126
    Create a Hidden Item   126
    Create Validation - Check Customer Credit Limit   127
    Create Validation - Can't Delete Customer with Orders   127
    Create Branch   128
Test Your Work   129
Summary   130

6. Products Setup
About Products Setup   132
Create Pages for Products Setup   134
Modify Products Main Page   136
    Create Region - Top 5 Products   141
Modify Product Details Page   143
    Create Region - Product Image   144
    Create Button - Remove Image   145
    Modify Item Attributes   146
    Create a Hidden Item   147
    Create Process - Delete Image   149
    Create Branch   149
Test Your Work   150
Summary   152

7. Manage Orders
About Orders Management   154
Create Order Master/Detail Pages   156
Modify Orders Master Page   158
    Delete and Re-create Region   158
    Modify Interactive Report   159
    Create Alternative Report   160
        Report View   160
        Chart View   163
        Group By View   164
    Create Public Report   165
        Report View   165
        Chart View   166
        Group By View   167
    Create Branch   170
    Understand the Branching Process   171
Modify Order Details Page   172
    Create/Modify Items   175
    Create Process - Add Rows   177

Test Your Work   177
How Tabular Forms Work   178
Create Page - Enter New Order   180
    Create Process - Create or Truncate Order Collection   186
    Create Dynamic Action - Hide/Show Customers   186
    Modify and Create Validations   187
    Test Your Work   189
Create Page - Select Items   190
    Cascading Style Sheets   191
    What is PL/SQL?   194
    Using HTML in PL/SQL Code   198
    Cursor FOR LOOP   200
    PL/SQL Code Explanation   201
    Create Process - Add Product to the Order Collection   214
    Create Process - Remove Product from the Order Collection   215
    Create Process - Place Order   216
    Create Branches   218
    Test Your Work   218
Create Product Info Page   219
Create Order Summary Page   223
Complete Testing   226
Summary   228

8. Graphical Reports
Oracle APEX Reports   230
Create a Global Page   231
Customer Orders Report   232
Sales by Category and Product Report   236
Sales by Category/Month Report   240
Order Calendar Report   242
Customer Map Report   245
Product Order Tree   248
Summary   254

9. Advanced Reporting
About Advanced Reporting   256
Install BI Publisher   258
Configure APEX to use BI Publisher as a Print Server   259
Enable Network Services in Oracle Database   259
Test the Print Server   261
Install BI Publisher Desktop   262
Create Monthly Order Review Report   263
    Create the Report Query   263
    Create Report Template in MS Word   264
    Format Report   265
    Conditional Formatting   266
    Summary Calculation   266
    Add a Summary Chart   267
    Add a Pivot Table   268
Upload Report Template to APEX   269

Run the Report   270
Create a Commercial Invoice   273
    Create Query for the Invoice   273
    Create Invoice Template in MS Word   274
    Upload Template to APEX   274
    Call Invoice from an APEX Page   275
    Test Your Work   276
Summary   278

10. Users Management

About Users Management   280
The Manage Users Page   280
    Create Validations   283
    Create Process - Add Row   284
The Reset Password Page   285
    Create Validation   288
    Create Process - Update Password   289
    Create Branch   289
Test Your Work   290
Hide the Administration Tab   292
Summary   292

11. Smartphone and Mobile Development

About Mobile Development   294
    Types of Mobile Applications   294
Create the Mobile Application Interface   296
Modify Mobile Application's Global Page   301
Create Footer Control List   301
Create Mobile Styles   302
The Mobile Home Page   304
    Create Mobile Menu   304
Create Customers Page   306
Create Maintain Customer Page   310
Create Products Main Page   312
Create Maintain Product Page   316
Create Order and Order Details Pages   318
Create Maintain Order Page   327
    Create Dynamic Action - Get List Price   329
Create Order Page   330
Create Select Order Items Page   333
Create Order Summary Page   338
Display Reports on Smartphones   341
    Create Reports List   341
    Customer Orders Report   341
    Sales by Category and Product Report   344
    Sales by Category/Month Report   348
    Order Calendar   350
Summary   352

12. Deploy and Access APEX Application
About Application Deployment   354
Export Application   355
Export Data   356
Export Selective Components   358
Lock and Unlock Application   358
Create a New Workspace   359
Import Application   360
Import the Application Logo   361
Remove Developers Toolbar   361
Import Data   362
Accessing the Application   363
    In Local Area Network (LAN)   364
    Through the Internet   365
    Dealing with Firewalls   365
Summary   366

About The Author

INDEX

PREFACE

The success of the first edition of this book motivated me to write the second one. The first edition was written with the objective to put a big picture of Oracle Application Express in front of the audience, and revolved around the sample application to demonstrate the practical aspect of the technology. The previous edition emphasized on the HOW area and didn't deeply elaborate the WHY part.

After getting valuable feedback from the respected audience, I spent ample time to revise my work with some more useful stuff. This book is written keeping in view those suggestions. Focusing on the current Oracle Application Express version (4.2), it contains the following new enhancements to show how to develop web applications with the help of this unique declarative rapid application development (RAD) tool.

- Mobile web application development
- Utilization of new themes and grid layouts in desktop and mobile web applications
- A new chapter to elaborate different areas of the technology
- Hands-on, step-by-step instructions with thorough explanations
- Improved user-friendly book layout

You'll create two flavors of a web application in this book: desktop and mobile. The desktop version teaches you many techniques that will aid you in your own development tasks. Once you complete the application, and fully understand the provided instructions, you'll be able to develop Internet facing applications as well as the conventional departmental applications with professional look in web interface. The mobile version, on the other hand, is really cool and fun. The chapter devoted to this platform shows how to create the same desktop application for mobile devices. To save development efforts and time, you'll be guided to use existing tested application pages from the desktop version for the mobile platform.

This work is produced with the intention to help those who are willing to learn how desktop and mobile web applications are developed, in minimal time frame. It is assumed that the users of this book have basic knowledge of SQL, PL/SQL, and have exposure to Oracle database objects.

From APEX introduction to application development, and from dual version development to its deployment, this book is the ultimate practical guide for you to enhance your skills in an area which is the need of the hour.

Download Book Code

Download the book's source code from:
http://www.creating-website.com/ApexBookCode.rar

- Riaz Ahmed
Author

Chapter 1
Develop Applications for Desktop & Smartphones

Chapter 1 - Develop Applications for Desktop & Smartphones

1.1 What are you going to create?

Oracle Application Express (APEX) is a browser-based rapid application development (RAD) tool that helps you create rich interactive Oracle-based web applications very quickly and with relatively little programming effort. A web application is an application that is accessed by users over a network such as the Internet or an intranet. It is an application software that is coded in a browser-supported programming language (such as JavaScript, combined with a browser-rendered markup language like HTML) and dependent on a common web browser to render the application. The popularity of web applications is due to the ubiquity of web browsers, which is the only requirement to access such applications. Another major reason behind the popularity of web applications is the ability to update and maintain these applications without distributing and installing software on potentially thousands of client devices.

Developing Web applications can be a real challenge as it's a multidisciplinary process. You have to be proficient in all the core technologies involved such as HTML, CSS, JavaScript on the client side; PHP or any other scripting language to interact with the database on the server side. Also, you've to take into account the type-less nature of the Web environment and above all, the need to put it all together in a manner that will allow the end users to execute their jobs efficiently and in a simplified manner.

Oracle Application Express is a hosted declarative development environment for developing and deploying database-centric web applications. Oracle Application Express accelerates the application development process. Thanks to its built-in features such as user interface themes, navigational controls, form handlers, and flexible reports that off-loads the extra burden of proficiency acquisition in the core technologies.

The format of this book is to introduce you to the art of building desktop and mobile web applications by iteratively developing the sample sales application from scratch, provided with Oracle Application Express. This application has been chosen as an example because you can learn most of the techniques from it for your own future work. The primary purpose of this book is to teach you how to use Oracle Application Express to realize your own development goals. Each chapter in this book explores a basic area of functionality and delivers the development techniques to achieve that functionality. By the time you reach the end of the examples in this book, you will have a clear understanding of Oracle Application Express and will be able to extend the application in almost any direction. There are a number of features that provide APEX a clear edge over other available RAD development tools. First of all APEX uses SQL and PL/SQL as core languages for development. Due to this ability, people who have been working with Oracle database can easily tread the path. Following are some of the major benefits of developing web applications in Oracle APEX:

- Declarative development is the most significant feature which makes Oracle APEX a good choice for rapid application development. Most of the tasks are performed with the help of built-in wizards that help you create different application pages. Each wizard walks you through the process of defining what you are expecting to achieve. After getting the input, the wizard data is stored as metadata in Oracle database tables. Later on, you can call page definition to modify or enhance the metadata to give your page the desired look. You can even add more functionalities by putting your own custom SQL and PL/SQL code. Once you're comfortable with Oracle APEX, you can ignore the wizards and generate your application directly. The Application Express engine renders applications in real time using the metadata. When you create or extend an application, Oracle Application Express creates or modifies metadata stored in database tables. When the application is run, the Application Express engine reads the metadata and then displays the application. See chapter 2 for more details on this topic.

- Another hefty feature provided in the current version (APEX 4.2) is the ability to create applications for mobile devices. Content to these devices are delivered through jQuery Mobile that is incorporated in APEX. To create mobile-based interface, a new specific theme is added to the collection that support mobile page transitions such as swipe, tap, and so on.

- A new theme (Theme 25) is provided with responsive design capability. With this design content is adjusted according to different screen dimensions and provides same user interface for desktop, tablet, and smartphones.

Being the future, mobile application development is the need of the hour. This platform will definitely aid the over burdened business professionals, facing increasing time constraints, to increase their productivity by enabling them to work from anywhere at any time. These applications will make the busy community more effective as the features they carry allow people of high cadre to stay informed and take correct in-time decisions even sitting away from their desks.

1.2 Understanding the Application

The application you will be creating in this book features an easy-to-use interface for adding, updating, deleting and viewing order and related products and customers information. Users can navigate among the pages using the Home, Customers, Products, Orders, and Reports tabs. When you log into the application, the following home page appears as shown in Figure 1-1. In addition to the desktop version, you'll be guided to create a mobile version of the same application so that it could be accessed on mobile devices such as smartphones and tablet.

Let's have a quick look at some of the major areas of our sample Sales Web Application to know what we're going to create.

Chapter 1 - Develop Applications for Desktop & Smartphones

1.2.1 The Home Page

Figure 1-1 Desktop Home Page

The Home page (Figure 1-1) is the first page a user will see when he/she successfully logs into the application. This page will be created in chapter 4. Let's first take a look at the tagged areas to acquaint ourselves with different sections of a page:

- A: Application Logo
- B: Navigation Bar
- C: Tabs
- D: Breadcrumb
- E-J: Regions
- K: Button
- L: Developers Toolbar

The Home page contains six regions (E-J):

- This Month's Sales
- Sales by Product
- Sales by Category
- Top Customers
- Top Products
- Top Orders by Date

This Month' Sales demonstrates the use of a Flash Dial chart. This chart displays a value based on an underlying SQL statement to graphically present current month's sales.

Sales by Product is a pie chart that shows sales share of each product in color-coded slices.

Sales by Category is a bar chart to present sale figures of the three categories setup in the database.

Top Customers is a report based on a SQL query and displays a subset of the information that appears on the Customers page. Users can link to additional details by clicking the customer name or by clicking the View Customer button (marked as K in Figure 1-1) in the upper right corner of the region. The button with the plus sign is used to create a new customer.

Top Products is also a report based on a SQL query. This report displays a subset of the information that displays on the Products page. Users can link to product details by clicking the product name or by clicking the View Products icon in the upper right corner of the region and can even create a new product using the Add Product button.

Top Orders by Date displays top orders by date and order amount. Clicking the right arrow button takes users to the main orders page while the first one allows them to create a new order.

Chapter 1 - Develop Applications for Desktop & Smartphones

1.2.2 Manage Customers

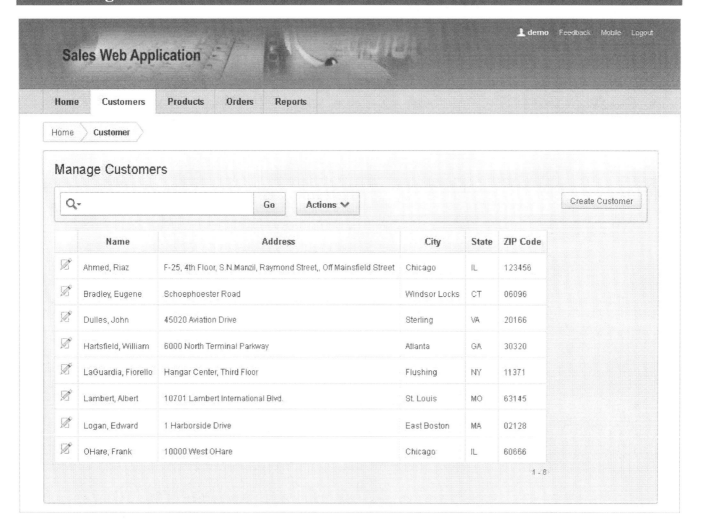

Figure 1-2 Desktop Main Customers Page

The Customers page (to be created in chapter 5) enables users to view and edit customer information. It is an interactive report for tracking customer information. To search for a customer, enter a customer name in the Search field and click Go. To sort the report by customer name, click the column heading and then select the Up or Down arrow to sort it either in ascending or descending mode.

You can change the appearance of the report using the Actions menu. To update existing customer information, click the **Edit** icon (the gray pencil icon to the left). To add a new customer, click the **Create Customer** button. After performing the former two actions, you'll be presented with the following Customer Details page. This page is used in the application to both modify record of an existing customer and to add a new one. In the previous case, the screen would resemble Figure 1-3 with an additional pane, **Orders for this Customer**, to display orders placed by the selected customer along with his/her profile.

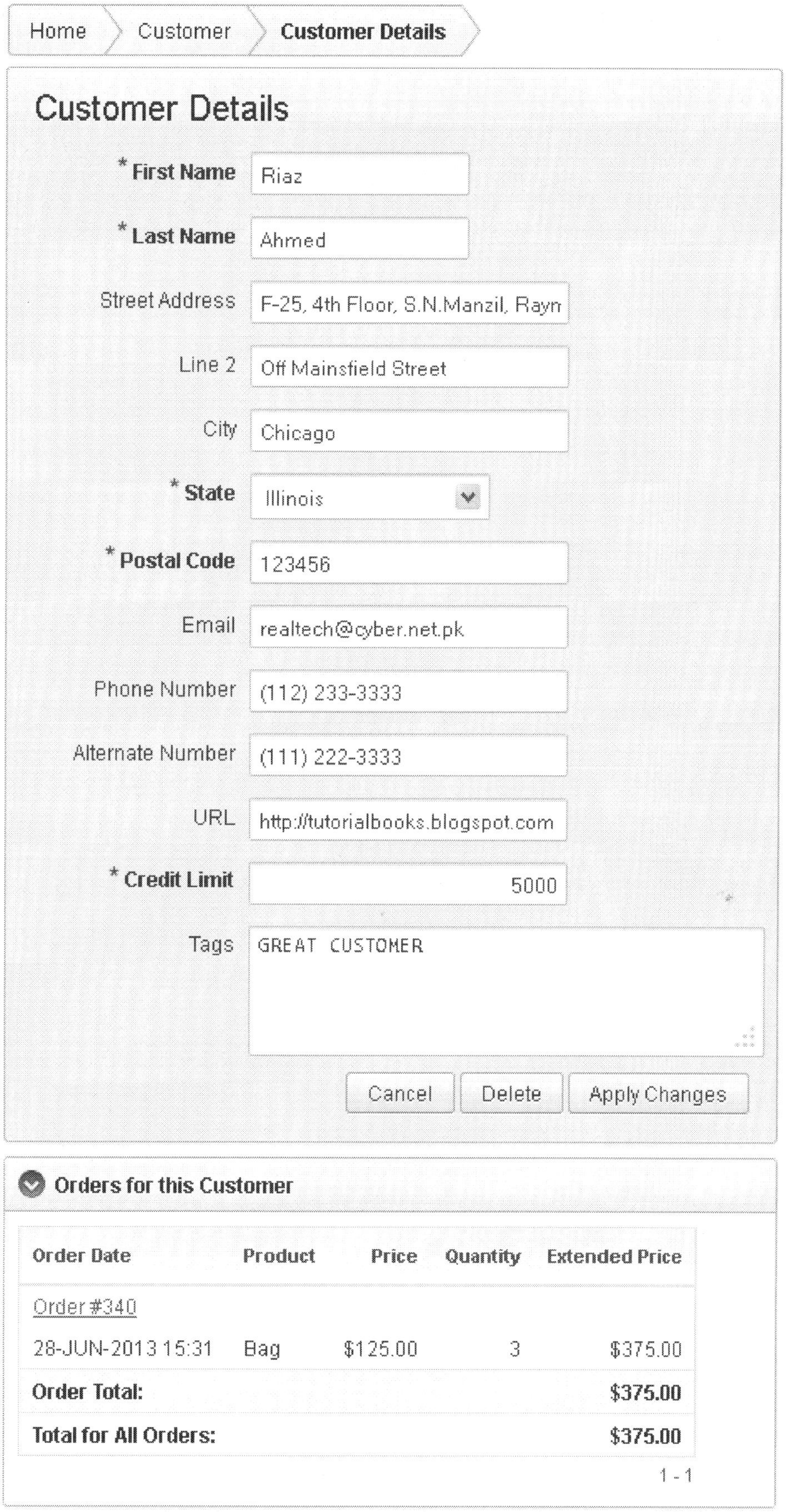

Figure 1-3 Desktop Customer Details Page

1.2.3 Setup Products

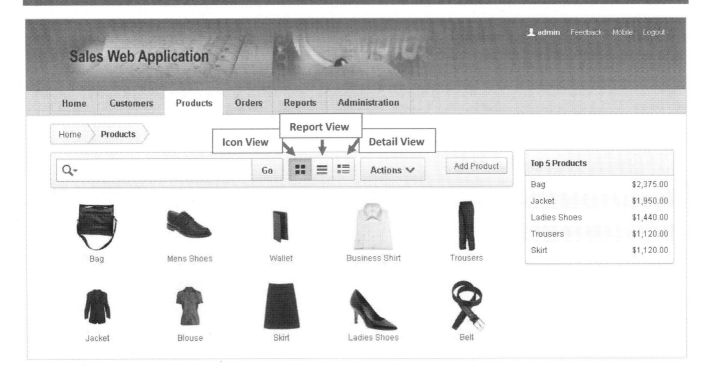

Figure 1-4 Desktop Main Products Page

The Products page (see chapter 6) enables users to view and edit product information. The Products page consists of two main regions:

- Products
- Top 5 Products

The main **Products** region displays product information. This region is based on a SQL query that uses a custom function for displaying images stored in the database. The page has three view options; Icon, Report, and Detail. By default, the page is displayed in **Icon view**. To edit product information in Icon view, click an image to call Product Details page (Figure 1-5).

To view the information in a report format, click the **View Report** icon. In Report view, you can sort the list by product category by clicking the column heading and then selecting the Up or Down arrow to sort it in ascending or descending mode. Users can change the appearance of the report using the Actions menu. To edit a product description, click the product image (in Icon View), edit button (in Report View), and product name link (in Detail View). To add a new product, click the **Add Product** button at the top of the page.

The second region, Top 5 Products, displays list of top five selling products. From development view point, this region is added to demonstrate placement of multiple regions on a single page and utilization of page area.

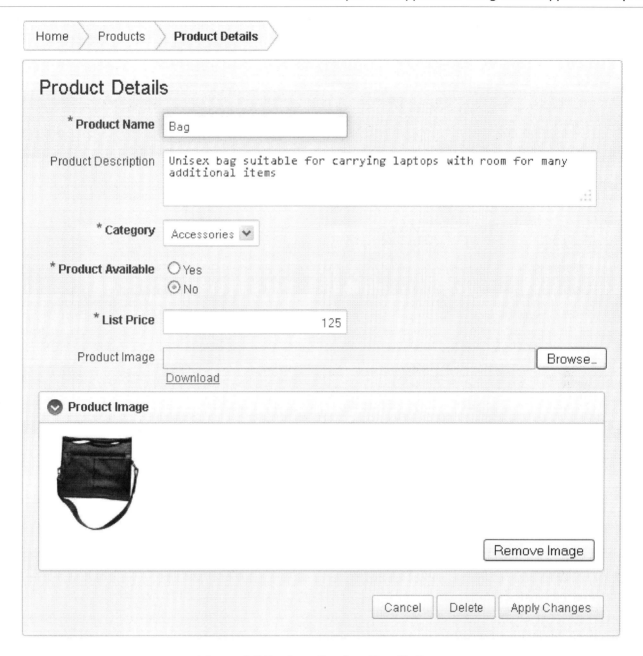

Figure 1-5 Desktop Product Details Page

1.2.4 Place Orders

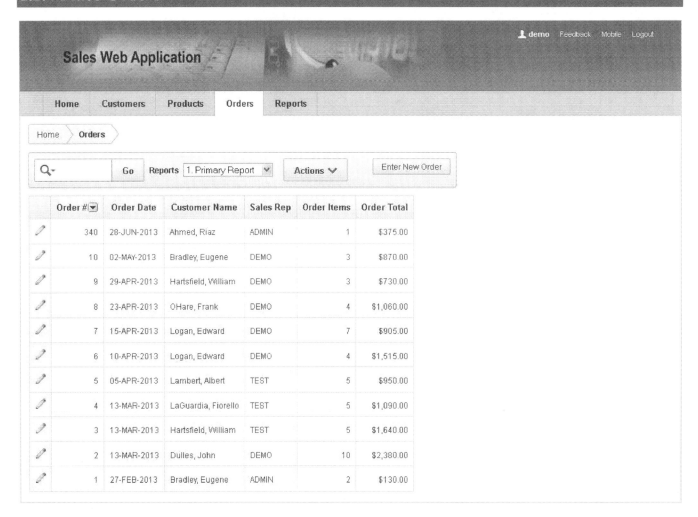

Figure 1-6 Desktop Main Orders Page

The Orders page enables users to view and edit customer orders. The Orders tab contain three interactive reports for tracking order information: Primary, Monthly Review, and Customer Review. To sort the report by column, click the column heading and then select the Up or Down arrow to sort the report in ascending or descending mode. You can change the appearance of the report using the Actions menu. To update existing order information, click the **Edit** icon to call Order Details page as shown in Figure 1-7. To add a new order, click the **Enter New Order** button. Unlike previous two page (Customers and Products), the Order module uses a different approach to enter a new order. It is based on a wizard comprising three steps: Select or enter a new customer, Add items to the new Order, and present the Order Summary. This module will be developed in chapter 7.

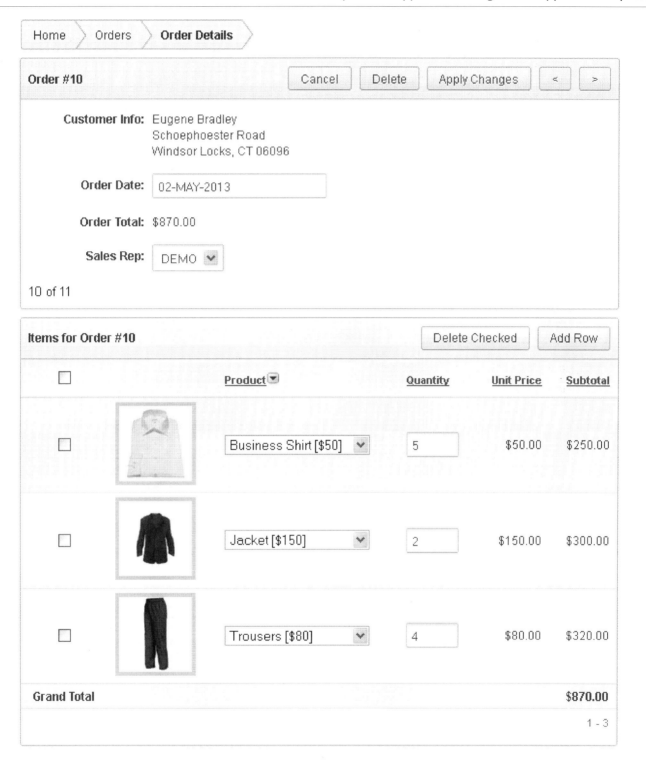

Figure 1-7 Desktop Order Details Page

1.2.5 Generate Graphical Reports

Figure 1-8

The Reports tab enables you to view information in various formats, including different types of charts, calendar, map, and tree. There are six graphical reports, listed under the Reports region on the left side of the page, that you can view by making a selection. Some of these reports are designed to demonstrate drill-down functionality. When a bar in the chart is clicked, you're taken to the details page to view respective underlying information. This module is created in chapter 8.

Create Rapid Web Application Using Oracle Application Express

1.2.6 Advanced Reporting

With advanced reporting, you can author, manage, and deliver all your reports and documents easier and faster. Using familiar desktop tools, you can create everything from pixel-perfect customer facing documents to critical management reports. View reports online or take a hard copy in various formats including PDF, MS Word, MS Excel and HTML. The reports shown below will be created in chapter 9.

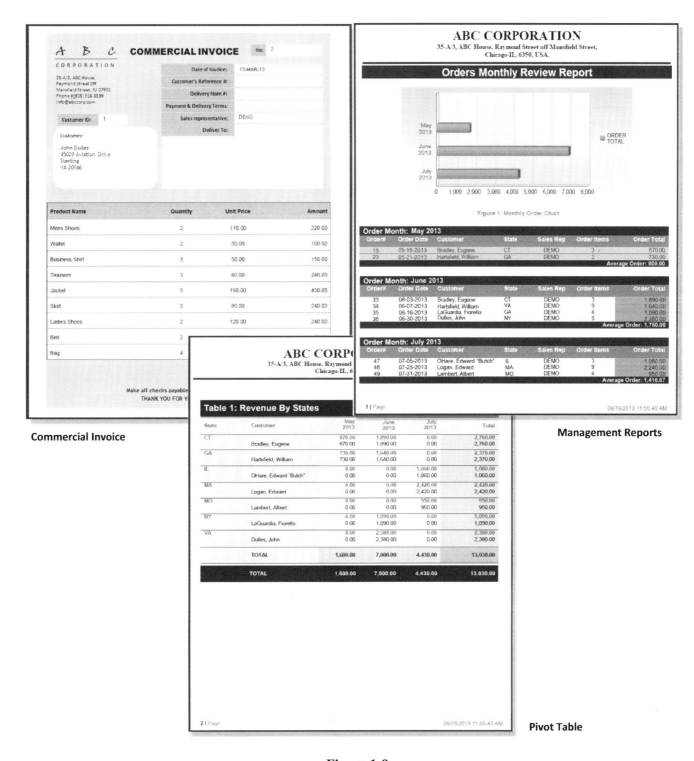

Commercial Invoice   **Management Reports**

Pivot Table

Figure 1-9

Chapter 1 - Develop Applications for Desktop & Smartphones

1.2.7 Users Management

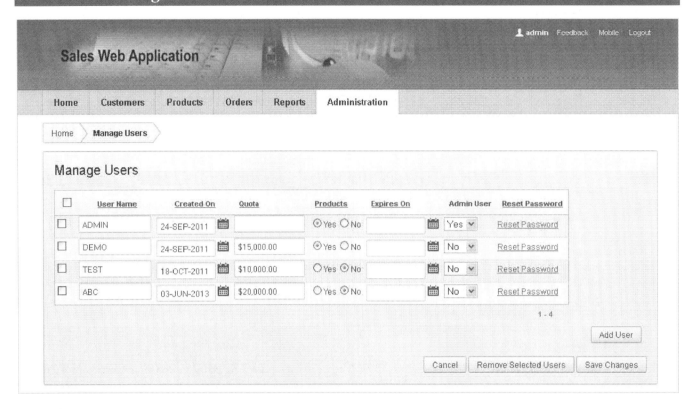

Figure 1-10

Application users are managed through the Administration tab. This tab is displayed only if you log in to the Application with the user name admin. The application makes use of a custom authentication scheme that stores user names and obfuscated passwords in a table. The Manage Users page enables you to manage additional users. To add a new user, click **Add User** at the bottom of the page. To delete a user, select the user and click **Remove Selected Users**. Similarly, the Reset Password link, provided with each user, will enable the administrator to update user password.

After getting an overview of the desktop version of our Sales Web Application, let's see the mobile version as well.

Create Rapid Web Application Using Oracle Application Express

1.2.8 Mobile Application

In the current APEX version (4.2), the most significant feature is the ability to develop applications specifically aimed at smartphones and tablets, such as iPhone, iPad, Android, and BlackBerry. Here are some glimpses of the mobile application that you'll create in this book.

Figure 1-11   Figure 1-12

Mobile Login Screen	Main Mobile Menu
Just like the desktop application, Oracle APEX creates few default pages for the mobile platform as well. The Login screen is one of those, which takes username and password to authenticate a user.	After the successful login attempt, you see the Home page of your mobile application containing the main mobile menu. Using this menu you can navigate to other pages of the application.

Chapter 1 - Develop Applications for Desktop & Smartphones

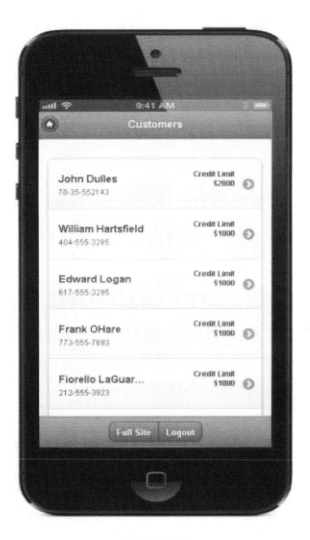

Figure 1-13

Figure 1-14

Customers Page
Selecting the customers option in the main menu brings you to this page to display list of existing customers. You can browse details of customers by tapping their names.

Maintain Customer
Modify and delete records of existing customers.

Create Rapid Web Application Using Oracle Application Express

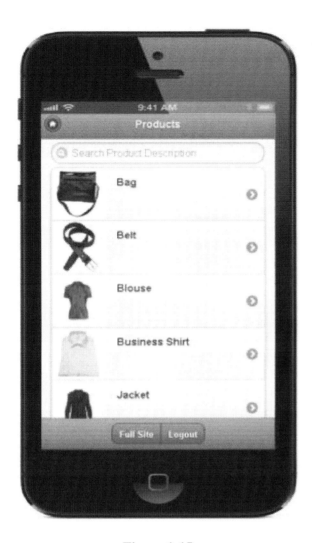

| Figure 1-15 | Figure 1-16 |

Products Page	Maintain Product
List products from the database with names and images.	Use this page either to modify or to delete an existing product.

Chapter 1 - Develop Applications for Desktop & Smartphones

Figure 1-17

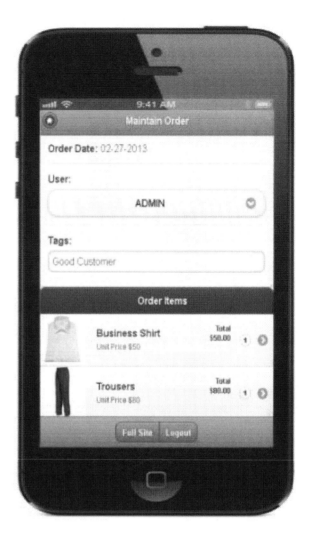

Figure 1-18

Orders Page	Maintain Order
Based on APEX Form on a Table with Report wizard this page displays a list of placed orders. Using the Enter New Order button you can create a new order. Modify or remove an order by clicking the corresponding number in the first column.	Tapping an order in the main orders page calls this one to display details of the selected order. You can add and remove items to and from an existing order.

Figure 1-19   Figure 1-20

Reports Page	Order Calendar
This page lists three graphical reports with an order calendar.	Marks days in a month to signify placed orders dates. Besides the month option, the second option (List) presents a different view of the report.

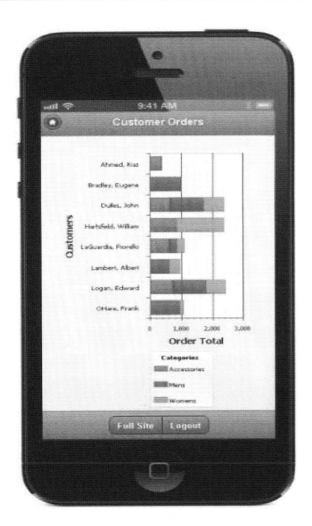 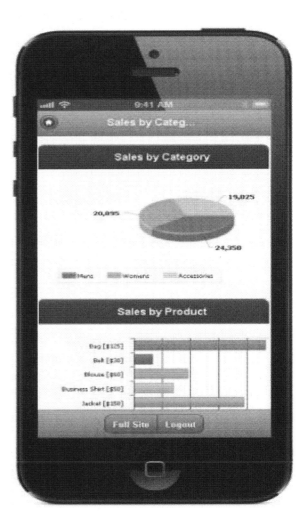

Figure 1-21 Figure 1-22

Mobile Application Reports
Presents data in graphical form using simple SQL queries with drill-down functionality. Just like the desktop version, you can present information in multiple regions.

1.3 Summary

This chapter provided you an overview about the subject matter of the book: a web-based data-centric application. You'll create this application in two flavors using the browser-based declarative development environment of Oracle APEX. The next chapter is aimed at providing some core concepts about Oracle APEX. Read the chapter thoroughly because the terms used in it are referenced throughout the book.

Chapter 2
Introduction to Oracle Application Express

2.1 What is APEX?

Oracle Application Express (Oracle APEX), is a rapid web application development tool for the Oracle database. It runs in an Oracle database instance and comes as a no-cost option with Oracle database. If you want to develop and deploy fast and secure professional applications then Oracle APEX must be your choice. The only requirements are a web browser and a little programming experience. Besides ease of use and flexibility, Oracle Application Express provides the qualities of an enterprise database, scalability, security, integrity, availability and above all the web development experience.

Oracle Application Express lives entirely within your Oracle database. It is comprised of nothing more than data in tables and large amount of PL/SQL code. The essence of Oracle Application Express is approximately 400+ tables and 200+ PL/SQL packages containing 425,000+ lines of code. The Application Express engine renders applications in real time from data stored in database tables. When you create or extend an application, Oracle Application Express creates or modifies metadata stored in database tables. When the application is run, the Application Express engine reads the metadata and displays the application.

Data-driven Applications: Develop any application through an easy declarative development process of Application Express. However, you can use HTML to extend the presentation of your client interfaces and add Oracle's standard PL/SQL procedural language to supply additional logical operations. With this productive tool you can build applications that report on database data. Create hyper text linked reports to easily link to other reports, charts, and data entry forms. Charts have built-in drill-down functionality, so that a user can get more detailed information on any of the sections of the chart with a simple mouse click. You can effectively communicate data using the charting engine by presenting SQL queries graphically. Use declarative form controls including shuttles, text editors, date pickers, checkboxes, radio groups, and select lists to manipulate data. Easily and instantly build opportunistic and departmental database applications with the help of simple wizards. This makes Application Express a natural replacement for multi-user desktop database applications. Create highly professional, secure, and scalable applications without scripting languages and complex framework.

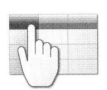

Online Reporting: Application Express provides a declarative programming environment, which means that no code is generated or compiled during development. You just interact through wizards and property sheets to build SQL-based reporting applications on existing database schemas. Reports and charts are defined with simple SQL queries, so some knowledge of SQL is very helpful. Besides, if procedural logic is needed, you can also write PL/SQL code. Oracle Application Express is a declarative tool and has a vast collection of pre-defined wizards, HTML objects, database handling utilities, page rendering and submission processes, navigation and branching options, and more. You can use all these options to build your database-centric web applications comprising web pages carrying forms, reports, charts, etc., with their layouts and business logic. The APEX engine translates it all into an HTML code for the client side, and SQL and PL/SQL code for the server side. If you do not get a solution from predefined options, you are allowed by APEX to create your own SQL and PL/SQL code for the server side, and HTML, CSS, and JavaScript code, for the client side.

Oracle APEX has the web-based application development environment to build web applications. You are not required to install any client software to develop, deploy, or run APEX applications. Following are the primary tools provided by Oracle APEX:

Application Builder – to create dynamic database driven web applications. This is the place where you create and modify your applications and pages. It comprises the following:
- **Applications:** This tab lists all applications is the current workspace and lets you create a new one.
- **Create:** Using this option in the Application Builder you can create two different types of applications: database applications and Websheet applications.
- **Import:** Used to import an entire application and related files.
- **Export:** Export application and component metadata to SQL script file format. You'll use Import and Export utilities in chapter 12 – Application Deployment.
- **Repository:** When you import an application and any related files into a target Oracle Application Express instance, the files are stored in the Export Repository. You can use the Export Repository to manage archived application exports, imports, and other files.
- **Migrate:** Use this option to migrate a Microsoft Access application or convert an Oracle Forms application to an Oracle Application Express application.

SQL Workshop – to browse your database objects and to run ad-hoc SQL queries, SQL Workshop is designed to allow Application Developers to maintain database objects such as tables, packages, functions, views, etc. It is beneficial in hosted environments like apex.oracle.com where direct access to underlying schemas is not provided. It has five basic components:
- **Object Browser:** to review and maintain DB Objects.
- **SQL Commands:** to run SQL queries.
- **SQL Scripts:** to upload and execute script files.
- **Utilities:** includes Query Builder, Data Workshop, Generate DDL, Schema Comparison and more.
- **RESTful Services:** to define Web Services using SQL and PL/SQL against the database.

Team Development – Team Development allows development teams to better manage their APEX projects by defining milestones, features, to-dos and bugs. Features, to-dos and bugs can be associated with specific applications and pages as necessary. Developers can readily configure feedback to allow their end-users to provide comments on applications. The feedback also captures relevant session state details and can be readily converted to a feature, to-do or bug.

Administration – Workspace administrators can administer their workspace and use the various reports to monitor activity. Manage Service allows them to request more space or access to another schema. Manage Users and Groups allows them to define developers and end-users.

2.2 Migrating to APEX

Velocity in the demand for new applications and functionality rises as businesses grow. As a developer, you are expected to rapidly respond to these needs. Over the years, desktop database and spreadsheet tools have enormously contributed to data management due to the ease and user friendliness these applications extend to their audience. Besides benefits, these applications have scalability and functionality limitations that not only results in dozens of different applications and data sources but also adds extra overhead in their maintenance. Due to these issues, organizations are unable to continue their standard practices, leaving mission-critical data at risk. These fragmented systems may also cause loss of business opportunity. Finally, significant amount of time and resource is required to put these data blocks together to get the desired information. In addition to above, the following points provide some more drawbacks of desktop applications:

- Installation of client software, such as Excel, on every machine
- Lack of data sharing with other applications
- Simultaneous data access inability in spreadsheets
- May not be the part of regular data backup
- Critical and confidential data can easily be moved via email or pocket storage devices

Having gone through the above stuff, it is clear that you need a tool that has the capability to cope with these shortfalls. The following list shows how APEX allows you to handle most of these issues:

- Central management of data and applications
- No installation of software is required on client machines, the only requirement is a supported browser
- Shared development and application access
- Being central, data and applications become a part of regular backup procedure
- Data and application access control, empowered by audit trail

The above glimpses have disclosed that APEX is capable of far more than just being an Excel or Access replacement. Give it a try by replacing your existing desktop applications with APEX application and enjoy the benefits that this robust technology offers.

2.3 About the Application Express Engine

Besides rendering and processing application pages, the APEX engine performs the following tasks:
- Session state management
- Authentication services
- Authorization services
- Page flow control
- Validation processing
- Rendering and page processing

2.4 Oracle Application Express Environments

The APEX environment has two broad categories:

Development Environment: Here you have complete control to build and test your applications as mentioned in this book.

Runtime Environment: After completing the development and testing phase, you implement your applications in a production environment where users can only run these applications and do not have the right to modify them.

2.5 About Browser Requirements

To view or develop Oracle Application Express applications, web browsers must support Java Script and the HTML 4.0 and CSS 1.0 standards. The following browsers are required to develop applications in Oracle Application Express:

- Microsoft Internet Explorer 7.0 or later version
- Mozilla Firefox 14 or later version
- Google Chrome 21 or later version
- Apple Safari 5.0 or later version

Chapter 2 – Introduction To Oracle Application Express

2.6 APEX Applications

In Oracle Application Express you build an application using Application Builder. There are two types of applications that you can create using the Application Builder: database applications and Websheet applications. The Create Application Wizard helps you create both database applications and Websheet applications. The main difference between these two types of applications is the intended audience. While database applications are geared towards application developers, Websheet applications are designed for end users with no development experience.

Database Applications

As the name implies, these type of applications interact with a backend database to store and retrieve data. It is a collection of pages linked together using tabs, buttons, or hypertext links. Pages are declaratively created through wizards. Each page can have multiple containers called regions. Each region can contain text, reports, charts, maps, web service content, calendars, or forms. Web forms hold items such as text fields, radio groups, check boxes, data pickers, list of values and more. In addition to these built-in types, you can create your own item types using plug-ins. When you build a database application, you can include different types of navigation controls, such as navigation bar entries, tabs, lists, breadcrumbs, and trees. Most of these navigation controls are shared components which means that you create them at the application level and use them in any page within your database application. All pages in a database application share a common session state that is transparently managed by APEX (more on sessions in a while).

Websheet Applications

Besides professional developers, APEX also cares for those who are not expert in the development field. It offers Websheet applications to such users to manage structured and unstructured data. Websheet applications are interactive web pages that combine text with data. These applications are highly dynamic and defined by their users. Websheet applications include navigation controls, search capabilities, and the ability to add annotations such as files, notes, and tags. Websheet applications can be secured using access control lists and several built-in authentication models. Pages can contain sections, reports, and data grids and everything can be linked together using navigation. All information is searchable and completely controlled by the end-user.

2.7 What is a Page?

A page is the basic building block of an application. When you build an application using Application Builder, you create pages that contain user interface elements, such as regions, items, tabs, lists, buttons and more. By default, page creation wizards automatically add controls to a Page Definition based on your selection. You can add more controls to a page later on by using the Page Definition interface and can also use the Create Page Wizard to add components such as report, chart, form, calendar, or tree in the Page Definition. You can create the following types of pages for your application:

Blank Page: Creates a page without any built-in functionality.

Form: Creates a form interface with which users can update a single row or multiple rows within a table.

Report: Used to present a SQL query in a formatted style. It has the following options:
- Classic Report – Creates a report based on a custom SQL SELECT statement or a PL/SQL function.
- Interactive Report – Creates an interactive report based on a custom SQL SELECT statement you provide. Users can alter the layout of report data by selecting specific columns, applying filters, highlighting, and sorting. They can also define breaks, aggregations, different charts, and their own computations. Note: Interactive reports are not supported by jQuery Mobile Smartphone.
- Report on Web Service Result – Creates a report on a Web Service result.
- Wizard Report – Users who do not possess any SQL knowledge can create a report using this option by simply selecting the appropriate schema, table, and columns.

Plug-ins: Creates a new page based on a region type plug-in. Plug-ins enable developers to declaratively extend, share, and reuse the built-in types available with Oracle Application Express.

Chart: Creates HTML5 and Flash graphical charts.

Map: Creates a Flash map based on the AnyChart AnyMap Interactive Maps Component.

Tree: Creates a tree to graphically communicate hierarchical or multiple level data.

Calendar: Generates a calendar with monthly, weekly, and daily views.

Feedback Page: Adds a feedback page. Feedback is the process of gathering real-time comments, enhancement requests, and bugs from your application users.

Login Page: Creates a login page.

Access Control: Creates a page containing an access control list, enabling developers to control access to an application, individual pages, or page components.

2.8 Global Page

It's a new feature incorporated in Oracle Application Express and functions as a master page in your application. You can define a separate Global Page, Login Page, and Home Page for each user interface. This facilitates different pages being shown to end users when they access the application from a mobile device as opposed to a desktop system. The Application Express engine renders all components you add to a Global page on every page within your application. You can further control whether the Application Express engine renders a component or runs a computation, validation, or process by defining conditions.

2.9 About the Page Definition

A Page Definition is the basic building block of a page. You use the Page Definition to view, create, and edit the controls and application logic that define a page. Each page can have buttons and fields (called items), which are grouped into containers called regions. Pages can also have application logic (or processes). You can branch from one page to the next using conditional navigation; perform calculations (called computations); perform validations (such as check customer's credit limit); and display reports, calendars, and charts. You view, create, and edit the controls that define a page by accessing the Page Definition.

The Page Definition appears and is divided into three main sections:

- **Page Rendering** lists user interface controls and logic that are executed when a page is rendered. Page Rendering is the process of generating a page from the database.
- **Page Processing** lists logic controls (such as computations and processes) that are evaluated and executed when the page is processed.
- **Shared Components** lists common components that can be used by one or more pages within an application.

2.10 Tree and Components Views

Application Express presents two ways to view a page when you call it in Page Definition:

Tree View: It displays page components such as regions, items, and processes in a tree hierarchy where nodes are grouped according to their sequence or how they are processed by Application Express engine while rendering or processing a page. Using this hierarchical approach you can see the exact execution point of a component.

Component View: Here, page elements and application logic are organized by component type.

While creating Page 11 (Enter New Order) in our sample application , you'll create a process named *Create or Truncate Order Collection* under Page Rendering and will set its process point to *On Load–Before Header*. In the Tree View, this process will appear at the top of the tree under the *Before Header* node whereas, if you look at it in the Component View, it will be placed at the bottom under the *Processes* section.

2.11 Understanding Applications and Processes

Before digging details of each of the above mentioned sections, let's first understand the concept behind APEX applications. Applications in APEX are created through Application Builder and each application consists of one or more pages that are linked together using tabs, buttons, or hypertext links. Usually each page carries items, buttons, and application logic. You can show forms, reports, chart, and calendars on these pages and can perform different types of calculations and validations. You also can control movement within an application using conditional navigation. You do all this declaratively using built-in wizards or through custom PL/SQL code.

2.12 How the Application Express Engine Renders and Processes Pages

The Application Express engine dynamically renders and processes pages based on data stored in Oracle database tables. To view a rendered version of your application, you request it from the Application Express engine. When you run an application, the Application Express engine relies on two processes:

Show Page is the page rendering process. It assembles all the page attributes (including regions, items, and buttons) into a viewable HTML page.

Accept Page performs page processing. It performs any computations, validations, processes, and branching.

When you request a page using a URL, the engine is running Show Page. When you submit a page, the Application Express engine is running Accept Page or performing page processing during which it saves the submitted values in the session cache and then performs any computations, validations, or processes.

2.13 About Page Rendering

In Oracle Application Express, web pages are generated from the database and this process is called page rendering. The Page Rendering section in the Page Definition interface allows you to control rendering of a page by updating attributes of different components such as the page itself, regions, items, buttons, and page processes. Page Rendering has the following subsections:

Page
Using this subsection you can control specific characteristics of a page by altering some attributes like the page name, its title, associated template, header/footer text, and an authorization scheme (as used in Page 8 – Manage Users – of our application).

Regions
You put items on a page under a specific region. A region is an area on a page that serves as a container for content. You can create multiple regions to visually segregate different sections on a page and to group page elements. A region may carry a SQL report or static HTML content which is determined by the region source. Each region can have its own template applied which controls their respective appearance.

Chapter 2 – Introduction To Oracle Application Express

Controlling Region Positioning

When you create a region, you must specify its position (or Display Point) on the page. You can choose either a default position (such as Page Template Body) or a user-defined position in the template (such as Page Template Region Position 1.) Using the flashlight icon next to the Display Point attribute, you can view the positions available on the current page template (as shown in the following figure) and select the required display point.

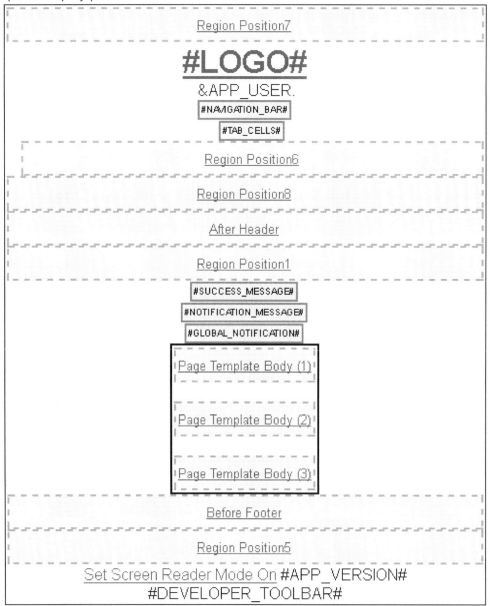

Figure 2-1 Region positions available on the current page template

Buttons

Just like desktop applications where you place buttons on your form to perform some actions, in web applications too, you can create buttons to submit a page or to take users to another page within the same site or to a different site. In the former case where a user submits a page, the APEX engine executes some processes associated with a particular button. You have three button options that you can add to a web page: HTML buttons, Image buttons, or a template. You can place buttons either in predefined region positions or with other items in a form.

Being an important component that controls the flow of database applications, buttons are created by running the Create Button wizard from the Page Definition. By placing buttons (such as Create, Delete, Cancel, Next, Previous and more) on your web page, you can post or process the provided information, or you can direct user to another page in the application or to another URL. Buttons are used to:

- Submit a page – For example, to save user input in a database table. When a button on a page is clicked, the page is submitted with a REQUEST value that carries the button name.
- Take user to another page within the same application with optional additional properties for resetting pagination, setting the request value, clearing cache, and setting item values, on the target page.
- Redirect to another URL.
- Do nothing – for example, if the button's behavior is defined in a Dynamic Action.
- Download Printable Report Query – This creates a Submit Page button and also a corresponding branch. When the button is clicked, the output is downloaded from the Report Query.

Items

You're familiar with page items that you see everywhere on the web. HTML form elements such as text fields (where you input some text like your id and password), select lists (from where you can select one or more available options), check boxes and more are called items. In Application Express some items are created for you by the wizard. Later on, you can modify the attributes of each item to provide the desired effect and behavior. For instance, you can set where a label should appear, how wide an item should be, its placement etc. APEX provides two categories of items: page items and application items. A page item is placed on a page and has associated attributes such as Name, Label, Display As, Alignment and more. In contrast, an application-level item is not associated with a page and therefore has no user interface properties. It is basically used as a global variable.

Processes

Processes are logic controls used to execute data manipulation language (DML) or PL/SQL. For example, you can use a process to populate session state at the time a page is rendered, to execute some type of logic (for example, using PL/SQL), or to make a call to the rendering engine. Typically a process performs an action at a specified point during the rendering or submission of the page. A page process is a unit of logic that runs when a specific event occurs, such as loading or submitting a page. From a functional perspective, there is no difference between page-level and application-level processes. The difference between these two process types is where the process is defined, that is at the page-level or at the application level. It's important to understand that the Processes associated with the Page Rendering phase are run by the APEX engine on the server side as part of building the HTML code for the application page.

Dynamic Actions

JavaScript is one of the most popular and widely used scripting language of the web and is used in billions of Web pages to add functionality, validate forms, communicate with the server, and much more. It is primarily a client-side scripting language for use in Web browsers. Its main focus is to help developers interact with Web pages and the Web browser window itself. APEX provides an alternate in shape of dynamic actions to create complex client-side behavior declaratively without the need for JavaScript. Actions are specified that execute on a defined set of conditions. While creating dynamic actions, you define which elements are affected by the action as well as how and when they are affected.

2.14 About Page Processing

Page processing is the process of submitting a page. A page is typically submitted when a user clicks a button. Use the Page Processing section of the Page Definition to specify application logic such as computations, validations, processes, and branches. In general, when viewing the Page Definition in Tree View, the Application Express engine runs this logic in the order it appears. The sections that follow describe each subsection under Page Processing.

Computations

Computations are APEX's declarative way of setting an item's values on the page or at the application level. These are units of logic used to assign session state to items and are executed at the time the page is processed. Both Page Rendering column and Page Processing column under the Page Definition carry a Computations section. Both these sections have the same mechanism that they apply using the same wizard. However, each computation has its own Computation Points, that determine whether the computation is associated with the page rendering phase (the SHOW page process) or the page submit phase (the ACCEPT page process).

Validations

Validations enable you to create logic controls to verify whether user input is valid. Validations are part of the Page Processing phase and are fired right after the Computations stage. It is a server-side mechanism designed to check and validate the quality, accuracy, and consistency of the page submitted data, prior to saving it into the database. For example, a validation can check whether a date entered into a target completion date field is in the future. In the case of validation errors, you can alert the users and allow them to correct the problems.

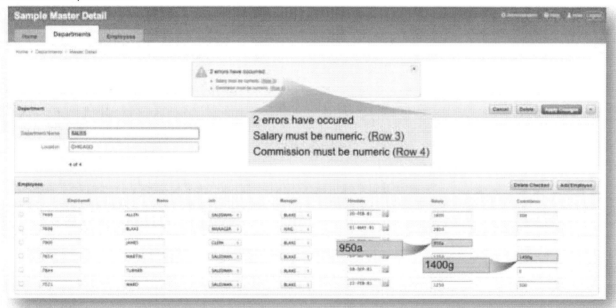

Figure 2-2

Processes

Processes are logic controls used to execute data manipulation language (DML) or PL/SQL. Processes are executed after the page is submitted.

Branches

Branches enable you to create logic controls that determine how the user navigates through the application.

2.15 About Shared Components

The right-hand section on the Page Definition is called Shared Components. It has eight sections (Tabs, List of Values, Breadcrumbs, Lists, Templates, Theme, Security, and Navigation Bar) containing common elements that can display or be applied on any page within an application. The Shared Components column on a specific page lists all the various shared components that have been used on that particular page. Note that Shared Components only display on the Page Definition after you add them. The sections that follow describe subsections that may display under Shared Components on the Page Definition.

Tabs

You might have seen a horizontal bar at the top of each website that helps you navigate to different pages within a particular site. Application Express provides you with similar type of navigation bar known as tabs. Tabs are an effective way to navigate users between pages of an application. Application builder includes two types of tabs: standard tabs and parent tabs.

Standard tabs are used when an application has only on level of tabs. A standard tab can have a one-to-one relationship with a page, or a standard tab can be the current tab for many pages. A standard tab set is associated with a specific page and page number. You can use standard tabs to link users to a specific page.

A parent tab acts as a container and hold a group of standard tabs under each option. Clicking a parent tab displays the corresponding standard tab, with the default page as the current page.

An application can have pages with no tabs, one level of tabs, and two levels of tabs. Standard tabs enable you to display only one level of tabs. To display two levels of tabs define both Parent tabs and Standard tabs. You can group tabs into collections called a tab set. Each tab must be part of a tab set.

Lists of Values

A list of values (abbreviated as LOV) are defined by running the LOV wizard. Once created, LOVs are stored in the List of Values repository and are utilized by page items. You can create two types of LOVs: static and dynamic. A static LOV displays and returns predefined values while a dynamic list is populated using a SQL query that fetches values from database tables. After creating an LOV you associate it to page items such as select list, radio group, check box etc.

Breadcrumbs

A breadcrumb is a hierarchical list of links that is rendered using a template. For example, you can display breadcrumbs as a list of links or as a breadcrumb path. A breadcrumb trail indicates where you are within the application from a hierarchical perspective. In addition, you can click a specific breadcrumb link to instantly view the page. You use breadcrumbs as a second level of navigation at the top of each page, complementing other user interface elements such as tabs and lists.

Lists

A list is a collection of links. For each list entry, you specify display text, a target URL, and other attributes that control when and how the list entry displays. Once created, you can add a list to any number of pages within an application by creating a region and specifying the region type as List. You control the display of the list and the appearance of all list entries by linking the list to a template. Lists are of two types:

Static Lists
When you create a static list you define a list entry label and a target (either a page or URL). You can add list entries when you create the list (creating from scratch), by copying existing entries, or by adding the list entries. You can control when list entries display by defining display conditions.

Dynamic Lists
Dynamic lists are based on a SQL query or a PL/SQL function executed at runtime. A dynamic list enables you to dynamically create styled list items that support mobile frameworks such as jQuery Mobile.

Themes and Templates
Instead of telling the Application Builder how to design and style your pages using HTML, CSS, and JavaScript code, which you may not be aware of, you only declaratively apply theme and templates that you want to use and the APEX engine does the rest of the job for you.

A theme is a named collection of templates that defines the look and feel of application user interface. Each theme contains templates for every type of application component and page control, including individual pages, regions, reports, lists, labels, menus, buttons, and list of values.

Templates control the look and feel of the pages in your application using snippets of HTML, CSS, JavaScript and image icons. As you create your application, you specify templates for pages, regions, reports, lists, labels, menus, buttons, and popup lists of values. Groups of templates are organized into named collections called themes.

The Application Builder also allows you to access the themes and template mechanism so that you can create new ones according to your own requirements, or amend existing ones.

Security
Security is an important feature when building applications, as it enables us to prevent unauthorized access and activity in our applications. Not all applications require security; a public website doesn't for example. However, for many applications, we need to be able to control who can run and gain access to them. Once a user is logged into our application, we also need to further control what functionality they have permission to access. In Application Express, these security features are implemented through the use of Authentication and Authorization Schemes. These schemes enable us to declaratively define security for our applications quickly and easily.

Navigation Bar
Just like tabs and lists, a navigation bar too is created to link users to various pages within an application. Typically, a navigation bar carries links such as log in, log out, feedback, help etc. and is placed according to the selected page template. While creating a navigation bar, you can specify an image name, text, display sequence, and target location. A navigation bar entry can be an image, text, or an image with text beneath it. Navigation bars are different from other shared components in that you do not need to reference them on a page-by-page basis. If your page template includes the #NAVIGATION_BAR# substitution string, the Application Express engine automatically includes any defined navigation bars when it renders the page.

Shortcuts

By using shortcuts you can avoid repetitive coding of HTML or PL/SQL functions. You can use a shortcut to define a page control such as a button, HTML text, a PL/SQL procedure, or HTML. Once defined, you can invoke a shortcut using specific syntax unique to the location in which the shortcut is used. Shortcuts can be referenced many times, thus reducing code redundancy.

When you create a shortcut, you must specify the type of shortcut you want to create. Oracle Application Express supports the following shortcut types:

- PL/SQL Function Body
- HTML Text
- HTML Text with Escaped Special Characters
- Image
- Text with JavaScript Escaped Single Quotes
- Message
- Message with JavaScript Escaped Special Quotes

Upload Images

You can reference images within your application by uploading them to the Images Repository. When you upload an image, you can specify whether it is available to all applications or to a specific application.

Upload Static Files

You can upload static files to your workspace using the Static File Repository. You can edit static files smaller than 30,000 bytes by selecting the file name. Otherwise, you must edit the file offline and upload it again.

Web Services

Web services enable applications to interact with one another over the web in a platform-neutral, language independent environment. In a typical Web services scenario, a business application sends a request to a service at a given URL by using the protocol over HTTP. The service receives the request, processes it, and returns a response. You can incorporate calls with external Web services in applications developed in Application Builder.

Web services are typically based on Simple Object Access Protocol (SOAP) or Representational State Transfer (REST) architectures. SOAP is a World Wide Web Consortium (W3C) standard protocol for sending and receiving requests and responses across the Internet. SOAP messages can be sent back and forth between a service provider and a service user in SOAP envelopes. RESTful Web services are resource oriented. The scope of the Web service is found in the URI and the method of the service is described by the HTTP method that is used such as GET, POST, PUT, HEAD, and DELETE.

SOAP offers two primary advantages:
- SOAP is based on XML, and therefore easy to use.
- SOAP messages are not blocked by firewalls because this protocol uses simple transport protocols, such as HTTP.

REST offers similar advantages:
- REST messages are also not blocked by firewalls because this protocol uses the HTTP protocol.
- REST requests do not require the overhead of XML and SOAP envelopes and inputs are typically provided in the URI.

Plug-ins

With the increase in Application Express usage the demand for specific features also surfaced. To meet these demands, the plug-ins framework was introduced in APEX 4.0 which allows developers to create their own plug-ins to add additional functionality in a supported and declarative way.

Usually a tool like Ajax is used to add custom functionality. The con of this approach is to place the code in different locations such as within the database, in external JavaScript files and so on. On the other hand, turning that code into a plug-in is more convenient to use and manage as the code resides in one object. With the help of open source jQuery components you can create plug-ins without generating huge amount of code manually.

Plug-ins are shared component objects that allow you to extend the functionality of item types, region types, dynamic actions, and process types. The plug-in architecture includes a declarative development environment that lets you create custom versions of these built-in objects. For example, you could create your own star rating item that allows your user to provide feedback using a one-to-five star graphic. This new item type could then be used across all your applications. The main part of a plug-in consists of PL/SQL code and can be supplemented with JavaScript and CSS code. A plug-in consists of one or more PL/SQL functions. These functions can either reside in the database (in a package or a set of functions) or be included within the plug-in.

The Plug-in OTN page has several different plug-ins developed by the APEX Development Team
http://www.oracle.com/technetwork/developer-tools/apex/application-express/apex-plug-ins-182042.html

Application Globalization

You can develop applications in Application Builder that can run concurrently in different languages. A single Oracle database instance and Oracle Application Express can support multiple database sessions customized to support different languages. In general, translating an application built in Application Builder involves the following steps:

- Map the primary and target application IDs
- Seed and export the text to a file for translation
- Translate the text in the file
- Apply the translated file
- Publish the translated file

2.16 Reports in APEX

Reports are an essential component of any application as they provide a way to query and view data stored in our database while providing the results in a meaningful format. Many applications need the ability to display information to the end user in the form of a report or a chart. Fortunately, APEX makes this extremely easy, allowing you to create reports and charts out of the box. In Oracle Application Express, a report is the formatted result of a SQL query. You can generate reports in a database application by selecting and running a built-in query, or by defining a report region based on a SQL query. Application Express includes a new charting engine, AnyCharts, which improves rendering time, generates better graphics, and allows for greater customization.

When creating a database application, you can include two types of reports: an interactive report or a classic report. The main difference between these two report types is that interactive reports enable the user to customize the appearance of the data through searching, filtering, sorting, column selection, highlighting, and other data manipulations.

Interactive Reports
The following is an example of an interactive report.

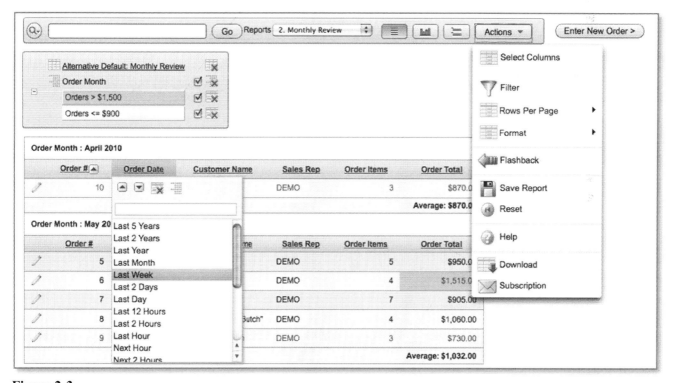

Figure 2-3

Interactive reports enable end users to create highly customized reports. Users can alter the report layout by hiding or exposing specific columns and applying filters, highlighting, and sorting. They can also define breaks, aggregations, charts, group bys, and add their own computations. Once customized, the report can be saved as either a private or public report. Each interactive report includes a search bar, Actions menu, Column Heading menu, and Edit icons in the first column of each row.

Chapter 2 – Introduction To Oracle Application Express

When using an interactive report you can:

- Include one interactive report per page
- Display 100 columns using report columns. You can edit additional columns using Tree view or paginating through Report Column Attributes.
- 1,000,000 rows per column heading filter (if no custom LOV is specified in the column attributes)
- Include 999 rows per column heading filter (if no custom LOV is specified in the column attributes)

Interactive Reports Save Options for Developers:

Primary Default (Developer only) – The Primary Default is the report that initially displays. Primary Default reports cannot be renamed or deleted.

Alternative Report (Developer only) – Enables developers to create multiple report layouts. Only developers can save, rename, or delete an Alternative Report.

Interactive Reports Save Options for End Users:

Public Report (End user and developer) – This report is viewable by all users. However, only the user who creates a public report can save, rename, or delete it. Although all users can view a public report, they can only save it under a new report name.

Private Report (End user and developer) – Only the user who creates the private report can view, save, rename, or delete it.

Classic Reports

In contrast, a classic report does not support the ability to create a highly customized report. The following is an example of a classic report built on top of the same data.

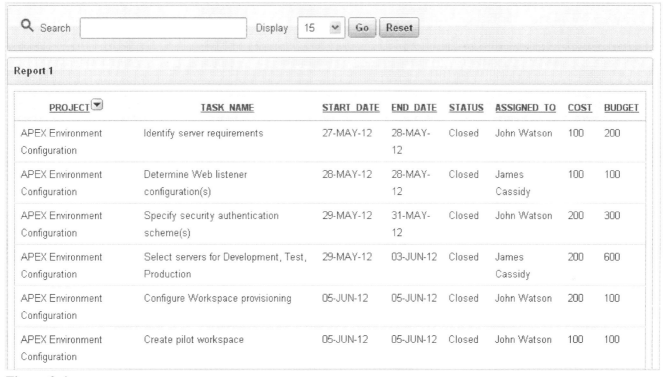

Figure 2-4

Classic reports support general keyword search capability, the ability to specify the number of rows that display, and basic column sorting. When using a classic report, you can view 100 columns using report columns. You can edit additional columns using Tree view or paginating through Report Column attributes.

Printing Report Regions

You can configure a classic report region to print by exporting it to several different formats. Oracle BI Publisher supports Adobe Portable Document Format (PDF), Microsoft Word Rich Text Format (RTF), or Microsoft Excel format (XLS), or Extensible Markup Language (XML). The supplied OC4J with Apache FOP alternative only supports PDF and XML. If you choose to use other third-party rendering engines, other output formats can also be configured.

By taking advantage of region report printing, your application users can view and print reports that have a predefined orientation, page size, column headings, and page header and footer. Interactive reports also have the ability to export to PDF, RTF, Microsoft Excel and Comma Separated Values (CSV). Note that for interactive reports, it is not possible to define a custom report layout. See chapter 9 – Advanced Reporting to create reports with custom layouts.

2.17 Understanding URL Syntax

Each application has its own unique ID and is referenced by this ID in URL. Similarly, you create pages in an application with respective numbers that uniquely identify each page. The Application Express engine assigns a session ID which is used as a key to the user's session state when an application is run. Following is the URL syntax example:

http://apex.abc.com/pls/apex/f?p=101:1:440323506685863558

This example indicates:
- apex.abc.com is the URL of the server
- pls is the indicator to use the mod_plsql cartridge
- apex is the database access descriptor (DAD) name. The DAD describes how HTTP Server connects to the database server so that it can fulfill an HTTP request. The default value is apex.
- f?p= is a prefix used by Oracle Application Express
- 101 is the application being called
- 1 is the page within the application to be displayed
- 440323506685863558 is the session number

Using f?p Syntax to Link Pages

You can create links between pages in your application using the following syntax:

f?p=App:Page:Session:Request:Debug:ClearCache:itemNames:itemValues:PrinterFriendly

Following are the arguments you can pass when using f?p syntax.

App: Indicates an application ID or alphanumeric alias.

Page: Indicates a page number or alphanumeric alias.

Session: Identifies a session ID. You can reference a session ID to create hypertext links to other pages that maintain the same session state by passing the session number. You can reference the session ID using the syntax:
- Short substitution string: &SESSION.
- PL/SQL: V('SESSION')
- Bind variable: :APP_SESSION

Request: Sets the value of REQUEST. Each application button sets the value of REQUEST to the name of the button which enables accept processing to reference the name of the button when a user clicks it. You can reference REQUEST using the syntax:
- Substitution string: &REQUEST.
- PL/SQL: V('REQUEST')
- Bind variable: :REQUEST

Debug: Displays application processing details. Valid values for the DEBUG flag include:
- YES.
- LEVELn
- NO

Setting this flag to YES displays details about application processing. Setting this flag to LEVELn (where n is between 1 and 9) controls the level of debug detail that displays. The value of YES equals LEVEL4.

You can reference the Debug flag using the following syntax:
- Short substitution string: &DEBUG.
- PL/SQL: V('DEBUG')
- Bind variable: :DEBUG

ClearCache: You use Clear Cache to make item values null. To do so, you provide a page number to clear items on that page. You can also clear cached items on multiple page by adding a list of page numbers separated by comma. Clearing a page's cache also resets any stateful processes on the page. Individual or comma-separated values can also include collection names to be reset or the keyword RP, which resets region pagination on the requested page. The keyword APP clears cache for all pages and all application-level items in the current application and removes sort preferences for the current user. The keyword SESSION achieves the same result as the APP keyword, but clears items associated with all applications that have been used in the current session.

itemNames: Comma-delimited list of item names used to set session state with a URL.

itemValues: List of item values used to set session state within a URL. Item values cannot include colons, but can contain commas if enclosed with backslashes. To pass a comma in an item value, enclose the characters with backslashes. For example:\123,45\

PrinterFriendly: Determines if the page is being rendered in printer friendly mode. If PrinterFriendly is set to Yes, then the page is rendered in printer friendly mode. The value of PrinterFriendly can be used in rendering conditions to remove elements such as regions from the page to optimize printed output. You can reference the printer friendly preference by using the following syntax:

V('PRINTER_FRIENDLY')

When referenced, the Application Express engine does not display tabs or navigation bars, and all items are displayed as text and not as form elements.

Making a Call in Application Express

It is important to understand how f?p syntax works. Application Builder includes many wizards that automatically create these references for you. However, you may have to create the syntax yourself in some situations. The following sections describe specific instances that use f?p syntax to link pages.

Calling a Page Using an Application and Page Alias

Application and page aliases must consist of valid Oracle identifiers, cannot contain any whitespace, and are not case-sensitive. The following example calls a page using an application and a page alias (instead of numbers) from within an application. It runs the page home of the application myapp and uses the current session ID.

f?p=myapp:home:&APP_SESSION.

Application aliases must be unique within a workspace. If an application in a different workspace has the same application alias, use the &c argument to specify the workspace name. For example:

f?p=common_alias:home:&APP_SESSION.&c=WORKSPACE_A

Calling a Page from a Button URL

When you create a button, you can specify a URL to redirect to when the user clicks the button. This example runs page 1 of application 101 and uses the current session ID.

f?p=101:1:&APP_SESSION.

Note that this is only one approach to using a button. This method bypasses page submission and acts as a hyperlink on the page. You can also have a button click submit a page. In that approach, clicking the button submits the page for processing, allowing forms to be submitted and session state to be saved.

2.18 Understanding Session State Management

Web applications use HTTP by which browsers talk to Web servers. Since HTTP doesn't maintain state, it is known as a stateless protocol. Here, your Web server reacts independently to each individual request it receives and has no way to link requests together even if it is logging requests. For example, a client browser requests a page from a web server. After rendering the page, the server closes the connection. When a subsequent request is forwarded from the same client, the web server doesn't know how to associate the current request with the previous one. To access values entered on one page on a subsequent page, the values must be stored as session state. It is very crucial to access and manage session state while designing an interactive, data-driven web application. Fortunately, Oracle Application Express transparently manages session state behind the scenes for every page and provides developers with the ability to get and set session state values from any page in the application. The session state information is easily referenced in static HTML or logic controls such as processes or validations.

What Is a Session?

In Web terminology, a session is a period of time during which a person visits a number of different Web sites using his or her browser. A session ends when the visitor quits the browser. From the perspective of a single website, the session runs from that person's first download of a page from the site through the last. Session tracking is a term that refers to keeping track of users as they move around a website. Application Express engine assigns a unique identifier also called session ID to each session. It does so to store and retrieve an application's working set of data (or session state) before and after each page view.

The Application Express engine stores session information in the database. Since sessions are completely independent of one another, the database can have any number of sessions. Similarly, there can be multiple instances of the same application being executed by a user in different browsers. From Application Express perspective, a session is the duration (either in minutes or hours) in which a user logs in to an application and logs out of it. During this period, the application express engine creates or reuses the session information with each page request.

What is a Session ID?

When a user requests a page, the Application Express engine uses session ID to get session state information from the database. You can see this ID as the third parameter in the requested URL as shown below:

http://apex.abc.com/pls/apex/f?p=101:1:440323506685863558

In the above example, the number 440323506685863558 is the session ID. In addition to URLs, you can see it in page's HTML POST data and in the contents of a session cookie. Application Express engine sets the cookie in the user's browser during authentication and keeps it there unless the user quits the application or closes the browser.

New session IDs are assigned by Application Express during authentication processing. Then, it records the authenticated user's identity with the session ID and continually checks the session ID in each page request's URL or POST data with the session cookie and the session record in the database. While the session ID is the key to session state, the session cookie and the session record safeguard the integrity of the session ID and the authentication status of the user.

Setting Session State

You set the value of an item in your application and therefore session state using the following methods:

- Form submission
- Bind variable
- Computation
- f?p syntax (See section 2.17 Understanding URL Syntax)

Form Submission

Suppose you created an application comprising two pages. One of those pages carries a registration form to receive input from the end user using several input items while the second one is used to display values obtained from the first one. After filling in the form, the user submits it to Application Express engine which captures all the entered values and stores them in session state. All this information can then be retrieved by the second page from session state by referencing the items associated with the fields on the page.

Bind Variable

In Oracle Application Express, bind variables are used in SQL statement or PL/SQL block to reference session state of specified items. In the following example, a page item named SEARCH_STRING is used as a bind variable to fetch all customer records matching the value specified in the page item.

SELECT * FROM customers WHERE last_name like '%' || :SEARCH_STRING || '%'

When using bind variable syntax, remember the following rules:

- Bind variable names must correspond to an item name.
- Bind variable names are not case-sensitive.
- Bind variable names cannot be longer than 30 characters.

Although page item and application item names can be up to 255 characters, if you intend to use an application item within SQL using bind variable syntax, the item name must be 30 characters or less.

Using Bind Variables in Regions Based on a SQL Query or LOV

If your region type is defined as a SQL Query, SQL Query (plsql function body returning SQL query), or list of values (LOV), you can reference session state using the following syntax:

:MY_ITEM

One common way to do this is to incorporate a session state variable in a WHERE clause. The following example shows how to bind the value of the item CUSTOMER_ID into a region defined from a SQL Query.

SELECT order_id, order_total FROM demo_orders WHERE customer_id = :CUSTOMER_ID

Using Bind Variables in Regions Based on PL/SQL

For region types defined as PL/SQL dynamic content, regions are constructed using PL/SQL anonymous block syntax. In other words, the beginning and ending keywords are used to enclose the PL/SQL block. For example:

```
IF :CUSTOMER_ID IS NOT NULL THEN
    INSERT INTO demo_customers (customer_id, cust_first_name, cust_last_name)
    VALUES (:P1_CUSTOMER_ID, :P1_CUST_FIRST_NAME, :P1_CUST_LAST_NAME)
END IF;
```

In this example, a customer record is added to the table demo_customers using three bind variables :P1_CUSTOMER_ID, :P1_CUST_FIRST_NAME, and :P1_CUST_LAST_NAME.

Computations

A common use of an application item is to store the value of the last page viewed in the application. By storing the value in an item, you can add a back button and then redirect the user to the page number captured by the computation. This type of computation works well, for example, when you need to enable users to back out of an error page.

The following is an example of a computation that stores the last page visited. In this example, the computation stores the last application page visited to an item named LAST_PAGE:

```
BEGIN
    :LAST_PAGE := nvl(:CURRENT_PAGE,:APP_PAGE_ID);
    :CURRENT_PAGE := :APP_PAGE_ID;
    RETURN :LAST_PAGE;
END;
```

Referencing Session State

You can reference item values stored in session state in regions, computations, processes, validations, and branches. An item can be a field, a text area, a password, a select list, or a check box. The following table describes the supported syntax for referencing item values.

Type	Syntax	Description

SQL	Standard item syntax:
	`:MY_ITEM`
	Syntax for items containing special characters:
	`:"MY_ITEM"`
		For items whose names are no longer than 30 characters, precede the item name with a colon (:). Use this syntax for references within a SQL query and within PL/SQL.
		To reference page items containing special, multibyte, or unicode characters, wrap the page item name in double quotation marks.

PL/SQL	`V('MY_ITEM')`	Use PL/SQL syntax to reference an item value using the V function.
PL/SQL	`NV('MY_NUMERIC_ITEM')`	Use standard PL/SQL syntax referencing the numeric item value using the NV function.

Static text (exact)	Standard item syntax:
	`&MY_ITEM.`
	Syntax for items containing special characters:
	`&"MY_ITEM".`
		For static text or an exact substitution, use the convention &ITEM_NAME followed by a period (.).
		To reference page items containing special, multibyte, or unicode characters, wrap the page item name in double quotation marks.

Clearing Session State

While developing an application, you often need to reset an item's value to null. In Application Express you can:

- Clear the cached values of page items by setting them to null
- Clear all pages in an application
- Clear session state for the current user

The above three session state clearance methods are further elaborated with some examples hereunder.

Clearing Cache by Item

Clearing cache for a single item resets the value of the item to null. For example, you might use this approach to make sure a specific item's value is null when a page is prepared for rendering. The following example uses standard f?p syntax to clear the cache for an item. This example calls page 7 of application 101 to clear an item named P7_CUSTOMER_ID. To do so, you need to place the item's name (P7_CUSTOMER_ID) in the ClearCache position of the f?p syntax to reset the value of the item to NULL. The NO flag used in the Debug position is added to not show debug information.

f?p=101:7:&APP_SESSION.::NO:P7_CUSTOMER_ID

Use a comma-separated list to reset values of multiple items as shown in the following example:

f?p=101:7:&APP_SESSION.::NO:P7_CUST_FIRST_NAME,P7_CUST_LAST_NAME

Clearing Cache by Page

Caching is the mechanism to preserve session state of page items. Just like clearing cache for individual items, you may need to clear the cache for all items on a page. For example, the order form page in your application is called using a link and you want to clear the cache for all items on this page for each new order.

f?p=101:3:&APP_SESSION.::NO:RP,3

This example clears the session cache for page 3 like this:
- Runs page 3 of application 101 and uses the current session ID
- Indicates to suppress debug information (NO)
- Clears all values maintained by the current session's cache for items on pages 3
- Resets region pagination (RP) on page 3 (the requested page)

The following example sets and passes values to multiple items.

f?p=101:3:&APP_SESSION.::NO:3:ITEM1,ITEM2,ITEM3:1234,,5678

Clearing Cache for an Entire Application

Using the Clear Cache argument "APP", you can clear an entire application's cache just like this:

f?p=App:Page:Session::NO:APP

Clearing Cache for the Current User Session

An alternate method to clear an application's cache is to set the Clear Cache argument using the keyword SESSION as:

f?p=6000:6004:12507785108488427528::NO:SESSION

2.19 Referencing Strings

In order to make your application more portable, Application Express provides many features. On top of the list are the Substitution Strings that help you avoid hard-coded references in your application. As you know, every application in APEX has its own unique ID and which is used to identify the application and the corresponding metadata within the Application Express repository. When you move these applications from your development environment to the production environment, and if you've hard-coded application references, you might be placed in an awkward situation. For example, you hard-coded the application ID (101) like this: f?p=101:1:&APP_SESSION. If you take this application to the production environment that already has an application that uses the same application ID, you'll be forced to use a different ID which will point all your links within the application to the wrong ID.

To avoid such situations, you should always use substitutions strings. You can avoid hard-coding the application ID by using the APP_ID substitutions string which identifies the ID of the currently executing application. With the substitution string, the URL looks like: f?p=&APP_ID.:1:&APP_SESSION. This approach makes your application more portable. We'll use substitution strings in our project and will discuss each one of them in detail.

The following table describes the supported syntax for referencing APP_ID. The substitution string reference type references page or application items using &ITEM. syntax.

Reference Type	Syntax
Bind variable	`:APP_ID`
Direct PL/SQL	`APEX_APPLICATION.G_FLOW_ID (A NUMBER)`
PL/SQL	`NV('APP_ID')`
Substitution string	`&APP_ID.`

2.20 Database Application Components and Controls

In Application Express, every database application uses some sort of components (such as forms, calendars, maps, and charts) and controls (such as buttons, list of values, shortcuts, and trees) to display and process data. Let's have a quick look at each of these useful components to see how they help in building a professional data-centric web application.

Forms

A Form is a useful component to manipulate data. Forms are included in database applications to update a single row in a table or multiple rows at once. Application Builder provides a variety of different types of forms for your application.

Form on a Procedure: Builds a form based on stored procedure arguments. Use this approach when you have implemented logic or data manipulation language (DML) in a stored procedure or package.

Form on a Table or View: Creates a form that enables users to update a single row in a database table.

Form on a Table with Report: Creates two pages. One page displays a report. Each row provides a link to the second page to enable users to update each record. Note: This wizard does not support tables having more than 127 columns. Selecting more than 127 columns generates an error.

Master Detail Form: Creates a form that displays a master row and multiple detail rows within a single HTML form. With this form, users can query, insert, update, and delete values from two tables or views.

Tabular Form: Creates a form in which users can update multiple rows in a database.

Form on a SQL Query: Creates a form based on the columns returned by a SQL query such as an EQUIJOIN.

Summary Page: Creates a read-only version of a form. Typically used to provide a confirmation page at the end of a wizard.

Form on Web Service: Creates a page with items based on a Web service definition. This wizard creates a user input form, a process to call the Web service, and a submit button.

Form and Report on Web Service: Creates a page with items based on a Web service definition. This wizard creates a user input form, a process to call the Web service, a submit button, and displays the results returned in a report.

Calendars

Application Builder includes a built-in wizard for generating a calendar with monthly, weekly, daily, and list views. Once you specify the table on which the calendar is based, you can create drill-down links to information stored in specific columns and enable drag and drop capability.

Application Builder supports two calendar types:

Easy Calendar creates a calendar based on the schema, table, and columns you specify. The wizard prompts you to select a date column and display column.

SQL Calendar creates a calendar based on a SQL query you provide. This SQL SELECT statement must include at least two columns: a date column and display column.

Maps

Application Builder includes built-in wizards for generating Flash maps on pages with a Desktop user interface. How you create a flash map depends upon whether you are adding the map to an existing page, or adding a map on a new page.

Flash map support in Oracle Application Express is based on the AnyChart AnyMap Interactive Maps Component. AnyMap is a flexible Macromedia Flash-based solution that enables developers to visualize geographical related data. Flash maps are rendered by a browser and require Flash Player 9 or later.

AnyChart stores map data in files with a *.amap extension, and supports 300 map files for the United States of America, Europe, Asia, Europe, Africa, Oceania, North America, and South America. To render a desired map, you select the map source in the wizard (for example, Germany) and the map XML automatically references the desired map source .amap file, germany.amap.

Trees

Trees are typically used where you wish to represent hierarchical information. Application Builder includes a built-in wizard for generating a tree. Trees use jsTree, a JavaScript-based, cross browser tree component that features theme support, optional keyboard navigation, and optional state saving. You can create a Tree from a query that specifies a hierarchical relationship by identifying an ID and parent ID column in a table or view. The tree query utilizes a START WITH .. CONNECT BY clause to generate the hierarchical query.

Charts

Oracle Application Express supports four types of graphical charts: Flash, HTML5, SVG and HTML. You use built-in wizards provided by the Application Builder to generate the following chart types:

- Dial Chart (Flash and HTML5)
- Multiple Series (Flash and HTML5)
- Range Chart (Flash and HTML5)
- Scatter Chart (Flash and HTML5)
- Candlestick Chart (Flash and HTML5)
- Gantt Chart (Flash Only)

Figure 2-5

HTML5 Charts

These charts are supported through AnyChart HTML5 Chart Component. Now you can create animated and compact interactive charts with the help of this component which is based on flexible Flash and JavaScript. HTML5 charts are rendered in SVG format using JavaScript chart engine. Most mobile devices do not support Flash; therefore, developers can now take advantage of the new HTML5 charting solution to incorporate charts in their mobile applications. The following mobile platforms browsers support HTML5 charts:

- Android: Versions 3.1, 3.2, 4.0, 4.0.3, and 4.1
- iOs (iPhone, iPad, iPod Touch): Safari 3.2 and higher is required

Flash Charts

Similar to HTML5 charts, the support for Flash charts is also based on AnyChart through its Flash Chart Component. These charts are rendered by browsers using the FLASH_PREFERRED rendering type. You must have Flash Player 9 or above to see them. In the absence of Flash Player, the chart engine is switched to HTML5 to display an SVG-based chart.

2.21 Controlling Access to Applications, Pages, and Page Components

You can control access to an application, individual pages, or page components by using a built-in feature of APEX that creates an access-control framework with three roles: Administrator, Edit, and View. This feature is based on a wizard and provides basic security for an application. However, to avoid the downsides of the built-in access control mechanism, you have to create a more robust custom mechanism, as you'll do in this book. For further details, see the final sections of this chapter.

2.22 Incorporating JavaScript into APEX Applications

Adding JavaScript to a web application is a great way to add features that mimic those found in client/server applications without sacrificing all the benefits of web deployment. Oracle Application Express includes multiple built-in interfaces especially designed for adding JavaScript.

2.23 Declarative Support for Building Mobile Web Applications

Mobile pages use jQuery Mobile through jQuery Mobile based themes and templates. The Application Builder is enhanced to support the declarative building of mobile applications. Among the numerous changes made are: Updated Create Application wizard to support generation of applications for Desktop or Mobile; Updated Create Page and Region wizards, to expose Components applicable to Mobile applications. By incorporating jQuery Mobile applications will render correctly on all mobile devices, old and new. Applications will run on iOS, Android, BlackBerry, Windows Mobile etc. For older devices that don't fully support HTML5 equivalent components will be rendered so that users can still maintain data. Updating charting engine allows defining HTML5 charts for mobile applications. Text fields can now have sub-types of Email, Phone and URL which will bring up appropriate keyboards on HTML5 compliant devices.

2.24 Sending Email from an Application

You can use the APEX_MAIL package to send an email from an Oracle Application Express application. This package is built on top of the Oracle supplied UTL_SMTP package. Because of this dependence, the UTL_SMTP package must be installed and functioning to use APEX_MAIL.

APEX_MAIL contains three procedures. Use APEX_MAIL.SEND to send an outbound email message from your application. Use APEX_MAIL.PUSH_QUEUE to deliver mail messages stored in APEX_MAIL_QUEUE. Use APEX_MAIL.ADD_ATTACHMENT to send an outbound email message from your application as an attachment.

Create Rapid Web Application Using Oracle Application Express

2.25 Finding Objects

You can search for items, pages, queries, tables, PL/SQL code, or images by clicking the Find icon on numerous pages within Application Builder.

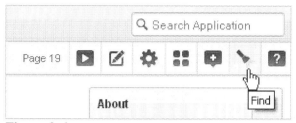

Figure 2-6

2.26 Packaged Applications

Oracle Application Express includes a number of packaged business applications, which are available free of charge, can be used as production applications and will be supported by Oracle. These applications enable customers to improve their business processes and secondly, a set of sample feature applications have been designed to help customers quickly understand specific capabilities of Application Express.

- Project Tracker
- Checklist Manager
- Customer Tracker
- Group Calendar
- Product Features
- Bug Tracker
- Asset Manager
- Document Library
- Survey Builder

The packaged applications are locked and can't be modified by customers. Customers who wish to modify a packaged applications or simply review its implementation will be able to unlock the application. Once unlocked, the application is no longer supported by Oracle and can no longer be updated. Customers can always return to a supported version by removing the unlocked copy and re-installing the locked version.

2.27 About Oracle Application Express Architecture

As pointed out earlier in this chapter that the core of Application Express is a collection of PL/SQL packages and several hundred database tables, in which all the metadata regarding developed applications are stored. Oracle Application Express consists of a metadata repository that stores the definitions of applications and an engine (called the Application Express engine) that renders and processes pages. It lives completely within your Oracle database.

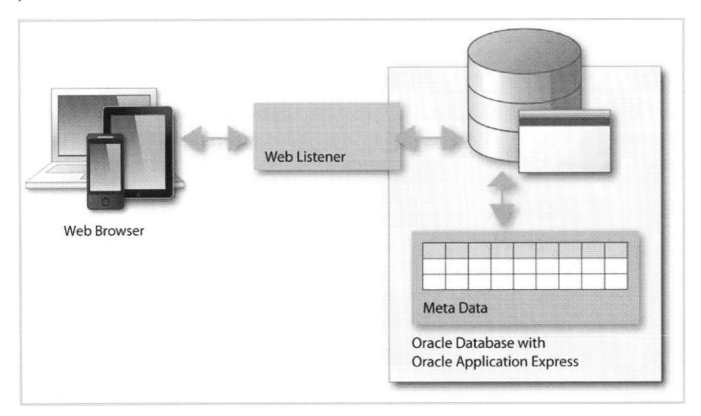

Figure 2-7

It is a simple 2-Tier architecture where browser goes through a web listener to the database – the web listener is only used to pipe requests and send responses. During run-time, the Application Express engine (in the database tier) queries the metadata tables and retrieves all the relevant information for a specific application page. Next, it generates the application page's HTML code. This page's code also includes the proper linkage to the CSS and JavaScript resources that support proper page functionality, layout, and styles. As soon as you update page definitions, the metadata can run immediately as there is no need to perform any code generation or file compilation.

In this simple architecture, we have the Application Express engine on one side running inside an Oracle database, and on the other side we have the user, accessing applications using a Web browser. In a 3-Tier architecture, the Application Express engine is accessed from a Web browser through a Web server. There are three choices of Web Server that can be used with Oracle Application Express:

1. Oracle Application Express Listener (APEX Listener)

The new Oracle APEX Listener is a J2EE based alternative for Oracle HTTP Server (OHS) and mod_plsql. The J2EE implementation offers increased functionality including a web based configuration, enhanced security, and file caching. The APEX Listener is built in Java and is installed into a J2EE Web Server. The APEX Listener is certified against Oracle Weblogic Server, Oracle Glassfish Server, and OC4J.

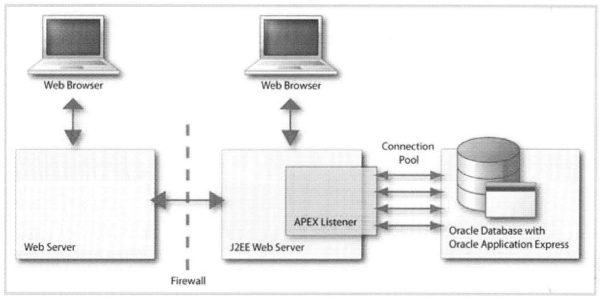

Figure 2-8 Oracle Application Express using the APEX Listener

2. Oracle HTTP Server (Apache) and mod_plsql

Oracle HTTP Server (OHS) is based on the well-known (open source) Apache HTTP server. OHS, with the mod_plsql module, is located between the client's Web browser and the Oracle database server. The Oracle HTTP Server can be installed on the same server as the database or installed on multiple servers, providing fault tolerance. The mod_plsql module communicates with the database by mapping the Web browser request into PL/SQL stored procedures in the database. In turn, the PL/SQL stored procedures can manipulate the data in the database tables and generate HTTP responses, which can include HTML code, to be displayed on the client Web browser. In order to communicate with the database, mod_plsql uses a DAD (Database Access Descriptor) file, which contains configuration parameters on how to connect with the database, which user and password to use, NLS parameters, and so on.

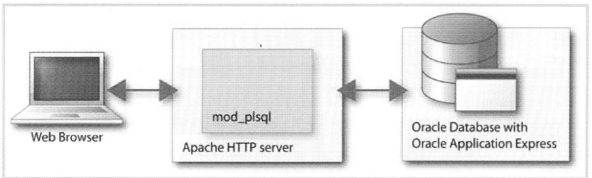

Figure 2-9 Oracle Application Express using the Oracle HTTP Server (Apache) with mod_plsql

mod_plsql provides support for deploying PL/SQL-based database applications on the World Wide Web. As part of the Oracle HTTP Server, it is the job of mod_plsql to interpret a URL sent by a Web browser to a Web server, call the appropriate PL/SQL subprograms to treat the browser request, then return the generated response to the browser. Typically, mod_plsql responds to a Web browser HTTP request by constructing an HTML page to display. Oracle HTTP Server uses the mod_plsql plug-in to communicate to the Oracle Application Express engine within Oracle Database. It functions as a communication broker between the Web server and the Oracle Application Express objects in Oracle Database. More specifically, it maps browser requests into database stored procedure calls over a SQL*Net connection. Note that this configuration consists of three tier architecture: a Web browser, Oracle HTTP Server (ohs) with mod_plsql, and an Oracle database containing Oracle Application Express.

3. Embedded PL/SQL Gateway (EPG)

Embedded PL/SQL Gateway is an integrated feature of the Oracle Database and runs in the XML Database HTTP Server. The EPG provides the Oracle Database with a Web Server and also the necessary infrastructure to create dynamic applications. It provides the equivalent core features of Oracle HTTP Server and mod_plsql. Oracle Database Express Edition (XE) also utilizes the EPG.

Because the HTTP Listener runs in the same database where Oracle Application Express is installed, it is not possible to separate the HTTP listener from the database. For this reason, Oracle does not recommend the embedded PL/SQL gateway for applications that run on the Internet. Additionally, the embedded PL/SQL gateway does not provide the same flexibility of configuration and detailed logging as Oracle HTTP Server with mod_plsql.

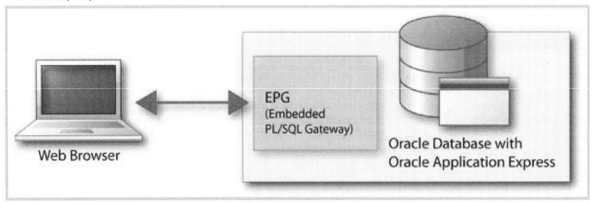

Figure 2-10 Oracle Application Express using the Embedded PL/SQL Gateway

2.28 Database Support

Oracle Application is distributed with:
- Oracle Enterprise Edition
- Oracle Standard Edition
- Oracle Standard Edition One
- Oracle XE

Supported Database Releases:
- 10gR2
- 11gR1 and 11gR2
- 12c

Application Express is available as a "No-Cost" feature in Oracle database which means you can build any number of applications and any number of users without additional licensing costs. As APEX is released more frequently than database (generally Oracle Corporation releases a new version of APEX annually), you should always update to the latest version of APEX available on OTN:
http://www.oracle.com/technetwork/developer-tools/apex/downloads/index.html. The next release will be APEX 5.0 with proposed features such as Modal Dialogs, multiple Tabular Forms on one page, Master-Detail-Detail support, and multiple Interactive Reports on one page.

2.29 APEX Development Environment

Oracle Application Express runs within the Oracle database environment. You have number of options on how you want to use APEX.

- Start developing on your laptop running Oracle XE. You can download a free copy of a developer edition of Oracle Database. We will use this approach in this book to create our Sales Web Application. In section 2.32, I will guide you to download and install Oracle Database XE and to upgrade existing Application Express version.

- Public Cloud – The Oracle Database Cloud Service is built on Oracle Database technology, running on the Oracle Exadata Database Machine, the best performing database platform in the world. The Database Cloud Service has three main components – RESTful Web service access, which allows access to the data in your Database Cloud Service through simple URIs, Oracle Application Express, for creating and deploying all varieties of applications in a browser-based environment, and a set of business productivity applications that can be installed with just a few clicks. The Database Cloud Service is simple to provision, simple to administer and simple to use to develop and deploy all types of applications. This simplicity of use is complemented by a simple pricing structure, based on only two metrics of storage and data transfer. In addition, the simplicity of the Oracle Cloud means lower costs for your own IT staff. Universal access to the components of the Oracle Cloud through a browser dramatically simplifies the maintenance overhead for your Cloud-based solutions. Applications delivered through the Oracle Cloud can be accessed from a wide variety of client platforms, including Windows, Apple or mobile devices.

- Private Cloud – This term refers to the data centers inside your company's firewall. Within your organization you can have a single Oracle Database supporting many departments with each having their own workspaces to build applications. Each of these workspaces can be granted access to one or more schemas as appropriate. The term may also apply to a private space dedicated to your company within a cloud provider's data center. Private clouds enable organizations to have complete control and visibility over security, regulatory compliance, service levels and functionality. Follow the link to have more information: http://apex.oracle.com

Oracle Application Express and your Oracle Application Express applications are built on technology that resides within an Oracle Database, so all your applications can be easily run on any Oracle platform – from the Oracle Database Cloud Service to your in-house data center to Oracle Database XE on your laptop. Once you have developed an application either on your PC or on the cloud, simply export the application, import into any other Oracle Database where you have the same version or later of Application Express installed. Deploy on the Oracle Database Cloud Service and then once your application gets wide utilization move it to your private cloud.

2.30 Application Deployment

In-house applications
- Deploy to APEX instance in company internal network
- Access from outside the network via VPN

Public-facing applications
- Deploy on APEX instance that's accessible from Internet
- Deploy to hosted site like the Oracle Cloud

2.31 What you need to develop the Sales Web Application?

You will create the Sales Web Application on your own computer. For this, you need to download Oracle Database Express Edition 11g Release 2. Oracle Database Express Edition (Oracle Database XE) is an entry-level, small-footprint database. It's free to develop, deploy, and distribute; fast to download; and simple to administer. Oracle XE comes bundled with APEX 4.0. In order to get benefits of the latest version, you have to download and upgrade APEX. A subsequent section will walk you through you on this. But first, you need to download and install Oracle XE Database.

Chapter 2 – Introduction To Oracle Application Express

2.32 Download and Install Oracle XE Database

Assuming you are using Windows XP SP2 or later, follow the sequence mentioned below to download Oracle Express Edition Database 11g Release 2:

1. Enter the following address in your browser to download the database:
   http://www.oracle.com/technetwork/products/express-edition/downloads/index.html

2. Accept the License Agreement.

3. Click on the link **Oracle Database Express Edition 11g Release 2 for Windows x32**.

4. Enter your Username and Password. If you don't have an account, sign up for a free Oracle Web account and repeat the download process.

5. Save File **OracleXE112_Win32.zip** on your computer.

6. Once downloaded, extract the .zip file, and launch the Setup file from the extracted Disk1 folder to start installation.

7. Follow the on-screen instructions to complete the installation.

> **NOTE: During the installation you are required to enter and confirm SYSTEM user password. Provide a password that you can easily remember since you'll need it in subsequent sections. I set it to** *manager*. **The Summary page provides the APEX port, 8080, as shown in the following figure. Your Installation might have configured a different port. This port is used in the URL to connect to the APEX environment like this:**
> **http://localhost:8080/apex**

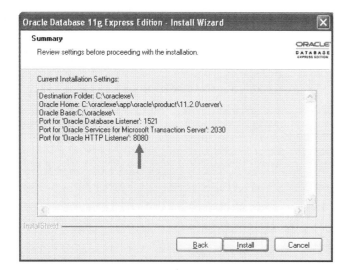

Figure 2-11

Create Rapid Web Application Using Oracle Application Express

2.33 Upgrade APEX

Oracle Database 11 g Express Edition (Oracle XE), that you just installed, includes Oracle Application Express release 4.0. In order to take advantage of the latest features you need to upgrade APEX to the most recent release. The following set of steps guide you how to do that:

1. Download the latest version of Application Express from the Oracle Technology Network.

   http://www.oracle.com/technetwork/developer-tools/apex/downloads/index.html

2. Unzip the downloaded zip file (apex_4.2.2_en.zip) and save its content under **c:\apex**. Make sure that all the files and folders go into **c:\apex** and not into **c:\apex\apex**.

3. Open a command prompt and type **cd c:\apex** and hit the Enter key. At **C:\apex>** type: **sqlplus /nolog** and hit the Enter key. At SQL> type: **CONNECT SYS as SYSDBA** and hit Enter. For Password, type **manager** and hit Enter. You'll be connected to your database. The following screen-shot illustrates this step.

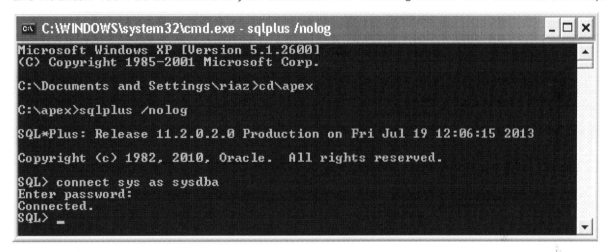

Figure 2-12

4. At the SQL> prompt type: **@apexins SYSAUX SYSAUX TEMP /i/** to install the latest Application Express version. The upgrade process may take approximately 30 minutes and will end-up with the message: Disconnected from Oracle Database 11g.

5. Log back into SQL*Plus (as above) and load images: SQL>**@apxldimg.sql C:** hit Enter.

6. Upgrade Application Express admin password: SQL>**@apxchpwd** hit Enter. Type password for Application Express ADMIN account. I entered and used **Manager_2013** in later sections of this book.

Chapter 2 – Introduction To Oracle Application Express

2.34 Create Workspace for Application

A workspace is a virtual private container allowing multiple users to work within the same Oracle Application Express installation while keeping their objects, data and applications private. You have to create a workspace before you create an application. It is necessary because you have to specify which workspace you want to connect to at the time of login. Without this piece of information, you are not allowed to enter Oracle Application Express.

1. Open a browser session and type http://localhost:8080/apex/apex_admin in the address bar to access the administrator's control panel.

2. In the Username box type **admin** and for password, type **Manager_2013**. The next screen asks you to change the admin user password. Accede to the request by entering Manager_2013 in the Current Password box and providing a new password in the next two boxes. I set this Application Express ADMIN password to Gemini_2013. Click **Apply Changes** and then the **Return** button.

3. The new login screen will come up with an additional Workspace box carrying the INTERNAL value. Making sure the Username is Admin, enter the new password you set in the previous step to login. This will bring up the admin control panel interface.

4. Click on the **Manage Workspace** icon.

5. Under Workspace Actions, select the option: **Create Workspace**.

6. In the Workspace Name box type **ASA** and click **Next**.

7. On Identify Schema page set the following attributes and click Next. A schema is the set of metadata (data dictionary) used by the database, typically generated using DDL statement. You should consider a schema to be the user account and collection of all objects therein. In this step you specified a schema ASA (Apex Sample Application) that APEX will create for you with some default objects including data tables carrying dummy data.

    Re-use existing schema? **No**
    Schema Name: **ASA**
    Schema Password: **asa**
    Space Quota (MB): 100 (accept the default values)

8. On Identify Administrator page set the following values and click Next. Note that currently you're logged in as APEX administrator whereas, in this step, you're creating administrator for the Sales Web Application workspace to manage workspace tasks such as creating the application, users and so on.

    Administrator Username: **ADMIN**
    Administrator Password: **asa**
    Email: **admin@abc.com**

9. Click the **Create Workspace** button followed by the **Done** button.

10. Click the **Logout** link located at the top right corner.

2.35 Start Building the Application

1. Login to the APEX development environment by entering **http://localhost:8080/apex** or **http://127.0.0.1:8080/apex** or **http://yourcomputerIP:8080/apex** in your browser. The localhost parameter specifies the server running your database. Since we have the database on the same machine, we'll set this parameter to localhost. In computer networking, localhost (meaning this computer) is the standard hostname given to the address of the loopback network interface. This mechanism is useful for programmers to test their software during development.

2. Enter **ASA** for Workspace, **Admin** for Username, the case-sensitive password (**asa**) that you set in step 8 in the previous section, and click the **login to Application Express** button. Once again, you'll be asked to change the admin user password. Do so as you did before. To follow the password complexity rules, put a strong password for example: Manager_2013. Click the Return button after successfully changing the password and login to the develop environment with the new password.

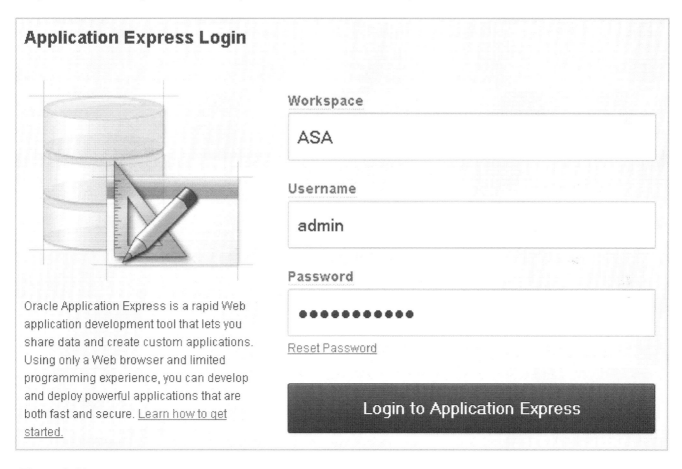

Figure 2-13

3. Click the **Application Builder** icon.

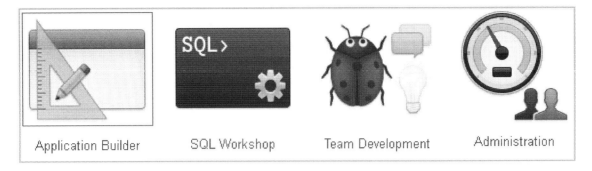

Figure 2-14

4. In the Application Builder page, click the **Create** button to create a new application.

Figure 2-15

5. Click the **Database** icon.

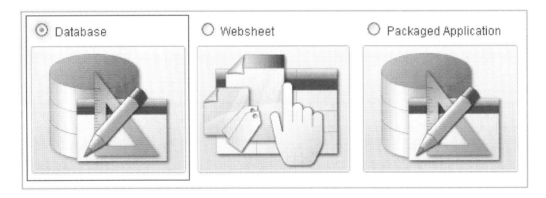

Figure 2-16

6. Enter **Sales Web Application** in the Name box and match other attribute values with those set in the following figure. Click **Next**.

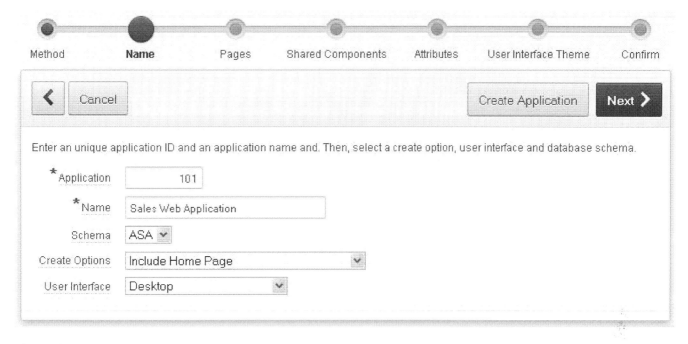

Figure 2-17

7. Accepting default values in the "Pages" page, click **Next** to move on.

8. In Shared Components Page, select **No** for **Copy Shared Components from Another Application** and click **Next**.

9. In the Attributes page, set Date and Time formats using the adjacent LOV buttons. Accept default values for Authentication Scheme and other attributes as shown in the figure below. Oracle APEX provides a number of predefined authentication mechanisms, including a built-in authentication framework and an extensible custom framework. In the selected default scheme (Application Express Accounts) users are managed and maintained in the APEX workspace. Note that in a subsequent section we will replace the default Application Express Authentication Scheme with custom authentication for this application. For the time being, click **Next** to proceed.

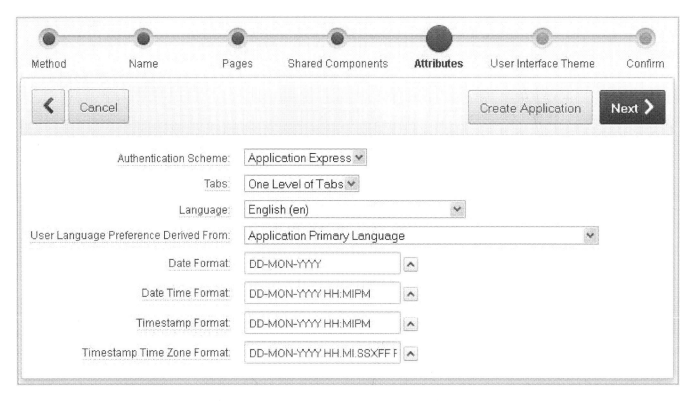

Figure 2-18

10. For User Interface Theme, select **Blue Responsive (Theme 25)** and click **Next**.

Figure 2-19

11. Click the **Create Application** button in the confirm page. Your screen should resemble the following figure. Note that APEX created the application with two pages, Page 1 (Home) and Page 101 (Login). This main application interface can be viewed differently using the three buttons: icon, report and detail. By default, the page (as shown in the figure below) is presented in report view with relevant details.

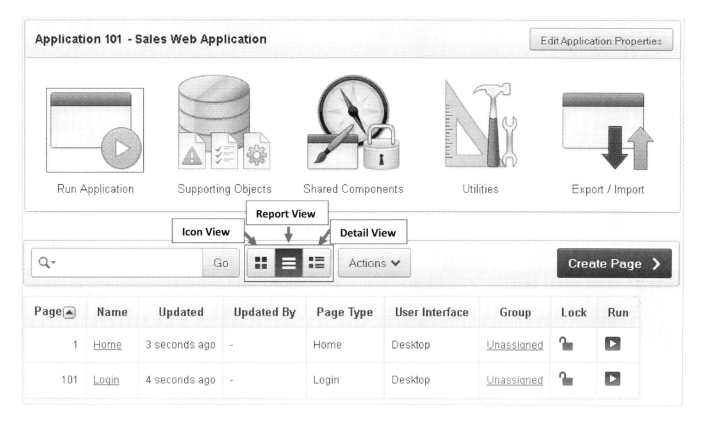

Figure 2-20

12. Click the **Run Application** icon. Type **admin** and **Manager_2013** for username and password, respectively. Click the **Login** button. You'll see the Home page of your application (as illustrated below) displaying the currently logged in user (admin) along with the Logout link. Click the **Logout** link and then the **Application 101** link at the bottom of your screen to move back to the development environment.

Figure 2-21

2.36 The Underlying Database Objects

In Step 7 of section 2.3.4 you requested APEX to create a new schema with the name ASA to hold database objects for your application. The following table lists those objects, created by APEX by default. In addition to creating the schema, APEX also creates underlying database objects (listed below) for the sample web application. View all these objects using the Object Browser utility under SQL Workshop.

Tables	Indexes	Sequences	Triggers
DEMO_CUSTOMERS	DEMO_CUSTOMERS_PK	DEMO_CUST_SEQ	DEMO_CUSTOMERS_BD
DEMO_ORDERS	DEMO_CUSTOMERS_UK	DEMO_ORDER_ITEMS_SEQ	DEMO_CUSTOMERS_BIU
DEMO_ORDER_ITEMS	DEMO_CUST_NAME_IX	DEMO_ORD_SEQ	DEMO_ORDER_ITEMS_AIUD_TOTAL
DEMO_PRODUCT_INFO	DEMO_PRODUCT_INFO_PK	DEMO_PROD_SEQ	DEMO_ORDER_ITEMS_BI
DEMO_STATES	DEMO_PRODUCT_INFO_UK		DEMO_ORDER_ITEMS_BIU_GET_PRICE
DEMO_TAGS			DEMO_PRODUCT_INFO_BD
			DEMO_PRODUCT_INFO_BIU
			DEMO_TAGS_BIU

2.37 Add Database Functions

After receiving login information, the APEX engine evaluates and executes the current authentication scheme (to be configured in the next chapter). The scheme makes a call to a function named CUSTOM_AUTH. In conjunction with the CUSTOM_HASH function, the function authenticates the user using his/her credentials stored in the DEMO_USERS table (to be created in the next section). Here are the two functions that you are required to store in your database to implement custom authentication mechanism. The CUSTOM_HASH function is a subordinate function to the CUSTOM_AUTH function and is called from the parent function to obfuscate users' password using hash algorithm. Besides assisting the custom authentication scheme, this function is used in section 10.3.9 in chapter 10 to obfuscate updated password.

CUSTOM_HASH Function

```
create or replace function custom_hash (p_username in varchar2, p_password in varchar2)
return varchar2
is
  l_password varchar2(4000);
  l_salt varchar2(4000) := 'XV1MH24EC1IHDCQHSS6XQ6QTJSANT3';
begin
-- This function should be wrapped, as the hash algorithm is exposed here.  You can change the value of l_salt or the
--method of which to call the DBMS_OBFUSCATOIN toolkit, but you must reset all of your passwords if you choose to do -
--this.
l_password := utl_raw.cast_to_raw(dbms_obfuscation_toolkit.md5
  (input_string => p_password || substr(l_salt,10,13) || p_username ||
    substr(l_salt, 4,10)));
return l_password;
end;
```

CUSTOM_AUTH Function

```
create or replace function custom_auth (p_username in VARCHAR2, p_password in VARCHAR2) return BOOLEAN is
  l_password varchar2(4000);
  l_stored_password varchar2(4000);
  l_expires_on date;
  l_count number;
begin
-- First, check to see if the user is in the user table
select count(*) into l_count from demo_users where user_name = p_username;
if l_count > 0 then
  -- Fetch the stored hashed password & expire date
  select password, expires_on into l_stored_password, l_expires_on
   from demo_users where user_name = p_username;

  -- Next, check whether the user's account is expired. If it isn't, execute the next statement, else return FALSE
  if l_expires_on > sysdate or l_expires_on is null then

    -- If the account is not expired, apply the custom hash function to the password
    l_password := custom_hash(p_username, p_password);

    -- Finally, compare them to see if they are the same and return either TRUE or FALSE
    if l_password = l_stored_password then
      return true;
    else
      return false;
    end if;
  else
    return false;
  end if;
else
  -- The username provided is not in the DEMO_USERS table
  return false;
end if;
end;
```

> The function receives username and password on line # 1 as parameters from the login form and compares this information with the values stored in the DEMO_USERS table after applying the CUSTOM_HASH function. If the provided information matches with the table values, the user is authenticated and is allowed to access the application.

Follow the instructions mentioned below to add the two database functions using SQL Scripts utility.

1. Save the above two functions as files (Custom_Hash.sql and Custom_Auth.sql) on your PC's desktop.
2. Select **SQL Scripts** from SQL Workshop.
3. Click the **Upload** button.
4. Click the **Browse** button, select **Custom_Hash.sql** file, and click **Open**.
5. Click **Upload**.
6. Repeat the same process for the Custom_Auth.sql file. After the upload, press the **Run** button individually for each file. This action will create and store the two functions in your database that you can see using SQL Workshop | Object Browser and selecting Functions from the drop-down list.

2.38 Create Demo_Users Table

While creating the application we used the default Application Express Authentication Scheme to access the application. In the next chapter, we will create a custom authentication scheme along with some Authorization schemes based on a table named DEMO_USERS. This table will carry all users of our application with their respective obfuscated passwords. The key components of this authentication scheme are CUSTOM_AUTH and CUSTOM_HASH functions. These two functions compare the given username and password to the stored values in the DEMO_USERS table. If there is a match, the user is authenticated to access the application. Besides authentication, the table also contains couple of columns (Products and Admin_User) to incorporate authorization. Follow the steps mentioned below to create this important table to fulfill the custom authentication and authorization requirements of our application. In SQL Commands under SQL Workshop, enter the following statements individually (ignoring the underlined text):

Statement # 1 – Create DEMO_USERS table:
```sql
CREATE TABLE "DEMO_USERS"
   (   "USER_ID" NUMBER,
       "USER_NAME" VARCHAR2(100),
       "PASSWORD" VARCHAR2(4000),
       "CREATED_ON" DATE,
       "QUOTA" NUMBER,
       "PRODUCTS" CHAR(1),
       "EXPIRES_ON" DATE,
       "ADMIN_USER" CHAR(1),
        CONSTRAINT "DEMO_USERS_PK" PRIMARY KEY ("USER_ID") ENABLE
   )
```

Statement # 2 – Create Trigger
```sql
CREATE OR REPLACE TRIGGER  "BI_DEMO_USERS"
BEFORE
insert on "DEMO_USERS"
for each row
begin
begin
 for c1 in (
   select DEMO_USERS_SEQ.nextval next_val
   from dual
 ) loop
   :new.USER_ID := c1.next_val;
   :new.admin_user := 'N';
   :new.created_on := sysdate;
 end loop;
end;
end;
```

Statement # 3 – Enable Trigger
```sql
ALTER TRIGGER "BI_DEMO_USERS" ENABLE
```

Statement # 4 – Create Another Trigger
CREATE OR REPLACE TRIGGER "DEMO_USERS_T1"
BEFORE
insert or update on "DEMO_USERS"
for each row
begin
:NEW.user_name := upper(:NEW.user_name);
end;

Statement # 5 – Enable Trigger
ALTER TRIGGER "DEMO_USERS_T1" ENABLE

Statement # 6 – Create Sequence to auto-generate User_ID column
CREATE SEQUENCE "DEMO_USERS_SEQ" MINVALUE 1 MAXVALUE 9999999999999999999999999999 INCREMENT BY 1 START WITH 121 CACHE 20 NOORDER NOCYCLE

Statement # 7 – Add Application Administrator Record
INSERT INTO demo_users (USER_NAME, PASSWORD, CREATED_ON, QUOTA, PRODUCTS, EXPIRES_ON, ADMIN_USER) values ('ADMIN','0CF8137A4E6A77A777C30D4AA85AC5DE', TO_DATE('01-01-2013','MM-DD-YYYY'), 0, 'Y', TO_DATE('12-31-2020','MM-DD-YYYY'),'Y')

Statement # 8 – Add Application Developer Record
INSERT INTO demo_users (USER_NAME, PASSWORD, CREATED_ON, QUOTA, PRODUCTS, EXPIRES_ON, ADMIN_USER) values ('DEMO','25F743BE60A13BC099A61DF1B8E734F7', TO_DATE('01-01-2013','MM-DD-YYYY'), 1000, 'Y', TO_DATE('12-31-2020','MM-DD-YYYY'), 'N')

Statement # 9 – Add Application User Record
INSERT INTO demo_users (USER_NAME, PASSWORD, CREATED_ON, QUOTA, PRODUCTS, EXPIRES_ON, ADMIN_USER) values ('TEST','988CB30F1EDE09BD710366F12475FED1', TO_DATE('01-01-2013','MM-DD-YYYY'), 2000, 'N', TO_DATE('12-31-2020','MM-DD-YYYY'), 'N')

After creating the custom authentication scheme in the next chapter, you'll use these three user accounts (statements 7,8 and 9) to access the application. Note that the Admin user you created using statement # 7 is different from the main Oracle APEX administrator. All the four users are listed below with their respective passwords for your understanding:

1. Application Express Administrator (ADMIN/Gemini_2013)
2. Application Workspace Administrator (ASA/ADMIN/Manager_2013)
3. Application Administrator (ADMIN/asa)
4. Application Developer (DEMO/demo)
5. Application End User (TEST/test)

2.39 Summary

This chapter introduced you to some of the important basic concepts of Oracle Application Express. Besides the theoretical stuff, you were guided to download and install the latest version of Oracle XE database and Oracle APEX. You also saw how to create workspaces for applications using the admin interface. You created the basic structure of your application with two default pages (you will work in detail on these pages in subsequent chapters to add useful content) and went through the underlying database objects that APEX created for you. Finally, to implement a custom security mechanism, you uploaded two database functions and created a table to hold application users' credentials.

In the next chapter, you will create the building blocks (the shared components) for your application. The Shared Components wizards allow us to define a variety of components that we can use, and re-use, throughout our application. In the coming chapters, our main focus will be on the practical aspect of this robust technology. Once you get familiar with Oracle Application Express, you can explore other areas on your own to become a master. The rest of the book will guide you to build a professional looking web-based data-centric desktop and mobile applications, which will provide you the techniques in building your own.

Chapter 3
Construct the Building Blocks

Chapter 3 – Construct The Building Blocks

3.1 The Shared Components

The Shared Components section of the Page Definition contains common elements that can display or be applied on any page within an application. Note that Shared Components are only displayed on the Page Definition after you add them. Following are the Shared Components that we are going to create individually for our application:

- 3.2   Tabs
- 3.3   Lists
- 3.4   Breadcrumbs
- 3.5   Navigation Bar Entries
- 3.6   Authentication Scheme
- 3.7   Authorization Scheme
- 3.8   List of Values (LOV)
- 3.9   Plug-ins
- 3.10   Images

If you are logged off, login to the application using http://localhost:8080/apex url in your browser's address bar. Enter the following credentials:

   Workspace: asa

   Username: admin

   Password: Manager_2013

1. Click on the **Application Builder** icon.

2. Click on the **Edit** button under **Sales Web Application**.

3. Click on the **Shared Components** icon.

Figure 3-1

3.2 Tabs

In this exercise we are going to create our application tabs. Tabs are an effective way to navigate between pages of an application. Application Builder includes two types of tabs: standard tabs and parent tabs. An application having only one level of tabs uses a standard tab set. A standard tab set is associated with a specific page. You can use standard tabs to link users to other pages within your application. A parent tab set functions as a container to hold a group of standard tabs. Parent tabs give users another level of navigation within the application. While creating the initial structure of the application in section 2.35, a tab set named TS1 carrying the Home tab (as shown in the following figure) was created for us. In the following set of steps you'll create the remaining tabs of your application.

1. In the Shared Components interface, click on the **Tabs** link 📄 Tabs under the Navigation section.

2. Click the tab **Manage Tabs**.

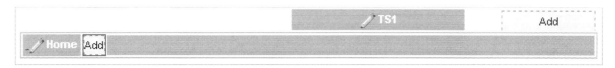

Figure 3-2

3. Click **Add** beside the existing Home entry to create a new tab with the help of a wizard.

4. Enter **Customers** in Tab Label, click **Next**.

5. Enter 2 for Tab Current for Page, click **Next**. The attribute identifies the page that makes this tab current. When the user clicks on this tab, the application will navigate to page number 2.

6. Enter 2 in Sequence box, click **Next**. It specifies the sequence for this component which determines the order in which the items will be rendered on page.

7. Accept the default condition type '**No Display Condition**' and click **Next**. A condition is specified by selecting a type from the provided list. The selected condition must be met in order for a component to be rendered or processed. You'll use this feature in the application for other components later on.

8. Click **Create Tab** button.

> **NOTE:** If you have problems running a page, try removing controls and components one at a time. Using this approach, you can quickly determine which control or component may be the source of your problem. You can disable a control or component by selecting the Never value for the Condition Type attribute.

This creates the second tab (Customers) for your application. Create the remaining application tabs (Products, Orders, Reports, and Administration) and set the attributes as shown in the following table. Once finished, your tabs should look like Figure 3-3. The attribute **Tab Also Current for Pages** means that the tab will be active for the listed page(s). For example, looking at the first entry in the table below, the values for this attribute has been left blank which means that the Home tab will be current only for the Home page (Page 1). Similarly, the second entry (Customers) has Page 7 (Customer Details) defined for this attribute which will make this tab current for both Page 2 and Page 7. Values for this attribute must be set after creating all the defined pages because at this stage setting values for it may generate a message like **Must specify an existing page** which indicates that the values for this attribute can only be set once you have created the specified page.

Tabs	Tab Label	Tab Current for Page	Sequence	Tab Also Current for Pages
Home	Home	1	1	
Customers	Customers	2	2	7
Products	Products	3	3	6
Orders	Orders	4	4	11,12,14,29
Reports	Reports	17	5	5,10,15,16,19
Administration	Administration	8	6	9

Table 3-1

Figure 3-3

3.3 Lists

After creating tabs, our next task is to create lists. A list is a collection of links that is rendered using a template. For each list entry, you specify display text, a target URL, and other attributes that control when and how the list entry displays. You control the display of the list and the appearance of all list entries by linking the list to a template.

3.3.1 Reports List

This list contains six links that lead to different graphical reports in our desktop application and appears on all pages associated with the Reports tab. See Figure 1-5 in chapter 1.

1. Go to Shared Components, Navigation Section – Lists, and click the **Create** button.

2. Select **From Scratch**. Enter **Reports List** for Name, select **Static** as the list Type, and click **Next**.

3. Enter the following values in Query or Static Values page:

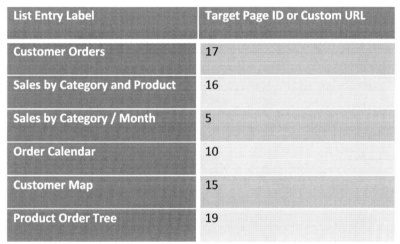

List Entry Label	Target Page ID or Custom URL
Customer Orders	17
Sales by Category and Product	16
Sales by Category / Month	5
Order Calendar	10
Customer Map	15
Product Order Tree	19

Table 3-2

4. Click **Next**, accept the default values in the next screen and click the **Create List** button. The wizard allowed you to create five entries. The sixth one – **Product Order Tree** – will be created like this:

5. In the main Lists interface, click the newly created **Reports List** icon.

Figure 3-4

6. Click the button: **Create List Entry**.

Chapter 3 – Construct The Building Blocks

7. Enter **Product Order Tree** in List Entry Label.

8. Enter **19** in the Page attribute under the Target section and click the **Create List Entry** button. That's it. Your Reports List should look like figure 3-5.

Sequence	Name	Parent Entry	Target
10	Customer Orders	-	f?p=&APP_ID.:17:&SESSION.:
20	Sales by Category and Product	-	f?p=&APP_ID.:16:&SESSION.:
30	Sales by Category / Month	-	f?p=&APP_ID.:5:&SESSION.:
40	Order Calendar	-	f?p=&APP_ID.:10:&SESSION.:
50	Customer Map	-	f?p=&APP_ID.:15:&SESSION.:
60	Product Order Tree	-	f?p=&APP_ID.:19:&SESSION.::&DEBUG.:::

Figure 3-5

3.3.2 Mobile Reports List

Create another list named Mobile Reports List for the mobile application. APEX provides a utility that lets you make a copy of an existing component. Here are the steps to create Mobile Reports List by making a copy of Reports List, you just created. See Figure 1-19 in chapter 1.

1. In the Shared Components interface, click **Lists** under the Navigation section.

2. Click on the recently created list: **Reports List**.

3. From the Tasks section to your right, select the option **Copy List**.

4. Select **List in this application** and move on.

5. Make sure that Reports List is shown in the Copy List option. Enter **Mobile Reports List** for New List Name and click the **Copy** button.

6. Move to the main Lists page and click **Mobile Reports List** you just copied. Click each link individually and set the Page attribute in the Target section as follows:

List Entry	Page
Customer Orders	209
Sales by Category and Product	210
Sales by Category / Month	211
Order Calendar	212

Table 3-3

3.3.3 Order Wizard List

This is another utilization of lists. Rather than associating list items to pages in the application, you'll use it for visual representation. This list is used while creating orders. In our application, we will create an order using a wizard in the following sequence:

    a) Identify Customer

    b) Select Items

    c) Order Summary

1. Go to **Shared Components** | **Navigation Section** | **Lists** and click the **Create** button.

2. Select the first option – **From Scratch** and click **Next**.

3. Type **Order Wizard** in the Name box, set Type to **Static** and click **Next**.

4. On the next page, enter the following values and click **Next**.

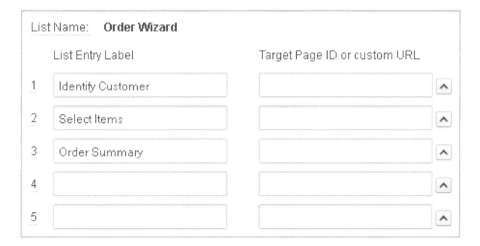

Figure 3-6

5. Click **Create List** button in the confirmation page.

6. Click the newly created **Order Wizard** list.

7. Edit each list item, set Target Type attribute to **No Target**. The target is either a page in the current application, or any valid URL. The No Target is being set because this list is intended to display the current order wizard step the user is on and not to call a page in the application. In the **Current List Entry** section, set **List Entry Current for Pages Type** to **Colon Delimited Page List** for all three list items, and set the **List Entry Current for Condition** attributes individually as shown below.

Attribute	Identify Customer	Select Items	Order Summary
List Entry Current for Condition	11	12	14

Table 3-4

Chapter 3 – Construct The Building Blocks

The attribute – List Entry Current for Pages Type – specifies when this list entry should be current. Based on the value of this attribute, you define a condition to evaluate. When this condition is true then the list item becomes current. Current items use the current template. Non-current items use the non current template. If the condition identified here is true then the item is current. You can cause a list item to use the current template which will give users a visual indication that the current list item is selected. The following figure illustrates the use of this list in our application. Being the first step in the order wizard, the Identify Customer list item is marked as current, while the remaining two non-current items are using the non current template.

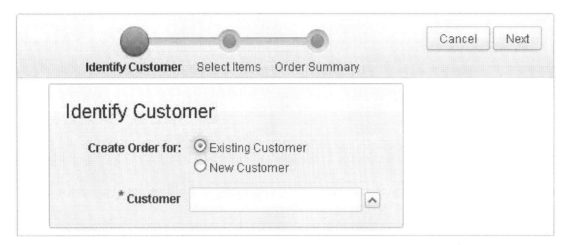

Figure 3-7

3.4 Breadcrumbs

Breadcrumbs provide hierarchical navigation to any number of levels. Breadcrumb entries are associated with pages and also identify a parent page. Here we will modify the default breadcrumb entry to give it a meaningful name. Rest of the breadcrumb entries will be defined while creating individual application pages. See Figure 1-1 in chapter 1 to see breadcrumb location on the web page.

1. Go to Shared Components and click **Breadcrumbs** under Navigation section.

2. Click the **Breadcrumb**  icon.

3. Click the button labeled **Edit Breadcrumb Name**.

4. Enter **Main Menu** in Breadcrumb Name box and click the **Apply Changes** button to save the new name.

3.5 Navigation Bar Entries

Use a navigation bar to link users to various pages within an application. Typically a navigation bar is used to enable users to log in, log out, or link to Help text. The location of a navigation bar depends upon the associated page template. A navigation bar icon enables you to display a link from an image or text. When you create a navigation bar icon you can specify an image name, text, display sequence, and target location (a URL or page).

The navigation bar in our application will have Mobile and Logout links. Besides, it will show the currently logged in user. In this exercise we are going to create these links. Please note that the Logout entry was created automatically when we initially created the application in the previous chapter.

Figure 3-8

3.5.1 Mobile Entry

This navigational bar entry will take users to the home page of the mobile application.

1. Go to Shared Components, click on **Navigation Bar Entries** in the Navigation section and click the **Create** button.

2. Select **From Scratch**.

3. For Entry Type, select **Navigation to URL** and click **Next**.

4. In Entry Label, type **Mobile** and click **Next**.

5. For Target is a attribute leave the default value **Page in this Application**. In Page attribute, type **HOME_JQM_SMARTPHONE** and click **Next**. HOME_JQM_SMARTPHONE is a Page Alias that we'll set for our mobile application's home page (Page 13) later on.

6. Click the **Create** button.

3.6 Authentication Schemes

Authentication is the process of identifying an individual, usually based on a user id and password. In a web application, you implement authentication to allow access only to authorized users. Form-based authentication in the most common type of authentication where a web form is presented to the user to provide his/her id and password. To prevent hackers from intercepting this sensitive information, a secure connection is used along with an encryption algorithm to send the information to the server.

To make your application secured you need to determine the identity of the user trying to access the application. As your first line of defense, provide a login form to the users where they input their identity along with password. For additional security you may also include an SSL certificate to your login page. An SSL Certificate (Secure Sockets Layer), also called a Digital Certificate, creates a secure link between a website and a visitor's browser.

With SSL, the browser encrypts all data that's sent to the server and decrypts all data that's received from the server. Similarly, the server encrypts all data that's sent to the browser and decrypts all data that's received from the browser. By ensuring that all data passed between the two remains private and secure, SSL encryption prevents hackers from stealing private information. SSL can also determine if data has been tampered with during transit and can also verify both client and server.

A digital secure certificate can be purchased from certification authorities (CA) like VeriSign, Thawte, Instantssl, Entrust etc. Once you get the certificate, provide it to your hosting provider who will set up the certificate in your Web server so that every time a page is accessed via the https protocol, it hits the secure server. Once that is set up, you can start building your Web pages that need to be secure.

In Oracle Application Express, the provided login details are validated against the selected scheme to check whether the user credentials are correct. The user is allowed to access the application after passing these checks. In APEX, this process is implemented through the use of following Authentication Schemes:

Application Express Accounts: Recall that we opted to use this scheme for our application while creating the blank structure of the application and provided Admin/Manager_2013 credentials to access the application (see Figure 2-18 in chapter 2). The application express engine authenticates this information using its built-in repository which stores and manages user accounts.

Database Accounts: This authentication scheme requires that a database user (schema) exists in the local database. When using this method, the user name and password of the database account is used to authenticate the user.

HTTP Header Variable: Authenticate externally, where the username is stored in a HTTP Header variable set by the web server.

LDAP Directory: Authentication of user/password with an authentication request to a Lightweight Directory Access Protocol (LDAP) server.

No Authentication (using DAD): This scheme authenticates users by adopting the current database user. This can be used in combination with a mod_plsql DAD configuration that uses basic authentication to set the database user session.

Open Door Credentials: Implementing this scheme allows all users to access the application just by entering a user name in the login page.

Oracle Application Server Single Sign-On: This delegates authentication to the Oracle AS Single Sign-On (SSO) Server. To use this authentication scheme, your site must have been registered as a partner application with the SSO server.

Custom: We will use this scheme in our application. It is based on the username and password values stored in the DEMO_USERS table and uses CUSTOM_AUTH and CUSTOM_HASH functions incorporated in chapter 2 section 2.37. Following the best practice method, you'll encrypt the data before storing it in the database. That way, if a hacker gains access to the database, he will not be able to easily read the password.

After the successful login attempt, the username is stored in a built-in substitution string named APP_USER which can be referenced in subsequent processes to retrieve the username of the current user. Follow the steps mentioned below to create the custom scheme.

1. Go to Shared Components.

2. Click the **Authentication Schemes** link under the Security section.

3. Edit the existing **Application Express Authentication** scheme.

4. Change the Name to **Custom Scheme**.

5. Select **Custom** from the Scheme Type drop down list.

6. Type **custom_auth** in Authentication Function Name under the Settings pane.

7. Click the **Apply Changes** button.

Figure 3-9

> **NOTE: In case of multiple schemes, the currently applied authentication scheme contains a check mark on its icon. Please make sure that the CUSTOM SCHEME we created in this exercise carries that check (as indicated in the above figure). If not, edit the scheme and click the Make Current Scheme button.**

Chapter 3 – Construct The Building Blocks

3.7 Authorization Schemes

Authorization schemes help you identify additional security beyond simple user authentication. For example users with administration rights may have access to more navigation bar icons, pages, and tabs than other users. This type of access right will be implemented in our application where the Administration tab will only be accessed by admin users.

3.7.1 Admin Users Scheme

This authorization scheme will be used in Page 8 of users management module in chapter 10 to allow access of this page only to the users with administrative privileges. It will be used in the same module to hide the administration tab altogether. The SELECT statement in point 6 fetches one row from the DEMO_USERS table by comparing currently logged in user (:APP_USER) with the corresponding value (user_name) in the table. In the WHERE clause, it also evaluates that the user is an administrator (admin_user='Y'). Note that we have a flag column named ADMIN_USER in the DEMO_USERS table which is populated with either Y (yes) or N (no) to signify whether the user is an administrator. If the logged in user is not an administrator, the query doesn't return a row and thus the message mentioned in point 7 is displayed. See chapter 10 where you create a new user and assign admin privileges.

1. Go to Shared Components.

2. Click **Authorization Schemes** under the Security section.

3. Click the **Create** button.

4. Select **From Scratch** and click **Next**.

5. Enter **Admin Users** in the Name box and select **Exists SQL Query** for Scheme Type.

6. In SQL Query type: **select 1 from demo_users where user_name = :APP_USER and admin_user = 'Y'**

7. In Identify error message type **You need to be an Admin User in order to view this page**. This message will be displayed to the unauthorized users who try to access this page.

8. Select **once per page view** under Evaluation Point. This attribute determines if the authorization scheme should be evaluated once per session or once per page view. Evaluating once per session is much more efficient. However, if the authorization check depends on changing session state or other factors that are not consistent over an entire session then you can choose to have the authorization scheme evaluated once per page view.

9. Click the **Create Authorization Scheme** button.

> **NOTE:** Whenever you create an authorization scheme a reciprocal opposite {NOT} scheme is created by APEX. For example, we just created Admin Users scheme, APEX created a reciprocal scheme{Not Admin Users} . You'll apply and test this reciprocal scheme after completing the Home page of the application in the next chapter .

3.7.2 Allow Product Modification Scheme

This scheme is similar to the previous one and is created to allow/disallow product information updates. Here too, we have a flag column named PRODUCTS in the DEMO_USERS table to control the modification process. A value of Y in this column allows the corresponding users modification rights to product content. The value N will revoke the right with the message shown in point 6 below.

1. In Authorization Scheme, click the **Create** button.

2. Select **From Scratch** and click **Next**.

3. Enter **Allow Product Modification** in the Name box.

4. Select **Exists SQL Query** for Scheme Type.

5. In SQL Query type: **select 1 from demo_users where user_name = :APP_USER and products = 'Y'**

6. In Identify error message type **You are not authorized to modify Product Information.**

7. Select **once per page view** under Evaluation Point.

8. Click the **Create Authorization Scheme** button.

3.7.3 Verify Order Ownership Scheme

The table DEMO_ORDERS store orders header information such as order number, date, customer ID and so on. It also stores information about the user who entered the order in a column named USER_NAME. This information is stored to evaluate order ownership and to allow modification rights to the person who actually created the order. This evaluation is done using a PL/SQL procedure (defined on the next page) which returns a Boolean value (true or false). The scheme is used in chapter 7 section 7.4.1. The error message defined in point 6 is displayed when the logged in user is not an administrator or doesn't possess order's ownership. The message is followed by the HTML <br> tag to add a line break, followed by the text 'Click', followed by HTML anchor element <a> which creates a link using the built-in substitution variables to assess current application id and session and takes the user back to the main orders page (Page 4).

1. In Authorization Scheme, click the **Create** button.

2. Select **From Scratch** and click **Next**.

3. Enter **Verify Order Ownership** in the Name box.

4. Select **PL/SQL Function Returning Boolean** for Scheme Type.

5. In PL/SQL Function Body, enter the PL/SQL function defined on the next page.

6. In Identify error message type: **You are not authorized to view this order!
 Click <a href="f?p=&APP_ID.:4:&SESSION.">here</a> to continue**

7. Select **once per page view** under Evaluation Point.

8. Click the **Create Authorization Scheme** button.

Line	PL/SQL Function
1	declare
2	l_count number;
3	begin
4	select count(*) into l_count from demo_orders
5	where order_id = :P29_ORDER_ID and user_name =
6	(select user_name from demo_users where user_name = :APP_USER);
7	if l_count > 0 or :APP_USER = 'ADMIN' then
8	return true;
9	else
10	:P29_ORDER_ID := 1;
11	return false;
12	end if;
13	end;

Line	Explanation
	PL/SQL variables are initialized in the DECLARE section. You can declare multiple variable in this section, with each variable declaration separated by a semicolon. The body of a PL/SQL block which contains program statements reside in the BEGIN section. The EXCEPTION section (not used in this code) contain statements to handle errors. PL/SQL code finishes with the END; reserve word.
1	Starts the PL/SQL function with a variable declaration.
2	The variable l_count is declared as a number.
3	The actual function begins.
4	Selects all records from DEMO_ORDERS table. The COUNT(*) built-in function returns an integer representing a count of the number of returned rows. The value of integer is stored in the variable l_count.
5-6	The WHERE clause holds filtering criteria and returns a single numeric value carrying number of records returned by the query based on the current order ID (order_id = :P29_ORDER_ID). Here, order_id is a table column that holds the value while :P29_ORDER_ID is the name of the page item referencing the order. The second condition matches the table column user_name value in the DEMO_ORDERS table with the current application user (:APP_USER). If you're logged in as Admin user and select order number 1, the query will return and store 1 in the variable l_count. But, if you're not logged in as Admin, the resulting value of the variable will be 0 because this order belongs to the Admin user.
7	The statement returns true if the value of l_count is greater than zero i.e. the order being called for modification belongs to the current user. The second portion in the IF conditional statement (:APP_USER = 'ADMIN') checks whether the current user is an administrator. Here, you're granting modification rights on all orders to the Admin user.
8	Combined together, the IF statement says: return true if the order belongs to the current user or if the user is an administrator, and allow him/her order modification rights.
9	The ELSE block is executed when none of the two conditions satisfy and
10-11	returns false after initiating the page item (:P29_ORDER_ID) with a value of 1.
12	IF condition terminated.
13	PL/SQL block completed.

3.8 List of Values (LOV)

List of values is used to control the values displayed and limits the user's selection. You can define two types of lists: Static and Dynamic. A static list of values is based on predefined display and return values. A dynamic list of values is based on a SQL query, executed at runtime. In the following exercise we are going to create both types of LOVs.

3.8.1 Categories LOV

In our application we have two types of setups: Categories and Products. The application uses three categories as shown in the figure below. Each product in the application falls under one of these categories. This LOV is created with the intention to provide three static values to the user while creating a product record to choose a category the product belongs to. This LOV is utilized in chapter 6 section 6.4.4, and chapter 11 section 11.10.

1. In Shared Components, click **Lists of Values** under the User Interface section. Lists of Values

2. Click the **Create** button.

3. Select the option **From Scratch** and click **Next**.

4. Enter **Categories** in the Name box, select **Static** as Type, and click **Next**.

5. **Fill in the values** as show in the following figure and click **Create List of Values** button.

Sequence	Display Value	Return Value
1	Mens	Mens
2	Womens	Womens
3	Accessories	Accessories

Figure 3-10

In the last step of the LOV wizard, you entered static Display and Return values. Values will display in the order entered. Return Value does not display, but is the value that is returned as a user selection to the Application Express engine. If you do not specify a Return Value then it is equal to the Display Value. You can display additional attributes including build option controls and item level conditional display by editing the List of Values.

3.8.2 Products with Price LOV

Similar to the categories list of value, this one also limits user's selection by displaying product names with prices during order creation. This time you'll generate the list dynamically with the help of a SQL statement. It is utilized in chapter 7 section 7.4.2 step 5.

1. Once again click the **Create** button in Lists of Values.

2. Select **From Scratch** and click **Next**.

3. Enter **Products with Price** in the Name box, select **Dynamic** as Type, Click **Next**.

4. In the Query box type:

    select htf.escape_sc(product_name) || ' [$' || list_price || ']' d, product_id r
    from demo_product_info
    where product_avail = 'Y'
    order by 1

    Escape_sc is a function which replaces characters that have special meaning in HTML with their escape sequence.

    converts occurrence of & to &amp
    converts occurrence of " to &quot
    converts occurrence of < to &lt
    converts occurrence of > to &gt

    To prevent XSS (Cross Site Scripting) attacks, you must call SYS.HTF.ESCAPE_SC to prevent embedded JavaScript code from being executed when you inject the string into the HTML page. The SYS prefix is used to signify Oracle's SYS schema. HTP and HTF are Oracle database packages that normally exist in the SYS schema and APEX relies on them.

5. Click **Create List of Values** button.

3.8.3 States LOV

This is a dynamic list and is based on a SQL SELECT query that fetches name of States from DEMO_STATES table. The query fetches both columns from the table. This LOV is used in chapter 5 section 5.4.4 and chapter 11 section 11.7 where it is attached to the state column in the customer form.

1. In Lists of Values, click the **Create** button.

2. Select the **From Scratch** option and click **Next**.

3. Enter **States** in the Name box, select **Dynamic** as Type, and click **Next**.

4. In the Query box type:

    select initcap(state_name) display_value, st return_value from demo_states order by 1

5. Click **Create List of Values** button

3.8.4 Y or N LOV

We have two flag columns in the DEMO_USERS table to authorize users to modify products and grant them administrative rights. These columns (PRODUCTS and ADMIN_USER) receive either Y (yes) or N (no) values to determine users rights. A Y value in the Products column allows users to handle the products setup module (chapter 6), while this value in the ADMIN_USER column specifies that the user is the application administrator. In chapter 10 section 10.2.2, we'll turn these columns into radio and select list input elements to grant or revoke administrative privileges. The list created in this section will be attached to the form's radio elements so that the administrator could select a single option. It is also used in the Product setup module (section 6.4.4) to specify whether the product is available or not.

11. In Lists of Values, click **Create**.

12. Select **From Scratch** and click **Next**.

13. Enter **Y or N** in the Name box, select **Static** as Type, and click **Next**.

14. **Fill in the values** as show in the following figure and click **Create List of Values**.

Sequence	Display Value	Return Value
1	Yes	Y
2	No	N
3		

Figure 3-11

3.8.5 New or Existing Customer LOV

This static list will be incorporated in the initial Order Wizard step to select either an existing customer or to create a new one.

1. In Lists of Values, click **Create**.

2. Select **From Scratch** and click **Next**.

3. Enter **NEW OR EXISTING CUSTOMER** in the Name box, select **Static** as Type, and click **Next**.

4. **Fill in the values** as show in the following figure and click **Create List of Values**.

List of Values Name:	NEW OR EXISTING CUSTOMER	
Sequence	Display Value	Return Value
1	Existing Customer	EXISTING
2	New Customer	NEW

Figure 3-12

Chapter 3 – Construct The Building Blocks

3.9 Plug-Ins

Plug-ins enable developers to declaratively extend, share, and reuse the built-in types available with Oracle Application Express. Oracle Application Express supports a set group of authentication scheme, authorization scheme, item, region, dynamic action, and process types. Plug-ins offer a means of augmenting these built-in types by declaratively creating and using new types in your application. Because plug-ins are designed for reuse, developers can export and import them to other workspaces and also share them with others. The process of implementing a plug-in involves the following steps:

1. Create a plug-in or import a plug-in in to your application workspace.
2. Edit or create an authorization scheme, item, region, process, or dynamic action type to use the plug-in.
3. Run your application to test the plug-in.

3.9.1 CSS Bar Chart Plug-In

You'll create a CSS Bar Chart in your application's Home page to show top orders by date. CSS Bar Chart is a plug-in developed by APEX community and is included in the source code of this book. You just need to import this plug-in to use it in the Home page. See chapter 4 section 4.3.6 for its utilization.

1. In Shared Components, click **Plug-ins** under User Interface section. Plug-ins

2. Click the **Import** button.

3. Click the **Browse** button, select **css_bar_chart.sql** file from the downloaded book source, and click the **Open** button. Make sure that the option Plug-in is selected in File Type.

4. Click **Next** to move on.

5. A message **The export file has been imported successfully** would appear. Click **Next** to install the file.

6. Select your application (Sales Web Application) from the **Install Into Application** list and click the **Install Plug-in** button. The plug-in (CSS Bar Chart) will be installed with a confirmation message.

3.9.2 Masked Field Plug-In

This is another plug-in that is included in the book's source code. In chapter 5 you'll create a form to enter and save customers profile. Besides other information, you'll store each customer's phone numbers in the relevant table. The purpose of this plug-in is to receive and store these phone numbers in (999) 999-9999 format. See chapter 5 section 5.4.5 for details.

1. Under Shared Components | Plug-ins, click the **Import** button.

2. Click the **Browse** button, select **masked_field.sql** file from the **book source** folder, and click the **Open** button. Make sure that File Type is set to Plug-in.

3. Click **Next** to move on.

4. A message **The export file has been imported successfully** would appear. Click **Next** to install the file.

5. Select Sales Web Application from the **Install Into Application** list and click the **Install Plug-in** button. The masked field plug-in will be installed with a confirmation message.

3.10 Images

You can reference images within your application by uploading them to the Images Repository. When you upload an image, you can specify whether it is available to all applications or a specific application. Images uploaded as shared components can be referenced throughout an application. They may include images for application tabs or buttons or may represent icons that, when clicked, allow users to modify or delete data. One important point to remember here is that the images uploaded to the images repository should not be directly related to the application's data such as images of products and employees. Such images must be stored in the application's schema alongside the data to which the image is related. You'll follow this approach in chapter 9 (Product Setup) to save each product's image along with other product information in a database table.

Application Express images are divided into two categories:

- **Workspace images** are available to all applications for a given workspace
- **Application images** are available for only one application

In the following set of steps, you'll add your application's logo to the images repository. The logo appears at the top of every page in the application.

1. In Shared Components, click **Images** under Files section. 🖼 Images

2. Click the **Create** button.

3. Select **Sales Web Application** from the Application drop down list.

4. Click the **Browse** button and select logo.PNG (provided with the book code).

Figure 3-13

5. Click the **upload** button. After uploading the image, you need to tell APEX to use this file as your application logo. To pass this information, execute the following steps.

6. In Shared Components click 🌐 Globalization Attributes under Globalization section.

7. Click the **User Interface** tab.

8. Select **Image** as Logo Type.

9. Enter **#APP_IMAGES#logo.PNG** in the Logo box (Use the correct case for the image file name and extension else the logo will not be displayed) and click the **Apply Changes** button. The substitution string (APP_IMAGES) is used to reference uploaded images, JavaScript, and cascading style sheets that are specific to a given application and are not shared over many applications. If you upload a file and make it specific to an application, then you must use this substitution string, or bind variable.

3.11 Summary

In this chapter you created all the components required by the application with relevant references. These shared components were created declaratively with the help of APEX wizards to demonstrate yet another great feature of this technology to tackle redundancy. From the next chapter you will be creating all the pages of your web application (starting with the Home page) and will see all the shared components in action. After creating an application page, the right-hand column on the Page Definition page includes eight sections that displays shared components (Tabs, List of Values, Breadcrumbs, Lists, Templates, Theme, Security, and Navigation Bar) and shows individual components that have been used on that particular page.

Chapter 4
The Home Page

Chapter 4 - The Home Page

4.1 About the Home Page

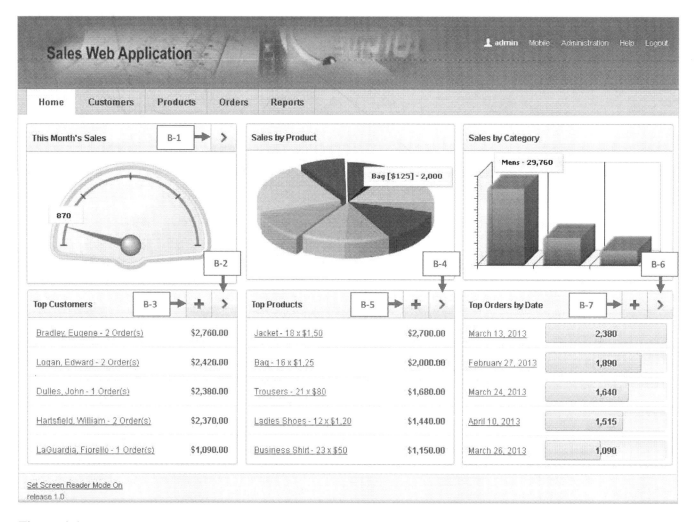

Figure 4-1

Every website on the internet has a home page. Technically referred to as the default page, it is the page that comes up when you call a website without mentioning a specific page. For example, if you call Oracle's official website using the URL www.oracle.com, the first page you see is the default or home page of the website. It is the page that represents the objective of a website. Similar to a website, a web application also carries this page. By default, Oracle APEX creates this page along with a login page, both for desktop and mobile applications. The desktop login page, that you used to access the application in the previous chapter, usually doesn't require any modification or enhancement. It comes with out-of-the-box functionalities and utilizes current authentication scheme to process the login request. The Home page, on the other hand, is created as a blank slate that you need to populate with content relevant to your application's theme. For instance, the Home page of your Sales Web Application will have stuff related to sales. See chapter 1 for further details on the Home page.

Let's experience the APEX declarative development environment by completing this page of our web application which is a dashboard and holds six regions to present different views of sales data.

4.2 Modify the Home Page

Before we delve into practical process, let's first acquaint ourselves with definitions of an APEX page. The Page Definition, as shown in the figure below, is the interface that you'll use to view, create, and edit application logic and controls on web pages. It has two views (Component and Tree) to browse the controls and logic and has three main sections (Rendering, Processing and Shared Components) each having sub-sections with Edit and Create icons to modify and add new controls and logic to a web page. See chapter 2 section 2.9 and 2.10 for further reading.

1. Type http://localhost:8080/apex in your browser's address bar and login to APEX using admin user's credentials. See chapter 2 section 2.38 for login information.

2. Click the **Application Builder** icon and then the **Edit** icon under Sales Web Application.

3. Click the **Home** link in the Name column (if you're browsing the page in Report view). This will bring up the definition page as shown in figure 4-2. Click the **Component View** button.

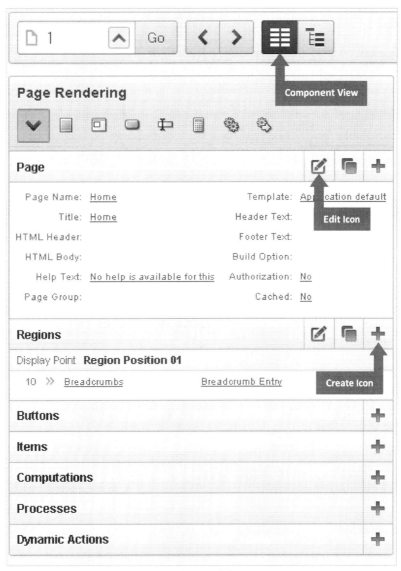

Figure 4-2

Chapter 4 – The Home Page

4.2.1 Modify Page Attributes

Modify Name and Title attributes of the Home page with meaningful labels. The Name attribute gives the page a meaningful name for recognition. The value defined in the Title attribute is displayed in the title bar of the browser window. The Application Express engine uses the title you specify here in place of the #TITLE# substitution string used in the page template. This title is inserted between the HTML tags <TITLE> and </TITLE>.

1. In **Page Rendering**, click the **Edit** icon in **Page section** (see Figure 4-2). Click the **Show All** tab and set the following attributes. After setting these attributes, click the **Apply Changes** button.

Attribute	Value
Name	Sales Web Application
Title	Sales Web Application

4.3 Create Regions

You put items on a page under a specific region. A region is an area on a page that serves as a container for content. You can create multiple regions to visually segregate different sections on a page and to group page elements. A region may carry a SQL report or static HTML content which is determined by the region source. Each region can have its own template applied which controls their respective appearance. For further details on regions, see section 2.13. The following sub-sections demonstrate how multiple regions are created on a page.

4.3.1 This Month's Sales

As the name implies, this region will present sales figures in graphical format (using a dial chart), for the current month. The chart is dynamically rendered based on a SQL Statement each time the page is viewed. The value 870 being displayed on the chart is the sales value for the current month derived from the SQL SELECT statement in step 9 and is displayed by enabling *Values* attribute in step 12 below. Similarly, the attribute *Major Ticks* is enabled to display marks on the gauge chart. Major tick marks are the small marks used to represent a point on an axis scale, they indicate major intervals of an axis scale. For example, we set *Major Interval* attribute to 2500 in step 12 which created four equal intervals on the chart. This attribute works in conjunction with the max value (10000) set in the SQL SELECT statement.

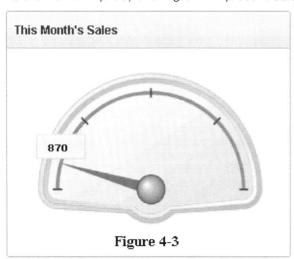

Figure 4-3

1. In the Regions section, delete the existing region named Breadcrumbs. APEX created this default entry at the time of application creation. Click the region name Breadcrumbs and then click the **Delete** button. Confirm deletion by clicking the **Delete Region** button.

2. Click the **Create** icon in the Regions section to create a new region.

3. In the Region page, click on the **Chart** icon.
4. From *Chart Rendering* list, select **HTML5 Chart**.
5. Click the **Gauges** option.
6. Select **Dial**.
7. Enter **This Month's Sales** in Title, select **Standard Region – No Padding** for Region Template (you're free to test other available options for Region Template). Enter **20** in Sequence and click the **Next** button.
8. Select **Look6** for *Color Scheme*, un-check the *Show Labels* box, and click **Next**. Use another scheme with a check on Show Labels to see the impact, after completing the exercise.
9. Enter the following SQL Query in the *Enter SQL Query or PL/SQL function returning a SQL Query* box. Click **Next**.

   select sum(o.order_total) total, 10000 max, 0 low
   from demo_orders o
   where order_timestamp >= to_date(to_char(sysdate,'YYYYMM')||'01','YYYYMMDD')

10. Click the **Create Region** button. You'll be taken back to the Page Definition where you'll see a new region with the name This Month's Sales under the Regions section. Click this link to call the region for the following modifications.

Attribute	Value
Start New Row	Yes
Column	Automatic
Column Span	4

11. Click the **Chart Attributes** tab on the same page to set the following chart attributes:

Attribute	Value
Chart Width	300
Chart Height	180
Values	Checked
Major Ticks	Checked
Major Interval	2500

12. Save your changes by clicking the **Apply Changes** button.

> **NOTE:** APEX enables you to test your work from time to time. For example, after completing this exercise in step 12, you can run the page (using the Run button) to check how the region appears on it.

This application is based on Theme 25 (new to APEX 4.2) that uses a grid layout (comprising 12 columns) to position page elements. The first attribute, in step 10, is set to Yes to put the region on a new row. Compare this value to the next region (Sales by Product), where it is set to No to place that region next to this one. The value Automatic in the Column attribute automatically finds a column position for the region. Since there exists no elements on the current row, column number 1 will be used as the starting place to position this region. As you can see in Figure 4-1, we have placed three regions on a single row. Equally divided in a 12 columns layout, each region spans 4 columns and this is the value we set for all the six regions on the Home page. This particular region will span from column number 1 to 4.

4.3.2 Sales by Product

This region is intended to show individual product sale figures using a pie chart. Hovering the mouse pointer over the pie slices display those figures, as illustrated below.

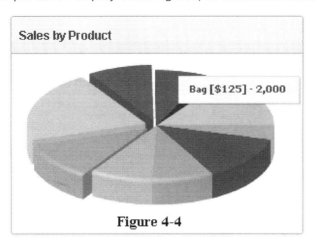

Figure 4-4

1. Click the **Create** ✚ icon in the Regions section to create a new Region.
2. In the Region page, click on the **Chart** icon.
3. From *Chart Rendering* list, select **Flash Chart** and click the **Pie & Doughnut** option. In order to view the Flash impact, you need to have Flash Player 9 or above installed on your PC.
4. Click on **3D pie**.
5. Enter **Sales by Product** in Title, select **Standard Region – No Padding** for Region Template, **30** in Sequence and click the **Next** button.
6. Select **Look6** for *Color Scheme*, un-check the *Show Labels* and *Show Values* boxes, and click **Next**.
7. Enter the following SQL Query in the *Enter SQL Query or PL/SQL function returning a SQL Query* box. Click **Next**.
   select null, p.product_name||' [$'||p.list_price||']' product, SUM(oi.quantity * oi.unit_price) sales
   from demo_order_items oi, demo_product_info p
   where oi.product_id = p.product_id
   group by p.product_id, p.product_name, p.list_price
   order by p.product_name desc
8. Click the **Create Region** button.
9. Click the link of the newly created region (Sales by Product) in the Regions section and set the following attributes. The region will be placed on the same row next to the existing one: This Month's Sales. The next column position (5) will be selected automatically. This region will also span 4 columns from 5-8.

Attribute	Value
Start New Row	No
Column	Automatic
New Column	Yes
Column Span	4

10. Click the **Chart Attributes** tab on the same page to set the following chart attributes:

Attribute	Value
Chart Width	300
Chart Height	180
Animation	Appear

> **NOTE:** You can define custom color scheme by adding your own colors to the chart with the help of color picker palette or by adding hex color values. Custom color scheme is used by setting the following two attributes:
> *Color Scheme*: Custom
> *Custom Colors*:
> 05FA05,#FF0000,#00ABFA,#87FA03,#FF8400, #DBF705,#0857F7,#7700FF,#112E01,#781200

11. Save your changes by clicking the **Apply Changes** button.

4.3.3 Sales by Category

This region demonstrates the use of bar charts and presents sale figures of each category through this chart type.

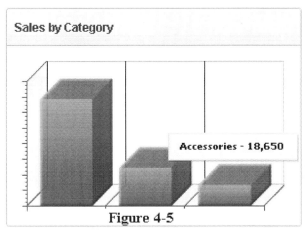

Figure 4-5

1. Click the **Create** icon in the Regions section to create a new Region.
2. In the Region page, click on the **Chart** icon.
3. From *Chart Rendering* list, select **Flash Chart**. And click the **Column** chart option.
4. Click on **3D Column**.
5. Enter **Sales by Category** in Title, select **Standard Region – No Padding** for Region Template, **40** in Sequence and click the **Next** button.
6. Select **Look6** for *Color Scheme*, un-check the *Show Labels* and *Show Values* boxes, and click **Next**.
7. Enter the following SQL Query in the *Enter SQL Query or PL/SQL function returning a SQL Query* box. Click **Next**.

   ```
   select null, p.category label, sum(o.order_total)
   from demo_orders o, demo_order_items oi, demo_product_info p
   where o.order_id = oi.order_id
   and oi.product_id = p.product_id
   group by category order by 3 desc
   ```

8. Click the **Create Region** button.
9. Click the link of the newly created region and set the following attributes.

Attribute	Value
Start New Row	No – used the same row
Column	Automatic – Next position is 9
New Column	Yes
Column Span	4 – The region will span from column 9-12

NOTE: In APEX you create a chart using a SQL query which has the following syntax:
SELECT link, label, value FROM ...
The link column helps you drill-down to further details. You'll use the link column in chapter 8 - Generate Graphical Reports. Right now the drill-down functionality is not being used, therefore, a null is put in the link position to follow the syntax rule.

10. Click the **Chart Attributes** tab on the same page to set the following chart attributes:

Attribute	Value
Chart Width	300
Chart Height	180
Animation	Appear

11. Save your changes by clicking the **Apply Changes** button.

Chapter 4 – The Home Page

4.3.4 Top Customers Region

This region will display top five customers with highest orders and will present the information in text format using the another option named Reports.

Top Customers

Bradley, Eugene - 2 Order(s)	$2,760.00
Logan, Edward - 2 Order(s)	$2,420.00
Dulles, John - 1 Order(s)	$2,380.00
Hartsfield, William - 2 Order(s)	$2,370.00
LaGuardia, Fiorello - 1 Order(s)	$1,090.00

Figure 4-6

1. Click the **Create** ✚ icon in the *Regions* section.
2. Click on the **Report** icon.
3. Select **Classic Report**.
4. Enter **Top Customers** in *Title*, select **Standard Region – No Padding** for *Region Template*, enter **30** in *Sequence*, and click **Next**
5. Enter the following SQL Query in *Enter SQL Query or PL/SQL function returning a SQL Query* and click **Next**.

```
select  b.cust_last_name || ', ' || b.cust_first_name || ' - '|| count(a.order_id) ||' Order(s)' customer_name, sum(a.order_total) order_total,  b.customer_id id
from demo_orders a, demo_customers b
where a.customer_id = b.customer_id
group by b.customer_id, b.cust_last_name || ', ' || b.cust_first_name
order by nvl(sum(a.order_total),0) desc
```

6. Click **Create Region**.
7. **Edit** the newly created region, *Top Customers*, and set the following attribute:

Attribute	Value
Start New Row	Yes – Put the region on a new row
Column	1 – Place it in column number 1
Column Span	4 – The region will span from column 1-4

8. Click on the **Report Attributes** tab on the same page and set the following attributes:

Attribute	Value
Heading Type	None – Eliminate column headings
Report Template	Template: 25. Two Column Portlet
Pagination Scheme	No Pagination Selected
Number or Rows	5
Maximum Rows Count	5

We set Heading Type to None to suppress column headings. In order to show the two columns (customer name and order total), we set Report template to two columns. Pagination is suppressed since we want to see only five records in the region. Often only a certain number of rows of a report display on a page. In order to include additional rows, the application user needs to navigate to the next page of the report. Pagination provides the user with information about the number of rows and the current position within the result set. Pagination also defines the style of links or buttons that are used to navigate to the next or previous page.

9. In Column Attribute section, edit column **Customer_Name** by clicking the pencil icon to its left.

10. Scroll down to **Column Link** section, set the following attributes and click the **apply changes** button.

Attribute	Value
Link Text	#CUSTOMER_NAME#
Page	7
Clear Cache	7
Item 1	P7_CUSTOMER_ID
Value	#ID#
Item 2	P7_BRANCH
Value	1

    The column link section provides us with the ability to specify attributes about the link we wish to create. The purpose of setting the above attributes is to place hyperlinks on customer name column to provide drill-down capability. We specified CUSTOMER_NAME column in the Link Text attribute. When you run this page, each customer's name would appear as a hyperlink and would call customer's profile page (Page 7) when you click any of these links. After specifying the Link Text, we set Page attribute to 7 which is the page we wish to navigate to. We also specified Items and the Values. Item 1 (P7_CUSTOMER_ID) refers to an item on Page 7 that will be populated with the value (#ID#) and passed to Page 7 from this Home page to display profile of the selected customer. The value of Item 2 (P7_BRANCH) is set to 1 which is referenced in the sole branch in Page 7 to bring you back to the Home page when you click Apply Changes button after editing a customer profile. If you set this value to something else, for instance 3, you'll be taken to the product setup page (Page 3).

    > **NOTE:** You can input the above values using the keyboard or by using the adjacent Pick Column/LOV icons to select values from the popup list. Also note that the above link will work after creating Page 7 in Chapter 5.

11. Edit the ORDER_TOTAL column. Using the LOV icon, set Number/Date format by selecting $5,234.10 from the popup list. This would apply number format mask to values in the ORDER_TOTAL column by prefixing a $ symbol and adding a thousand separator. Click **Apply Changes**.

12. Un-check the **Show** column corresponding to the ID column in the Column Attribute section to hide it at runtime. Apply the change.

Chapter 4 – The Home Page

4.3.5 Top Products Region

This region is similar to Top Customers and displays five top selling products.

Top Products

Jacket - 18 x $1.50	$2,700.00
Bag - 16 x $1.25	$2,000.00
Trousers - 21 x $80	$1,680.00
Ladies Shoes - 12 x $1.20	$1,440.00
Business Shirt - 23 x $50	$1,150.00

Figure 4-7

1. Once again, click the **Create** + icon in the Regions section.
2. Click on **Report**.
3. Click on **Classic Report**.
4. Enter **Top Products** in *Title*, select Standard Region – No Padding for *Region Template*, enter **40** in *Sequence*, and click **Next**.
5. Enter the following SQL Query in *Enter SQL Query or PL/SQL function returning a SQL Query* and click **Next**.

```
Select p.product_name||' - '||SUM(oi.quantity)||' x '||to_char(p.list_price,'L999G99')||'' product,
       SUM(oi.quantity * oi.unit_price) sales, p.product_id
from demo_order_items oi, demo_product_info p
where oi.product_id = p.product_id
group by p.Product_id, p.product_name, p.list_price
order by 2 desc
```

6. Click **Create Region**.
7. **Edit** the newly created region and set the following attribute:

Attribute	Value
Start New Row	No – Place the region to the right of the previous one
Column	5 – Instead of using Automatic, we used an alternate method by specifically mentioning the column number
Column Span	4 – Span the region from column 5-8

8. Click on the **Report Attributes** tab and set the following attributes:

Attribute	Value
Heading Type	None
Report Template	Template: 25. Two Column Portlet
Pagination Scheme	No Pagination Selected
Number or Rows	5
Maximum Rows Count	5

9. In Column Attributes section, edit the **Product** column by clicking the pencil icon to its left.
10. Go to **Column Link** section, set the following attributes and **apply changes**.

Attribute	Value
Link Text	#PRODUCT#
Page	6
Clear Cache	6
Item 1	P6_PRODUCT_ID
Value	#PRODUCT_ID#
Item 2	P7_BRANCH
Value	1

11. Edit the **SALES** column. Using the LOV icon, set Number/Date format by selecting **$5,234.10** from the popup list. Click **Apply Changes**.
12. Un-check the **Show** column corresponding to the PRODUCT_ID column in the Column Attribute section to hide it at runtime. Apply the change. Again, Page 6 which is referenced in the Link Column section will be displayed when you create it in chapter 6.

4.3.6 Top Orders by Date

This region will display top five orders by date from the database using a CSS Bar Chart plug-in that we imported in chapter 2 section 3.9.1.

Figure 4-8

1. Click the Create + icon in the Regions section to create a new region.
2. This time, select the **Plug-ins** option.
3. Select the option **CSS Bar Chart** and click **Next**.
4. For Title, enter **Top orders by Date**, select **Standard Region – No Padding** for *Region Template*, enter **50** in *Sequence*, and click **Next**.
5. Enter the following SQL Query in the Region Source and click **Next**:

```
select to_char(o.order_timestamp,'Month DD, YYYY') order_day, SUM(o.order_total) sales,
'f?p=&APP_ID.:4:'||:app_session||':::RIR,4:IREQ_ORDER_DATE:'||trunc(order_timestamp) the_link
from demo_orders o
group by to_char(o.order_timestamp,'Month DD, YYYY'), order_timestamp
order by 2 desc
```

6. In the *Display As* drop down list, select **Value with absolute bar width**, enter **5** for *Maximum Rows* attribute and click the **Create Region** button.
7. **Edit** the newly created region by clicking its name in the Page Definition and set the following attribute:

Attribute	Value
Start New Row	No
Column	9
Column Span	4

8. Click **Apply Changes**.

In the SQL SELECT statement, on the previous page, you are creating links to redirect to Page 4 – Orders (an interactive report) using APEX f?p syntax to display list of orders for the selected date. Unlike classic reports which typically use page items as report parameters, the data in an interactive report is driven by declarative filters. In the syntax, the RIR string (short for Reset Interactive Report) is used in the Clear Cache position to reset the interactive report. This is equivalent to the end user selecting the Reset option from the interactive report Actions menu on the target page. This argument returns the report to its default settings specified by the developer or saved by the user. Next, you used the IR string along with the operator EQ followed by a filter _ORDER_DATE:trunc(order_timestamp) to create a filter on the report. The TRUNC (date) function returns date with the time portion of the day truncated. To create a filter on an interactive report in a link, use the string **IR<operator>_<target column alias>** in the ItemNames section of the URL, and pass the filter value in the corresponding location in the ItemValues section of the URL. See section 2.17 in chapter 2 on APEX f?p syntax. Other operators that you can use to filter an interactive report include:

- EQ = Equals (the default operator)
- LT = Less than
- GT = Greater than
- LTE = Less than or equal to
- GTE = Greater than or equal to
- LIKE = SQL LIKE operator
- N = Null

The output of the above SQL statement would be something like this:

ORDER_DAY	SALES	THE_LINK
March 13, 2013	2730	f?p=4500:4:16438278322244:::RIR,4:IREQ_ORDER_DATE:03/13/2013
March 13, 2013	2380	f?p=4500:4:16438278322244:::RIR,4:IREQ_ORDER_DATE:03/13/2013
April 10, 2013	1515	f?p=4500:4:16438278322244:::RIR,4:IREQ_ORDER_DATE:04/10/2013
April 23, 2013	1060	f?p=4500:4:16438278322244:::RIR,4:IREQ_ORDER_DATE:04/23/2013
April 05, 2013	950	f?p=4500:4:16438278322244:::RIR,4:IREQ_ORDER_DATE:04/05/2013
More than 10 rows available. Increase rows selector to view more rows.		

Figure 4-9

After completing Page 4 (Orders) in chapter 7, when you run the Home page and click any of the appearing date links, the interactive report defined on the target page will appear with a filter applied as shown below.

Order Date = 3/13/2013

Order #	Customer Name	Sales Rep	Order Items	Order Total	Tags	Order Date	Order Month
0004	LaGuardia, Fiorello	TEST	5	$1,090.00	-	3/13/2013	March 2013
0003	Hartsfield, William	TEST	5	$1,640.00	-	3/13/2013	March 2013
0002	Dulles, John	DEMO	10	$2,380.00	LARGE ORDER	3/13/2013	March 2013

Figure 4-10

Chapter 4 – The Home Page

4.4 Create Buttons

After creating all the regions, your next task is to create buttons on top of each region. These buttons provide drill-down functionality and takes user to relevant pages to dig further details for the provided summarized information. Each region will have a pair of buttons (add and view) to create a new record and to browse further details of the provided information. You'll be redirected to the relevant page when you click any of these buttons. For instance, if you click the Add Customer button in the Top Customers region, you will be redirected to Customer Details page (Page 7).

4.4.1 View Orders For This Month

The first region on the Home page, containing a dial chart, will have a single button to drill into current month's order details. Follow the steps mentioned below to create this button. After completion, a button with the tooltip "View order for this month" will be added to the top of the region. This button is marked as B-1 in Figure 4-1.

1. Click the **Create** icon in the Buttons section to create a new button.

2. From the available options in *Select a region for the button*, select **This Month's Sales (20)** and click **Next**. The button will be placed in the selected region.

3. Select the option: **Create a button in a region position**. This attribute work in conjunction with point 5 to position the button.

4. Enter **VIEW_MONTH_ORDERS** for *Button Name*, **View Orders for this Month** for *Label*, set *Button Style* to **Template Based Button**, set *Button Template* to **Large Button - Icon Only**, click **Next**.

5. Set *Sequence* to **10**, button *Position* to **Region Template Position #CREATE#** and click **Next**. Position is a select list field that allows us to choose the location of the button. You can choose a location that is relative to the region itself, like Above Region, or Bottom of Region; or you can choose a predefined location inside the region that correlates with a specific Substitution String in the region template, such as Region Template Position #EDIT#.

6. Set *Action* to **Redirect to Page in this Application**, enter **4** in *Page*, **RIR,4** in *Clear Cache*, **IRGTE_ORDER_DATE** in *Set these items*, and **&P1_THIS_MONTH.** – including the terminating period (.) – in *With these values* and click **Next**. The Action attribute is triggered when you click the button and redirects you to Page 4 (Orders) to see a list carrying current month's orders after resetting Page 4. This time you applied the filter using the greater than or equal to operator on the interactive report (IRGTE). You set the value for the filter using the value held in a hidden item: &P1_THIS_MONTH. This item is created in section 4.5 ahead to get the current month. In this point you adopted the alternate method to create a declarative link to the interactive report. See point 5 and associated details in the section 4.3.6.

7. Click **Create Button**.

8. Edit the newly created button and enter **rightarrow insetButton** for *Button CSS Classes* in the Attributes section. Styles the button and puts a right arrow icon on it.

9. Click **Apply Changes**.

4.4.2 View Customers

You'll place two buttons in the Top Customers region. This is the first one to view list of customers and is marked as B-2 in Figure 4-1.

1. Click the **Create** icon in the Buttons section to create a new button.

2. From the available option in *Select a region for the button*, select **Top Customers (30)** and click **Next**.

3. Select the option: **Create a button in a region position**.

4. Enter **VIEW_CUSTOMERS** for *Button Name*, **View Customers** for *Label*, set *Button Style* to **Template Based Button**, set *Button Template* to **Large Button – Icon Only**, click **Next**.

5. Set *Sequence* to **20**, button *Position* to **Region Template Position #CREATE#** and click **Next**.

6. Set *Action* to **Redirect to Page in this Application**, enter **2** in *Page* and click **Next**.

7. Click **Create Button**.

8. Edit the newly created button and enter **rightarrow insetButton** for *Button CSS Classes* in the Attributes section.

9. Click **Apply Changes**.

Chapter 4 – The Home Page

4.4.3 Add Customer

This button is marked as B-3 in Figure 4-1 and is used to add a new customer record.

1. Click the **Create** icon in the Buttons section.

2. From the available option in *Select a region for the button*, select **Top Customers (30)** and click **Next**.

3. Select the option: **Create a button in a region position**.

4. Enter **ADD_CUSTOMER** for *Button Name*, **Add Customer** for *Label*, set *Button Style* to **Template Based Button**, set *Button Template* to **Large Button – Icon Only**, click **Next**.

5. Set sequence to **30** and button *Position* to **Region Template Position #EDIT#** and click **Next**.

6. Set *Action* to **Redirect to Page in this Application**, enter **7** in *Page*, put a check mark on *reset pagination for this page*, enter **7** in *Clear Cache*, **P7_BRANCH** in *Set these items*, and **1** in *With these values*. Click **Next**.

7. Click **Create Button**.

8. Edit the newly created button and enter **plus insetButton** for *Button CSS Classes* in the Attributes section to place a plus icon on the button.

9. Click **Apply Changes**.

Explanation Step 6:
When this button is clicked, the user is redirected to Page 7 – Maintain Customer. P7_BRANCH is a hidden item on the target page which is created to hold number of the calling page. For example, the value of 1 is the number assigned to the Home page. When the redirect action is performed, this value is stored in the item P7_BRANCH to inform Page 7 that it was called from Page 1. After creating a new customer record, the target page (Page 7) returns the flow to the Home page. It does so using a branch process based on P7_BRANCH hidden item. This step is repeated for all 'Add' buttons on the Home page with respective branch values to control the application flow. See chapter 5 section 5.4.6 (hidden item) and section 5.5 (branch).

4.4.4 View Products

This button leads you to the main products page to view list of products. It is marked as B-4 in Figure 4-1.

1. Click the **Create** + icon in the Buttons section.

2. From the available option in *Select a region for the button*, select **Top Products (40)** and click **Next**.

3. Select the option: **Create a button in a region position**.

4. Enter VIEW_PRODUCTS for *Button Name*, **View Products** for *Label*, set *Button Style* to **Template Based Button**, set *Button Template* to **Large Button – Icon Only**, click **Next**.

5. Set *Sequence* to **40** and button *Position* to **Region Template Position #CREATE#** and click **Next**.

6. Set *Action* to **Redirect to Page in this Application**, enter **3** in *Page* and click **Next**.

7. Click **Create Button**.

8. Edit the newly created button and enter **rightarrow insetButton** for *Button CSS Classes* in the Attributes section.

9. Click **Apply Changes**.

4.4.5 Add Product

It calls Page 6 to add a new product and is marked as B-5 in Figure 4-1.

1. Click the **Create** + icon in the Buttons section.

2. From the available option in *Select a region for the button*, select **Top Products (40)** and click **Next**.

3. Select the option: **Create a button in a region position**.

4. Enter ADD_PRODUCT for *Button Name*, **Add Product** for *Label*, set *Button Style* to **Template Based Button**, set *Button Template* to **Large Button – Icon Only**, click **Next**.

5. Set *Sequence* to **50** and button *Position* to **Region Template Position #EDIT#** and click **Next**.

6. Set *Action* to **Redirect to Page in this Application**, enter **6** in *Page*, put a check mark on *reset pagination for this page*, enter **6** in *Clear Cache*, **P6_BRANCH** in *Set these items*, and **1** in *With these values* and click **Next**.

7. Click **Create Button**.

8. Edit the newly created button and enter **plus insetButton** for *Button CSS Classes* in the Attributes section.

9. Click **Apply Changes**.

Chapter 4 – The Home Page

4.4.6 View Orders

This button is marked as B-6 in Figure 4-1 and is used to view list of all orders.

1. Click the **Create** icon in the Buttons section.

2. From the available option in *Select a region for the button*, select **Top Orders by Date (50)** and click **Next**.

3. Select the option: **Create a button in a region position**.

4. Enter **VIEW_ORDERS** for *Button Name*, **View Orders** for *Label*, set *Button Style* to **Template Based Button**, set *Button Template* to **Large Button – Icon Only**, click **Next**.

5. Set *Sequence* to **60** and button *Position* to **Region Template Position #CREATE#** and click **Next**.

6. Set *Action* to **Redirect to Page in this Application**, enter **4** in *Page* and click **Next**.

7. Click **Create Button**.

8. Edit the newly created button and enter **rightarrow insetButton** for *Button CSS Classes* in the Attributes section.

9. Click **Apply Changes**.

4.4.7 Add Order

This one calls Order Wizard module (to be created in chapter 7) to place an order. It is marked as B-7 in Figure 4-1.

1. Click the **Create** icon in the Buttons section.

2. From the available option in *Select a region for the button*, select **Top Orders by Date (50)** and click **Next**.

3. Select the option: **Create a button in a region position**.

4. Enter **ADD_ORDER** for *Button Name*, **Add Order** for *Label*, set *Button Style* to **Template Based Button**, set *Button Template* to **Large Button – Icon Only**, click **Next**.

5. Set *Sequence* to **70** and button *Position* to **Region Template Position #EDIT#** and click **Next**.

6. Set *Action* to **Redirect to Page in this Application**, enter **11** in *Page*, put a check mark on *reset pagination for this page*, enter **11** in *Clear Cache*, **P11_BRANCH** in *Set these items*, and **1** in *With these values* and click **Next**.

7. Click **Create Button**.

8. Edit the newly created button and enter **plus insetButton** for *Button CSS Classes* in the Attributes section.

9. Click **Apply Changes**.

Note that all the three "Add" buttons used the same branching technique, to return users to the Home page if they click any button on the target pages.

At this stage, all the seven buttons are placed at their proper locations with the expected functionalities and are ready for partial test. To remind you again, these buttons will be productive only after creating all relevant pages indicated in the attribute *Redirect to Page in this Application*.

4.5 Create Hidden Item - P1_THIS_MONTH

In this section you'll create a hidden item named P1_THIS_MONTH under the Items section to evaluate first day of the current month with the help of a SQL query. This item is used in section 4.4.1.

1. In the Items section, click the Create ✚ icon.

2. Select the **Hidden** option. Hidden items are rendered on the page, but they are invisible to the users. These items are usually created to pass values between application pages.

3. Enter **P1_THIS_MONTH** for *Item Name*, accept the default value for Sequence, select **This Month's Sales** for *Region*, and click **Next**.

4. Click **Next** to accept the default value (Yes) for *Value Protected* attribute. Specifying Yes will prevent the hidden value from being manipulated when the page is posted.

5. On the Source page, set *Source Type* to **SQL Query (return single value)** and enter the following query in *Item Source Value*: **select to_char(to_date(to_char(sysdate ,'YYMM')||'01','YYMMDD'),'DS') from dual**

   The query returns first day of the current month from the system in the short date (DS) format. Assuming the current system date is July 30, 2013, the query will return: 7/1/2013

6. Click the **Create Item** button.

Chapter 4 – The Home Page

4.6 Test Your Work

The Home page is ready to launch. Let's give it a try. Before running, have a look at the page definition. The important thing to note here is that you performed all the tasks in Page Rendering section to create and modify controls, the Shared Components area was populated automatically by APEX based on your component and attribute selections.

Click the RUN button in Page Definition. As mentioned earlier the links on this page will not work right now since the corresponding pages are not available at the moment and will be created in subsequent chapters. After completing Chapter 7, you can check the functionality of these links and the seven buttons we created here in this chapter.

One more thing that I deem necessary at this stage is to test the reciprocal entry of the Admin Users authorization scheme that was generated automatically by APEX in chapter 3 section 3.7.1. In Page Definition, click This Month's Sales link. Scroll down to the security section, and set Authorization Scheme to {Not Admin Users}. Apply the change and run the Home page. The setting you just made will hide the region, if you're logged in as Admin. Log in as some other user and see that the region re-appears because the show condition is applied for users other than Admin.

4.7 Summary

Congratulations! You've created your first professional looking page in APEX. This chapter provided you with the flavor of declarative development where you just responded to some wizard questions to create a page you desired. Later on, you modified some attributes to customize the look and feel of this page. This is the uniqueness and beauty of Oracle Application Express that allows you to create pages rapidly without writing tons of code.

Let's summarize the techniques you went through in this chapter. Here is the list of some major areas you worked upon to modify the application's Home page:

- Created a dashboard to presented data for management information.
- Presented data graphically as well as in text format.
- Created multiple types of regions on different positions to display data from the database.
- Used a 12 columns grid layout to position page elements.
- Created links to display details.
- Implemented drilldown functionality to switch to other pages in the application using links and buttons.

Chapter 5
Manage Customers

Chapter 5 – Manage Customers

5.1 About Customer Management

Customer management module has a significant role in any sales application. Either it be a small sales order application or a huge supply chain management system, it aids in customer profiling and helps us view and analyze customers' information from different perspectives. In this chapter, you'll learn the basics of this huge topic and will see how this vital module is created with the help of APEX wizard and how to change the module interface by tweaking some attributes. This module will allow you to:

- Browse and search customer records
- Modify customers profile
- Add record of a new customer to the database
- Remove a customer from the database
- View details of orders placed by each customer under their profile

You'll be creating two pages with the help of APEX wizard to view and edit customer information. The first one (Page 2 Figure 5-1) will display a list of all customers from the back-end database table using a SELECT SQL query, while the second one (Page 7 Figure 5-3) will present a form to enter a new customer, modify record of an existing customer, or delete a customer's record. Those customers who have some existing orders cannot be removed from the database. When a customer's record is called for modification, all the orders placed by that customer are shown under his profile. Each order carries a link which helps you navigate to the order's detail page. Let's start the practical work and have some more on the exciting declarative development environment offered by Oracle Application Express.

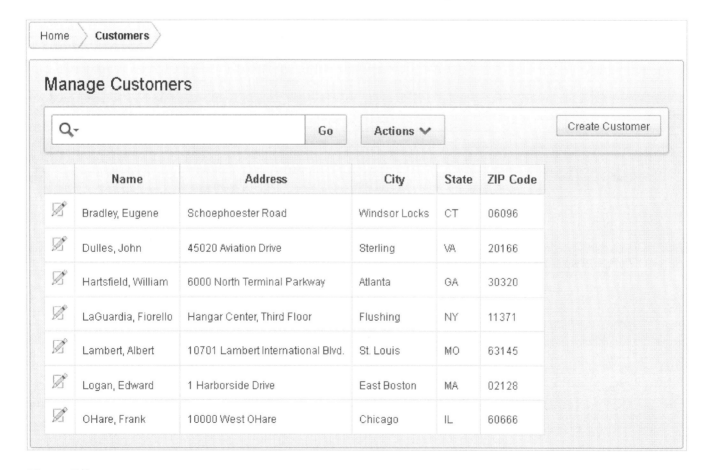

Figure 5-1

1. If logged off, login to APEX using: http://localhost:8080/apex
2. Click the **Application Builder** icon.
3. Open Sales Web Application by clicking the **Edit** icon.

5.2 Create Pages to Manage Customers

The Home page of our application was created by APEX, initially at the time the application was created. Rest of the application pages will be created manually with the help of wizards and copy utilities.

1. Click the **Create Page** [Create Page >] button. You'll use this button throughout the exercises presented in this book to create new application pages.
2. Click on the **Form** option. The initial wizard screen allows you to select a single option from a collection of multiple choices. Since you're creating a form to enter customer details, you'll select the Form option.
3. Select **Form on a Table with Report**. This screen presents sub-categories of forms and requires a single selection the form will base on. Here, you selected *Form on a Table with Report*, which means that a form will be created and attached to a backend database table for data manipulation. Besides, a report will also be added. Coupled together, the above steps inform APEX to generate two page. The first page (Page 2 – Customers) will show an interactive report as shown in Figure 5-1, while the second page (Page 7 – Customer Details) will present a form to add, modify or delete a customer record. Subsequent inputs are received by the wizard based on these initial selections.
4. On the next page (Report), set the following attributes and click **Next**.

Attribute	Value
Implementation	Interactive
Page Number	2
Page Name	Customers
Region Title	Manage Customers
Region Template	Alert Region
Breadcrumb	Main Menu
Entry Name	Customers
Parent Entry	Home

For the report implementation type, you can either choose Classic to create SQL Report, or Interactive to create Interactive Report. For more details on interactive and classic reports, see section 2.16. In Application Express each page is identified with a unique number. The main page of this module (showing an interactive report) will be recognized by number 2, whereas the form page will have number 7. Just like numbers, a page is provided a unique title for visual recognition. The title of the sole region on this page is also set to uniquely identify it on the page. Recall that we created six regions in chapter 4, each with a unique title. The Template attribute is set to Alert Region which renders the region with a grayish background. Switch the attribute to other options to see the impact. A breadcrumb shared component was created initially by the Application Builder when you created this application in chapter 2, and was modified later on to give it a more meaningful name: Main Menu. In this step you selected the same breadcrumb component and added an entry name (Customers) to it. You also specified Home as the parent entry. These settings will generate a breadcrumb for Page 2 (Customers) like this: Home > Customers (see Figure 5-1). After creating this entry you can instantly switch back to the parent entry (the Home page) from either the Customers or the Customer Details page at runtime.

5. On Data Source page, select **ASA** in Table/View Owner, select **DEMO_CUSTOMERS** for Table/View Name and click **Next**. After defining the main criteria for the page, you're asked to specify the schema to connect to for data manipulation. Once you select the schema, all tables within the schema are populated in the adjacent drop-down list. Note that in the current scenario you can select only one table from the provided list.

6. In the Tabs page, select the third option **Use an existing tab set and reuse an existing tab within that tab set**, select the *Tab Set* TS1, for *Use Tab* select **T_CUSTOMERS** and click **Next**. The values selected for these attributes are obvious. When you select the third option, couple of more options appear on your screen. The sole tab set (TS1) was created in chapter 3 section 3.2 carrying individual tabs. For this page you will select the tab labeled T_CUSTOMER. Recall that you provided the label Customer while creating the second tab in section 3.2. The prefix T_ (short for tab), was added by APEX to identify the entry as a tab.

7. In this step you select the desired columns from the DEMO_CUSTOMERS table to display on the main interactive report. By default, the Report Columns page selects all the columns from the defined table. Leave the following columns in the right pane to include them in the report and exclude others by moving them to the left pane using ctrl+click and the left arrow icon. These are the columns that we want to show on the interactive report.

    Cust_First_Name, **Cust_Last_Name**, **Cust_Street_Address1**, **Cust_Street_Address2**, **Cust_City**, **Cust_State**, and **Cust_Postal_Code**

8. Click **Next**.

9. You'll be presented with a list of Edit Link Images. Select any edit link image and click **Next**. The icon you select here will appear in the first column of the interactive report (for each record) as an edit link. When clicked, the link will call Page 7 where you can either modify or delete a customer's record.

10. In the **Form Page**, set the following attributes and click **Next**. The wizard will create a child page (Page 7) named Customer Details that will be linked to the main Customers page (Page 2) and will be called to create a new customer or to edit record of an existing customer. The remaining steps in the wizard receive input for Page 7.

Attribute	Value
Page Number	7
Page Name	Customer Details
Region Title	Customer Details

11. For *Primary Key Type*, select the second option **Select Primary Key Column(s)** and set *Primary Key Column 1* attribute to **CUSTOMER_ID**. Click **Next**.

12. Select the option *Existing sequence*, set *Sequence* to **DEMO_CUST_SEQ**, and click **Next**. The above two steps specify the primary key and the database sequence object the key will generate from. In step 11, you set CUSTOMER_ID as the primary key. A primary key is a column or set of columns that uniquely identify a record in a table. In step 12, you selected the option *Existing sequence* and defined DEMO_CUST_SEQ as the existing sequence. A sequence is a database object that automatically generate primary key values for every new customer record.

13. Include all the columns from the DEMO_CUSTOMERS table to Page 7 by clicking the double right arrow icon: ≫. Click **Next**. You selected all the columns from the customers table. All these columns will appear in the entry form on Page 7.

14. Select **Yes** for *Insert, Update,* and *Delete* and click **Next**. With the Yes option selected, you inform APEX to declaratively create the three processes for this form page. To avoid any of these processes, select the No option. For example, to prevent users from deleting data from this form, select No for the Delete option. This will prevent the Delete button from appearing on the form.

15. On the final confirmation page, click the **Create** button. A message *The Form and Report have been created successfully* will be displayed.

16. Click the **Application 101** breadcrumb and see the two new pages, Customers and Customer Details, with their respective page numbers.

> **NOTE:** We will use **Application 101** throughout this book for our Sales Web Application ID.

Chapter 5 - Manage Customers

5.3 Modify Customers Page - Page 2

The second page of this module holds an interactive report which is generated by the wizard with some default values such as SQL SELECT statement and corresponding column names. In the following steps you will change these values to generate some meaningful output.

5.3.1 Modify Region Attributes

1. In the main Application 101 page, click the **Customers** page.

2. Click Manage Customers under the Regions section. The standard method to modify attributes of a page component is to click the corresponding link. This action calls the attributes page of the selected page component for alteration.

3. Enter the following SQL statement in *Region Source* replacing the existing one. The auto generated SELECT SQL statement is replaced with a custom statement that uses the concatenation operator '||' to join columns. The new statement joins last and first name of customers into a single column. The new concatenated column is named customer name. Similarly, the address columns are combined into customer address.

   select customer_id,
   cust_last_name || ', ' || cust_first_name customer_name, CUST_STREET_ADDRESS1 ||
   decode(CUST_STREET_ADDRESS2, null, null, ', ' || CUST_STREET_ADDRESS2) customer_address,
   cust_city,
   cust_state,
   cust_postal_code
   from demo_customers

   The DECODE function has the functionality of an IF-THEN-ELSE statement. It compares expression to each search value one by one. If expression is equal to a search, then Oracle Database returns the corresponding result. If no match is found, then Oracle returns default. If default is omitted, then Oracle returns null. In the above statement, the Decode function assesses if the returned value of second street address is null, store null to the result; otherwise, concatenate it to the first address. The following syntax and example of the Decode function elaborates it further.

   Decode Syntax:
   decode(expression , search , result [, search , result]... [, default])

   Example of Decode Function:
   Select customer_name,
   decode(customer_id, 1, 'A', 2, 'B', 3, 'C', 'D') result
   From customers;

The equivalent IF-THEN-ELSE statement for the above Decode function would be:

```
IF customer_id = 1 THEN
result := 'A';
ELSIF customer_id = 2 THEN
result := 'B';
ELSIF customer_id = 3 THEN
result := 'C';
ELSE
result := 'D';
END IF;
```

4. Set *Template* to **Alert Region** in the *User Interface* section.
5. Click **Apply Changes** twice to confirm the change request for interactive report query. Note that if you added columns to the query, they will not be displayed when the report is run. You will need to use the actions menu and either select the columns or the Reset option. If you removed any columns from the query, it will disable existing filters, highlight rules, and other report settings referencing those columns.
6. Click **Run**.
7. Click on the **Actions** menu `Actions ∨` and then on **Select Columns**. Make sure all the columns appear in *Display in Report* section. If not, move all the columns to it. Using the arrow icons (to your right), arrange columns in the following order:

    Customer Name, Address, City, State, and Postal Code
8. Click the **Apply** button.
9. Click **Edit Page2** in the Developer Toolbar at the bottom of your screen to call its definitions.
10. Click <u>Interactive Report</u> next to the Manage Customers link under Regions. Interactive Report modification involves renaming of default column headings into meaningful labels, as instructed in the next step.
11. Set meaningful **headings** for all columns as follows:

    Name, Address, City, State, and Zip Code
12. Make sure that the value for the attribute *Display Text As* for CUSTOMER_ID column is set to Hidden to hide the column at runtime. Click the **Apply Changes** button. Primary Key columns are added to database tables to enforce data integrity and are not displayed in applications. This is why we set the hidden attribute to not show the CUSTOMER_ID column on the page.

Chapter 5 - Manage Customers

5.3.2 Modify Button Attributes

The following modifications are applied to the Create button. This is a default button created by the wizard to add a new customer record.

1. Click the link Create Redirect to page 7 under Buttons section, set the following attributes and **Apply Changes**:

Attribute	Value
Button Name	NEW
Text Label/Alt	Create Customer
Button Alignment	Left

2. Click **Run** to test Page 2 which will look like Figure 5-1.
3. Click the **Create Customer** button. Customer Details page (Page 7) should come up.

5.4 Modify Customer Details Page - Page 7

With Page 7 being displayed in your browser, click the link **Edit Page 7** in Developer Toolbar at the bottom of your screen to modify this page.

5.4.1 Modify Region - Customer Details

1. Click Customer Details in regions, set the following attributes and apply changes:

Attribute	Value
Display Point	Page Template Body (2)
Template	Alert Region
Start New Row	Yes
Column	4
Column Span	6

   NOTE: The Display Point attribute identifies where the region displays within the page. Regions are rendered in order of sequence number within a Display Point. Click the View icon to see the page layout and select a position. The possible display points for a region are determined by the page-level template (which is a page attribute). If no page-level template is selected, the default page-level template, defined in the Application Definition, is used.

5.4.2 Create Region - Orders for this Customer

You can always create new regions on a page to display additional content. This region is created with the same intention to display details of orders placed by a selected customer, as shown in Figure 5-3. This region will not be displayed while creating a new customer.

1. Click **Create** in Regions section.
2. Click **Report**. A report region is used in APEX to display the results of a SQL Query in a formatted HTML table within a page.
3. Click on **Classic Report**. You select this option to create a report based on a custom SQL SELECT statement or a PL/SQL function.
4. In *Display Attributes* set the following attribute values and click **Next**.

Attribute	Value
Title	Orders for this Customer
Region Template	Hide and Show Region (Hidden)
Display Point	Page Template Body (2)
Sequence	20

NOTE: The selected template (Hide and Show Region) creates a region which you can hide and show at runtime. By default, the region will be hidden. To expand or hide a region, click the arrow icon.

5. In *Enter SQL Query or PL/SQL function returning a SQL Query* box enter the following statement:

```
select
'Order #' || o.order_id order_number,
o.order_id,
p.product_name,
oi.quantity,
oi.unit_price,
(oi.quantity * oi.unit_price) ext_price,
o.order_timestamp
from demo_orders o, demo_order_items oi, demo_product_info p
where customer_id = :P7_CUSTOMER_ID
and o.order_id = oi.order_id
and oi.product_id = p.product_id
order by o.order_id, o.order_timestamp
```

6. Click **Next**.
7. In Report Attributes, set the following values and click **Next** to move on:

Attribute	Value
Report Template	template: 25. Standard - Alternative
Break Columns	Column 1

NOTE: The report derived from the SQL statement in Step 5, will have a break on column number 1 (Order #). A break column acts as a header for corresponding records. See Figure 5-3.

8. In Condition Type select **Value of Item in Expression 1 Is NOT NULL**. Enter P7_CUSTOMER_ID in Expression 1, and click the **Create Region** button. This condition evaluates whether to display the region on the page. The region will only be displayed when the item P7_CUSTOMER_ID, defined in Expression 1, carries some value. A null value in this page item indicates creation of new record which, of course, eliminates region's display.

9. Edit the newly created region: Orders for this Customer and set the following attributes:

Attribute	Value
Start New Row	Yes
Column	4
Column Span	6

10. Click on the *Report Attributes* tab. Change **Column Attributes** as shown in the following figure. Arrange the column using the pointers located on the right side to move columns up and down:

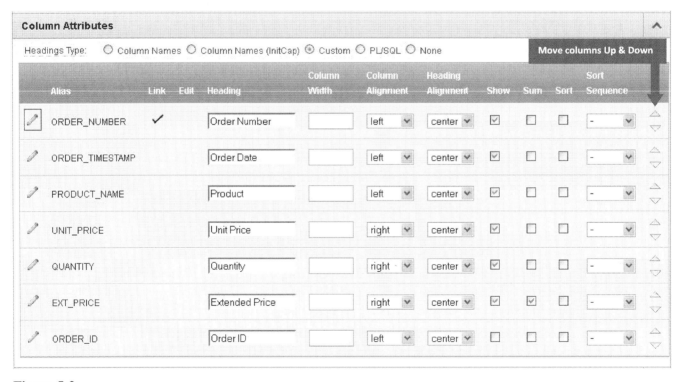

Figure 5-2

11. Click on the **Edit** link ✎ corresponding to the order number column. Scroll down to *Column Link* section and set the following attributes. These attributes are set to present the order number column as a link. At runtime, you'll see each order number like this: Order #1. When you click any of these links, the Order Details page (Page 29) will appear with all the details of the selected order.

The same technique was used in chapter 4 section 4.3.4 (The Home page) where you created similar links to call details pages. Check out the section for more information on the following attributes. Don't forget to apply these changes.

Attribute	Value
Link Text	#ORDER_NUMBER#
Page	29
Clear Cache	29
Item 1	P29_ORDER_ID
Value	#ORDER_ID#

12. Edit the following columns to present price figures in the defined format. Modify and save the changes individually.

Colum	Attribute	Value
Unit Price	Number/Date Format	Using the LOV button select $5,234.10 format
Extended Price	Number/Date Format	Using the LOV button select $5,234.10 format

13. In the *Report Attributes* tab, scroll down to **Break Formatting** section and set these attributes and **Apply Changes**. Using the Break Formatting attribute, you can control if a specific column repeats and how column breaks appear when printed. For example, suppose your report displays employee information by department number. If multiple employees are members of the same department, you can increase the readability by specifying the department number only appear once. To visually understand the above attributes, see the second region in Figure 5-3.

Attribute	Value
Report Sum Label	Total for All Orders:
Break Columns	First Column (already set through the wizard)
Break Column Style	Repeat Headings on Break
Display this text on report breaks	Order Total:

14. Save region attributes by clicking the **Apply Changes** button.

5.4.3 Modify Item Attributes

Click each item in the ITEMS section and apply the following attributes. If Value Required is set to Yes and the page item is visible, Oracle Application Express automatically performs a NOT NULL validation when the page is submitted. If set to No, no validation is performed and a NULL value is accepted.

Item	Label	Value Required
P7_CUST_FIRST_NAME	First Name	Yes
P7_CUST_LAST_NAME	Last Name	Yes
P7_CUST_STREET_ADDRESS1	Street Address	
P7_CUST_STREET_ADDRESS2	Line 2	
P7_CUST_CITY	City	
P7_CUST_POSTAL_CODE	Postal Code	Yes
P7_CUST_EMAIL	Email	
P7_PHONE_NUMBER1	Phone Number	
P7_PHONE_NUMBER2	Alternate Number	
P7_URL	URL	
P7_CREDIT_LIMIT	Credit Limit	Yes
P7_TAGS	Tags	

5.4.4 Change Item Type and Attach LOV

You might have noticed that we didn't modify any attribute for the STATE column in the above table. In the following set of steps you'll work on this column, first by altering its type from Text to a Select List, and then attaching an LOV to it. APEX allows you to change an item's type from its default state to another desirable type. For example, the P7_CUST_STATE item was generated as a text type by the wizard. Now, we wish to change this item to a Select List to hold predefined list of states. To display this list, you'll attach the STATES LOV to this item. Recall that we created this LOV in chapter 3 section 3.8.3. That list will be screwed up with this field so that the user could save a valid State value to the database.

1. Click on **P7_CUST_STATE** item.
2. Change *Display As* from Text to **Select List**.
3. Enter **State** in Label.
4. Set Template to **Required (Horizontal - Right Aligned)**. This attribute will align the label to the right and will have an asterisk (*) mark that signifies a mandatory field. Note that this attribute was set by the wizard for first and last name columns. Set this attribute for postal code and credit limit as well to display them as mandatory fields.
5. Set *Value Required* to **Yes**. If set to Yes and the page item is visible, Application Express will automatically perform a NOT NULL validation when the page is submitted and will ask you to input a value in the field. This attribute works in conjunction with the previous one - Required (Horizontal - Right Aligned) - for mandatory fields on a page.
6. Select **STATES** in *Named LOV*.
7. Set *Display Extra Values* to **No**. An item may have a session state value which does not occur in its list of values definition. Select whether this list of values should display this extra session state value. If you choose not to display this extra session state value and there is no matching value in the list of values definition, the first value will be the selected value. For instance, while creating a new record you will see the first value from the list (-Choose State-) set in step 9 below.
8. Set *Display Null Value* to **Yes**.
9. Enter **-Choose State-** in *Null Display Value*.
10. Click **Apply Changes**.

5.4.5 Apply Input Mask to Items

We imported a plug-in named masked field in chapter 3 section 3.9.2 to receive telephone numbers of customers in (999) 999-9999 format. Here, you'll replace the default text type with the imported plug-in by setting the Display As attribute to Masked Field. The input mask is defined by a format made up of mask literals and mask definitions. Any character not in the definitions list below is considered a mask literal and cannot be modified by the user. For example a mask of (999) 999-9999 with a placeholder of "#" will be displayed to the user as (###) ###-####. As the user types in the value, the hashes will be replaced by the numbers entered and the parenthesis, space, and dash will remain untouched. The placeholder is displayed for all enterable characters (mask definitions) in the input field. Amend/add the following attributes to store the two phone numbers in the desired format.

Attribute	Value
Display As	Masked Field v1.0 [Plug-in]
Input Mask	(999) 999-9999
Placeholder	_

5.4.6 Create a Hidden Item

This hidden item is being created to remember the application flow. It receives item values from the calling page. For instance, the Customer Orders report (Page 17) in chapter 8 section 8.3 (step 7) passes two branch values —customer id (201) and the calling page number (17) — when a chart bar is clicked to display details of the selected customer. The first parameter requests the target page (Page 7) to display details of the chosen customer, while the second parameter informs about the calling page.

The consequent URL is formed like this:
http://localhost:8080/apex/f?p=101:7:13989489520905:::7:P7_CUSTOMER_ID,P7_BRANCH:201,17
After receiving the focus, the target page (Page 7) displays details of the selected customer. When the user clicks a button, he/she is taken back to page 17.

1. Click **Create** to add an item.
2. Select the **Hidden** option.
3. For *Item Name* type, **P7_BRANCH** and for *Region*, select **Customer Details**. Click **Next**.
4. In the Settings page, set *Value Protected* to **No**.
5. Click the **Create Item** button in the final page.
6. Modify this item. Scroll down to the Default section and enter **2** for *Default Value*. The default value is used when the item's value is not derived from session state and when the source value is null. In the current scenario, the main Customers page (Page 2) is set if the source value is not found. See section 5.5 ahead for relevant details on branching.

5.4.7 Create Validation - Check Customer Credit Limit

Validations enable you to create logic controls to verify whether user input is valid. In this part, you'll create a validation to check customers credit limit. The customer form contains a field named Credit Limit which is used to assign a cap to each customer with a figure of $5,000. If you enter a value more than the assigned cap, you'll be prevented by presenting the message specified in step 7.

1. Click the **Create** button in the Validation section under Page Processing.
2. Click on the **Page** option to create a page level validation.
3. Enter **Check Credit Limit** in *Validation Name*, click **Next**.
4. Select **PL/SQL**.
5. Select **PL/SQL Expression** and click **Next**.
6. In *Validation Code* enter :P7_CREDIT_LIMIT <= 5000
7. In Error Message, enter the following text and click **Next**:
   A customer's Credit Limit must be less than or equal to $5,000
8. Finish the wizard by clicking the **Create Validation** button.

> **NOTE:** Validations are of two types. Validations specific to a single item are page item validations. Validations that apply to an entire page are page validations. Validations are either specific to a given field (either a single page item or tabular form column validation) or, they are not field specific (either a page or tabular form row validation). Here we used the later one.

5.4.8 Create Validation - Can't Delete Customer with Orders

This is the second validation to prevent deletion of those customers who have placed orders. This check is performed to retain application's integrity from the front-end. The validation is performed using a custom PL/SQL function which returns either a true or a false value. The return value is based on a SELECT query which returns false if records exist for the selected customer. If the returned value is false, the message mentioned in point 7 is displayed and the record deletion process is prevented. The validation is associated to the DELETE button in step 8, which means that the validation will be performed only when the Delete button is pressed.

1. Click the **Create** button again in the Validation section.
2. Select the **Page** option.
3. In *Validation Name*, enter **Can't Delete Customer with Orders** and click **Next**.
4. Select the **PL/SQL** option.
5. Select **Function Returning Boolean** and click **Next**.
6. In *Validation Code* enter the following code:

   ```
   begin
     for c1 in (select 'x' from demo_orders where customer_id = :P7_CUSTOMER_ID) loop
       RETURN FALSE;
     end loop;
       RETURN TRUE;
   end;
   ```

7. In *Error Message* enter, **Can't delete customer with existing orders** and click **Next**.
8. Select **DELETE (Delete)** from the *When Button Pressed* list.
9. Click the **Create Validation** button.

Chapter 5 - Manage Customers

5.5 Create Branch

In APEX, application flow is implemented and controlled through branches. The Branches section is part of the Page Processing column. In order to control the application flow process, at least one valid branch must exist on every application page to guide the APEX engine where to go next. Keep in mind that it is not the only source to control the application flow. Tabs, buttons, links, PL/SQL and JavaScript code are some other means to serve the purpose.

In section 5.4.6 above, you created a hidden item named P7_BRANCH to receive number of the calling page to remember the application flow and set the default value to 2 which moves the user back to the main Customers page (Page 2). Note that the current Customer Details page is called from two sources: the Home page and the main Customers page. In chapter 4 section 4.3.4, the region Top Customers calls this page when you click the name of a customer in that region. While creating that region you created a column link and initialized P7_BRANCH item with a value (1 – ID of the Home page). Secondly, you call it using its parent page either to modify/delete a customer record or to create a new one. To assess inflow from the parent page, you set 2 as the default value for the hidden item. To override the default value when the page is called from the Home page, you need to create a flexible mechanism which could evaluate exact page number. In this section you'll create a branch to turn the flow back to the calling page.

1. In the Branches section delete the existing branch (**Go To Page 2** – created by the wizard) by clicking its link and then the Delete button on the ensuing page.
2. Click the **Create** button under the Branches section to create a new branch.
3. For *Branch Type*, select **Branch to Page Identified by Item (Use Item Name)**. Leave other attributes to their default values and click **Next**.
4. On the Target page, select or enter **P7_BRANCH** in *Identify item* box to inform APEX to branch to the page held in this item.
5. Click the **Create Branch** Button.

After creating the branch when you call this page from the Home page, the value 1 is forwarded in the hidden item P7_BRANCH. When you click any of the provided button on the page, the branch you just created moves you back to the Home page after assessing the hidden item value. Similarly, when you call it from the main Customers page, the branch uses the default value (2).

Note that the Action attribute of the Cancel button on the Customer Details page is created with the default attribute Redirect to page 2. In order to utilize the branching mechanism, you need to replace the static value (2) for the Page attribute (under the Action When Button Clicked section) with a substitution string i.e. &P7_BRANCH. – with the terminating period (.).

5.6 Test Your Work

Before running the customer module, let's have a look at the definitions of the two pages. Call Page 2 – Customers and closely look at the third section: Shared Components. The entries contained in this section were automatically generated by APEX based on your selections in the wizard steps. Similarly, the Create Customer button (in the Page Rendering section) was generated by the wizard with a default action to redirect users to the appropriate page (Page 7), when this button is clicked. If you see definition of Page 7, you'll see some more auto-generated buttons with default functionalities. Just like buttons, APEX performs many other tasks transparently without us writing a single line of code. For instance, in Page 7 click the Edit button in the Page section and scroll down to the Function and Global Variable Declaration section. Here you'll see a global variable defined as var htmldb_delete_message. This variable was generated automatically along with a corresponding shortcut named DELETE CONFIRM MSG (in Shared Components) to control the record deletion process by presenting a confirmation dialog box before deleting a customer's record. Moreover, the wizard created a branch (Go To Page) under Page Processing to take the user back to the main page (Page 2) after he/she clicks any of the four buttons created for this page. The branch was later replaced with a custom mechanism to control the application flow. These are some of the beauties of declarative development that not only allow us to develop, test, and deploy a web based data-centric application using a web browser, but on the same time it doesn't limit our abilities to manually enter specific and tailored code, both on the client and server sides to answer our specific needs.

Perform one last step prior to testing this module. Go to the main Shared Components interface and click on the **Tabs** option under the Navigation section. Edit the Customers tab and enter 7 for **Tab Also Current for Pages** attribute. Save the change and run the application. Click the Home tab and then the Customers tab. You'll see the page (Page 2 – Customers) as shown in Figure 5-1 carrying an interactive report. As you can see, the page has only one region (Manage Customers). The region has a search bar comprising a magnifying glass, a text area, and a button labeled Go. This bar allows you to search a string in the report appearing underneath. The magnifying glass is a drop down list. You can use this list to limit your search to a specific column. Type **albert** in the text area and click the Go button. You'll see a row displaying record of Albert Lambert. Click the remove filter icon to reinstate the report to its previous state. The Actions menu has several options that we'll apply in chapter 7. The Create Customer button calls the second page of this module (Page 7) to enter profile of a new customer. You can also see the edit icon, you selected in the wizard, in the first column of the table for each record. If you want to modify a specific record, click the corresponding edit icon. Again, you'll be taken to the form page (Page 7) where all the fields will be populated with relevant information from the database. Click the edit icon for Eugene Bradley. Your page should look like Figure 5-3. The page has two regions. The upper region, Customer Details, displays customer's profile while the lower region, Orders for this Customer, contains all the orders placed by Bradley. If you click the link Order # 1, the system will try to open the orders page (Page 29) and will return an error since that page has not been created so far.

You are free to test your work. Try by adding, modifying, and deleting a new customer. Try to delete Eugene Bradley; you won't be able to do that because there are some orders placed by this customer and the validation that you created in section 5.4.8 will prevent the deletion process. Also check the credit limit validation by entering a value more than 5000 in the Credit Limit box. Note that whenever you leave Customer Details page (by clicking any of the provided three buttons), you'll be taken back to the calling page and this is because of the branching mechanism you implemented for this module.

Chapter 5 - Manage Customers

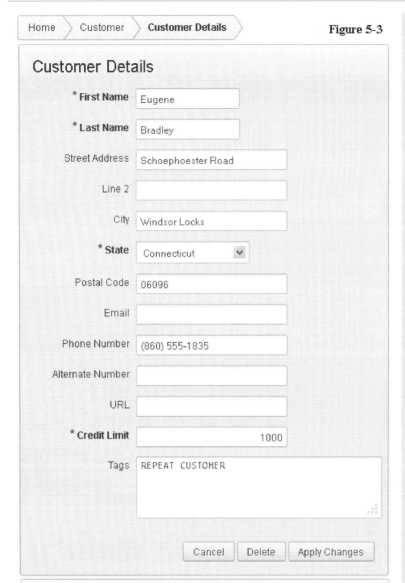

Figure 5-3

5.7 Summary

Let's go through the summary of this chapter to see what we grasped in it. We learned the following techniques while performing various exercises in this chapter:

- Declaratively created report and form pages and linked them together.
- Used interactive and classic reports.
- Created multiple regions to show order details for the selected customer.
- Changed type of an item and attached a list of value.
- Created validations to prevent customer record deletion having existing orders and to check customers' credit limits.
- Implemented branching mechanism to control the application flow.

The next chapter discusses how to manage products in a database application with some more useful techniques to explore APEX.

Chapter 6
Products Setup

Chapter 6 – Products Setup

6.1 About Products Setup

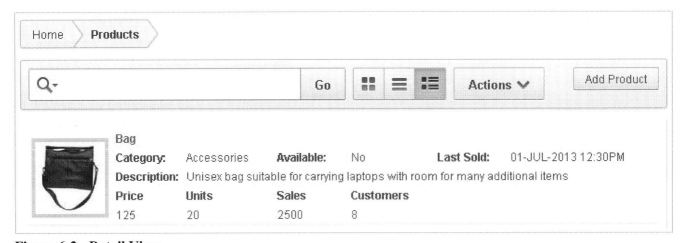

Figure 6-1 - Report View

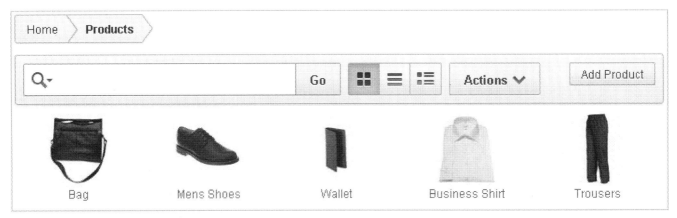

Figure 6-2 - Detail View

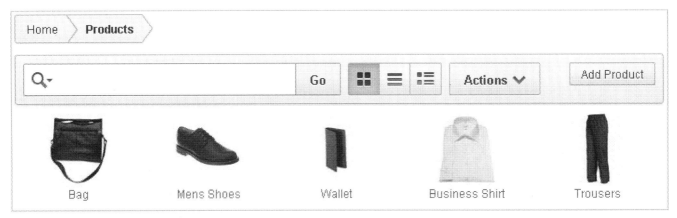

Figure 6-3 - Icon View

Just like the Customers module, you'll create a Products module that will allow you to manage products information. This module will also have two pages: Products and Product Details. The main products page (Page 3) will have three different views as shown on the previous page. The wizard will create the Report View version that you'll modify with a custom SQL statement. The remaining two views (Detail and Icon) are placed on the page by enabling respective attributes found under the main Products region. Once you enable these view, their respective icons appear on the main Search bar. Using these icons you can switch among different views of the interactive report.

The Product Details page (Page 6) will be created to add, modify, and delete a product. To create these two pages you'll follow the same approach as you did in the previous chapter. Since most of the steps are similar to those already briefed in the Customers Management chapter, we'll elaborate the bits new to this module.

The new stuff added to this module includes: image handling and styling. This module is based on DEMO_PRODUCT_INFO table in the database. Among conventional columns exists the following four special columns to handle images in the database. A question arises here: why do we need extra columns? BLOBs fall outside the range of normal data, and, in a normal scenario, require specialized processing to handle their use. The APEX environment has eliminated the need to perform all that specialized processing with these additional columns. Your APEX application will use these columns to properly process images in the BLOB column.

> **PRODUCT_IMAGE:** This column uses BLOB data type. A BLOB (Binary Large Object) is an Oracle data type that can hold up to 4 GB of data. BLOB's are handy for storing digitized information (e.g., images, audio, video).
>
> **MIMETYPE:** A Multipurpose Internet Mail Extension (MIME) type identifies the format of a file. The MIME type enables applications to read the file. Applications such as Internet browsers and email applications use the MIME type to handle files of different types. For example, an email application can use the MIME type to detect what type of file is in a file attached to an email. Many systems use MIME types to identify the format of arbitrary files on the file system. MIME types are composed of a top-level media type followed by a subtype identifier, separated by a forward slash character (/). An example of a MIME type is image/jpeg. The media type in this example is image and the subtype identifier is jpeg. The top-level media type is a general categorization about the content of the file, while the subtype identifier specifically identifies the format of the file.
>
> **FILENAME:** A case sensitive column name used to store the filename of the BLOB (e.g. bag.jpg).
>
> **IMAGE_LAST_UPDATE:** A case sensitive column name used to store the last update date of the BLOB.

Besides image handling, you'll also learn the technique to incorporate style sheet in an APEX page. Web browsers refer to Cascading Style Sheets (CSS) to define the appearance and layout of text and other material.

Chapter 6 – Products Setup

6.2 Create Pages for Products Setup

The following set of steps use the same approach you followed in the previous chapter to create an interactive report with a form. Login to APEX using the usual URL http://localhost:8080/apex. Click on **Application Builder** and then click the **Edit** button under Sales Web Application.

1. Click the **Create Page**  button.
2. Click on the **Form** option.
3. Select **Form on a Table with Report**. For details, see the Customer Management chapter.
4. On the Report Page, set the following attributes and click **Next**. These attributes were also discussed in chapter 5.

Attribute	Value
Implementation	Interactive
Page Number	3
Page Name	Products
Region Title	Manage Products
Region Template	No Template
Breadcrumb	Main Menu
Entry Name	Products
Parent Entry	Home

5. On Data Source page, select **ASA** in Table/View Owner, select **DEMO_PRODUCT_INFO** for Table/View Name and click **Next**.
6. On the Tabs page, select the third option **Use an existing tab set and reuse an existing tab within that tab set**, select Tab Set **TS1**, for Use Tab select **T_PRODUCTS** and click **Next**. The tab T_PRODUCTS will be active for this module.
7. On Report Columns page, leave the following columns in the right pane and exclude others by moving them to the left pane using ctrl+click and the left arrow icon.

    Product_Name, Product_Description, Category, Product_Avail, List_Price, and Product_Image

8. Click **Next**.
9. Select any edit link image or keep the default option selected and click **Next**.
10. On **Form Page** set the following attributes and click **Next**. This page will have a form to add, update, or delete product records.

Attribute	Value
Page Number	6
Page Name	Product Details
Region Title	Product Details
Region Template	Alert Region

134

11. For *Primary Key Type*, select the second option **Select Primary Key Column(s)**. Set *Primary Key Column 1* to **PRODUCT_ID**. Click **Next**. PRODUCT_ID is the primary key column which uniquely identifies a product and is populated using a database sequence object (DEMO_PROD_SEQ).

12. Select the option *Existing sequence*, set *Sequence* to **DEMO_PROD_SEQ**, and click **Next**.

13. Include all the columns from the DEMO_PRODUCT_INFO table to Page 6 except **MIMETYPE, FILENAME,** and **IMAGE_LAST_UPDATE**. Click **Next**.

14. Select **Yes** for *Insert, Update,* and *Delete* and click **Next**.

15. In the final Confirm page, click the **Create** button. A message *The Form and Report have been created successfully* will be displayed.

16. Go to application's home by clicking the **Application 101** breadcrumb. You'll see the two new pages, Products (Page 3) and Product Details (Page 6) with their respective page numbers. As you saw, we used the same procedure to create the initial structure for this module as we did for the Customers module. In the upcoming exercises you will undergo some new techniques to transform these pages and provide them a professional look.

Chapter 6 – Products Setup

6.3 Modify Products Page - Page 3

6.3.1 Modify Region Attributes

1. Click the **Products** page (Page 3) for few modifications.

2. In the Regions section, click the Products region link 📄 Products.

3. Replace the existing SELECT statement with the following in Region Source:

   select **p.product_id, p.product_name, p.product_description, p.category,**
       decode(p.product_avail, 'Y','Yes','N','No') **product_avail,**
       p.list_price,
       (select sum(quantity) from demo_order_items where product_id = p.product_id) **units,**
       (select sum(quantity * p.list_price) from demo_order_items where product_id = p.product_id) **sales,**
       (select count(o.customer_id) from demo_orders o, demo_order_items t
         where o.order_id = t.order_id and t.product_id = p.product_id group by p.product_id) **customers,**
       (select max(o.order_timestamp) od from demo_orders o, demo_order_items i
         where o.order_id = i.order_id and i.product_id = p.product_id) **last_date_sold,**
       p.product_id **img,**
       'f?p='||:app_id||':6:'||:app_session||':::P6_PRODUCT_ID:'||p.product_id **icon_link,**
       decode(nvl(dbms_lob.getlength(p.product_image),0),0,null,
         '<img style="border: 4px solid #CCC; -moz-border-radius: 4px; -webkit-border-radius: 4px;" '||'src="'||
         apex_util.get_blob_file_src('P6_PRODUCT_IMAGE',p.product_id)|| '" height="75" width="75"
         alt="Product Image" title="Product Image" />') **detail_img,**
       decode(nvl(dbms_lob.getlength(p.product_image),0),0,null,
           apex_util.get_blob_file_src('P6_PRODUCT_IMAGE',p.product_id)) **detail_img_no_style**
   from demo_product_info p

Output of this statement is illustrated in Figure 6-4 for the Bag product. The icon link column is formed using the APEX syntax to create a link. This link is used to call Product Details (Page 6). The detail_img column holds images of products. We used HTML <img> tag to form this column in conjunction with a built-in function. APEX_UTIL.GET_BLOB_FILE_SRC is an APEX function which provides the ability to more specifically format the display of the image (with height and width attributes). The image is styled using CSS inline styling method. The getlength function of the dbms_lob package (dbms_lob.getlength) is used to estimate the size of a BLOB column in the table. The selection of the BLOB size is made to facilitate the inclusion of a download link in a report. If the length is 0, the BLOB is NULL and no download link is displayed. See Figure 6-6 at the end of this chapter.

Figure 6-4

4. Set *Display Point* to **Page Template Body(1)**.

5. In Grid Layout, set the following attributes and apply changes. The Column Span value leaves 3 columns on the right side to display a list of top 5 products. See the previous chapter to learn more about Grid Layout settings.

Attribute	Value
Start New Row	Yes
Column	1
Column Span	9

6. Confirm changes by clicking the **Apply Changes** button.

7. Click **Run** and click the Products tab.

8. Click the Actions menu `Actions ∨`, click **Select Columns**. Make sure all the columns (except Description) appear in *Display in Report section*. If not, move all the columns to it. Using the arrow icons, arrange columns in the desired order and click the **Apply** button.

Chapter 6 – Products Setup

9. Click on the **Actions** menu again. Select **Save Report**. From the *Save* drop-down list, select **As Default Report Settings**. Set *Default Report Type* to **Primary** and click **Apply**. Developers can save two types of default interactive report: primary and alternative. Both reports display on the Report list on the search bar. The primary default report (you just saved) cannot be renamed or deleted. For details on interactive report, see chapter 2 section 2.16.
10. Click **Edit Page3** in the Developer Toolbar at the bottom of your screen.
11. In the Regions section, click on the Interactive Report link Interactive Report.
12. In Column Attributes, set meaningful **headings** for all columns as follows:

    Name, Description, Category, Available, Price, Units, Sales, Customers, Last Sold, Image, Icon Link, Image Detail, Detail Img No style

13. Edit the following columns individually using the edit ✎ link, set the following attributes and save your changes. Columns 1, 2, and 4 are marked as hidden and will not be shown on the page. Your APEX application will use these columns while handling the images, but you should not display them in the report pages. These columns were derived through the SQL SELECT statement in step 3.

Column	Attribute	Value
IMG	Display Type	Hidden
ICON_LINK	Display Type	Hidden
DETAIL_IMG	Display Type	Standard Report Column
DETAIL_IMG_NO_STYLE	Display Type	Hidden

14. Scroll down to **Icon View** section and set the following attributes. By default, most interactive reports display as a report. You can optionally display columns as icons. When configured, a View Icons icon displays on the Search bar (see Figure 6-3). To use Icon view, you must identify the columns used to identify the icon, the label, and the target (that is, the link). As a best practice, set these columns to display as hidden since they are typically not useful for end users.

Attribute	Value
Icon View Enabled	Yes
Columns Per Row	5 – to display 5 images on a single row
Link Column	ICON_LINK
Image Source Column	DETAIL_IMG_NO_STYLE
Label Column	PRODUCT_NAME
Image Attributes	Width="75" height="75"

15. In **Detail View** section set *Detail View Enabled* to **Yes**. By default, interactive reports are displayed as a report (Figure 6-1). You can optionally display details about each column by enabling the Detail View option. When configured, a *View Details* icon displays on the Search bar (see Figure 6-2).

16. In **Before Rows** enter the following code. This attribute of the Detail View enables you to enter HTML code to be displayed before report rows. For example, you can you the <TABLE> element to put the database content in row/column format. Besides adding HTML code, styling information can also be incorporated using this attribute. The <style> tag is used to define style information for an HTML document. Inside the <style> element you specify how HTML elements should render in a browser. A cascading style sheet (CSS) provides a way to control the style of a web page without changing its structure. When used properly, a CSS separates visual attributes such as color, margins, and fonts from the structure of the HTML document. Oracle Application Express includes themes that contain templates that reference their own CSS. The style rules defined in each CSS for a particular theme also determine the way reports and regions display. The code below uses custom CSS rules to override the default APEX Interactive Report (apexir) styles.

```
<style>
   table.apexir_WORKSHEET_CUSTOM {
      border: none !important;
      box-shadow: none;
      -moz-box-shadow: none;
      -webkit-box-shadow: none;}

   .apexir_WORKSHEET_DATA td {
      border-bottom: none !important;}

   table.reportDetail td {
      padding: 2px 4px !important;
      border: none !important;
      font: 11px/16px Arial, sans-serif;}

   table.reportDetail td.separator {
      background: #F0F0F0 !important;
      padding: 0 !important;
      height: 1px !important;
      padding: 0;
      line-height: 2px !important;
      overflow: hidden;}

   table.reportDetail td h1 {margin: 0 !important}

   table.reportDetail td img {
      margin-top: 8px;
      border: 4px solid #CCC;
      -moz-border-radius: 4px;
      -webkit-border-radius: 4px;}
</style>
<table class="reportDetail">
```

> **NOTE:** Remember that all APEX pages are HTML pages controlled by HTML attributes and cascading style sheet (CSS) settings. When you create an interactive report, Oracle APEX renders it based on CSS classes associated with the current theme. Each APEX interactive report component has a CSS style definition that may be changed by applying standard CSS techniques to override the defaults. Such changes may be applied to a single interactive report, to a page template to effect changes across several interactive reports, or to all page templates of a theme to enforce a common look and feel for all reports in an application.
>
> In the current step, you are changing the appearance of the report by overriding built-in styles for the table and subordinate elements.

Chapter 6 – Products Setup

17. In **For Each Row** enter the following code. The code is applied to each record. In every <td> element you are referencing interactive report columns and labels with the help of a special substitution string (#) and are styling each record using inline CSS method. You used the substitution string to reference column names and labels as #PRODUCT_NAME# and #CATEGORY_LABEL#, respectively.

    ```
    <tr>
      <td rowspan="5" valign="top"><img width="75" height="75" src="#DETAIL_IMG_NO_STYLE#"></td>
      <td colspan="6">
        <h1><a href="#ICON_LINK#"><strong>#PRODUCT_NAME#</strong></a></h1>
      </td>
    </tr>
    <tr>
      <td><strong>#CATEGORY_LABEL#:</strong></td><td>#CATEGORY#</td>
      <td><strong>#PRODUCT_AVAIL_LABEL#:</strong></td><td>#PRODUCT_AVAIL#</td>
      <td><strong>#LAST_DATE_SOLD_LABEL#:</strong></td><td>#LAST_DATE_SOLD#</td>
    </tr>
    <tr>
      <td align="left"><strong>#PRODUCT_DESCRIPTION_LABEL#:</strong></td>
      <td colspan="5">#PRODUCT_DESCRIPTION#</td>
    </tr>
    <tr>
      <td style="padding-bottom: 0px;"><strong>#LIST_PRICE_LABEL#</strong></td>
      <td style="padding-bottom: 0px;"><strong>#UNITS_LABEL#</strong></td>
      <td style="padding-bottom: 0px;"><strong>#SALES_LABEL#</strong></td>
      <td style="padding-bottom: 0px;"><strong>#CUSTOMERS_LABEL#</strong></td>
    </tr>
    <tr>
      <td style="padding-top: 0px;">#LIST_PRICE#</td>
      <td style="padding-top: 0px;">#UNITS#</td>
      <td style="padding-top: 0px;">#SALES#</td>
      <td style="padding-top: 0px;">#CUSTOMERS#</td>
    </tr>
    <tr>
      <td colspan="7" class="separator"></td>
    </tr>
    ```

18. In **After Rows** enter </table>. In this attribute you enter the HTML to be displayed after report rows. Here, you used the closing table tag </TABLE> to end the table.

19. Click the **Apply Changes** button. Have a look at Figure 6-2 to observe the rules applied in the above steps.

6.3.2 Create Region – Top 5 Products

This region will display list of top five products on the right side of the page, as shown in Figure 6-5 below.

1. Click the **Create** button in the Regions section.

2. Select **Report**.

3. Click on **Classic Report**.

4. Enter **Top 5 Products** in Title, select **Standard Region – No Padding** in Region Template, select **Page Template Body (1)** in Display Point, 20 in Sequence and click **Next**.

5. In **Enter SQL Query or PL/SQL function returning a SQL Query** write the following statement and click **Next**.

   SELECT b.product_name, SUM(a.quantity * b.list_price)
   FROM DEMO_ORDER_ITEMS a, DEMO_PRODUCT_INFO b
   WHERE a.product_id = b.product_id
   GROUP BY b.product_name
   ORDER BY 2 desc

6. For *Report Template* select **template: 25. Borderless Report**, enter 5 for *Rows per Page*, and click **Next**.

7. Click the **Create Region** button.

8. **Edit** the newly created region, scroll down to the Grid Layout section and set the following attributes. Recall that we used initial 9 columns for the main region. This one will use the remaining 3 i.e. from 10-12.

Attribute	Value
Start New Row	No
Column	10
Column Span	Automatic

9. Click the **Report Attributes** tab on the same page to set the following attributes. Apply the changes.

Attribute	Value
Heading Type	None
Pagination Scheme	No Pagination Selected
Maximum Row Count	5

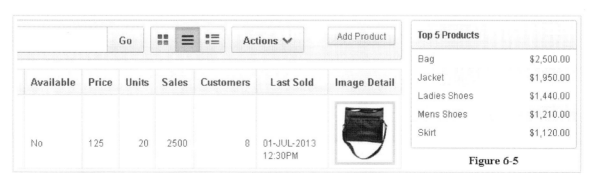

Figure 6-5

Chapter 6 – Products Setup

6.3.3 Modify Button Attributes

In this section you'll apply an authorization scheme to the Create button (modified as Add Product in step 1 below) to prevent unauthorized users from creating a product record.

1. Click Create Redirect to page 6 under Buttons section, set the following attributes and **Apply Changes**:

Attribute	Value
Text Label/Alt	Add Product
Authorization Scheme	Allow Product Modification

2. Click **Run** to test Page 3. The page will look like Figure 6-1. There are 3 different views of this interactive report (Icon, Report, and Detail), click each one of them and see the output.

3. Click the **Add Product** button. Product Details page (Page 6) will come up.

Click the **Logout** link at the top of the page. Login as **test/test**. Click the **Products** tab. Note that the **Add Product** button disappeared from the page and it is just because of the authorization scheme you set for the button in step 1 above. This scheme was created in chapter 3 section 3.7.2 to prevent product manipulation. Also recall that there is a column named Product in the DEMO_USERS table which controls this process. The value 'N' in this column indicates that the user in not allowed to manage products. On the other hand, the value 'Y' allows the corresponding user to add, modify, and delete products. TEST is an application users, created in chapter 2 section 2.38 (SQL Statement # 9), who is not allowed to perform any manipulation action on products.

In this section the authorization scheme was applied only to a single page item i.e. the **Add Product** button. In the next section, you'll apply it to the whole page to prevent add, modify, and delete operations.

6.4 Modify Product Details Page - Page 6

Click **Edit Page 6** in Developer Toolbar to modify this page.

6.4.1 Modify Page Attributes

1. Click the edit button in the Page section. Click on the **Show All** tab, scroll down to the Security section and set Authorization Scheme to **Allow Product Modification** . Click the **Apply Changes** button.

This setting ensures that only authorized users can access the page to modify products. Test the page-wide authorization by logging into the application as test/test. Go to the Products page and click any products link from any view to call the Products Detail page (Page 6). A message will appear saying **You are not authorized to modify Product Information. Access denied by Page security check.** Click the OK button to move back.

The previous two exercises demonstrated how to implement security on application pages and individual page items. By combining together the DEMO_PRODUCT_INFO table, the Allow Product Modification scheme and the Authorization Scheme attribute, you enforced a policy of authorized access to individual application components.

Chapter 6 – Products Setup

6.4.2 Create Region – Product Image

To show the image of the selected product on the Product Details page, we will create an HTML region. Note that this section will only create a blank region to hold an image. The image will be added to it in a subsequent section.

1. To create the new region, click the **Create** button in the Regions section.
2. Click on the first option: **HTML**.
3. Again, click the first **HTML** option to select it as the region container type.
4. Enter **Product Image** in Title, select **Hide and Show Region (Expanded)** for Region Template, for Parent Region select **Product Details**, set Sequence to **20** and click **Next** twice.
5. In Condition Type select **PL/SQL Function Body Returning a Boolean** and enter the following block in Expression 1:

    ```
    a    declare
    b    begin
    c      if :P6_PRODUCT_ID is not null then
    d        for c1 in (select nvl(dbms_lob.getlength(product_image),0) A
    e                   from demo_product_info
    f                   where product_id = :P6_PRODUCT_ID)
    g        loop
    h          if c1.A > 0 then
    i            return true;
    j          end if;
    k        end loop;
    l      end if;
    m      return false;
    n    end;
    ```

> **NOTE:** Page items are referenced in PL/SQL block using bind variables i.e. a colon(:) prefixed to the item name, as used in point c - :P6_PRODUCT_iD

Code Explained

Almost every APEX wizard concludes on the condition page. This page carries a list of predefined condition types. In the current scenario, you set a condition based on a PL/SQL function which returns a single Boolean value: True or False. If the code returns True, the region is displayed carrying image of the selected product. After selecting a condition type, you inform APEX to execute the PL/SQL code defined in the Expression 1 attribute.

The code first executes an IF condition (point c) to check whether the product ID is not null by evaluating the value of the page item P6_PRODUCT_ID. If the value is null, the flow of the code is transferred to point m, where a false value is returned and the function is terminated. If there exists a value for the product ID, then point d is executed which creates a FOR loop to loop through all records in the DEMO_PRODUCT_INFO table to find the record (and consequently the image) of the selected product (point d-k). In point h, another IF condition is used to assess whether the image is found. If so, a true value is returned in point i and the function is terminated.

6. Click the **Create Region** button. In order to display the region in the center of the 12 columns grid, modify the region and set the value of *Column* attribute to **3** and *Column Span* to **8** in the Grid Layout section.

6.4.3 Create Button Remove Image

An image can be removed from the Product Details page by clicking this button. It is attached to a process (Delete Image) defined in section 6.5 ahead.

1. Click **Create** in the Buttons section.
2. Select **Product Image** region to place the button in. Click **Next**.
3. Click on the first option: **Create a button in a region position**.
4. Enter **DELETE_IMAGE** in Button Name, enter **Remove Image** in Label and click **Next**.
5. Select **Below Region** in Position. This attribute identifies where the button displays. See Figure 6-6 to see the placement.
6. Keep the default values for *Action* and *Execute Validations* to **Submit Page** and **Yes** respectively and click **Next**. If the page is submitted and the Execute Validations attribute is set to Yes, all validations defined for the page along with the built-in ones are executed to check for required values and to verify valid number or date. If set to No, none of the defined validations nor the built-in ones will be executed.
7. Click the **Create Button**.

Chapter 6 – Products Setup

6.4.4 Modify Items Attributes

1. In Page Definition, click the item **P6_PRODUCT_NAME**.
2. In the User Interface Section, set the Template for this item to **Required (Horizontal – Right Aligned)**.
3. Scroll down to the Settings section, set Value Required to **Yes**.

As mentioned in the Customers module, the first attribute marks mandatory fields on a page with an asterisk (*), while the second one ensures that the marked fields are not null. Set these attributes for P6_CATEGORY, P6_PRODUCT_AVAIL, and P6_LIST_PRICE as well.

We created a list of values (CATEGORIES) in Chapter 3 section 3.8.1. Here we're going to use that list to display pre-defined values of categories through an LOV. First, you will change the Category field from Text to a Select List, and then you'll define the list of values (LOV) the item will bound to. Recall that you used this process in the Manage Customers module to display STATES LOV.

1. Click **P6_CATEGORY** item.
2. Change *Display As* from Text to **Select List**.
3. Scroll down to the List of Values section and select **CATEGORIES** in Named LOV.
4. Set Display Extra Values to **No**.
5. Click **Apply Changes**.

Next, you will change Product Available field to Radio Group with two options Yes and No. This LOV was also created in chapter 3 section 3.8.4. Just like the previous steps, here as well, you're changing item type from text to a new one: Radio Group. At runtime, this item will show two options (as shown in the Figure 6-6) to specify whether the product is available or not. If you ignore this exercise and leave the item to its default type, users may enter whatever value they like, compromising application's integrity. This is a good example to restraint users to select valid values.

1. Click **P6_PRODUCT_AVAIL** item.
2. Change *Display As* from Text to **Radio Group**.
3. Set Label to **Product Available**.
4. In the List of Values section, select **Y OR N** in Named LOV.
5. Set Display Extra Values to **No**.
6. Scroll down to Default section and type **Y** in Default value.
7. Click **Apply Changes**.

Modify attributes of item P6_PRODUCT_IMAGE to handle product image.

1. Click **P6_PRODUCT_IMAGE** item.
2. In HTML Table Cell Attributes, click the **LOV** button and select **nowrap="nowrap"**.
3. In Settings section, set Storage Type to **BLOB column specified in item Source attribute**. The Storage Type attribute specifies where the uploaded file should be stored at. It has two values:
   - BLOB column specified in item source attribute – Stores the uploaded file in the table used by the "Automatic Row Processing (DML)" process and the column specified in the item source attribute. The column has to be of data type BLOB. If the file gets downloaded, the table name of the "DML Fetch" process is used.
   - Table WWV_FLOW_FILES – Stores the uploaded file in the table WWV_FLOW_FILES. To access the file use: select * from wwv_flow_files where name = :<enter page item name>;
4. Enter **MIMETYPE** in MIME Type Column (all in caps).
5. Enter **FILENAME** in Filename Column (all in caps).
6. Enter **IMAGE_LAST_UPDATE** in BLOB Last Updated Column (all in caps).
7. Click **Apply Changes**.

6.4.5 Create a Hidden Item

Create a hidden item just like the one you created in Customer Details Page in the previous chapter. This hidden item is referenced in a graphical report page – PAGE 16 (Sales by Category and Product) – to assess the application flow.

1. Click **Create** to add an item.
2. Select the **Hidden** option.
3. For Item Name type, **P6_BRANCH**. Select **Product Details** for Region. Click **Next**.
4. On the Settings page, set *Value Protected* to **No**.
5. Click the **Create Item** button in the final page.
6. Modify this item. Scroll down to the Default section and enter **3** in Default value. The default value is used when the item's value is not derived from session state and when the source value is null. In the current scenario, the main Products page (Page 3) is set if the source value is not found.

6.4.6 Create Item – IMAGE

In this section you will create a new item named Image to display product image in the HTML region created in section 6.4.2.

1. Click **Create** in Items section.
2. Click on **Display Only** icon.
3. Type **P6_IMAGE** in Item Name.
4. Select **Product Image** for Region and click **Next**.
5. **Clear** the Label box. Do not apply any template to this item by selecting the first value –**Select a Template**–. By not applying any template the image will appear in a default place i.e. to the left inside the region. Click **Next**.
6. Set Show Line Breaks to **No**. Leave Save Session State and Based On to No and Page Item Value, respectively. Click **Next**.
7. Select **PL/SQL Function Body** in Source Type and enter the following code in Item Source value:

    return '<img src="'||apex_util.get_blob_file_src('P6_PRODUCT_IMAGE',:P6_PRODUCT_ID)||'" />';
8. Click **Create Item** button.
9. **Edit** the newly created item and scroll down to Conditions section.
10. Select **Exists (SQL query returns at least one row)** in Condition Type.
11. In Expression 1 enter:

    SELECT mimetype from demo_product_info where product_id = :P6_PRODUCT_ID and mimetype like 'image%'
12. Scroll down to Security section and set *Escape special characters* to **No**.
13. Click **Apply Changes**.

6.5 Create Process Delete Image Under Page Processing

In section 6.4.3 you placed a button (Remove Image) in the Product Image region to delete an image. In step 6 of this section, you are referencing the same button to execute the current process only when that particular button is processed.

1. Click **Create** in Processes under Page Processing section.
2. Select the first option: **PL/SQL**.
3. Type **DELETE IMAGE** in Name, **20** in Sequence. For execution point, keep the default option: On Submit – After Computations and Validations, and click **Next**. This select list field for the execution point allows us to determine the process point of the Application Process. The selected processing point is a part of the Page Processing phase.
4. In enter **PL/SQL Page Process** enter the following code and click **Next**:

   ```
   update demo_product_info
   set product_image = null,
   mimetype = null,
   filename=null,
   image_last_update=null
   where product_id = :P6_PRODUCT_ID;
   ```

   NOTE: To remove the image, you are required to just replace contents of relevant columns with null.

5. In Success Message type: **Product image deleted**. Click **Next**.
6. In When Button Pressed select **DELETE_IMAGE (Remove Image)**.
7. Click **Create Process**.

6.6 Create Branch

Create a branch just like the one you created in the previous chapter to manage application flow.

1. In the Branches section delete the existing branch (**Go To Page 3**) by clicking its link and then the Delete button on the ensuing page.
2. Click the **Create** button under the Branches section to create a new branch.
3. For *Branch Type*, select **Branch to Page Identified by Item (Use Item Name)**. Leave other attributes to their default values and click **Next**.
4. On the Target page, select or enter **P6_BRANCH** in *Identify item* box to inform APEX to branch to the page held in this item.
5. Click the **Create Branch** Button.

Note that the Action attribute of the Cancel button on the Product Details page is created with the default attribute Redirect to page 3. In order to utilize the branch mechanism, you need to replace the static value (3) for the Page attribute (under the Action When Button Clicked section) with a substitution string i.e. &P6_BRANCH. – with the terminating period (.)

Chapter 6 – Products Setup

6.7 Test Your Work

Click the Run button and then the Home tab. Click the Products tab. Click the three buttons individually to see different views of the products module. Click the **View Icons** button. You'll see small icons of products as illustrated in Figure 6-3 at the start of this chapter. Each product is presented as a linked icon. If you click any icon, you'll be taken to another page (Page 6) where you'll see details of the selected product. Click the Report View icon. The Report View presents data in a tabular form. Here you can access the details page with the edit icon appearing in the first column for each product. Click the Detail View icon. This View presents products information from a different perspective. You can access details of a product by clicking its name. This view was styled in section 6.3.1 steps 16-18. Also note that the region Top 5 Products appears to the right of your screen in all three views.

Click any product's name to call the Product Details page (as illustrated in Figure 6-6). The main region (Product Details) was created by the wizard incorporating all relevant fields. The child region (Product Image) appears within the parent region. This region was created in section 6.4.2. Similarly, note that the Remove Image button (you created in section 6.4.3) appears within the child region.

Create a new product record using the Add Product button on the main Products page. Click the browse button and select any small image file to test image upload. Fill in all the fields except List Price. Try to save this record by pressing the Create button. A message will appear at the top of your screen asking you to put some value in the List Price box. Now, provide some alpha-numeric value like abc123 in the List Price. Again, an appropriate message will come up reminding you to put a numeric value. This time add a numeric value and save the record. You'll see the new product appearing among others with the image you uploaded. Edit this record and see the image appearing in the defined region. Change the category of this product, switch availability to the other option and apply changes. Call the product again and observe that the product now reflects the changes you just made. Click the Remove Image button and see what happens. Click the Delete button and then the OK button in the confirmation box. The product will vanish from the list. The Delete button was created by the wizard with the necessary process.

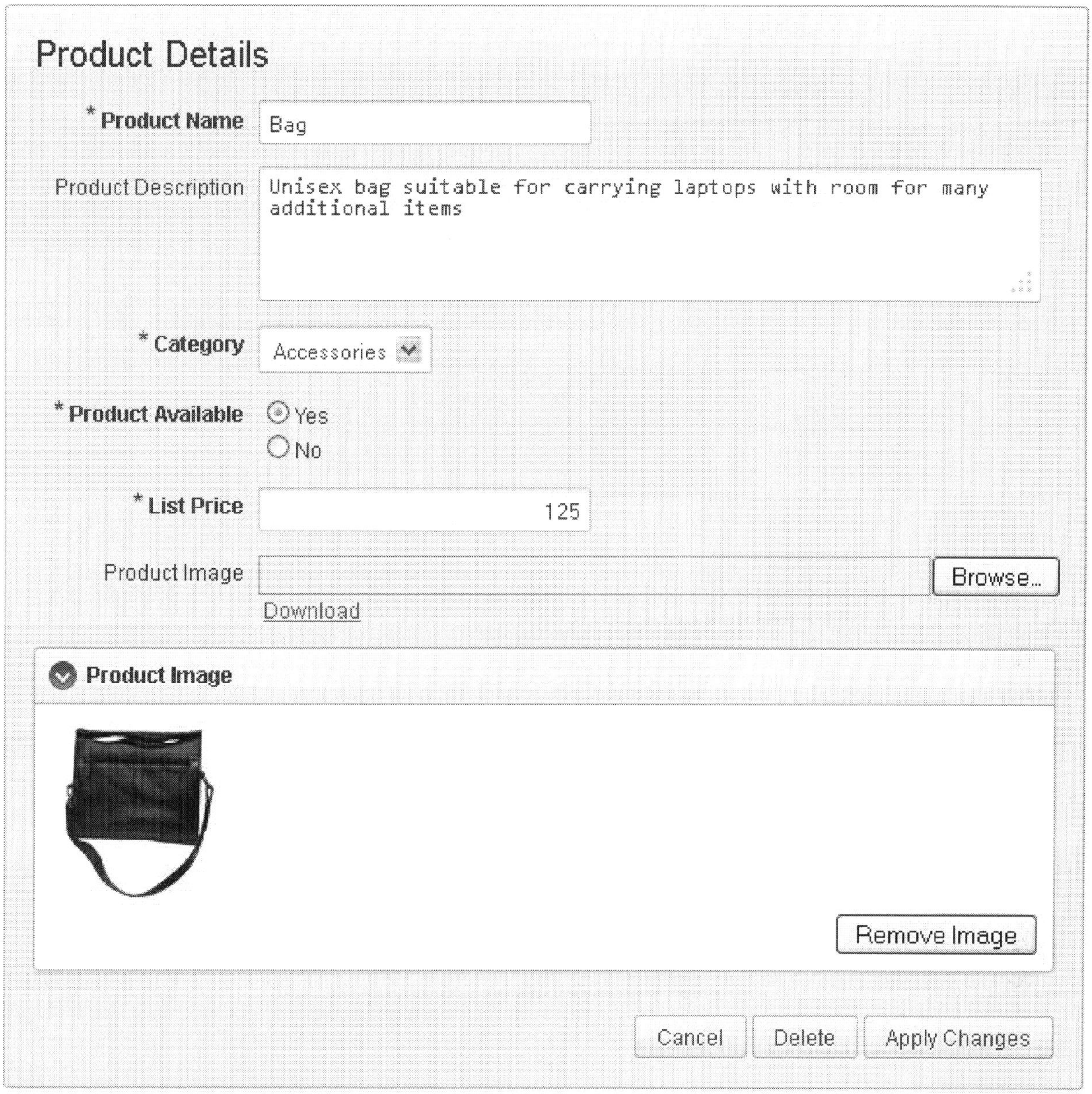
Product Details
* Product Name
Bag
Product Description
Unisex bag suitable for carrying laptops with room for many additional items
* Category
Accessories
* Product Available
Yes
No
* List Price
125
Product Image
Browse...
Download
Product Image
Remove Image
Cancel
Delete
Apply Changes

Figure 6-6

Chapter 6 – Products Setup

6.8 Summary

In this chapter you were taught some more skills that will assist you in developing your own applications. Most importantly, you knew the techniques to handle, store, and retrieve images to and from database tables. Play around with this module by tweaking the saved attributes to see the resulting effect on the two pages. This way you will learn some new things, not covered in this chapter. Of course, you can always restore the attributes to their original values by referencing the exercises provided in the chapter. An important point to consider here is that a module of this caliber would have taken plenty of time and effort to develop using conventional tools. With Oracle APEX declarative development, you created it in couple of hours. Let's wrap up the chapter and see the techniques you went through in it.

- How to create Icon, Report, and Detail views to present products catalog.
- Created a child within a parent region to show relevant information.
- Image handling. Uploaded, deleted, and viewed images to and from database tables.
- Changed default input types to Select List and Radio Group and attached LOVs.
- Used dynamic and static LOVs to store legitimate data in tables.

Chapter 7
Manage Orders

Chapter 7 – Manage Orders

7.1 About Orders Management

This chapter will teach you how to create professional looking order forms. Orders from customers will be taken through a sequence of forms (wizard). The first form will allow user to select an existing customer or create a new one. In the second step, user will select products to order and the last step will show summary of the placed order. Once an order is created, you can view, modify, and delete it through the Order Details page using the edit icon in the orders main page (Page 4). Couple of other pages will be created as well to create a new customer, if one does not exist, and to display product information such as Description, Category and Price in a popup window during order placement. See more details and screen shots on this module in chapter 1 – section 1.2.4. Following is the list of pages that you are going to create in this chapter:

Page No.	Page Name	Purpose
4	Orders	The main page to display all existing orders
29	Order Details	Display a complete order with details
11	Enter New Order - Identify Customer (Wizard Step 1)	Select an existing customer or create a new one
12	Select Order Items (Wizard Step 2)	Add products to an order
20	Product Info	Show details of a product in a popup window
14	Order Summary (Wizard Step 3)	Show summary of the placed order

You'll build this module sequentially in the order specified above. The first two pages (Page 4 and 29) will be created initially using a new wizard option: Master/Detail form. Both these pages are not part of the Order Wizard and will be utilized for order modification and deletion, once an order is recorded. Page 4 is similar to the pages you created in Customer and Product modules and lists all placed orders, while Page 29 will be used to manipulate order details. For example, you can call an order in a usual way using the edit link in the master page. The called order will appear in the details page where you can:

- Add/Remove products to and from an order
- Delete the order itself

The purpose of each chapter in this book is to teach you some new feature. Here as well, you'll get some new stuff. This chapter will walk you through to get detailed practical exposure to the techniques this module contains. After completing the two main pages, you will work on actual order wizard steps and will create other pages of the module. Recall that in the previous chapter you modified the main interactive report (Page 3) to create couple of more views (Icon and Detail), and used the Actions menu to select and sort table columns (section 6.3.1 – step 8). The bar which carried the three icons to access these reports also carried a Search box that you used to search a customer record in chapter 5 – section 5.6. In this chapter, you will be exposed to many other utilities provided under the Actions menu. But first, let's create the two main pages using the conventional route.

Figure 7-1

Chapter 7 – Manage Orders

7.2 Create Order Master and Order Detail Pages

1. Click the **Create Page** button in Application 101 interface.
2. Select the **Form** option.
3. Click on **Master Detail Form** (a new feature introduced in this chapter).
4. Select **ASA** in Table/View Owner, select **DEMO_ORDERS** (table) in Table/View Name, select **all columns** using the double arrow icon ⪢ and click **Next**. Here, you selected the parent table which contains the master information for each order.
5. Select **ASA** in Table/View Owner, select **DEMO_ORDER_ITEMS** (table) in Table/View Name, select **all columns** using ⪢, and click **Next**. This is the relational child table, which carries line item information for each order.
6. Select primary key columns for the specified Master and Detail pages in the Define Primary Key page as illustrated below and click **Next**.

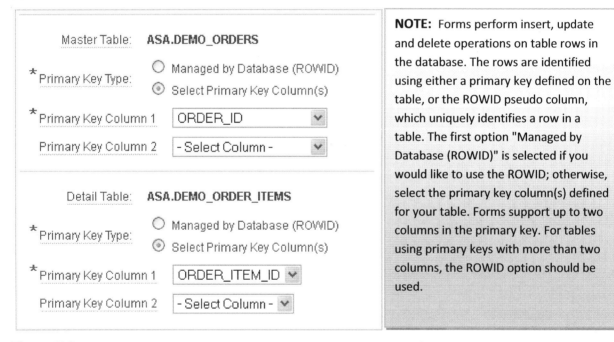

Figure 7-2

7. Click **Existing Sequence** icon, select **DEMO_ORD_SEQ** for Sequence, and click **Next**. In this step, you selected the method by which the master table primary key is populated and chose the database sequence object to populate the primary key. The same option, with different sequences, was selected in the previous two chapters.
8. Repeat the same process for the child table. Click **Existing Sequence** icon, select **DEMO_ORDER_ITEMS_SEQ** for Sequence, and click **Next**.

9. Click **Next** to accept the default options on Define Master page. This step determines whether to include master row navigation. The default is Yes. If you include master row navigation, define navigation order column(s). If a navigation order column is not defined, the master update form will navigate by the primary key column. By default, this wizard creates a master report page. You can choose to not create master report page if you already have a report page.

10. Click **Next** to accept the default layout. This step selects the layout of master detail pages. The first (default) option, *Edit detail as tabular form on same page*, creates a two page master detail while the second one, *Edit detail on separate page*, creates a three page master detail.

11. Set Page Attributes and Breadcrumb sections as shown in Figure 7-3 and click **Next**. This page specifies master and detail page information. If the pages you specify do not exist, the pages will be created for you. Click the **Home link** to select it as Parent Entry.

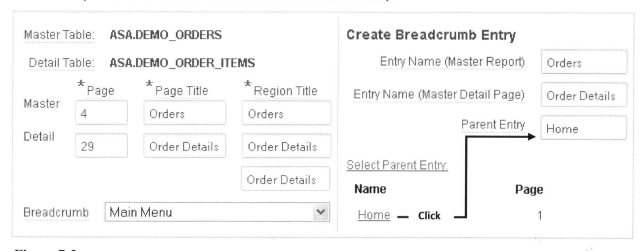

Figure 7-3

12. In Tab Options, click the third option **Use an existing tab set and reuse an existing tab within that tab set**, set Tab Set to **TS1**, select T_ORDERS:label="ORDERS" in Tab Names, and click **Next**.

13. Click the **Create** button. You'll be informed through a message that the master detail pages have been created successfully.

Click the **Run Page** button to check the two pages. The first page (Page 4) that you see will be an interactive report under the Orders breadcrumb. It is similar to those you created in the previous chapters, and opted to create here as well in step 9. It has a default Create button that is used to created a new order. Click the edit link in front of any record to call the details page (Page 29). Besides usual buttons, it has two navigational buttons (on far right) that helps you move forward and backward to browse orders. The Order Timestamp field is supplemented with a Date Picker control. The page carries two additional buttons in the details section to delete and add products. At first glance, the page looks complete but, from a professional perspective, it feels a bit clumsy. Execute the steps in the following sections to give these pages a more desirable look. Click the Orders breadcrumb. This will bring up the main orders report page. Click Edit Page 4 link located at the bottom. This should bring up page definition for Page 4.

Chapter 7 – Manage Orders

7.3 Modify Orders Page - Page 4

7.3.1 Delete and Re-Create the Default Orders Region

You need to delete the default Orders region to create a new region with the same name and with interactive functionality.

1. Click Orders Orders in the Regions section and click the **Delete** button. You'll be asked whether to delete the corresponding Create button (placed by the wizard), associated with the region. Opt to not delete the button. Click the **Delete Region** button to remove the region from the page.

2. Click **Create** in the Regions section.

3. Select the **Report** option.

4. Select **Interactive Report**.

5. In Create Region set the following attributes and click **Next**.

Attribute	Value
Title	Orders
Region Template	No Template
Display Point	Page Template Body (3)
Sequence	10

6. In **Enter a SQL SELECT Statement** type the following statement to create the report with desired columns and values:

   ```
   select
     o.order_id,
     to_date(to_char(o.order_timestamp,'mm yyyy'), 'mm yyyy') order_month,
     trunc(o.order_timestamp) order_date,
     o.user_name sales_rep,
     o.order_total,
     c.cust_last_name || ', ' || c.cust_first_name customer_name,
     (select count(*) from demo_order_items oi where oi.order_id = o.order_id) order_items
   from
     demo_orders o,
     demo_customers c
   where
     o.customer_id = c.customer_id
   ```

7. Click the **Create Region** button.

8. Call the region for modification by clicking the **Interactive Report** link.

9. In Column Attributes, set meaningful **headings** for all integrated report columns as follows:
   Order #, Order Month, Order Date, Customer Name, Sales Rep, Order Items, Order Total

10. Edit **ORDER_MONTH** column and enter **Month YYYY** in Number/Date Format. Click **Apply Changes**. The Number/Date Format attribute is used to apply formatting masks for dates and numbers in the column.
11. Edit **ORDER_TOTAL** column and select **$5,234.10** for Number/Date Format and apply changes.
12. Scroll down to Search Bar section and put a check on **Save Public Report** to include this option in the Actions menu at runtime.
13. Scroll down to **Link Column** section. Set Link Column attribute to **Link to Custom Target**. Enter 29 in *Page* and *Clear Cache*, in *Item 1* click the find item icon and select P29_ORDER_ID for *Name* and #ORDER_ID# for *Value*. The link column is included as the first column in the report and cannot be hidden by the user. The link column can navigate to either a single row detail view of the selected row, another page within the application or the provided URL. In this step you selected a value to navigate to the Order Details page (Page 29) after clearing the cache, and forwarded the order ID value using a substitution string (#ORDER_ID#) to the corresponding called page item (P29_ORDER_ID). Based on this ID value the called page displays details of the selected order.
14. Click **Apply Changes**.

7.3.2 Modify the Interactive Report

Perform the following steps to change the look and feel of the initial interactive report. After performing these steps, the interactive report will be saved as the Default Primary Report which cannot be renamed or deleted. Note that these modifications are made using the Actions menu at runtime.

1. Click **Run** to run Page 4.
2. Click **Actions** and then **Select Columns**.
3. Move **Order Month** column to *Do Not Display* pane. This way you can show/hide report columns.
4. Using the arrow on the screen to your right, sort the columns in *Display in Report* section as under:
   Order #, Order Date, Customer Name, Sales Rep, Order Items, and Order Total
5. Click **Apply**.
6. To display most current orders on top, click the **Actions** menu | **Format** | **Sort**. In the Sort grid, select the **Order #** column in the first row, set the corresponding Direction to **Descending**, and click **Apply**.
7. Click **Actions, Save Report, As Default Report Setting**, select **Primary** and click **Apply**. Perform this step whenever you make changes to a report; otherwise, your modifications will not be reflected the next time you log in to the application. In Interactive Reports, you can apply a number of filters, highlights, and other customizations. Rather than having to re-enter these customizations each time the report is run, you tell APEX to remember them so that they are applied automatically on every next run. Every application user can save multiple reports of their own, based on the defined default primary report.

Chapter 7 – Manage Orders

7.3.3 Create Alternative Report

Alternative report enables developers to create multiple report layouts. Only developers can save, rename, or delete an Alternative Report. This report (named Monthly Review) will base on the default primary report and will be rendered in a different layout using Control Break utility on Order Month column. Perform the following steps to create three different views of alternative report, with *1. Primary Report* selected in the Search bar.

A. Report View

1. Click **Actions | Save Report | As Default Report Setting |** select **Alternative**, in the Name box enter **Monthly Review** and click **Apply**.

2. In Reports drop down list select the alternative report: **2. Monthly Review**.

3. Click **Actions** and then **Select Columns**.

4. Move **Order Month** to *Display in Report* section and click **Apply**. You had eliminated this column in the previous section. But now, it will be shown in the Monthly Review alternative report.

5. Click **Actions | Format | Control Break**. Under Column, select **Order Month** in the first row, set Status to **Enabled** and click **Apply**.

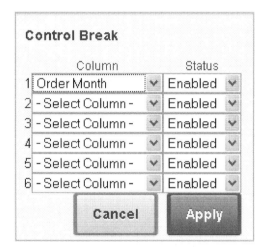

NOTE: The control break feature enables grouping to be added to our report on one or more columns. The Column attribute defines which column to group on and the Status attribute determines whether the control break is active or not. When the report is run, you will see that report results are grouped by the Order Month column and the created Control Break column will be listed under the Search Bar. A checkbox is displayed next to the control break column and is used to turn the control break on or off. The control break can be deleted from the report by clicking the delete icon.

Figure 7-4

6. Click **Actions | Format | Highlight**. Type **Orders > $2,000** in *Name*, set *Highlight Type* to **Cell**, click **[green]** for *Background Color*, click **[red]** for *Text Color*, in *Highlight Condition* set *Column* to **Order Total**, *Operator* to **>** (greater than), *Expression* to **2000** and click **Apply**. To distinguish important data, Oracle APEX provides you with conditional highlighting feature in interactive reports. The highlight feature in Interactive Reports enables users to display data in different colors based on a condition. You can define multiple highlights conditions for a report. In this step, you're asking APEX to highlight the Order Total column in the report with green background and red text color where the value of this column is greater than 2000. Since you set the Highlight Type to Cell, the condition will apply only to the Order Total column.

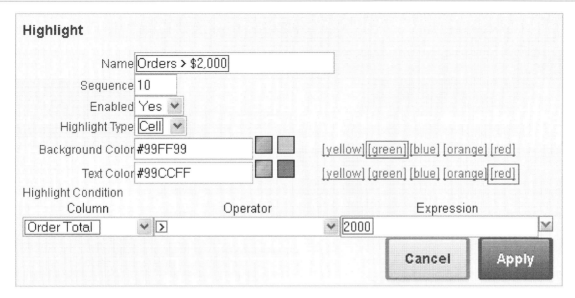

Figure 7-5

7. Click **Actions | Format | Highlight**. Type **Orders <= $900** in *Name*, set *Highlight Type* to **Row,** click [yellow] for *Background Color*, click [Red] for *Text Color*, in *Highlight Condition* set *Column* to **Order Total**, *Operator* to **<=** (less than or equal to), *Expression* to **900** and click **Apply**. This step is similar to the previous one with different parameters. In contrast to the previous action, where only a single cell was highlighted, this one highlights complete row with yellow background and red text color and applies it to all rows in the report with Order Total equaling $900 or less.

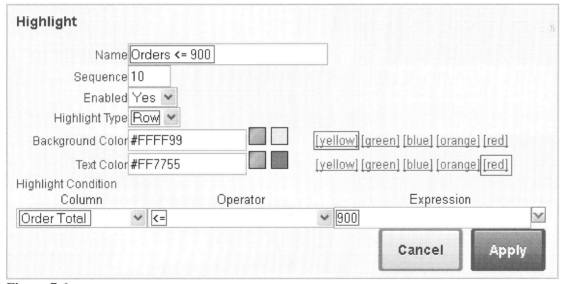

Figure 7-6

8. Click **Actions | Format | Sort**. Under Column, select **Order #** in the first row and click **Apply**.

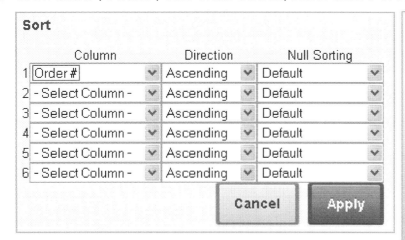

NOTE: The Sort feature enables a custom sort order to be applied to the results of a report. You can select which report columns to sort by using the Column attribute. The Direction attribute will determine if the column is sorted in ascending or descending order. The Null Sorting attribute controls whether null values in the column are displayed first or last. Report results can also be sorted by clicking individual report column headings when viewing the report.

Figure 7-7

The resulting output should look like the following figure.

Order Month : March 2013

	Order #	Order Date	Customer Name	Sales Rep	Order Items	Order Total
🖉	2	13-MAR-2013	Dulles, John	DEMO	Order > $2,000	$2,380.00
🖉	3	24-MAR-2013	Hartsfield, William	DEMO	5	$1,640.00
🖉	4	26-MAR-2013	LaGuardia, Fiorello	DEMO	5	$1,090.00

Order Month : April 2013

	Order #	Order Date	Customer Name	Sales Rep	Order Items	Order Total
🖉	5	05-APR-2013	Lambert, Albert	DEMO	5	$950.00
🖉	6	10-APR-2013	Logan, Edward	DEMO	4	$1,515.00
🖉	7	15-APR-2013	Logan, Edward	DEMO	7	$905.00
🖉	8	23-APR-2013	OHare, Frank	DEMO	4	$1,060.00
🖉	9	29-APR-2013	Hartsfield, William	DEMO	3	$730.00

Order Month : May 2013 — Order <= $900 shown in RED with Yellow background

	Order #	Order Date	Customer Name	Sales Rep	Order Items	Order Total
🖉	10	02-MAY-2013	Bradley, Eugene	DEMO	3	$870.00

Figure 7-8

B. Chart View

You can generate charts in Interactive Reports based on the results of the report. You can specify the type of chart together with the data in the report you wish to chart. In the following exercise, you will create a horizontal bar chart to present monthly sales figures using the Order Month column for the chart labels and a sum of the Order Total column for the chart values.

1. Click **Actions | Format | Chart**.
2. Select the **1st** option (horizontal bar) in *Chart Type*.
3. Select **Order Month** for *Label*.
4. Enter **Period** in *Axis Title for Label*.
5. Select **Order Total** for *Value*.
6. Enter **Total Orders Amount** in *Axis Title for Value*.
7. Select **Sum** as *Function*.
8. Select **Label-Ascending** for *Sort*.
9. Click **Apply**.

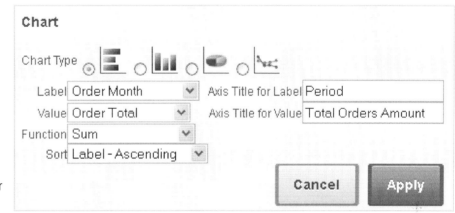

Figure 7-9

The chart should look like Figure 7-10. Note that the Search bar now has two icons: View Report and View Chart. If the chart doesn't appear, click the View Chart icon in the search bar. Move your mouse over each bar to see total amount for the month.

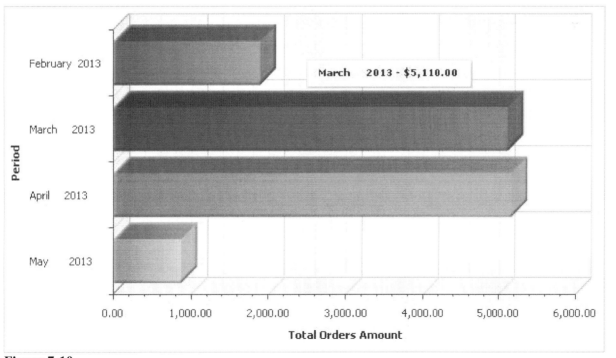

Figure 7-10

Chapter 7 – Manage Orders

C. Group By View

Group By enables users to group the result set by one or more columns and perform mathematical computations against the columns. Once users define the group by, a corresponding icon is placed in the Search bar which they can use to switch among the three report views.

1. Click the View Report icon ▤ to switch back to the report view.
2. Click **Actions | Format | Group By**.
3. Set attributes as show in the following figure and click **Apply**.

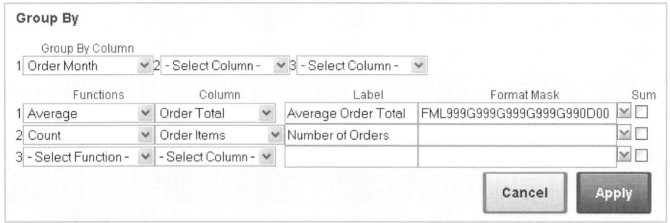

Figure 7-11

The output should look like the figure illustrated below. Note that a third icon View Group by will be added to the main report bar. To sort the output on the Order Month column, click on the **Actions** menu | Format | **Group By Sort**. In the Group By Sort grid, select the **Order Month** column in the first row and click **Apply**.

Order Month ▲	Average Order Total	Number of Orders
February 2013	$1,890.00	1
March 2013	$1,703.33	3
April 2013	$1,032.00	5
May 2013	$426.00	5

Figure 7-12

4. Click on the **Actions** menu and select the **Save Report** option.
5. Select **As Default Report Setting**.
6. This time select the option: **Alternative**. The Name of the report should be **Monthly Review**.
7. Click **Apply**.

7.3.4 Create Public Report

This type of report can be saved, renamed, or deleted by the end user who created it. Other users can view and save the layout as another report. Follow the instructions below to create the three views: Report, Chart, and Group by of a public report.

A. Report View

1. Select the default **1. Primary Report** from the Reports drop-down list in the Search bar.
2. From the **Actions** menu, select the **Save Report** option.
3. From the Save dropdown list select **As Named Report**. Users can create multiple variations of a report and save them as named reports, for either public or private viewing.
4. For report Name enter **Customer Review**, put a check on Public and click the **Apply** button. A new report group (Public) will be added to the Reports list in the Search bar carrying the report Customer Review. When you click the **Apply** button, the report is displayed on your screen.
5. With report **1. Customer Review** appearing on your screen, click **Actions | Format | Control Break**.
6. Select **Customer Name** in the first row under Column, set Status to **Enabled** and click **Apply**.

Figure 7-13

The output should be like this.

Customer Name : Bradley, Eugene

	Order #	Order Date	Sales Rep	Order Items	Order Total
✎	10	02-MAY-2013	DEMO	3	$870.00
✎	1	27-FEB-2013	DEMO	3	$1,890.00

Customer Name : Dulles, John

	Order #	Order Date	Sales Rep	Order Items	Order Total
✎	2	13-MAR-2013	DEMO	10	$2,380.00

Figure 7-14

Chapter 7 – Manage Orders

B. Chart View

1. Click **Actions** | **Format** | **Chart**.
2. In Chart Type, select the first option (horizontal).
3. Select **Customer Name** for *Label*.
4. Enter **Customer** in *Axis Title for Label*.
5. Select **Order Total** for *Value*.
6. Enter **Average Order Total** in *Axis Title for Value*.
7. Select **Average** for *Function*.
8. Select **Label–Ascending** for *Sort*.
9. Click **Apply**.

Figure 7-15

The output should look similar to this figure.

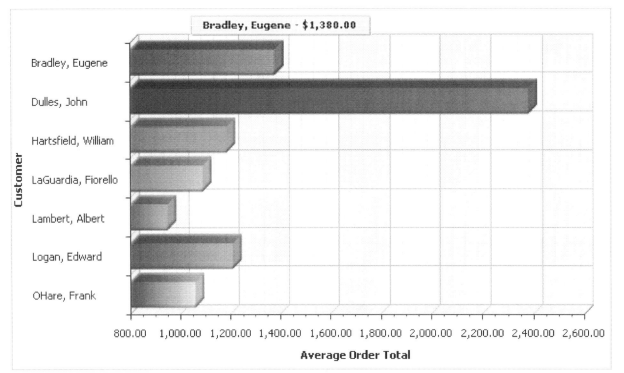

Figure 7-16

NOTE: This chart uses the Average function (as compared to the Sum function used in the previous exercise). The customer, Eugene Bradley, has placed two orders amounting to $2,760. The average for this customer comes to $1,380 (2,760/2) and this is what you see when you move your mouse over the bar representing this customer.

C. Group By View

1. Click on the **Report View** icon to switch back.
2. Click **Actions | Format | Group By**.
3. Set attributes as show in the following illustration. Don't forget to put check marks in the Sum column.
4. Click **Apply**.

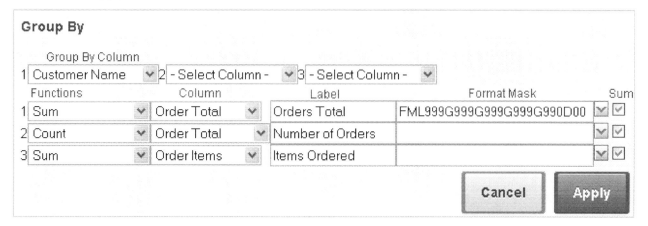

Figure 7-17

The following is the output for the selections you made. In this view, you utilized Sum and Count functions on two columns: Order Total and Order Items. This view displays total amount of orders placed by each customer with number of orders and the total number of items ordered.

Customer Name	Orders Total	Number of Orders	Items Ordered
Dulles, John	$2,380.00	1	10
OHare, Frank	$1,060.00	1	4
Logan, Edward	$2,420.00	2	11
Lambert, Albert	$950.00	1	5
Hartsfield, William	$2,370.00	2	8
LaGuardia, Fiorello	$1,090.00	1	5
Bradley, Eugene	$2,760.00	2	6
	$13,030.00	10	49

Figure 7-18

Chapter 7 – Manage Orders

7.3.5 Modify Button – Create

You deleted the default region in section 7.3.1 and re-created it. Recall that while deleting the old region, you were asked to delete the Create button associated with it, that you denied. In this section you'll associate this button with the new Orders region.

1. Click **Edit Page 4** in Developer Toolbar.
2. Click the **Create** CREATE link in the Button region to modify this default button, set the following attributes and **apply changes**:

Attribute	Value
Button Name	ENTER_NEW_ORDER
Text Label/Alt	Enter New Order
Display Region	Order (10)
Button Position	Right of Interactive Report Search Bar
Action	Submit Page

By setting the Display Region attribute to Order, you instructed to put the create button in the new region to the right of Search bar. The Action attribute was initially set to *Redirect to Page in this Application* by the wizard with a value of 29 for Page. While testing the default behavior of this page earlier, you were taken to Page 29 (Order Details) when you clicked this button. By setting the above attributes, you altered the process with the page submission mechanism that works in association with branching. The Submit Page action submits the current page with a REQUEST value equal to the Button Name. At this stage, after setting the Action attribute to Submit Page, if you run the page and click the Enter New Order button, no action will be performed. This is because you didn't mention what to do when the page is submitted, and that is what you are going to do next.

7.3.6 Delete Computation – P29_ORDER_ID

Once an order is generated, the Order Details page (Page 29) is used to modify or delete the order. This page was created by the Master/Detail Form wizard and was associated with DEMO_ORDER_ITEMS table. The primary key of this table is ORDER_ITEM_ID, whereas the column ORDER_ID is the foreign key to associate an order with its headers in the master table (DEMO_ORDERS). To associate the two tables, the wizard created a computation item: P29_ORDER_ID. The purpose of this computation was to assign the order ID value to the identified item and pass it on to Page 29. We do not need this item because we intend to process the order with the help of a wizard. For this purpose, you deleted the default region associated with this item and replaced it with an interactive report region.

1. Click P29_ORDER_ID under Computations in Page Processing section.
2. Click **Delete** button and then confirm deletion.

Chapter 7 – Manage Orders

7.3.7 Create a Branch

The two default order pages were created with a behavior to call the details page from the master page, whereas, we would like to record an order through a series of steps, as mentioned earlier in this chapter. Here we are going to create a new branch to initiate the Order wizard – page 11 when ENTER_NEW_ORDER button is pressed. Branches enable you to create logic controls that determine how the user navigates through the application.

1. Under Page Processing area, click the **Create** button in the Branches section.

2. In the Branch Attribute page, set Sequence to **10**, Branch Point to **On Submit: After Processing (After Computation, Validation, and Processing)**, and Branch Type to **Branch to Page or URL**. Click **Next**. The branching point used here is the most common one and takes place as the last step of the ACCEPT process and informs the APEX engine to take the next step i.e. branch to the specified page.

3. Set Branch Target to **Page in this Application**. Enter **11** in Page, put a check on **include process success message**, enter **11** in Clear Cache, enter **P11_BRANCH** for Set these items, enter **4** in With these values and click **Next**. Page 11 is the target page that we wish to call when Page 4 is submitted through the sole Enter New Order button on this page. Page 11 will be created in a subsequent section to select a customer. We also created a session state for an item (P11_BRANCH a hidden item to be created on Page 11) with a value 4. This declaration will be associated with the Cancel button on Page 11. When you click the Enter New Order button, the value of the current page i.e. 4 is stored in the session state to remember the application flow. An action will be created using the P11_BRANCH item for the Cancel button (on Page 11) that will return you to Page 4. See section 7.6.7 and 7.6.11 for related information.

4. Select **ENTER_NEW_ORDER** for When Button Pressed and click **Create Branch**. The branch is associated to the Enter New Order button. Now, if you run Page 4 and click the button, the page is submitted with a page not found error message. The message will never appear once Page 11 is there.

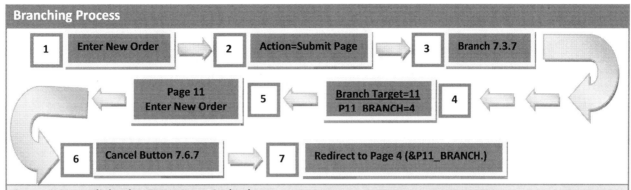

1.	User clicks the Enter New Order button.
2.	The Action (Submit Page) associated with this button is triggered and,
3.	Executes instructions set in the branch.
4.	The branch switches the flow to Page 11 after setting session state for P11_BRANCH - a hidden item on Page 11.
5.	Page 11 appears on the screen.
6.	User clicks the Cancel button on Page 11.
7.	The Action attribute (Redirect to page in this application), defined in the Cancel button in section 7.6.7 calls Page 4. It evaluates the page number (4) from the value of P11-BRANCH. This hidden item carries a value (4) that it received from the session state set in step 4.

Chapter 7 – Manage Orders

7.4 Modify Order Details Page - Page 29

7.4.1 Modify Page Attributes

1. Enter **29** in the Page box and click the **Go** button to call page 29. It is a shortcut to call definitions of a page, especially in applications with large number of pages.

2. In the Page Rendering area, click the **Edit** icon under Page section.

3. Scroll down to the CSS section. Add the following inline rule.

    table.uReport tr td {vertical-align: middle !important;}

    Inline styling is a method in which a style attribute is directly added to the relevant element. In the current scenario, you've applied this method to the <td> HTML element. The <td> element represents table cells and holds data. The Order Details page has two regions. The upper region displays master information from the DEMO_ORDERS table, while the lower region shows details of items associated with an order from DEMO_ORDER_ITEMS database table. Data in the lower region is presented by APEX using a Table HTML element. A table is a set of data elements (values) that is organized using a model of vertical columns and horizontal rows, the cell being the unit where a row and column intersect. By default, the data in each row is aligned at the bottom. The above rule will align it in the middle of the cell. See Figure 7-21 at the end of this section.

4. Scroll down to Security section and set Authorization Scheme to **Verify Order Ownership**. This scheme was created in chapter 3, section 3.7.3 to allow order manipulation rights only to the user who created the order. You'll test the functionality of this scheme at the end of this section.

5. Click **Apply Changes**.

7.4.2 Modify Region Attributes

1. Click the HTML region **Order Details** in the Regions section, set the following attributes and **apply changes**. The value, set for the Title attribute, consists of two parts. The first one (Order #), is a string concatenated to a page item (P29_ORDER_ID) which carries the order number. Combined together, the string is presented as: Order # 1 (see Figure 7-21). The Column Span attribute is set to 8 to span the region from column 3-10, leaving two columns on both sides to centralize the region.

Attribute	Value
Title	Order #&P29_ORDER_ID. (put the terminating period)
Template	Form Region
Display Point	Page Template Body (2)
Start new Row	Yes
Column	3
Column Span	8

2. Click the **Order Details** Report region and set the following attributes:

Attribute	Value
Title	Items for Order #&P29_ORDER_ID.
Display Point	Page Template Body (2)
Template	Standard Region - No Padding
Item Display Position	Below Content
Start New Row	Yes
Column	3
Column Span	8
Condition Type	-No Condition-

NOTE: The Item Display Position attribute determines if page items are displayed above or below the main region content.

3. In Region Source replace existing SQL statement with:

```
select oi.order_item_id,
    oi.order_id,
    oi.product_id,
    oi.unit_price,
    oi.quantity,
    (oi.unit_price * oi.quantity) extended_price,
    dbms_lob.getlength(product_image) product_image ,
    decode(nvl(dbms_lob.getlength(pi.product_image),0),0,null,
    '<img style="border: 4px solid #CCC; -moz-border-radius: 4px; -webkit-border-radius: 4px;"
     '||'src="'|| apex_util.get_blob_file_src('P6_PRODUCT_IMAGE',pi.product_id)|| '" height="75"
     width="75" alt="Product Image" title="Product Image" />')  detail_img
from DEMO_ORDER_ITEMS oi, DEMO_PRODUCT_INFO pi
where oi.ORDER_ID = :P29_ORDER_ID
and oi.product_id = pi.product_id (+)
```

4. Click the **Report Attributes** tab on the same page.

5. Under Column Attributes edit each column and set the following attributes. The default Display As value for UNIT_PRICE is Text which allows end user to modify price of a product and that is eliminated by changing the value to Display as Text. With this value set, the price column is displayed as text and the values contained within this column are not editable. For Product ID column, we changed two attributes. First, we set the Display As attribute to Select List. Secondly, we associated an LOV (Products with Price) to it. This LOV was created in chapter 3 section 3.8.2 to display list of products along with respective prices.

Column	Attribute	Value
UNIT_PRICE	Display As	Display as Text (escape special characters, does not save state)
	Format Mask	$5,234.10
PRODUCT_ID	Display As	Select List (named LOV)
	Named LOV	Products with Price
QUANTITY	Element Width	8
EXTENDED PRICE	Format Mask	$5,234.10
PRODUCT_IMAGE	Display As	Standard Report Column
DETAIL_IMG	Display As	Standard Report Column

Chapter 7 – Manage Orders

6. In Column Attributes change Headings, Alignment, Show, Sum, and Sort to match Figure 7-19. The check mark in the Sum column for Extended Price is put to show grand total for the selected order (see Figure 7-21).

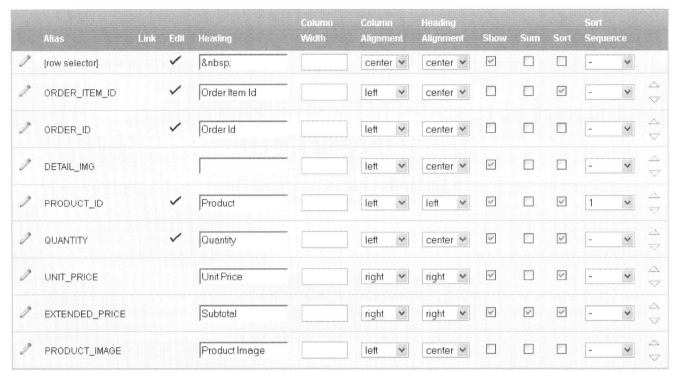

Figure 7-19

7. Scroll down to the Break Formatting section and type **Grand Total** in Report Sum Label attribute.
8. Click **Apply Changes**.

7.4.3 Modify Button

1. Click **Add Row** button (last in the button region).
2. Set Action to **Submit Page** under Action When Button Clicked section and **Apply Changes**. This button is referenced in Add Row process (section 7.4.6) to add a blank row for a new order item.

7.4.4 Create/Modify Items

1. Click **Create** in Items.

2. Select the **Display Only** item. As the name suggests, the data carried in this item cannot be manipulated. It is being created to display complete name of a customer, address, city, state, and postal code in the order's master section. See Figure 7-21.

3. Enter P29_CUSTOMER_INFO in Item Name, **10** in Sequence, set Region to **Order #&P29_ORDER_ID.**, and click **Next**.

4. Enter <b>Customer Info:</b> in Label, keep the value **Optional (Horizontal – Right Aligned)** for Template, and click **Next**. The <b> HTML tag will present the label in bold.

5. Set Show Line Breaks to **No** and keep default values for Save Session State and Based On to No and Page Item Value, respectively. Click **Next**.

6. Set Source Type to **SQL Query (return single value)** and enter the following query in Source Value:

    ```
    select htf.escape_sc(cust_first_name) || ' ' || htf.escape_sc(cust_last_name) || '<br />' ||
    htf.escape_sc(cust_street_address1) || decode(cust_street_address2, null, null, '<br />' ||
    htf.escape_sc(cust_street_address2)) || '</br>' || htf.escape_sc(cust_city) || ', ' ||
    htf.escape_sc(cust_state) || ' ' || htf.escape_sc(cust_postal_code) from demo_customers
    where customer_id = :P29_CUSTOMER_ID
    ```

7. Click **Create Item**.

Edit all the items individually and set the corresponding attributes shown under each item.

8. Edit the newly created item, P29_CUSTOMER_INFO, scroll down to Security section and set Escape special characters to **No**.

9. P29_ORDER_TIMESTAMP

Attribute	Value
Display As	Date Picker
Sequence	20
Label	<b>Order Date:</b>

10. P29_ORDER_TOTAL

Attribute	Value
Display As	Display Only
Sequence	30
Label	<b>Order Total:</b>
Save Session State	Yes
Show Line Break	No
Format Mask	Select $5,234.10 format

Chapter 7 – Manage Orders

11. **P29_USER_NAME**

Attribute	Value
Display As	Select List
Sequence	40
Label	<b>Sales Rep:</b>
Display Extra Values	No (If set to Yes, additional values from session state also appear in the list)
List of Value Definition	select distinct user_name d, user_id r from demo_users order by 1
Help Text	Use this list to change the Sales Representative associated with this order.

In the Help Text attribute you specify help text for an item. The help text may be used to provide field level, context sensitive help. At run-time you will see a small help icon ❷ in-front of this item which, upon click, will show the above help in a popup window.

12. **P29_ORDER_ID_NEXT** (Next and Previous buttons are created by Master/Detail form wizard process to navigate among orders. These two buttons are placed in the master section (see Figure 7-21).

Attribute	Value
Sequence	50

13. **P29_ORDER_ID_PREV**

Attribute	Value
Sequence	60

14. **P29_ORDER_ID_COUNT**

Attribute	Value
Sequence	70
Show Line Breaks	No

15. **P29_CUSTOMER_ID**

Attribute	Value
Display As	Hidden
Sequence	80
Value Protected	No

16. **P29_ORDER_ID**

Attribute	Value
Sequence	90
Value Protected	No

7.4.5 Remove Validations

Remove validations **UNIT PRICE not null** and **UNIT PRICE must be numeric**. We removed these two validations because product prices are controlled through Manage Products module.

7.4.6 Create Process – Add Rows

1. Click **Create** in Processes section under Page Processing area.
2. On the Process Type page, select **Items for Order#&P29_ORDER_ID.** in the *Tabular Form* list, select the option **Data Manipulation** and click **Next**.
3. From the provided three categories for data manipulation process, select **Add rows to tabular form** and click **Next**.
4. Enter **AddRows** in Name, **80** in Sequence and click **Next**.
5. Enter **1** in Number of Rows. Click **Next**. This attribute adds specified number of rows when Add Row button is clicked.
6. In Failure Message enter **Unable to add rows**.
7. Select **APPLY_CHANGES_ADD (ADD ROW)** for When Button Pressed. The process will execute when the button labeled Add Row (modified in section 7.4.3) is clicked.
8. Click **Create Process**.

> **NOTE:** Data Manipulation process types are frequently used by wizards to support data manipulation language (DML) actions. Application Builder supports the following declarative data manipulation processes:
>
> - Select Automatic Row Fetch and Automatic Row Processing (DML) to create an automatic data manipulation language (DML) process.
> - Use Multi Row Update and Multi Row Delete with tabular forms.
> - Use Add Rows to Tabular Form with a tabular form.
>
> A Tabular Form is an grid-like interface with rows and columns to display, create, update, and delete multiple records. See the lower pane in Figure 7-21.

7.5 Test Your Work

Enter the application as DEMO user. Click the Run button and then the Home tab. Click the Orders tab. The page should look like Figure 7-20. Click the edit link in front of Order # 9. Order Details page resembling Figure 7-21 appears. Try to navigate forward and backward using the Next and Previous buttons. During this navigation process, you'll be obstructed with a message (You are not authorized to view this order!), if you try to access a record entered either by Test or by the Admin user. The message is displayed by the authorization scheme you implemented for Order Details page in section 7.4.1. Look at the following screen shot. Order # 1 and Order # 3 belong to ADMIN and TEST, respectively. Since you're logged in as DEMO, you can't view these orders. Try adding more products, delete a few and check the page's functionality. At the moment, you can only use these two pages to manipulate existing orders. In the next sections, you will create some more pages to enter new orders.

Chapter 7 – Manage Orders

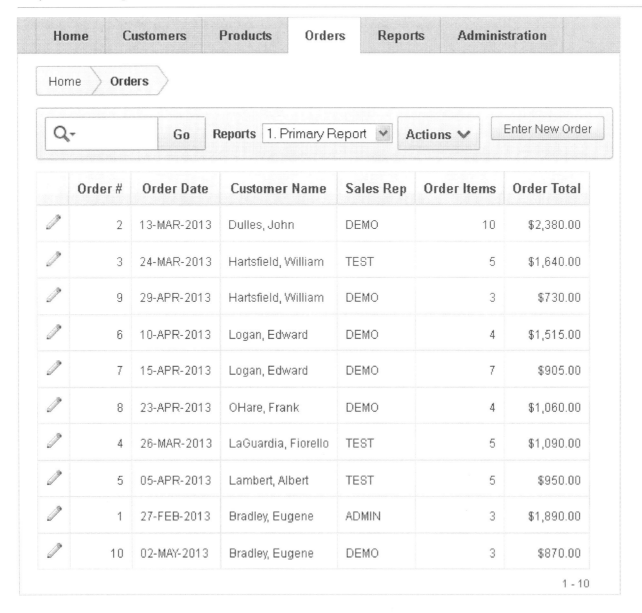

Figure 7-20

How Tabular Forms Work

Tabular forms are based on a SQL query in which the query columns are tied to the underlying table columns. Unlike a single record form, tabular forms do not store data in session state. When a tabular form page is submitted, the tabular form data is processed using built-in data manipulation language (DML), or a custom PL/SQL page processes.
A tabular form with automatic DML has two processes for multi-row operations:

- A Multi Row Update (MRU) process performs create and update operations
- Multi Row Delete (MRD) process deletes requests on one or more rows

MRU and MRD processes reference the underlying table name and the primary key columns. The primary key columns must be part of the tabular form SQL query, and the report columns must be either hidden or display-only (save state) in order for the DML processes to be able to identify the correct records. For new records, the primary key values must be NULL to be identified as new records. Delete operations are performed by referencing row number of the row to be deleted. Users can check one or more rows on the current page and when they click the Delete button, the row numbers identify the corresponding primary key value(s) and the matching rows are deleted.

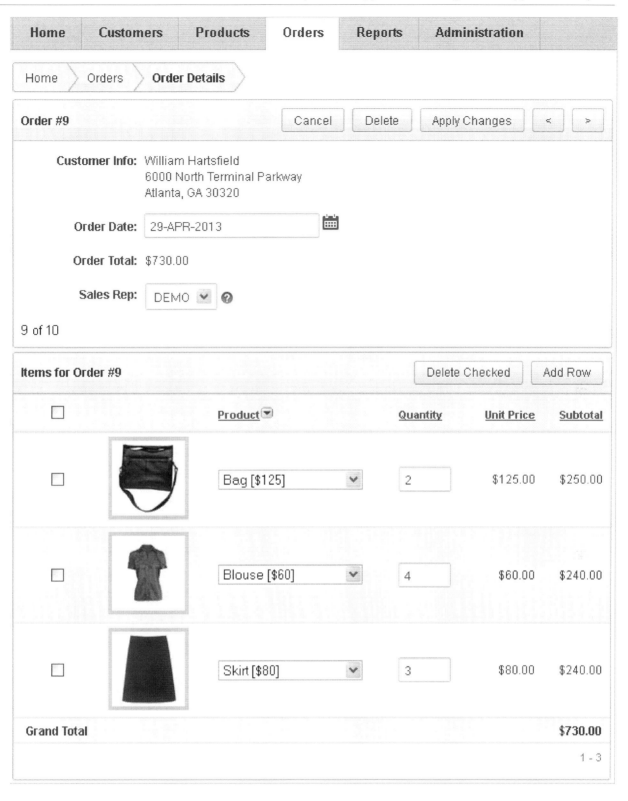

Figure 7-21

Chapter 7 – Manage Orders

7.6 Create Page Enter New Order - Page 11

As mentioned earlier, the user will go through a series of steps to enter a new order. You identified and created these steps in Order Wizard list in Chapter 3 section 3.3.3. The top region in the following figure reflects those steps. The rest of this chapter will guide you to create those three pages individually. In this exercise you will create Page 11 – Enter New Order. The order recording process is initiated when you click Enter New Order button on the Orders page (Page 4). The sole branch you created in Page 4 (section 7.3.7), redirects you to Page 11 where you identify a customer who has placed the order. Besides selecting an existing customer, you can also create record of a new customer from this page. The LOV button corresponding to the **Customer** text box calls a list of existing customer from which you can select a customer. If you select the **New Customer** option, a region (New Customer Details) will be shown under the existing region. By default, this region is hidden and becomes visible when you click on the New Customer option. This functionality is controlled by a dynamic action (Hide/Show Customer), which will also be created for this page. In addition to various techniques taught in this part, you'll create this page from an existing page. Recall that you created a page named Customer Details (Page 7) in the Manage Customer chapter to generate a new customer record. Here, you'll make a copy of that page and will tweak it for the current scenario. Let's see how it is done.

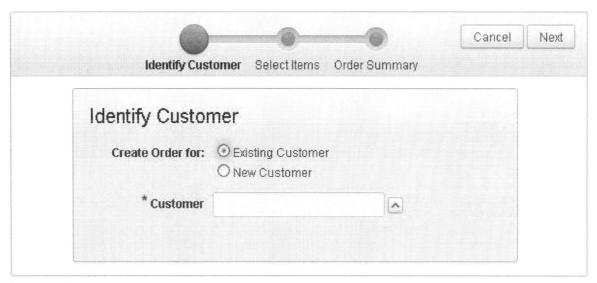

Figure 7-22

1. In Application's main page click on the **Customer Details – Page 7** link.
2. Click on the **Create** menu [Create ▼] to your right and select **New page as a copy** option.
3. For *Create a page as a copy of*, select the option **Page in this application** and click **Next**.
4. Fill in the following values in *Page To Copy* and click **Next**.

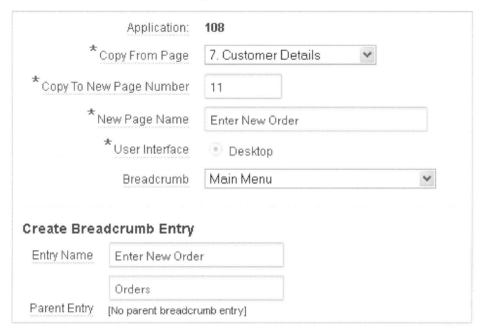

Figure 7-23

5. In the New Names page, do not change anything at this stage and click **Next**.
6. On the Tabs Option page, select **Use an existing tab set and reuse an existing tab within that tab set.**, **TS1** for Tab Set, **T_ORDERS** for Use Tab, and click **Next**.
7. Click **Finish**.
8. Click on the **Edit Page** icon.

Look at the Page Definition. All the elements from Page 7 appeared on the new page, especially the items section carrying all the input elements to create a new customer record. This is the section we needed on our new page to spare some time. There are some elements, such as the Orders for this Customer region, not required in the current development and will be removed in appropriate exercises.

7.6.1 Modify Page Attributes

1. Click **Edit** under Page section.
2. Set Page Template to **One Level Tabs – Wizard Page**, remove the variable htmldb_delete_message from Function and Global Variable Declaration section, and **Apply changes**. The selected page template creates a region to hold the order progress list as shown in Figure 7-22. The variable (htmldb_delete_message) is an auto-generated variable and is associated with the customer record deletion process, handled transparently by APEX. It is removed because the customer record deletion process is not required here. You create Shortcuts in APEX to write frequently used code once and then reference it in many places within your application. The variable (you just removed) is associated to a built-in shortcut named DELETE_CONFIRM_MSG to display a confirmation message whenever the Delete button is clicked on any page of the application. When you click the Delete button, the APEX JavaScript function, which is created automatically with the page carrying the Delete button, sends a DELETE request along with the variable (htmldb_delete_message), initialized in the page's Global Variable Declaration section. This variable contains a reference to the shortcut DELETE_CONFIRM_MSG, which holds a message: Would you like to perform this delete action?
3. Click on the link **Orders for this Customer** under Regions, click the **Delete** button and confirm region deletion. This region was used in Page 7 to display details of orders placed by a customer. Since it is not required, we removed it from the new page.

7.6.2 Create Region – Identify Customer

1. Click **Create** in Regions section.
2. Select the first **HTML** option.
3. On the Region selection page, click on **HTML** to select it as the type of region container.
4. Enter **Identify Customer** in Title, select **Alert Region** in Region Template, set Display Point to **Page Template Body (3)**, Sequence to **20**, and click **Next**.
5. Click **Create Region**.
6. **Modify** the region. In the Grid Layout section, set Column to **4** and Column Span to **6**. This will place the region in the center of the page with all contained elements.

7.6.3 Create Region – Existing Customer

1. Click **Create** in Regions section.
2. Select the first **HTML** option.
3. On the Region selection page, click on **HTML** to select it as the type of region container.
4. Enter **Existing Customer** in Title, select **DIV Region with ID** in Region Template, for Parent Region select **Identify Customer**, enter **30** in Sequence, and click **Next**.
5. Click **Create Region**.

7.6.4 Edit Region - Customer Details

1. Click **Customer Details** link ⓘ Customer Details to edit this region.
2. Enter **New Customer Details** in Title, **30** in Sequence, select **Identify Customer** as the Parent Region, set Template to **DIV Region with ID** and click **Apply Changes**.

7.6.5 Create Region – Order Progress

1. Click **Create** in Regions section.
2. Select the **List** option.
3. Enter **Order Progress** in Title, Set Region Template to **No Template**, Display Point to **Page Template Region Position 2**, Sequence to **50**, and click **Next**.
4. On Source page, select **Order Wizard** for List and **Horizontal Wizard Progress List** for List Template. Click **Next**. The Order Wizard list was created in chapter 3 – section 3.3.3.
5. Click **Create Region**.

7.6.6 Create Region – Buttons

1. Click **Create** in Regions section.
2. Select the first **HTML** option.
3. On the Region selection page, click on **HTML** to select it as the type of region container.
4. Enter **Buttons** in Title, select **Wizard Buttons** in Region Template, for Display Point select **Page Template Region Position 2**, enter **60** in Sequence, and click **Next**. Note that you selected the same Display Point as selected for the Order Progress region. Look at Figure 7-22 and see that the two buttons (Cancel and Next) contained in this region are displayed next to the Order Progress list. Since this region is sequenced higher, it is placed after the Order Progress list.
5. Click **Create Region**.

Chapter 7 – Manage Orders

7.6.7 Modify Button – Cancel

1. Set Display in Region to **Buttons** and Button Position to **Region Template Position #NEXT#**.
2. Scroll down to the Action When Button Clicked section. In Action, select **Redirect to Page in this Application** and enter &P11_BRANCH. in Page. Save the changes. The substitution string (&P11_BRANCH.) will be referenced by a hidden item (P11_BRANCH – to be created in section 7.6.11) to remember the application flow. In the current scenario, this item holds a value 4, assigned to it in section 7.3.7 step 3, to take users back to Page 4 when the Cancel button is clicked.

7.6.8 Delete Processes and Button

1. Click the link **Can't Delete Customer with Orders** under Validations, click the **Delete** button and confirm deletion. Using the same technique, delete **Get PK**, **Process Row of DEMO_CUSTOMERS**, and **reset page** processes.
2. Also remove **Delete**, **Apply Changes**, and **Create** buttons from the Buttons section.

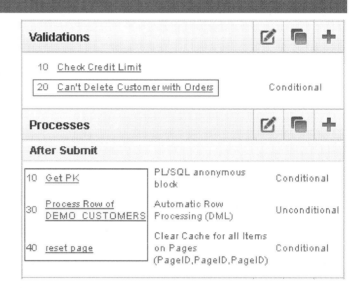

7.6.9 Create Button – Next

1. Click **Create** in Buttons section.
2. Select the **Buttons** region and click **Next**.
3. Click **Create a button in a region position**.
4. Enter **NEXT** in Name, **Next** in Label, set Button Style to **Template Based Button** and Button Template to **Button**. Click **Next**.
5. Select **Region Template Position #NEXT#** for Position and click **Next**.
6. Leave Action to **Submit Page** and Execute Validations to **Yes**. Click **Next**.
7. Click **Create Button**.

7.6.10 Modify Item – P11_CUSTOMER_ID

1. In the Items section, click on P11_CUSTOMER_ID.
2. Set Name attribute to **P11_CUSTOMER_ID_XYZ**. Set Condition Type to **Never**. This item is renamed and suppressed from being rendered because a new item (of POP LOV type) with the same name is created in the next section to display a list of customers to select one from.

7.6.11 Create Items

1. Click **Create** in Items section.
2. Select the **Radio Group** option.
3. Enter **P11_CUSTOMER_OPTIONS** in Item Name, enter **5** in Sequence, select **Identify Customer** in Region, and click **Next**.
4. Enter **Create Order for:** in Label and click **Next**.
5. Leave the attributes to their default values in the Settings page and move on.
6. Using the LOV button, select **NEW OR EXISTING CUSTOMER** for Named LOV and click **Next**. Note that this LOV was created in chapter 3 – section 3.8.5 with two static values.
7. Enter **EXISTING** in Item Source Value and Default boxes.
8. Click **Create Item** button.
9. Create a second Item.
10. Click on **Popup LOV**.
11. Enter **P11_CUSTOMER_ID** in Item Name, enter **6** in Sequence, select **Existing Customer** in Region, and click **Next**.
12. Enter **Customer** in Label, select **Required (Horizontal – Right Aligned)** in Template, click **Next**.
13. Set Value Required to **Yes**, click **Next**.
14. Set Display Null Value to **No** and enter the following statement in List of Values Query. This statement concatenates customer's last and first name into an alias column named d, and corresponding ID value in column r. At runtime, when you select a customer from this list, the concatenated name appears in the text box, while the ID is stored for subsequent process.

    select cust_last_name || ', ' || cust_first_name d, customer_id r from demo_customers
    order by cust_last_name

15. Click **Next** and then **Create Item**.
16. Create the last item.
17. Select the **Hidden** option.
18. For Item Name type, **P11_BRANCH** and for Region, select **New Customer Details**. Click **Next**.
19. In the Settings page, set Value Protected to **No**.
20. Click the **Create Item** button in the final page. See sections 7.3.7 and 7.6.7 for relevant details.

7.6.12 Delete Process

1. In the Page Rendering area click on **Fetch Row from DEMO CUSTOMERS,** click on the **Delete** button and confirm process deletion. This is a default process, not required in the current scenario.

Chapter 7 – Manage Orders

7.6.13 Create Process - Create or Truncate Order Collection

When developing web applications in APEX, you often need a mechanism to temporarily store an unknown number of items in a temporary location. The most common example of this is an online shopping cart where a user adds unknown number of items. To cope with this situation in APEX, you use collections to store variable information. Before using a collection, it is necessary to initialize it in the context of the current application session. After clicking the Enter New Order button, you're brought to this page (Page 11), and this is where your collection (ORDER) is initialized using a PL/SQL process that fires Before Header when the user enters into the interface of Page 11. See sections 7.8.2 and 7.8.9 for relevant details on collections.

1. Under Page Rendering, click the **Create** button in Processes section.
2. Select the first option **PL/SQL**.
3. Enter **Create or Truncate Order Collection** in Name, Keep the default process point i.e. **On Load – Before Header**, and click **Next**.
4. In PL/SQL Page Process enter:

    apex_collection.create_or_truncate_collection (p_collection_name => 'ORDER');

5. Click the **Create Process** button.

7.6.14 Create Dynamic Action (Page Rendering)

1. Click **Create** in Dynamic Actions under Page Rendering.
2. Enter **Hide/Show Customers** for Name and click **Next**.
3. The next page (When) asks you when you would like the Dynamic Action to fire. Set the following values:

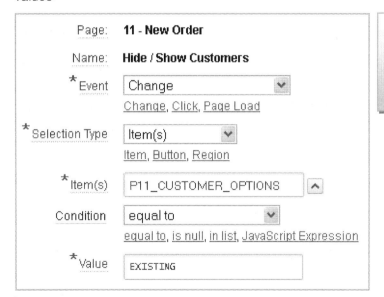

NOTE: The setting in point 3 informs APEX to fire the dynamic action when a user changes (Event) the page radio group item (Selection Type) P11_CUSTOMER_OPTIONS (Item), from New Customer to Existing.

Figure 7-24

4. In the True Action page, select **Show** for Action. Make sure that the options Fire On Page Load and Generate Opposite False Action are checked. Click **Next**.

5. In the final Affected Elements page, where you select which page elements you want the dynamic action to control, select **Region** for Selection Type and **Existing Customers** for Region.
6. Click the **Create Dynamic Actions** button. Click the newly created dynamic action, scroll down to the True Actions section. This section will contain an entry with a Show action for the Existing Customer region. The action will be fired when the condition defined in the 'When' section is met i.e. when the user selects the default Existing option from the available two options defined in the radio group item. A reciprocal False Action was also created by the wizard that is opposite to the True Action.
7. Modify the Hide/Show Customers dynamic action. Scroll down to the True Actions section.
8. Click the button **Add True Action**. Select **Hide** for Action, **Region** for Selection Type, **New Customer Details** for Region and click the **Create** button. This action hides the New Customer Details region when you select the Existing radio option.
9. Click the button **Add False Action**. Select **Show** for Action, **Region** for Selection Type, **New Customer Details** for Region and click the **Create** button. This action is opposite to the previous step and displays the New Customer region when the New Customer option is selected.
10. Click the **Apply Changes** button.

If you run the page at this stage, you'll see that the item P11_CUSTOMER_ID (carried in the region Existing Customer) is shown on the page. Now, select the New Customer option. The item P11_CUSTOMER_ID disappears from the page and the New Customer region becomes visible. Select the Existing Customer option again, the item becomes visible and the region hides.

7.6.15 Modify Validation – Check Credit Limit

In the Page Processing section click the link for **Check Credit Limit**. Set its Sequence to **100** and save the change.

7.6.16 Create Validation – Customer ID Not Null

1. In the Validations section, click **Create**.
2. For validation level, select **Page Item**.
3. select the option **Existing Customer: 6. P11_CUSTOMER_ID (Customer)** as the item to be validate.
4. In Sequence type **10** and in Validation Name type **P11_CUSTOMER_ID Not Null**. Click **Next**.
5. For validation type, select **Not Null**.
6. In the Error Message box, type the item's label substitution string with a text message like this: **#LABEL# must have some value**. Click **Next**.
7. On the Conditions page, select **Value of Item/Column in Expression 1 = Expression 2** for Condition Type. Enter **P11_CUSTOMER_OPTIONS** for Expression 1 and **EXISTING** for Expression 2. Click **Create Validation**. Combined together, the condition is formed like this: P11_CUSTOMER_OPTIONS=EXISTING

Chapter 7 – Manage Orders

7.6.17 Create Validation – First Name Not Null

This validation will check whether the name of a new customer is provided. It is fired only when the New Customer option is selected in the first order wizard step.

1. **Create** another validation.
2. For validation level, select **Page Item**.
3. Select item **New Customer Details: 20. P11_CUST_FIRST_NAME (First Name)**.
4. In Sequence type **20** and in Validation Name type **First Name Not Null**. Click **Next**.
5. For validation type, select **Not Null**.
6. In the Error Message box, type **#LABEL# must have some value** and click **Next**.
7. On the Conditions page, select **Value of Item/Column in Expression 1 = Expression 2** for Condition Type. Enter **P11_CUSTOMER_OPTIONS** for Expression 1 and **NEW** for Expression 2. Click **Create Validation**.

Using the steps performed in the above section, create validations for Last Name, State, Postal Code, and Credit Limit items. Set Sequence for Credit Limit validation to 80.

7.6.18 Create Validation – Phone Number Format

1. **Create** the final validation.
2. For validation level, select **Page Item**.
3. select item **New Customer Details: 100. P11_PHONE_NUMBER1 (Phone Number)**.
4. In Sequence type **60** and in Validation Name type **Invalid Phone 1 Format**. Click **Next**.
5. For validation type, select **Regular Expression**.
6. Click on the **Phone Number** link. This will add an expression ^\(?[[:digit:]]{3}\)?[-.][[:digit:]]{3}[-.][[:digit:]]{4}$ to Regular Expression to receive phone number in the specified format i.e. (999) 999-9999. In Error Message, type: **Phone number format not recognized. Use (xxx) xxx-xxxx format.**
7. On the Conditions page, select **Value of Item/Column in Expression 1 = Expression 2** for Condition Type. Enter **P11_CUSTOMER_OPTIONS** for Expression 1 and **NEW** for Expression 2. Click **Create Validation**.

Create a similar validation for P11_PHONE_NUMBER2 item with sequence=70. Next, set Value Required attribute to **No** for P11_CUSTOMER_ID (in Existing Customer Region), P11_CUST_FIRST_NAME, P11_CUST_LAST_NAME, P11_CUST_STATE, P11_CUST_POSTAL_CODE, and P11_CREDIT_LIMIT. The Value Required attributes for these items were inherited from Page 7 where they were set to Yes during the page creation, to mark them as mandatory. In the above two sections, you used an alternate method to manually control the validation process for these items.

7.6.19 Modify Branch

When the Next button (section 7.6.9) is clicked, the defined button action (submit page) triggers after performing all validations (defined prior to this section). The submit page process executes instructions specified in this branch and moves the user to the next order wizard step. Before calling Page 12 (Select Items), it assigns Page 11 to the hidden item P12_BRANCH to control the application flow.

1. Click the sole branch link Go To Page.
2. Set Page and Clear Cache attributes to **12**, enter **P12_BRANCH** in Set these items, **11** for With these values, and click **Apply Changes**.

7.7 Test Your Work

Click Run | Home | Orders and click Enter New Order button. Your page should look like Figure 7-22 shown section 7.6. Select Existing Customer and Click the LOV button to call list of customers. This list was created in section 7.6.11. Note that each customer name is displayed as a link. Click on a link to select a customer. The name of the selected customer appears in the Customer box. This is how an existing customer is selected for an order. Now, click the New Customer option, the Dynamic Action created in section 7.6.14 invokes and performs two actions. First, it hides the Customer box and LOV. Second, it shows a form similar to the one you created in chapter 5 to add a new customer record. Click the Next button without putting any value in the provided form. You'll see an inline message box appearing with five errors. This is the procedure you handled in the validation sections. At this stage if you click the Next button, a Page Not Found error message will come up indicating that Page 12 doesn't exist. Your next task is to create Page 12 where you'll select products for an order.

Chapter 7 – Manage Orders

7.8 Create Select Items Page - Pages 12

Having identified the customer, the second step in the order wizard is to add products to the order. In this exercise you will create Page 12 of the application to select order items and enter the required quantities.

1. Click **Application 101** in the Developer's Toolbar.
2. Click the **Create Page** button.
3. Click **Blank Page** icon. In this exercise you're using a new option (blank page) to create a page. Using this option you can create and customize a page according to your specific needs.
4. Enter **12** in Page Number and click **Next**.
5. Complete the next screen as show in the following figure and click **Next**.

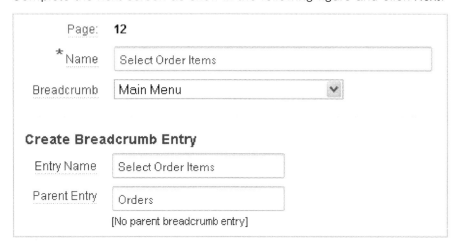

Figure 7-25

6. Click **Use an existing tab set and reuse an existing tab within that tab set.**, select **TS1**, select **T_ORDERS:label="ORDERS"**, and click **Next**.
7. Click **Finish**.
8. Click **Edit Page**.

7.8.1 Modify Page Attributes

In the previous chapter you styled the Detail View of the interactive report to customize its look. Here as well, you will apply styling rules to give the page a professional touch. Previously, you added rules to a single page element: the HTML table. In the following exercise you'll apply rules to the whole page. Before getting your feet wet, go through the following topic to understand Cascading Style Sheets (CSS).

Cascading Style Sheets

A cascading style sheet (CSS) provides a way to control the style of a Web page without changing its structure. When used properly, a CSS separates visual attributes such as color, margins, and fonts from the structure of the HTML document. Go through free CSS tutorials on http://www.w3schools.com/.

In this chapter, you are going to use CSS to style Page 12 (Select Items – Figure 7-26). On this page you will add class attributes to PL/SQL code and will reference them in CSS in the HTML Header section. Before moving on to understand the actual functionality, let's first take a look at a simple example on how to use class attribute in an HTML document. The class attribute is mostly used to point to a class in a style sheet. The syntax is <element class="classname">.

```html
<html>
  <head>
    <style type="text/css">
      h1.header {color:blue;}
      p.styledpara {color:red;}
    </style>
  </head>
  <body>
    <h1 class="header">Class Referenced in CSS</h1>
    <p>A normal paragraph.</p>
    <p class="styledpara">Note that this is an important paragraph.</p>
  </body>
</html>
```

The body of this page contains three sections:
1. <h1 class="header">Class Referenced in CSS</h1>. The text, "Class Referenced in CSS", is enclosed in h1 html tag. It is called level 1 heading and is the most important heading in a document; it is usually used to indicate the title of the document. The text is preceded by a class, named "header".
Considering the above class syntax, here, h1 is the element and header is the classname. Combined together (element.classname), this class is referenced in the style section using a CSS rule – **h1.header {color:blue;}** – to present the heading in blue color. A CSS rule has two main parts: a selector, and one or more declarations. The selector is normally the HTML element you want to style. Each declaration consists of a property and a value. The property is the style attribute you want to change. Each property has a value. In the above h1.header {color:blue;} rule, h1 is the selector, followed by the classname (header), followed by the declaration: {color:blue;}.
2. <p>A normal paragraph.</p> – A plain paragraph without any style applied to it. HTML documents are divided into paragraphs and paragraphs are defined with the <p> tag. <p> is called the start tag or opening tag while </p> is called the end or closing tag.
3. <p class="styledpara">Note that this is an important paragraph.</p>. A paragraph with a class, named "styledpara". In the style section, the selector "p" followed by the classname "styledpara" having declaration{color:red;} is referencing this section to present the paragraph text in red color.

Now that you have understood how CSS is used in web pages, let's figure out how it is used in APEX.

Chapter 7 – Manage Orders

1. Click **Edit** in the Page section.
2. Set Page Template to **One Level Tabs – Wizard Page**.
3. Enter the following code in the **inline** box under CSS section and **Apply Changes**. CSS rules entered in this box is applied to all the referenced elements on the current page.

Rule #	Rule	PL/SQL Ref.
	A - CustomerInfo	
1	div.CustomerInfo strong{font:bold 12px/16px Arial,sans-serif;display:block;width:120px;}	11,22
2	div.CustomerInfo p{display:block;margin:0; font: normal 12px/16px Arial, sans-serif;}	12-19,23-30
	B - Products	
3	div.Products{clear:both;margin:16px 0 0 0;padding:0 8px 0 0;}	36-42
4	div.Products table{border:1px solid #CCC;border-bottom:none;}	37,47
5	div.Products table th{background-color:#DDD;color:#000;font:bold 12px/16px Arial,sans-serif;padding:4px 10px;text-align:right;border-bottom:1px solid #CCC;}	37,47
6	div.Products table td{border-bottom:1px solid #CCC;font:normal 12px/16px Arial,sans-serif; padding:4px 10px;text-align:right;}	39
7	div.Products table td a{color:#000;}	39
8	div.Products .left{text-align:left;}	37,39,47
	C - CartItem	
9	div.CartItem{padding:8px 8px 0 8px;font:normal 11px/14px Arial,sans-serif;}	53-59
10	div.CartItem a{color:#000;}	54-55
11	div.CartItem span{display:block;text-align:right;padding:8px 0 0;}	56-57
12	div.CartItem span.subtotal{font-weight:bold;}	58
	D - CartTotal	
13	div.CartTotal{margin-top:8px;padding:8px;border-top:1px dotted #AAA;}	65-68
14	div.CartTotal span{display:block;text-align:right;font:normal 11px/14px Arial,sans-serif;padding:0 0 4px 0;}	66
15	div.CartTotal p{padding:0;margin:0;font:normal 11px/14px Arial,sans-serif;position:relative;}	66
16	div.CartTotal p.CartTotal{font:bold 12px/14px Arial,sans-serif;padding:8px 0 0;}	67
17	div.CartTotal p.CartTotal span{font:bold 12px/14px Arial,sans-serif;padding:8px 0 0 0;}	67
18	div.CartTotal p span{padding:0;position:absolute;right:0;top:0;}	66

Cascading Style Sheet (CSS) Rules

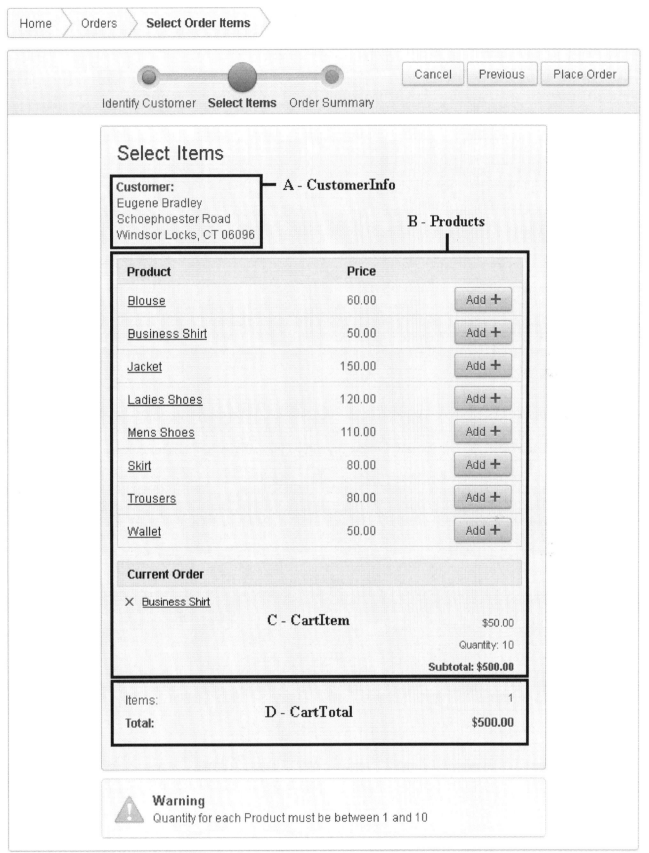

Figure 7-26 - CSS rules applied to the Select Items page

7.8.2 Create Region – Select Items

The region being created in this section is based on a custom PL/SQL code. The code references CSS rules (defined in the previous section) to design the Select Items page as illustrated in Figure 7-26.

What is PL/SQL?

PL/SQL stands for Procedural Language/Structured Query Language. It is a programming language that uses detailed sequential instructions to process data. A PL/SQL program combines SQL command (such as Select and Update) with procedural commands for tasks, such as manipulating variable values, evaluating IF/THEN logic structure, and creating loop structures that repeat instructions multiple times until the condition satisfies the defined criteria. PL/SQL was expressly designed for this purpose.

The structure of a PL/SQL program block is:

> Declare
>   Variable declaration
> Begin
>   Program statements
> Exception
>   Error-handling statements
> End;

PL/SQL program variables are declared in the program's declaration section using the data declaration syntax shown earlier. The beginning of the declaration section is marked with the reserved word DECLARE. You can declare multiple variables in the declaration section. The body of a PL/SQL block consists of program statements, which can be assigned statements, conditional statements, loop statements, and so on, that lie between the BEGIN and EXCEPTION statements. The exception section contains program statements for error handling. Finally, PL/SQL programs end with the END; statement.

In a PL/SQL program block, the DECLARE and EXCEPTION sections are optional. If there are no variables to declare, you can omit the DECLARE section and start the program with the BEGIN command.

1. Click **Create** in Regions section.
2. Click the **PL/SQL Dynamic Content** icon.
3. Enter **Select Items** in Title, select **No Template** for Region Template and click **Next**.
4. In PL/SQL Source type the following code and click **Create Region**. Enter the code defined in the PL/SQL code column. The first column (CSS Rule) references the rules, defined in the previous section. These rules are applied to the injected HTML elements in the following PL/SQL code. The second column is populated with a serial number, assigned to each PL/SQL code. These numbers are referenced in the explanation section (book's page number 201).

CSS Rule	Line No.	PL/SQL Code
	1	declare
	2	l_customer_id varchar2(30) := :P11_CUSTOMER_ID;
	3	begin
	4	--
	5	-- **display customer information**
	6	--
	7	sys.htp.p('<div class="CustomerInfo">');
	8	if :P11_CUSTOMER_OPTIONS = 'EXISTING' then
	9	for x in (select * from demo_customers where customer_id = l_customer_id) loop
	10	sys.htp.p('<div class="CustomerInfo">');
1	11	sys.htp.p('<strong>Customer:</strong>');
	12	sys.htp.p('<p>');
	13	sys.htp.p(sys.htf.escape_sc(x.cust_first_name) || ' ' || sys.htf.escape_sc(x.cust_last_name) || ' ');
	14	sys.htp.p(sys.htf.escape_sc(x.cust_street_address1) || ' ');
	15	if x.cust_street_address2 is not null then
2	16	sys.htp.p(sys.htf.escape_sc(x.cust_street_address2) || ' ');
	17	end if;
	18	sys.htp.p(sys.htf.escape_sc(x.cust_city) || ', ' || sys.htf.escape_sc(x.cust_state) || ' ' || sys.htf.escape_sc(x.cust_postal_code));
	19	sys.htp.p('</p>');
	20	end loop;
	21	else
1	22	sys.htp.p('<strong>Customer:</strong>');
	23	sys.htp.p('<p>');
	24	sys.htp.p(sys.htf.escape_sc(:P11_CUST_FIRST_NAME) || ' ' || sys.htf.escape_sc(:P11_CUST_LAST_NAME) || ' ');
	25	sys.htp.p(sys.htf.escape_sc(:P11_CUST_STREET_ADDRESS1) || ' ');
	26	if :P11_CUST_STREET_ADDRESS2 is not null then
2	27	sys.htp.p(sys.htf.escape_sc(:P11_CUST_STREET_ADDRESS2) || ' ');
	28	end if;
	29	sys.htp.p(sys.htf.escape_sc(:P11_CUST_CITY) || ', ' || sys.htf.escape_sc(:P11_CUST_STATE) || ' ' || sys.htf.escape_sc(:P11_CUST_POSTAL_CODE));
	30	sys.htp.p('</p>');
	31	end if;
	32	sys.htp.p('</div>');

Chapter 7 – Manage Orders

CSS Rule	Line	PL/SQL Code
	33	--
	34	**-- display products**
	35	--
3	36	sys.htp.p('<div class="Products" >');
4	37	sys.htp.p('<table width="100%" cellspacing="0" cellpadding="0" border="0"> <thead>
5,8		<tr><th class="left">Product</th><th>Price</th><th></th></tr> </thead> <tbody>');
	38	for c1 in (select product_id, product_name, list_price, 'Add to Cart' add_to_order from demo_product_info where product_avail = 'Y' order by product_name) loop
6, 7, 8	39	sys.htp.p('<tr><td class="left"><a href="javascript:popUp2('''||apex_util.prepare_url('f?p=&APP_ID.:20:'||:app_session||':ADD:::P20_PRODUCT_ID:'|| sys.htf.escape_sc(c1.product_id))||''',"700","400");">' || sys.htf.escape_sc(c1.product_name)||'</a></td> <td>'||trim(to_char(c1.list_price,'999G999G990D00')) || '</td> <td><a href="'||apex_util.prepare_url('f?p=&APP_ID.:12:'||:app_session||':ADD:::P12_PRODUCT_ID:'|| c1.product_id)||'" class="uButton uAltButton iconButton plus"><span>Add<i class="iR"></i></span></a></td> </tr>');
	40	end loop;
	41	sys.htp.p('</tbody></table>');
	42	sys.htp.p('</div>');

Create Rapid Web Applications Using Oracle Application Express

CSS Rule	Line	PL/SQL Code
	43	--
	44	**-- display current order**
	45	--
3	46	sys.htp.p('<div class="Products" >');
4	47	sys.htp.p('<table width="100%" cellspacing="0" cellpadding="0" border="0">
		<thead>
8		<tr><th class="left">Current Order</th></tr>
		</thead>
		</table>
4		<table width="100%" cellspacing="0" cellpadding="0" border="0">
		<tbody>');
	48	declare
	49	c number := 0; t number := 0;
	50	begin
	51	-- loop over cart values
	52	for c1 in (select c001 pid, c002 i, to_number(c003) p, count(c002) q, sum(c003) ep, 'Remove' remove
		from apex_collections
		where collection_name = 'ORDER'
		group by c001, c002, c003
		order by c002)
		loop
9	53	sys.htp.p('<div class="CartItem">
10	54	<a href="'|| apex_util.prepare_url('f?p=&APP_ID.:12:&SESSION.:REMOVE:::P12_PRODUCT_ID:'||sys.htf.escape_sc(c1.pid))||'"><img src="#IMAGE_PREFIX#delete.gif" alt="Remove from cart" title="Remove from cart" /></a>
10	55	<a href="javascript:popUp2('"||apex_util.prepare_url('f?p=&APP_ID.:20:'||:app_session||':ADD:::P20_PRODUCT_ID:'|| sys.htf.escape_sc(c1.pid))||'","700","400");">'||sys.htf.escape_sc(c1.i)||'</a>
11	56	<span>'||trim(to_char(c1.p,'$999G999G999D00'))||'</span>
	57	<span>Quantity: '||c1.q||'</span>
12	58	<span class="subtotal">Subtotal: '||trim(to_char(c1.ep,'$999G999G999D00'))||'</span>
	59	</div>');
	60	c := c + 1;
	61	t := t + c1.ep;
	62	end loop;
	63	sys.htp.p('</tbody></table>');

Chapter 7 – Manage Orders

CSS Rule	Line	PL/SQL Code
	64	if c > 0 then
13,14	65	sys.htp.p('<div class="CartTotal">
15,16	66	<p>Items: <span>'||c||'</span></p>
17,18	67	<p class="CartTotal">Total: <span>'||trim(to_char(t,'$999G999G999D00'))||'</span></p>
	68	</div>');
	69	else
	70	sys.htp.p('<div class="alertMessage info" style="margin-top: 8px;">');
	71	sys.htp.p('<img src="#IMAGE_PREFIX#f_spacer.gif">');
	72	sys.htp.p('<div class="innerMessage">');
	73	sys.htp.p('<h3>Note</h3>');
	74	sys.htp.p('<p>You have no items in your current order.</p>');
	75	sys.htp.p('</div>');
	76	sys.htp.p('</div>');
	77	end if;
	78	end;
	79	sys.htp.p('</div>');
	80	end;

> **NOTE:** The ELSE block (lines 70-76) is executed when the user tries to move on without selecting a product in the current order. The block uses a built-in class (alertMessage info) that carries an image (f_spacer.gif) followed by a message (lines 73-74).

In the above PL/SQL code you merged some HTML elements to deliver the page in your browser. Before getting into the code details, let's first acquaint ourselves with some specific terms and objects used in the PL/SQL code.

Using HTML in PL/SQL Code

Oracle Application Express installs with your Oracle database and is comprised of data in tables and PL/SQL code. Whether you are running the Oracle Application Express development environment or an application you built using Oracle Application Express, the process is the same. Your browser sends a URL request that is translated into the appropriate Oracle Application Express PL/SQL call. After the database processes the PL/SQL, the results are relayed back to your browser as HTML. This cycle happens each time you either request or submit a page.

Specific HTML content not handled by Oracle Application Express (forms, reports, and charts) are generated using the PL/SQL region type. You can use PL/SQL to have more control over dynamically generated HTML within a region, as you did here. Let's see how these two core technologies are used together.

htp and htf Packages:

htp (hypertext procedures) and htf (hypertext functions) packages generate HTML tags. These packages translate PL/SQL into HTML that is understood by a Web browser. For instance, the htp.anchor procedure generates the HTML anchor tag, <a>. The following PL/SQL block generate a simple HTML document:

```
Create or replace procedure hello AS
BEGIN
    htp.htmlopen;              -- generates <HTML>
    htp.headopen;              -- generates <HEAD>
    htp.title('Hello');        -- generates <TITLE>Hello</TITLE>
    htp.headclose;             -- generates </HEAD>
    htp.bodyopen;              -- generates <BODY>
    htp.header(1, 'Hello');    -- generates <H1>Hello</H1>
    htp.bodyclose;             -- generates </BODY>
    htp.htmlclose;             -- generates </HTML>
END;
```

Oracle provided the htp.p tag to allow you to override any PL/SQL-HTML procedure or even a tag that did not exist. If a developer wishes to use a new HTML tag or simply is unaware of the PL/SQL analog to the html tag, he/she can use the htp.p procedure.

For every htp procedure that generates HTML tags, there is a corresponding htf function with identical parameters. The function versions do not directly generate output in your web page. Instead, they pass their output as return values to the statements that invoked them.

htp.p / htp.print:
Generates the specified parameter as a string

htp.p('<p>'):
Indicates that the text that comes after the tag is to be formatted as a paragraph

Customer::
Renders the text they surround in bold

htf.escape_sc:
Escape_sc is a function which replaces characters that have special meaning in HTML with their escape sequence.

converts occurrence of & to &amp
converts occurrence of " to &quot
converts occurrence of < to &lt
converts occurrence of > to &gt

To prevent XSS (Cross Site Scripting) attacks, you must call SYS.HTF.ESCAPE_SC to prevent embedded JavaScript code from being executed when you inject the string into the HTML page. The SYS prefix is used to signify Oracle's SYS schema. The HTP and HTF packages normally exist in the SYS schema and APEX relies on them.

Cursor FOR LOOP Statement

The cursor FOR LOOP statement implicitly declares its loop index as a record variable of the row type that a specified cursor returns, and then opens a cursor. With each iteration, the cursor FOR LOOP statement fetches a row from the result set into the record. When there are no more rows to fetch, the cursor FOR LOOP statement closes the cursor. The cursor also closes if a statement inside the loop transfers control outside the loop or raises an exception.

The cursor FOR LOOP statement lets you run a SELECT statement and then immediately loop through the rows of the result set. This statement can use either an implicit or explicit cursor.

If you use the SELECT statement only in the cursor FOR LOOP statement, then specify the SELECT statement inside the cursor FOR LOOP statement, as in Example A. This form of the cursor FOR LOOP statement uses an implicit cursor, and is called an implicit cursor FOR LOOP statement. Because the implicit cursor is internal to the statement, you cannot reference it with the name SQL.

Example A – Implicit Cursor FOR LOOP Statement

```
BEGIN
  FOR item IN (
    SELECT last_name, job_id
    FROM employees
    WHERE job_id LIKE '%CLERK%' AND manager_id > 120
    ORDER BY last_name
  )
  LOOP
    DBMS_OUTPUT.PUT_LINE ('Name = ' || item.last_name || ', Job = ' || item.job_id);
  END LOOP;
END;
/
```

Output:
Name = Atkinson, Job = ST_CLERK
Name = Bell, Job = SH_CLERK
Name = Bissot, Job = ST_CLERK
...
Name = Walsh, Job = SH_CLERK

If you use the SELECT statement multiple times in the same PL/SQL unit, then define an explicit cursor for it and specify that cursor in the cursor FOR LOOP statement, as in Example B. This form of the cursor FOR LOOP statement is called an explicit cursor FOR LOOP statement. You can use the same explicit cursor elsewhere in the same PL/SQL unit.

Example B – Explicit Cursor FOR LOOP Statement

```
DECLARE
  CURSOR c1 IS
    SELECT last_name, job_id FROM employees
    WHERE job_id LIKE '%CLERK%' AND manager_id > 120
    ORDER BY last_name;
BEGIN
  FOR item IN c1
  LOOP
    DBMS_OUTPUT.PUT_LINE ('Name = ' || item.last_name || ', Job = ' || item.job_id);
  END LOOP;
END;
/
```

Output:
Name = Atkinson, Job = ST_CLERK
Name = Bell, Job = SH_CLERK
Name = Bissot, Job = ST_CLERK
...
Name = Walsh, Job = SH_CLERK

PL/SQL CODE EXPLANATION

Display Customer Information (Lines 7-32)

This procedure fetches information of the selected customer and presents it in a desirable format (as shown in Figure 7-26) using the CSS rules defined under the class CustomerInfo.

Declare (Line: 1)
This is the parent PL/SQL block. A nested block is also used under Display Current Order section on line:48.

l_customer_id varchar2(30) := :P11_CUSTOMER_ID; (Line: 2)
Assigns customer ID from the previous order step (Page 11) to the variable l_customer_id. This variable is used ahead in a SQL statement to fetch details of the selected customer. In PL/SQL, := is called the assignment operator. The value of the variable that is being assigned the new value is placed on the left side of the assignment operator, and the value is placed on the right side of the operator.

:P11_CUSTOMER_ID is called a bind variable. Bind variables are substituion variables that are used in place of literals. You can use bind variables syntax anywhere in Oracle Application Express where you are using SQL or PL/SQL to reference session state of a specified item. For example:

SELECT * FROM employees WHERE last_name like '%' || :SEARCH_STRING || '%'

In this example, the search string is a page item. If the region type is defined as SQL Query, you can reference the value using standard SQL bind variable syntax. Using bind variables ensures that parsed representations of SQL queries are reused by the database, optimizing memory usage by the server.

The use of bind variables is encouraged in APEX. Bind variables help you protect your Oracle APEX application from SQL injection attacks. Bind variables work in much the same way as passing data to a stored procedure. Bind variables automatically treat all input data as "flat" data and never mistake it for SQL code. Besides the prevention of SQL injection attacks, there are other performance-related benefits to its use.

You declare a field item as a bind variable by prefixing a colon character (:), like this:
:P11_CUSTOMER_OPTIONS

When using bind variable syntax, remember the following rules:

- Bind variable names must correspond to an item name.
- Bind variable names are not case-sensitive.
- Bind variable names cannot be longer than 30 characters (that is, they must be a valid Oracle identifier).

Although page item and application item names can be up to 255 characters, if you intend to use an application item within SQL using bind variable syntax, the item name must be 30 characters or less.

Begin (Line: 3)
Read **What is PL/SQL** at the beginning of this section.

Chapter 7 – Manage Orders

The code block, from line number 7 to 32, creates the first section on the page (marked as A in Figure 7-26) using the <div> HTML element, and styles it using Rule 1 and 2. The code between lines 9-20 is executed when the user selects an existing customer from the previous wizard step.

sys.htp.p('<div class="CustomerInfo">'); (Line: 7)
The <div> tag defines a division or a section in an HTML document. This is the opening tag which references the CustomerInfo class in CSS rules to format the following elements. The ending tag is defined on Line 32.

for x in (select * from demo_customers where customer_id = l_customer_id) loop (Line: 9)
Initiates the FOR loop to locate and fetch record of the selected customer from the demo_customers table.

sys.htp.p('<strong>Customer:</strong>'); (Line: 11)
Displays the label "Customer:" in bold.

sys.htp.p('<p>'); (Line: 12)
The paragraph opening tag ending on Line 19.

sys.htp.p(sys.htf.escape_sc(x.cust_first_name) || ' ' || sys.htf.escape_sc(x.cust_last_name) || '<br />'); (Line: 13)
Concatenates customer's first and last names using the concatenation characters (||). The <br /> tag inserts a single line break.

sys.htp.p(sys.htf.escape_sc(x.cust_street_address1) || '<br />'); (Line: 14)
Show customer's first address on a new line.

if x.cust_street_address2 is not null then (Lines: 15-17)
  sys.htp.p(sys.htf.escape_sc(x.cust_street_address2) || '<br />');
end if;
It's a condition to check whether the customer's second address is not null. If it's not, print it on a new line.

sys.htp.p(sys.htf.escape_sc(x.cust_city) || ', ' || sys.htf.escapte_sc(x.cust_state) || ' ' || sys.htf.escape_sc(x.cust_postal_code)); (Line: 18)
Displays city, state and postal code data on the same row separating each other with a comma and a blank space.

sys.htp.p('</p>'); (Line: 19)
The paragraph end tag.

end loop; (Line: 20)
The loop terminates here after fetching details of an existing customer from the database table.

sys.htp.p('</div>'); (Line: 32)
The div tag terminates here. The output of this section is illustrated in Figure 7-26: A – CustomerInfo. The ELSE block (line 22-30) is executed when a new customer is added to the database from the order interface. In that situation, all the values on the current page are fetched from Page 11.

Display Products (Lines: 36-42)

Here you create a section on your web page to display all products along with their prices and include an option which allows users to add products to their cart.

sys.htp.p('<div class="Products" >'); (Line: 36)
Creates a division based on the Products class. HTML elements under this division are styled using rules 3-8.

sys.htp.p('<table width="100%" cellspacing="0" cellpadding="0" border="0"> (Line: 37)
Here you are initiating to draw an HTML table. The <table> tag defines an HTML table. An HTML table consists of the <table> element and one or more <tr>, <th>, and <td> elements. The <tr> element defines a table row, the <th> element defines a table header, and the <td> element defines a table cell. The Width attribute specifies the width of the table. Setting 100% width instructs the browser to consume the full screen width to display the table element.

<thead> (Line: 37)
   <tr><th class="left">Product</th><th>Price</th><th></th></tr>
</thead>
The <thead> tag is used to group header content in an HTML table. The <thead> element is used in conjunction with the <tbody> and <tfoot> elements to specify each part of a table (header, body, footer). The <tr> tag creates a row for column heading. The three <th> tags specify the headings i.e. Product, Price, and leaving the thrid column heading blank. The specific declaration (class="left") is included that points towards the CSS rule (8) **div.Products .left{text-align:left;}** to align the title of the first column (Product) to the left. The second column (Price) is styled using a general rule (5).

<tbody>'); (Line: 37)
The <tbody> tag is used to group the body content in an HTML table. This section spans till line 41, and is marked as B in Figure 7-26.

for c1 in (select product_id, product_name, list_price, 'Add to Cart' add_to_order
from demo_product_info
where product_avail = 'Y'
order by product_name) loop (Line: 38)
The FOR loop fetches Product ID, Product Name, and List Price columns from the products table. To display the Add button in the table, we appended a column aliased add_to_order and populated all rows with a constant value 'Add to Cart'. For information on FOR LOOP see Cursor FOR LOOP Statement section earlier in this section.

```
sys.htp.p('<tr><td class="left"><a
href="javascript:popUp2('''||apex_util.prepare_url('f?p=&APP_ID.:20:'||:app_session||':ADD:::
P20_PRODUCT_ID:'||
sys.htf.escape_sc(c1.product_id))||''',''700'',''400'');">' || sys.htf.escape_sc(c1.product_name)||'</a></td>
<td>'||trim(to_char(c1.list_price,'999G999G990D00')) || '</td>
<td><a
href="'||apex_util.prepare_url('f?p=&APP_ID.:12:'||:app_session||':ADD:::P12_PRODUCT_ID:'||
c1.product_id)||'" class="uButton uAltButton iconButton plus"> <span>Add<iclass="iR"></i></span></a></td>
</tr>'); (Line: 39)
```

This line displays product name (as a link) with respective price, in two separate columns. The product column is styled using Rule 8, while the price column is styled using Rule 5. The product column is presented as a link using the HTML anchor tag <a>. An anchor can be used in two ways:

1. To create a link to another document, by using the href attribute.
2. To create a bookmark inside a document, by using the name attribute.

It is usually referred to as a link or a hyperlink. The most important attribute of the <a> element is the href attribute, which specifies the URL of the page the link goes to. In the current scenario, the first link calls a JavaScript function to open Page 20 in a popup window to display details of the selected product. The second link places a button (ADD+) in the third column of the table using a built-in class. When this button is clicked, the product it represents is moved to the Current Order section with the help of a process (Add Product to the Order Collection) defined in section 7.8.9.

The c1 prefix in front of column names, points to the FOR LOOP cursor. The TRIM function in the expression trim(to_char(c1.list_price,'999G999G990D00')) takes a character expression and returns that expression with leading and/or trailing pad characters removed. This expression initially formats the list price column to add thousand separators and decimal place. Next, it converts the numeric price value to text expression using the TO_CHAR function and finally applies the TRIM function. The TO_CHAR function converts a DATETIME, number, or NTEXT expression to a TEXT expression in a specified format. The tables that follow lists the elements of a number format model that we used above, with some examples.

Element	Example	Description
0	0999	Returns leading zeros.
	9990	Returns trailing zeros.
9	9999	Returns value with the specified number of digits with a leading space if positive or with a leading minus if negative. Leading zeros are blank, except for a zero value, which returns a zero for the integer part of the fixed-point number.
D	99D99	Returns in the specified position the decimal character, which is the current value of the NLS_NUMERIC_CHARACTER parameter. The default is a period (.).
G	9G999	Returns in the specified position the group separator (the current value of the NLS_NUMERIC_CHARACTER parameter. The default is comma [,]). You can specify multiple group separators in a number format model. Use the following SQL statement to check the current value for decimal and group separator characters: select value from v$nls_parameters where parameter='NLS_NUMERIC_CHARACTERS';

The code,
`<a href="'||apex_util.prepare_url('f?p=&APP_ID.:12:'||:app_session||':ADD:::P12_PRODUCT_ID:'|| c1.product_id)||'" class="uButton uAltButton iconButton plus"> <span>Add<iclass="iR"></i></span></a>`
creates a link with an ADD request. The value of REQUEST is the name of the button the user clicks, or the name of the tab the user selects. For example, suppose you have a button with a name of CHANGE, and a label Apply Change. When a user clicks the button, the value of REQUEST is CHANGE. In section 7.8.9, you will create the following process named **Add product to the order collection**.

```
for x in (select p.rowid, p.* from demo_product_info p where product_id = :P12_PRODUCT_ID)
loop
  select count(*)
  into l_count
  from wwv_flow_collections
  where collection_name = 'ORDER'
  and c001 = x.product_id;
  if l_count >= 10 then
    exit;
  end if;
  apex_collection.add_member(p_collection_name => 'ORDER',
    p_c001 => x.product_id,
    p_c002 => x.product_name,
    p_c003 => x.list_price,
    p_c004 => 1,
    p_c010 => x.rowid);
end loop;
```

During the process creation, you'll select **Request=Expression 1** in Condition Type and will enter **ADD** in Expression 1. The ADD request in the above <a> tag is referencing the same expression. When a user clicks the ADD button on the web page, the URL sends the ADD request to the above process along with the selected product ID. In turn, the process adds the product to the Current Order section. The URL generated from this code looks something like this at runtime:
http://localhost:8080/apex/f?p=101:12:13238397476902:ADD:::P12_PRODUCT_ID:10

end loop; (Line: 40)
End of FOR loop.

sys.htp.p('</tbody></table>'); (Line: 41)
Table and body closing tags.

sys.htp.p('</div>'); (Line: 42)
The closing div tag.

> **Note:** Oracle provides a utility function to enable developers to use PL/SQL to generate anchors to application pages using the f?p syntax. Use APEX_UTIL.PREPARE_URL whenever PL/SQL in the application produces f?p anchors that might require a zero session ID.

Chapter 7 – Manage Orders

Display Current Order (Lines: 46-79)

This section acts as a shopping cart. Products selected by users are placed in this section.

sys.htp.p('<div class="Products" >'); (Line: 46)
Defines the <div> tag and utilizes the Products class referenced in rules 3-8.

sys.htp.p('<table width="100%" cellspacing="0" cellpadding="0" border="0">
  <thead>
    <tr><th class="left">Current Order</th></tr>
  </thead>
</table> (Line: 47)
Displays section heading as follows in the first row of a separate table.

Current Order

Declare (Line: 48)
This is the nested or child block. To nest a block means to embed one or more PL/SQL block inside another PL/SQL block to have better control over program's execution.

c number := 0; t number := 0; (Line: 49)
Declared two numeric counter variables and initialized them with zero. The variable c is used to evaluate whether any product is selected in the current order while the variable t stores total value for the order.

Begin (Line: 50)

for c1 in (select c001 pid, c002 i, to_number(c003) p, count(c002) q, sum(c003) ep, 'Remove' remove
from apex_collections
where collection_name = 'ORDER'
group by c001, c002, c003
order by c001)
loop (Line: 52)
Collection enables you to temporarily capture one or more non-scalar values. You can use collections to store rows and columns currently in session state so they can be accessed, manipulated, or processed during a use's specific session. You can think of a collection as a bucket in which you temporarily store and name rows of information.

Every collection contains a named list of data elements (or members) which can have up to 50 character attributes (varchar2 (4000)), 5 number, 5 date, 1 XML type, 1 BLOB, and 1 CLOB attribute. You insert, update, and delete collection information using the PL/SQL API APEX_COLLECTION.

When you create a new collection, you must give it a name that cannot exceed 255 characters. Note that collection names are not case-sensitive and will be converted to uppercase. Once the collection is named, you can access the values (members of a collection) in the collection by running a SQL query against the database view APEX_COLLECTIONS.

The APEX_COLLECTIONS view has the following definition:

COLLECTION_NAME	NOT NULL VARCHAR2(255)
SEQ_ID	NOT NULL NUMBER
C001	VARCHAR2(4000)
C002	VARCHAR2(4000)
C003	VARCHAR2(4000)
C004	VARCHAR2(4000)
C005	VARCHAR2(4000)
...	
C050	VARCHAR2(4000)
N001	NUMBER
N002	NUMBER
N003	NUMBER
N004	NUMBER
N005	NUMBER
CLOB001	CLOB
BLOB001	BLOB
XMLTYPE001	XMLTYPE
MD5_ORIGINAL	VARCHAR2(4000)

Use the APEX_COLLECTIONS view in an application just as you would use any other table or view in an application, for example:

SELECT c001, c002, c003, n001, clob001 FROM APEX_collections WHERE collection_name = 'DEPARTMENTS'

Note that you can't read apex_collection using external tools. A collection is related to an APEX session and not available outside of it. However, using the following statement you can query WWV_FLOW_COLLECTION_MEMBERS$. It is into this table that APEX stores its collection data. Add Men Shoes to the Current Order section on the Select Items page. Connect to the SQL Command Line utility as sys/manager and issue the following statement in a SQL Command Line session:

Select c001,c002,c003,c004 from APEX_040200.wwv_flow_collection_members$;
Output:
   c001=9 (product id), c002=Men Shoes (product), c003=110 (list price), and c004=1 (quantity)

The CREATE_OR_TRUNCATE_COLLECTION method creates a new collection if the named collection does not exist. If the named collection already exists, this method truncates it. Truncating a collection empties it, but leaves it in place.

In section 7.6.13, we created a process named **Create or Truncate Order Collection** under page rendering section and used the following statement to create a collection named ORDER:

apex_collection.create_or_truncate_collection (p_collection_name => 'ORDER');

Chapter 7 – Manage Orders

In the above (For C1 in) loop, we're selecting records from the same ORDER collection. Columns from apex_collections in the SELECT statement correspond to:

Column	Corresponds To
C001 – pid	Product ID (9)
C002 – i	Product Name (Men Shoes)
C003 – p	List Price (110)
C002 – q	Quantity (1)
C003 – ep	Extended Price (110) This value will increase with each Add button click to accumulate price of a product.

sys.htp.p('<div class="CartItem"> (Line: 53)
This line references another class (CartItem) to style the actual Current Order section.

<a href="'||apex_util.prepare_url('f?p=&APP_ID.:12:&SESSION.:REMOVE:::P12_PRODUCT_ID:'||sys.htf.escape_sc(c1.pid))||'"><img src="#IMAGE_PREFIX#delete.gif" alt="Remove from cart" title="Remove from cart" /></a>   (Line: 54)

The above <a> tag creates a link with a REMOVE request. This time it uses product ID from the collection. In section 7.8.9 (B), there is a process named **Remove product from the order collection** (as shown below) where the request expression is set to REMOVE.

```
for x in
 (select seq_id, c001 from apex_collections
   where collection_name = 'ORDER' and c001 = :P12_PRODUCT_ID)
loop
apex_collection.delete_member(p_collection_name => 'ORDER', p_seq => x.seq_id);
end loop;
```

In HTML, images are defined with the <img> tag. The <img> tag has no closing tag. To display an image on a page, you need to use the src attribute. Src stands for "source". The value of the src attribute is the URL of the image you want to display.

Syntax for defining an image:
<img src="url" alt="some_text"/>

The URL points to the location where the image is stored. The value of IMAGE_PREFIX determines the virtual path the Web server uses to point to the images directory distributed with Oracle Application Express. We used "delete.gif" that is displayed in front of product name. The required alt attribute specifies an alternate text for an image, if the image cannot be displayed.

When a user clicks the remove link [X] in the Current Order section, the above URL sends the REMOVE request to the above process along with the product ID. The DELETE_MEMBER procedure deletes a specified member from a given named collection using the p_seq => x.seq_id parameter which is the sequence ID of the collection member to be deleted.

```
<a href="javascript:popUp2('''||apex_util.prepare_url('f?p=&APP_ID.:20:'||:app_session||':ADD:::P20_PRODUCT_ID:'|| sys.htf.escape_sc(c1.pid))||''',''700'',''400'');">'||sys.htf.escape_sc(c1.i)||'</a>
```
(Line: 55)

The above link allows you to see product details in the Current Order section as well and calls the popup window through the JavaScript function. c1.pid is the product ID passed on to the function. c1.i is concatenated in the URL to display product name as a link.

```
<span>'||trim(to_char(c1.p,'$999G999G999D00'))||'</span>
```
(Line: 56)
```
<span>Quantity: '||c1.q||'</span>
```
(Line: 57)
```
<span class="subtotal">Subtotal: '||trim(to_char(c1.ep,'$999G999G999D00'))||'</span>
```
(Line: 58)

The above three lines display price, quantity, and sub-total of the selected product in the Current Order section as shown below:

```
            $125.00
         Quantity: 10
   Subtotal: $1,250.00
```

`</div>');` (Line: 59)

The ending div tag.

`c := c + 1;` (Line: 60)

This counter increments the value of c with 1 at the end of each loop. The variable c is used to calculate number of items selected in the current order.

`t := t + c1.ep;` (Line: 61)

Similar to the variable c, t is also incremented to sum up extended price (c1.ep) in order to calculate total order value.

```
if c > 0 then
   sys.htp.p('<div class="CartTotal">
     <p>Items: <span>'||c||'</span></p>
     <p class="CartTotal">Total: <span>'||trim(to_char(t,'$999G999G999D00'))||'</span></p>
   </div>');
else
  sys.htp.p('<div class="alertMessage info" style="margin-top: 8px;">');
    sys.htp.p('<img src="#IMAGE_PREFIX#f_spacer.gif">');
    sys.htp.p('<div class="innerMessage">');
      sys.htp.p('<h3>Note</h3>');
      sys.htp.p('<p>You have no items in your current order.</p>');
    sys.htp.p('</div>');
  sys.htp.p('</div>');
end if;
```
(Line: 64-77)

The condition (IF c > 0) evaluates whether a product is selected in the current order. A value other than zero in this variable indicates addition of product(s). If the current order has some items added, show the label Total: along with the value, which is stored in the variable t. If no items are selected, show the message defined in the else block using built-in classes.

Chapter 7 – Manage Orders

7.8.3 Create Region – Maximum Product Quantity

Usually you create validations under page processing section to verify legitimate input from a user. Alerts are displayed in built-in region to inform users about the error(s). In this section, you're introduced to a new technique to deliver the same result. Here, you'll create an HTML region to display a message when the user tries to surpass the maximum quantity limit (10) set for each product in a single order. The HTML code in the region source is similar to the one used in the ELSE block of the PL/SQL code above.

1. Click **Create** in Regions section.
2. Select **HTML** for region type.
3. Select **HTML** as region container.
4. In Title, type **Maximum Product Quantity**. Set Region Template to **No Template**, Display Point to **Page Template Body (3)**, Sequence to **30**, and click **Next**.
5. In HTML Text Region Source, type the following code to display a message at the bottom of the page using built-in classes:

   ```html
   <div class="alertMessage yellow">
     <img src="#IMAGE_PREFIX#f_spacer.gif">
     <div class="innerMessage">
       <h3>Warning</h3>
       <p>Quantity for each Product must be between 1 and 10</p>
     </div>
   </div>
   ```

6. Click **Next**.
7. For Condition Type select **PL/SQL Function Body Returning a Boolean** and enter the following code in Expression 1. The code loops through every record in the APEX collection (ORDER) to evaluate quantity of each product. If the quantity of any product is greater than 10, the block terminates and returns a true Boolean value, which consequently display the message defined in step5.

   ```plsql
   begin
     for c1 in (select c001 pid, sum(c004) prod_count
                from wwv_flow_collections
                where collection_name = 'ORDER'
                group by c001)
     loop
       if c1.prod_count >= 10 then
         return true;
       end if;
     end loop;
     return false;
   end;
   ```

8. Click **Next** and then **Create Region**.

7.8.4 Create Region – Order Progress

This region will display the three steps used to enter an order. It is a visual presentation to show the current order step.

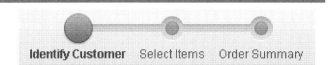

1. Click **Create** in Regions section
2. Click the **List** icon
3. Enter **Order Progress** in Title, select **No Template** for Region Template, select **Page Template Region Position 2** for Display Point, enter **40** in Sequence, and click **Next**.
4. Select **Order Wizard** for List and **Horizontal Wizard Progress List** for List Template. Click **Next**. The Order Wizard list you selected in this step was created in chapter 3 section 3.3.3. The list contains the three order steps, illustrated in the above figure.
5. Click **Create Region**.

7.8.5 Create Region – Buttons

It is an HTML region to hold three buttons: Cancel, Previous, and Place Order. These buttons are created in the next section.

1. Click **Create** in Regions section.
2. Select the first **HTML** option.
3. On the Region selection page, click on **HTML** to select it as the type of region container.
4. Enter **Buttons** in Title, select **Wizard Buttons** in Region Template, for Display Point select **Page Template Region Position 2**, enter **50** in Sequence, and click **Next**.
5. Click **Create Region**.

Chapter 7 – Manage Orders

7.8.6 Create Buttons

1. Click **Create** in Buttons section.
2. Select the **Buttons** region (created above) and click **Next**.
3. Click **Create a button in a region position**.
4. Enter **CANCEL** in Name, **Cancel** in Label, set Button Style to **Template Based Button** and Button Template to **Button**. Click **Next**.
5. Select **Region Template Position #NEXT#** for Position and click **Next**.
6. Leave Action to **Submit Page**, set Execute Validations to **No**, and click **Next**.
7. Click **Create Button**. This button is referenced in section 7.8.10 steps 6–10 to switch back to Page 4.
8. **Create** a second button.
9. Select the **Buttons** region and click **Next**.
10. Click **Create a button in a region position**.
11. Enter **PREVIOUS** in Name, **Previous** in Label, set Button Style to **Template Based Button** and Button Template to **Button**. Click **Next**.
12. Select **Region Template Position #NEXT#** for Position and click **Next**.
13. Leave Action to **Submit Page** and set Execute Validations to **No**. Click **Next**.
14. Click **Create Button**. This button is associated to a branch in section 7.8.10 steps 11–14 to move the user back to the previous page in the order wizard.
15. **Create** the third button.
16. Select the **Buttons** region and click **Next**.
17. Click **Create a button in a region position**.
18. Enter **PLACE_ORDER** in Name, **Place Order** in Label, set Button Style to **Template Based Button** and Button Template to **Button**. Click **Next**.
19. Select **Region Template Position #NEXT#** for Position and click **Next**.
20. Leave Action to **Submit Page** and Execute Validations to **Yes**. Click **Next**.
21. Click **Create Button**.
22. For Condition Type, select **Exists (SQL query returns at least one row)** and in Expression 1 enter the following SQL SELECT statement. When this button is clicked at runtime, the Submit Page action is executed which validates this condition. The SELECT statement check whether there exist at least one record in the ORDER collection. If so, the order is placed and the user is allowed to proceed to the next wizard step. This button is referenced in section 7.8.10 step 1–5.

    select 1 from apex_collections where collection_name = 'ORDER'
23. Click **Create Button**.

7.8.7 Create Items

1. Click **Create** in Items section.
2. Click **Hidden**.
3. Enter **P12_PRODUCT_ID** in Item Name, select **Select Items** in Region, enter **10** in Sequence, and click **Next**.
4. Select **No** for Value Protected, click **Next**. This item is referenced in section 7.8.8 to hold product ID while manipulating the ORDER collection.
5. Click **Create Item**.
6. **Create** another Item.
7. Select **Hidden**.
8. Type **P12_BRANCH** for Item Name, enter **20** in Sequence, set Region to **Select Items**, and click **Next**.
9. Keep Value Protected to **Yes** and click **Next**.
10. Click the **Create Item** button. This item is referenced in section 7.8.10 steps 11–14 to move to the previous order step.

Chapter 7 – Manage Orders

7.8.8 Create Processes (Page Rendering)

The two processes created in this section handle the routine to either add a product to the Current Order section or remove one from it. The add_member function references the collection (ORDER created in section 7.6.13) to populate the collection with a new product. On book's page 197, the link defined on line 55 of the PL/SQL code forwards an ADD request, which is entertained here after evaluating the request in step 6 below.

Similarly, the delete_member function is just opposite to the add_member function. It is called by a link (defined on book's page 197 line 54), which carries the REMOVE request. The request is evaluated by the condition set in Step 6. If the request matches, the selected product is deleted from the ORDER collection.

A. Add Product to the Order Collection

1. Click **Create** in Processes section under Page Rendering.
2. Click **PL/SQL**
3. Enter **Add product to the order collection** in Name, keep the default value for process Point to **On Load – Before Header** and click **Next**.
4. Enter the following code in PL/SQL Page Process and click **Next**:

    ```
    declare
      l_count number := 0;
    begin
    for x in (select p.rowid, p.* from demo_product_info p where product_id = :P12_PRODUCT_ID)
    loop
      select count(*)
      into l_count
      from wwv_flow_collections
      where collection_name = 'ORDER'
      and c001 = x.product_id;
      if l_count >= 10 then
        exit;
      end if;
      apex_collection.add_member(p_collection_name => 'ORDER',
        p_c001 => x.product_id,
        p_c002 => x.product_name,
        p_c003 => x.list_price,
        p_c004 => 1,
        p_c010 => x.rowid);
    end loop;
    end;
    ```

5. Click **Next** to leave messages blank.
6. Select **Request=Expression 1** in Condition Type and enter **ADD** in Expression 1.
7. Click the **Create Process** button.

B. Remove Product from the Order Collection

1. Click **Create** to create another Process.
2. Click **PL/SQL**.
3. Enter **Remove product from the order collection** in Name, set Sequence to **20**, keep the default value for process Point to **On Load – Before Header**, and click **Next**.
4. Enter the following code in PL/SQL Page Process and click **Next**:

   ```
   for x in
     (select seq_id, c001 from apex_collections
       where collection_name = 'ORDER' and c001 = :P12_PRODUCT_ID)
   loop
   apex_collection.delete_member(p_collection_name => 'ORDER', p_seq => x.seq_id);
   end loop;
   ```

5. Click **Next** to leave messages blank.
6. Select **Request=Expression 1** in Condition Type and enter **REMOVE** in Expression 1.
7. Click **Create Process**.

7.8.9 Create Process – Place Order

After selecting products for an order, the user click the Place Order button. The process defined in this section is associated with that button. The PL/SQL code specified in this process adds new customer and order information in relevant database tables using SQL INSERT statements. After committing the DML statement, the process truncates the ORDER collection.

1. Click **Create** in Processes section under Page Processing.
2. Click **PL/SQL**.
3. Enter **Place Order** in Name, keep the process Point to **On Submit – After Computations and Validations**, and click **Next**.
4. Enter the code defined on the next page in PL/SQL Page Process and click **Next**.
5. Click **Next** to leave messages blank.
6. Select **PLACE_ORDER** in When Button Pressed.
7. Click the **Create Process** button.

```
declare
   l_order_id   number;
   l_customer_id varchar2(30) := :P11_CUSTOMER_ID;
begin
-- Create New Customer
   if :P11_CUSTOMER_OPTIONS = 'NEW' then
      insert into DEMO_CUSTOMERS (
         CUST_FIRST_NAME, CUST_LAST_NAME, CUST_STREET_ADDRESS1,
         CUST_STREET_ADDRESS2, CUST_CITY, CUST_STATE, CUST_POSTAL_CODE,
         CUST_EMAIL, PHONE_NUMBER1, PHONE_NUMBER2, URL, CREDIT_LIMIT, TAGS)
      values (
         :P11_CUST_FIRST_NAME, :P11_CUST_LAST_NAME, :P11_CUST_STREET_ADDRESS1,
         :P11_CUST_STREET_ADDRESS2, :P11_CUST_CITY, :P11_CUST_STATE,
         :P11_CUST_POSTAL_CODE, :P11_CUST_EMAIL, :P11_PHONE_NUMBER1,
         :P11_PHONE_NUMBER2, :P11_URL, :P11_CREDIT_LIMIT, :P11_TAGS)
      returning customer_id into l_customer_id;
      :P11_CUSTOMER_ID := l_customer_id;
   end if;
-- Insert a row into the Order Header table
   insert into demo_orders(customer_id, order_total, order_timestamp, user_name)
   values  (l_customer_id, null, systimestamp, upper(:APP_USER))
   returning order_id into l_order_id;
   commit;
-- Loop through the ORDER collection and insert rows into the Order Line Item table
   for x in (select c001, c003, sum(c004) c004 from apex_collections
             where collection_name = 'ORDER' group by c001, c003) loop
      insert into demo_order_items(order_item_id, order_id, product_id, unit_price, quantity)
         values (null, l_order_id, to_number(x.c001), to_number(x.c003),to_number(x.c004));
   end loop;
   commit;
-- Set the item P14_ORDER_ID to the order which was just placed
   :P14_ORDER_ID := l_order_id;
-- Truncate the collection after the order has been placed
   apex_collection.truncate_collection(p_collection_name => 'ORDER');
end;
```

Chapter 7 – Manage Orders

7.8.10 Create Branches

1. Click **Create** in Branches.
2. Click **Next** to accept default Branch Point (On Submit: After Processing (After Computation, Validation, and Processing) and Branch Type (Branch to Page or URL) values .
3. Keep Branch Target selected to Page in this Application, enter **14** in Page, **put a check** on include process success message, and click **Next**.
4. Select **PLACE_ORDER** for When Button Pressed.
5. Click **Create Branch**.
6. **Create** another branch.
7. Click **Next** to accept default Branch Point and Branch Type values.
8. Keep Branch Target selected to Page in this Application, enter **4** in Page, **put a check** on include process success message, and click **Next**.
9. Select **CANCEL (Cancel)** in When Button Pressed.
10. Click **Create Branch**.
11. **Create** the final branch.
12. In the Branch Attributes page, set Sequence to **30**, select **Branch to Page Identified by Item (Use Item Name)** for Branch Type, and click **Next**.
13. In the Identify item box, type **P12_BRANCH** and click **Next**.
14. Select **PREVIOUS** for When Button Pressed and click the **Create Branch** button.

7.9 Test Your Work

Navigate to the Orders page using the Home tab route and click the button Enter New Order. Select a customer using the Existing Customer option and click Next. Initially you'll observe that the Place Order button (created in section 7.8.6) isn't there on the page. This is because of the condition you set while creating this button, which prevents it from appearing on the page if you haven't selected at least one product in an order. Click the Add + button next to Business Shirt to add it to Current Order pane. The Place Order button now becomes visible. Click the Add button for Business Shirt again and see increase in Quantity and Total. Note that if you click the Add button more than ten times for a single product, you get a warning message like: Quantity for each Product must be between 1 and 10. This is the HTML Text element that you created in section 7.8.3 that is displayed with the defined message whenever you try to raise the quantity of a product from the threshold value. Add few more products and observe the change in the Current Order section. Click the cross sign ✕ to remove a product from the section.

Click the Place Order button. This action will result in an error (**ERR-1002 Unable to find item ID for item "P14_ORDER_ID" in application "101"**) indicating missing Page 14 – the Order Summary page. Similarly, if you click on Business Shirt link, you will get an error saying Page "20" not found which refers to Product Information page – Page 20. In the next sections you will create these two pages to complete the order placement module.

7.10 Create Product Info Page - Page 20

In the previous exercise, you created a page to add products to the order. You can allow user to also check details of each product such as Description, Category, and Price before placing orders. In this exercise, you are going to create a page (Page 20), which will show the above details in a popup window.

1. Click **Application 101** in the Developer's Toolbar.
2. Click the **Create Page** button.
3. Click on **Blank Page** icon.
4. Enter **20** in Page Number and click **Next**.
5. Enter **Product Info** in Name, leave the default value –**do not use breadcrumbs on page**– selected in Breadcrumb and click **Next**.
6. Select **Do not use tabs** and click **Next**.
7. Click **Finish**.
8. Click **Edit Page**.

7.10.1 Modify Page Attributes

1. Click **Edit** under Page section.
2. In Display Attributes section, set Page Template to **Popup**.
3. Click **Apply Changes**.

Chapter 7 – Manage Orders

7.10.2 Create Region – Product Image

This region is created in the popup window page to fetch and display the image of the selected product from the database using conventional means, you went through earlier.

1. Click **Create** in Regions section.

2. Click the **Report** icon.

3. Click on **Classic Report** icon.

4. Enter **Product Image** in Title, select **No Template** for Region Template, select **Page Template Body (2)** for Display Point, and click **Next**.

5. In Enter SQL Query type the following statement:

    select decode(nvl(dbms_lob.getlength(product_image),0),0,null,'<img src="'||apex_util.get_blob_file_src('P6_PRODUCT_IMAGE',product_id)||'" />') image
    from demo_product_info
    where product_id = :P20_PRODUCT_ID

6. Click **Create Region**.

7. Click the **Report** link next to Product Image ▤ Product Image Report.

8. Set Headings Type to **None**.

9. Using the edit link ✎ modify the sole IMAGE column.

10. Select **Standard Report Column** for Display As and apply changes.

11. In Report Attributes, set Report Template to **default: HTML (standard)**, Pagination Scheme to **No Pagination Selected**, and Enable Partial Page Refresh to **No**.

12. Click **Apply Changes**.

7.10.3 Create Region – Product Information

Product details such as name, description, category, and list price are fetched using a SQL SELECT statement to display in the popup window.

1. Click **Create** to create another region.
2. Click the **Report** icon.
3. Click on **Classic Report** icon.
4. Enter **Product Information** in Title, select **Standard Region** for Region Template, select **Page Template Body (2)** for Display Point, and click **Next**.
5. In Enter SQL Query write the following statement:

    select product_name,
    product_description,
    category,
    list_price
    from demo_product_info where product_id = :P20_PRODUCT_ID

6. Click **Create Region**.
7. Click the **Report** link next to Product Information region.
8. Set Column Attributes as show in Figure 6-20.

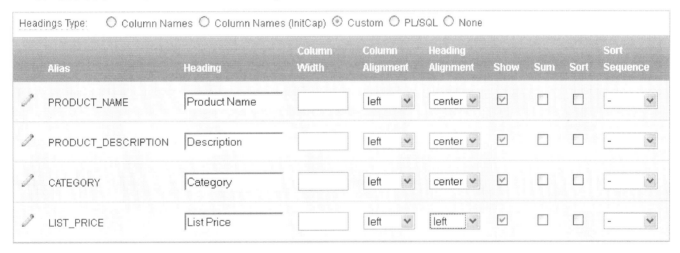

Figure 7-27

9. Set Report Template to **default: vertical report, look 2 (exclude null columns)**, Pagination Scheme to **No Pagination Selected**, and Enable Partial Page Refresh to **No**.
10. Click **Apply Changes**.

Chapter 7 – Manage Orders

7.10.4 Create Button – Close

A close button will be placed to close the popup window.

1. Click **Create** in Buttons section.
2. Click on **Product Information** in Select a Region for the button and click **Next**.
3. Click **Create a button in a region position**.
4. Enter **CLOSE** in Button Name, **Close** in Label, select **HTML Button** in Button Style, and click **Next**.
5. Click **Next** to accept default values in Display Properties page.
6. Select **Redirect to URL** in Action and enter **javascript:window.close()** in URL Target to close the browser window with the close() method..
7. Click **Create Button**.

7.10.5 Create Item

1. Click **Create** in Items section.
2. Click **Hidden**.
3. Enter **P20_PRODUCT_ID** in Item Name, select **Product Information** in Region, and click **Next**. This item represents Product ID. The link created in the PL/SQL code (line 55) populates this item with the id of the selected product, and which is referenced in the SELECT statement in sections 7.10.2 and 7.10.3 to fetch and show the product's details.
4. Select **No** for Value Protected, click **Next**.
5. Click **Create Item**.

7.11 Test Your Work

Click the Application101 breadcrumb, click Run Application and navigate to the Orders page. Click Enter New Order button. Select an Existing Customer using the LOV and click Next. Click the Business Shirt link under the Products column. A popup window like Figure 7-28 should appear. Click the Close button to switch back. Click some more product links to test your work.

Figure 7-28

7.12 Create Order Summary Page - Page 14

After adding products to the Order form, user clicks the Place Order button. The next page, Order Summary, comes up to show details of the placed order. In this section, you are going to create this page which will have the number 14 and will be the last step in the order creation wizard.

1. Click **Application 101** in the Developer's Toolbar.
2. Click the **Create Page** button.
3. Select **Blank Page**.
4. Enter **14** in Page Number and click **Next**.
5. Complete the next screen as show in the following figure and click **Next**.

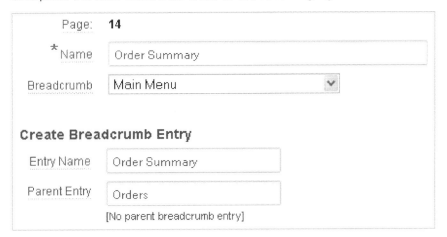

Figure 7-29

6. Click **Use an existing tab set and reuse an existing tab within that tab set**, select **TS1** in Tab Set, select **T_ORDERS:label="ORDERS"** for Use Tab, and click **Next**.
7. Click **Finish**.
8. Click **Edit Page**.

7.12.1 Modify Page Attributes

1. Click the **Edit** button under the Page section.
2. Set Page Template to **One Level Tabs - Wizard Page**.
3. Click **Apply Changes**.

Chapter 7 – Manage Orders

7.12.2 Create Region – Order Summary

1. Click **Create** under Regions.
2. Click on **HTML**.
3. Select the **HTML** option again.
4. Enter **Order Summary** in Title, set Region Template to **No Template**, Display Point to **Page Template Body (3)**, Sequence to 20, and click **Next**.
5. Click **Create Region**.

7.12.3 Create Region – Order Header

1. Click **Create** to create the second region.
2. Click the icon: **PL/SQL Dynamic Content**.
3. Enter **Order Header** in Title, select **No Template** for Region Template, select **Order Summary** for Parent Region, enter 30 in Sequence, and click **Next**.
4. In PL/SQL Source type the following code:

```
begin
for x in (select c.cust_first_name, c.cust_last_name, cust_street_address1,
cust_street_address2, cust_city, cust_state, cust_postal_code from demo_customers c,
demo_orders o
where c.customer_id = o.customer_id and o.order_id = :P14_ORDER_ID)
loop
  htp.p('<span style="font-size:16px;font-weight:bold;">ORDER #' ||
sys.htf.escape_sc(:P14_ORDER_ID) || '</span><br />');
  htp.p(sys.htf.escape_sc(x.cust_first_name) || ' ' || sys.htf.escape_sc(x.cust_last_name) ||
'<br />');
  htp.p(sys.htf.escape_sc(x.cust_street_address1) || '<br />');
  if x.cust_street_address2 is not null then
    htp.p(sys.htf.escape_sc(x.cust_street_address2) || '<br />');
  end if;
  htp.p(sys.htf.escape_sc(x.cust_city) || ', ' || sys.htf.escape_sc(x.cust_state) || ' ' ||
sys.htf.escape_sc(x.cust_postal_code) || '<br /><br />');
end loop;
end;
```

5. Click **Create Region**.

7.12.4 Create Region – Order Lines

1. Click **Create** in region to create third region.
2. Click the **Report** icon.
3. Select **Classic Report**.
4. Enter **Order Lines** in Title, select **No Template** for Region Template, select **Order Summary** for Parent Region, enter **40** in Sequence, and click **Next**.
5. In Enter SQL Query write the following statement:

    select p.product_name, oi.unit_price, oi.quantity, (oi.unit_price * oi.quantity) exteneded_price
    from demo_order_items oi, demo_product_info p
    where oi.product_id = p.product_id and oi.order_id = :P14_ORDER_ID

6. Click **Create Region**.
7. Click the **Report** link next to the newly created region and modify Column Attributes as shown below. Also set display format for Price and Subtotal columns using the edit link as done previously.

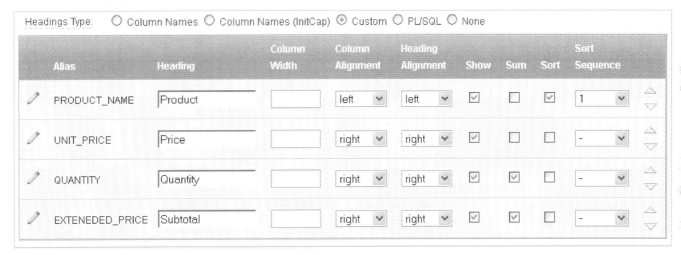

Figure 7-30

8. In the Layout and Pagination section, set Report Template to **template:25.Standard**, Pagination Scheme to **-No Pagination Selected-**, and Enable Partial Page Refresh to **No**. Scroll down to the Break Formatting section and enter **Report Total** in Report Sum Label box. Click **Apply Changes**.

7.12.5 Create Region – Order Progress

1. **Create** the fourth region.
2. Click the **List** icon.
3. Enter **Order Progress** in Title, select **No Template** for Region Template, select **Page Template Region Position 2** for Display Point, enter **50** in Sequence, and click **Next**.
4. As usual, select **Order Wizard** for List and **Horizontal Wizard Progress List** for List Template. Click **Next**.
5. Click **Create Region**.

Chapter 7 – Manage Orders

7.12.6 Create Region – Buttons

1. Click **Create** in Regions section.
2. Select the first **HTML** option.
3. On the Region selection page, click on **HTML** to select it as the type of region container.
4. Enter **Buttons** in Title, select **Wizard Buttons** in Region Template, for Display Point select **Page Template Region Position 2**, enter **60** in Sequence, and click **Next**.
5. Click **Create Region**.

7.12.7 Create Button

1. Click **Create** in Buttons section.
2. Select the region **Buttons** and click **Next**.
3. Click **Create a button in a region position**.
4. Enter **RETURN** in Button Name and **View Orders** in Label. Set Button Style to **Template Based Button** and Button Template to **Button**. Click **Next**.
5. Select **Region Template Position #NEXT#** in Position and click **Next**.
6. Select **Redirect to Page in this Application** for Action and enter **4** in Page. Put a check on **reset pagination** for this page.
7. Click **Create Button**.

7.12.8 Create Item

1. Click **Create** in Items section.
2. Select the **Hidden** item option.
3. Enter **P14_ORDER_ID** in Item Name, select **Order Lines** in Region, and click **Next**.
4. Select **No** for Value Protected, click **Next**.
5. Click **Create Item**.

7.13 Complete Testing

Congratulation! You have completed the most tiresome but interesting chapter of the book. This chapter taught you many techniques summarized at the end. Right now, you are going to test the whole work performed in this chapter.

1. Move to the application's **Home page**.
2. Click the **Orders tab** and then click the **Enter New Order** button.
3. Select **New Customer**.
4. **Fill in the New Customer form** using your own name, address etc. and click **Next**.
5. In Select Item page **add few products** to the Current Order pane.

6. Click the button **Place Order**. Order Summary Page resembling Figure 7-31 should appear.

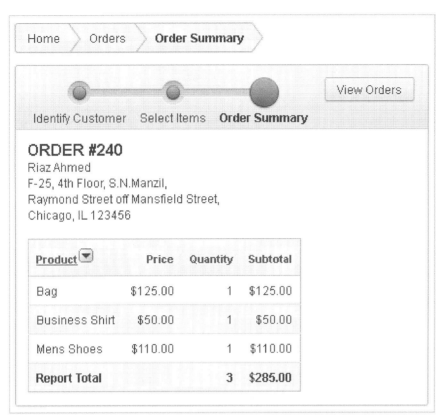

Figure 7-31

7. Click **View Orders** button in the Order Summary Page to return to Orders main page. The newly created order will appear in the orders list.

8. Click the edit link to modify the new order. The Order Details page (Page 29) should come up. Try to add or remove products on this page and save your modifications.

9. Try to delete an order created by another user. You cannot even see the details page of that order and will be prevented with a message: You are not authorized to view this order! The authorization scheme Verify Order Ownership controls this process and allows order alteration only to the user who created the order, besides Administrators.

7.14 Summary

Usually an application comprises two basic segments: input and output. The input process receives data from users and stores it in relevant tables in the database. In the last three chapters (including this one), you added data to the database using different input methods. You selected a new option (Master/Detail form) and applied a custom technique to receive input in this chapter. In the next couple of chapters, you'll be working on the report segment, where you will generate graphical reports with the help of APEX wizards, and few custom reports using Oracle BI Publisher and MS Word. Let's wrap up this chapter with the list of demonstrated features.

- How to create wizards to perform a series of tasks.
- Demonstrated the use of another APEX feature: Master/Detail forms.
- Created Primary and Alternative reports.
- Created Public Reports.
- Created a page as a copy of an existing application page.
- Generated reports, charts, and group by views from a primary interactive report.
- Demonstrated the use of Control Break, Highlight, and Aggregate functions from the Action menu.
- Drill-down to data entry page from report.
- Graphical presentation of data.
- Added processes under Page Rendering section.
- Created a new customer without leaving the order interface.
- Utilized Dynamic Actions to Show/Hide page item and region.
- How to add custom styles (CSS) to APEX pages.
- Use of PL/SQL and HTML code in APEX pages to add custom functionalities.
- Call a popup window to display additional information.

Chapter 8
Graphical Reports

Chapter 8 – Graphical Reports

8.1 About Oracle APEX Reports

Presenting data in Oracle APEX, either graphically or in text format, is as easy as creating the input forms. While creating the Order module in the previous chapter, you have had some glimpses of these report types and had some hands-on exposure while working on the interactive reports. Again, the wizards make it so easy to create flexible and powerful reports in Oracle Application Express. In this chapter you will take a step forward and will create the following reports to graphically present the data:

Report	Purpose	Page No.
Customer Orders	Show total orders placed by each customer	17
Sales By Category and Product	Display sales for category and products	16
Sales by Category / Month	Total monthly sales for each category	5
Order Calendar	Show orders in a calendar view	10
Customer Map	Show orders in different states with the help of a map	15
Product Order Tree	Display orders data in a tree view	19

Following are the options you'll avail to produce the above reports.

- **Hints** – Specify whether to display hint text on your chart. Hint text displays when a user's mouse hovers over the chart's data.
- **Values** – Specify whether to display values on your chart. Values are derived from your chart query and display next to your chart data.
- **Labels** – Specify whether to display labels on your chart. Labels are derived from your chart query and display along a chart axis.
- **Show Scrollbars** – Specify whether to display a scrollbar on your chart. Choose X-Axis to display the X-Axis scrollbar on the chart. Choose Y-Axis to display the Y-Axis scrollbar on the chart. Choose Both to display a scrollbar for both axes on the chart.
- **Show Grid** – Specify whether to display a value grid on your chart. Choose X-Axis to display the X-Axis grid on the chart. Choose Y-Axis to display the Y-Axis grid on the chart. Choose Both to display the grid for both axes on the chart.
- **Show Legend** – Specify whether to display a legend for your chart. Choose Left, Right, Top, Bottom or Float to specify where to display the legend.
- **Color Scheme** – Select a pre-built color scheme for your chart. Charts with a single series use one color for each datapoint, while charts with multiple series use one color for each series. The Look 7 scheme will use the AnyChart default palette of colors, applying a different color to each datapoint in a single series. If you wish to define your own color schemes, you can select Custom option and define your own set of colors in Custom Colors.

8.2 Create a Global Page

Prior to creating reports, you will create the reports menu. This menu will be displayed to the left on all report pages. In order to achieve this task, you need to create a Global Page. Global Page components are displayed on all pages if their region's display point is contained within the selected page template. Conditional Display attributes can be used to suppress display. This is a very simple and effective way of sharing APEX objects throughout the application. In this exercise you will create a Global Page for your application to display the Reports List created in chapter 3 section 3.3.1. Since Global Page components are shared across the application, you are going to put a condition to display the reports list only on pages related to the Reports tab.

1. Click the **Create Page** button.
2. Click on **Global Page** icon.
3. Enter **100** in Page Number and click **Finish**. Global Page definitions should appear.
4. Click **Create** ➕ in Regions section.
5. Select the **List** option.
6. Enter **Reports** in Title, set Template to **Standard Region**, Display Point to **Page Template Body (3)** and click **Next**.
7. Set List to **Reports List** and List Template to **Vertical Sidebar List**. The Reports List was created in chapter 3 section 3.3.1. It carries six links that lead to different graphical reports in our desktop application.
8. Set Condition Type to **Current Page Is Contained Within Expression 1 (comma delimited list of pages)** and enter **5,10,15,16,17,19** in Expression 1 and click the **Create Region** button. The Expression 1 attributes specifies the six report pages. When you call these reports (under the Reports tab), the condition evaluates to true, and displays the Reports List on the page.

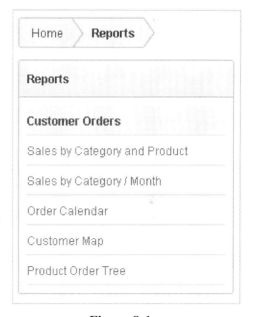

Figure 8-1

9. Modify the region and set Grid Layout attributes as follows:

   Start New Row: **Yes**

   Column: **1**

   Column Span: **Automatic**

Chapter 8 – Graphical Reports

8.3 Customer Orders Report - Page 17

This graphical report is based on a horizontal bar chart to display the amount of orders placed by each customer. Each bar in the chart has multiple slices that represent amount of different orders. When you move your mouse over these slices, a tooltip displays the corresponding amount. The chart will be created with drill-down functionality. That is, when you click a slice, you'll be take to Page 7 where you will see profile of the selected customer with all his/her orders appearing underneath.

1. Create a new page.
2. Click **Blank Page** icon.
3. Enter **17** in Page Number, click **Next**.
4. Fill in the next page as shown in the following figure and click **Next**.

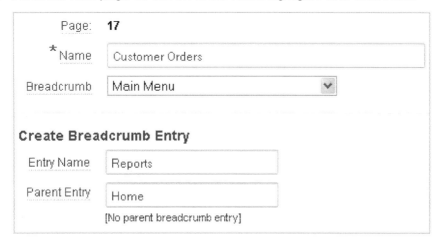

Figure 8-2

5. Select **Use an existing tab set and reuse an existing tab within that tab set**, select **TS1** for Tab Set, **T_REPORTS** for Use Tab, and click **Next**. You'll use the reports tab (T_REPORTS) in this chapter to associate all reports with this tab.
6. Click **Finish**.
7. Click **Edit Page** icon.
8. Click the link **One Level Tabs – Left Sidebar** and set the template to **One Level Tabs – No Sidebar**. The default setting is changed to adjust the chart on this page along with the Reports List. If you keep the default template, some room will be created to the left side and the chart will go off the screen.

8.3.1 Create Region - Customer Orders

Create a region to hold the chart.

1. Click the **Create** button in the Regions section.
2. Click **Chart**.
3. Select **Flash Chart** for Chart Rendering and click on **Horizontal Bar** option. See chapter 2 section 2.20 for details on APEX charts.

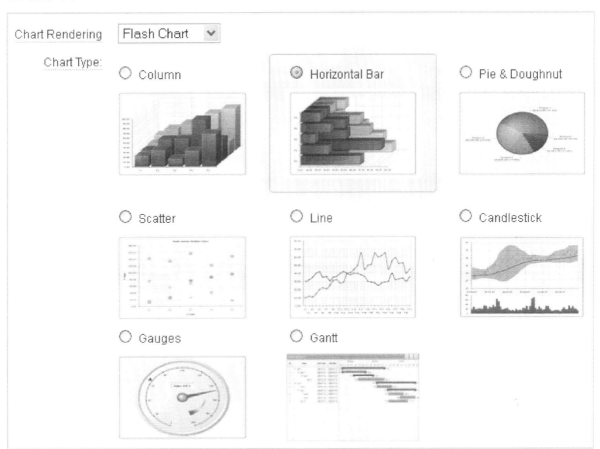

Figure 8-3

4. Click on **3D Stacked Bar Chart**.

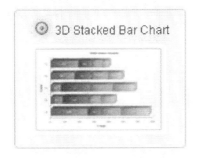

5. Enter **Customer Orders** in Title, select **No Template** for Region Template, select **Page Template Body** (3) for Display Point, and click **Next**.

Chapter 8 – Graphical Reports

6. In Display Attributes settings, input titles for X and Y axes, select options as shown in the figure below, and click **Next**.

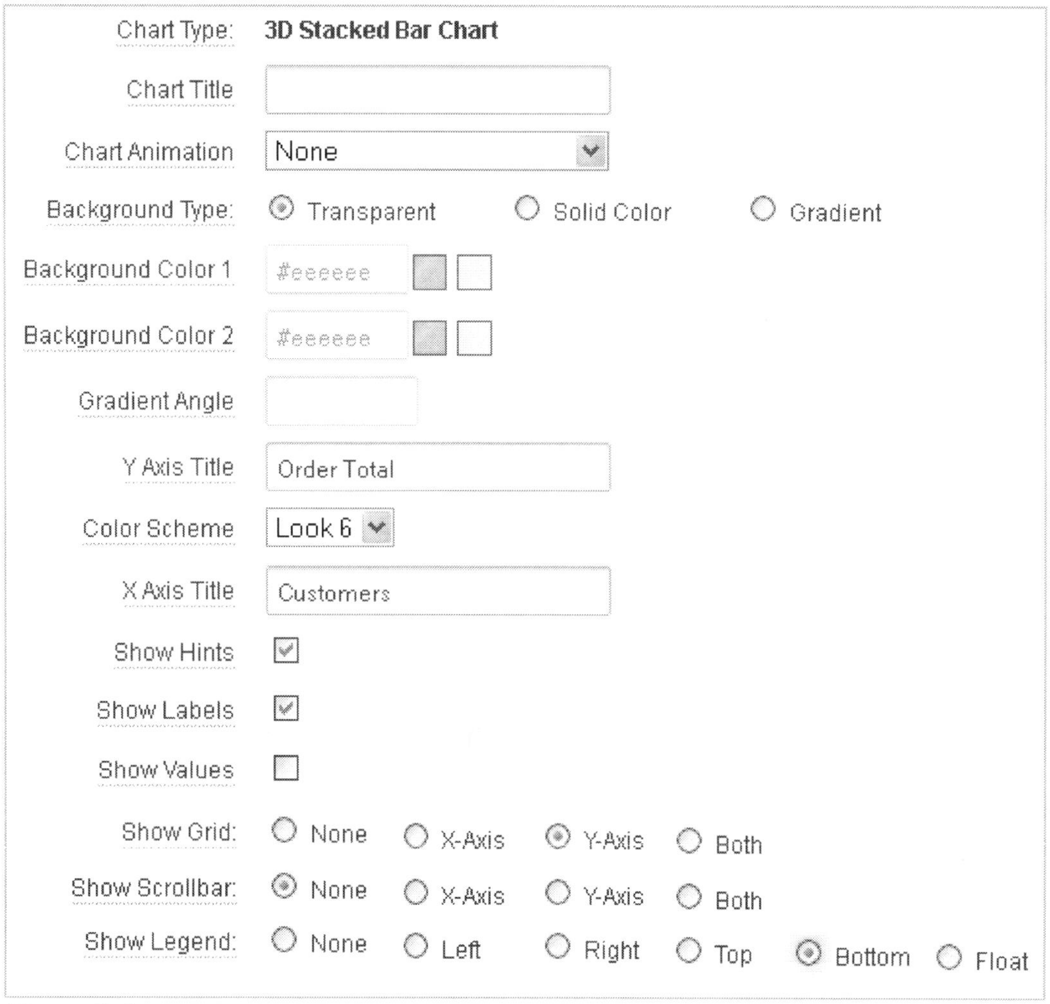

Figure 8-4

7. In Enter SQL Query, put the following statement. The first column is created as a link. As mentioned earlier, when you click a chart slice, you're drilled down to Page 7 to browser further details. The final portion of the URL – P7_BRANCH:'||c.customer_id||',17:' – sets P7_BRANCH (a hidden item on Page 7) with two values: customer id and current page number (17). These parameters are passed to show details of the selected customer and to remember the application flow. When you click any button (for example Cancel) on Page 7, you're returned to Page 17.

```
select apex_util.prepare_url('
        f?p=&APP_ID.:7:'||:app_session||':::7:P7_CUSTOMER_ID,P7_BRANCH:'||
        c.customer_id||',17:') link,
        c.cust_last_name||', '||c.cust_first_name Customer_Name,
        sum (decode(p.category,'Accessories',oi.quantity * oi.unit_price,0)) "Accessories",
        sum (decode(p.category,'Mens',oi.quantity * oi.unit_price,0)) "Mens",
        sum (decode(p.category,'Womens',oi.quantity * oi.unit_price,0)) "Womens"
from demo_customers c, demo_orders o, demo_order_items oi, demo_product_info p
where c.customer_id = o.customer_id and o.order_id = oi.order_id and oi.product_id = p.product_id
group by c.customer_id, c.cust_last_name, c.cust_first_name
order by c.cust_last_name
```

8. Click **Create Region**.
9. Click **Customer Orders** link in Regions to modify couple of attributes.
10. Set Grid Layout like this:

    Start New Row: **No**

    Column: **4**

    Column Span: **Automatic**

11. Click the **Chart Attributes** tab.
12. Scroll down to Legend Settings, enter **Categories** in Legend Title and select **Horizontal** for Legend Element Layout.
13. Click **Apply Changes**.
14. Click **Run** to test your work.

Move your cursor over the chart bars and different portions within a particular bar. You will see a tooltip showing order amount of the corresponding customer. Move your mouse over the three legends at the bottom to see the highlighted effect in the main chart. Observe the Reports menu to the left. This is the Reports List Shared Component created in chapter 3 section 3.3.1, incorporated in the Global Page in section 8.2, and appears only on the defined six report pages, including the current one.

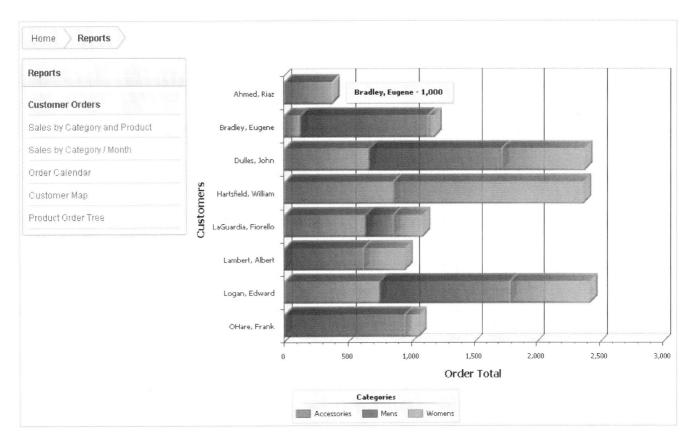

Figure 8-5

Chapter 8 – Graphical Reports

8.4 Sales by Category and Product Report - Page 16

In this report, you'll present Category and Product sales data in two different regions with different charting options.

1. Create a **Blank Page** numbered 16.
2. Fill in the attributes as shown in Figure 8-6 and click **Next**.

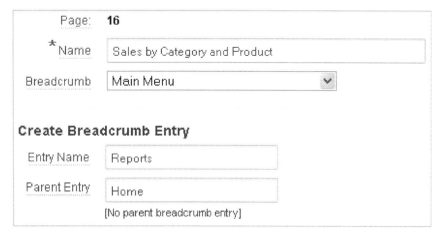

Figure 8-6

3. Select **Use an existing tab set and reuse an existing tab within that tab set**, select **TS1** for Tab Set, **T_REPORTS** for Use Tab, and click **Next**.
4. Click **Finish**.
5. Click **Edit Page** icon.
6. Click the link **One Level Tabs – Left Sidebar** and set the template to **One Level Tabs – No Sidebar** to change the page template.

8.4.1 Create Region – Sales by Category

Create the first region to present category sales in a pie chart.

1. Create a region.
2. Click **Chart**.
3. Select **Flash Chart** and click on **Pie and Doughnut** option.
4. Click on **3D Pie**.
5. Enter **Sales by Category** in Title, select **Standard Region** for Region Template, select **Page Template Body (3)** for Display Point, and click **Next**.

6. In Display Attributes settings, set the attributes as shown below and click **Next**.

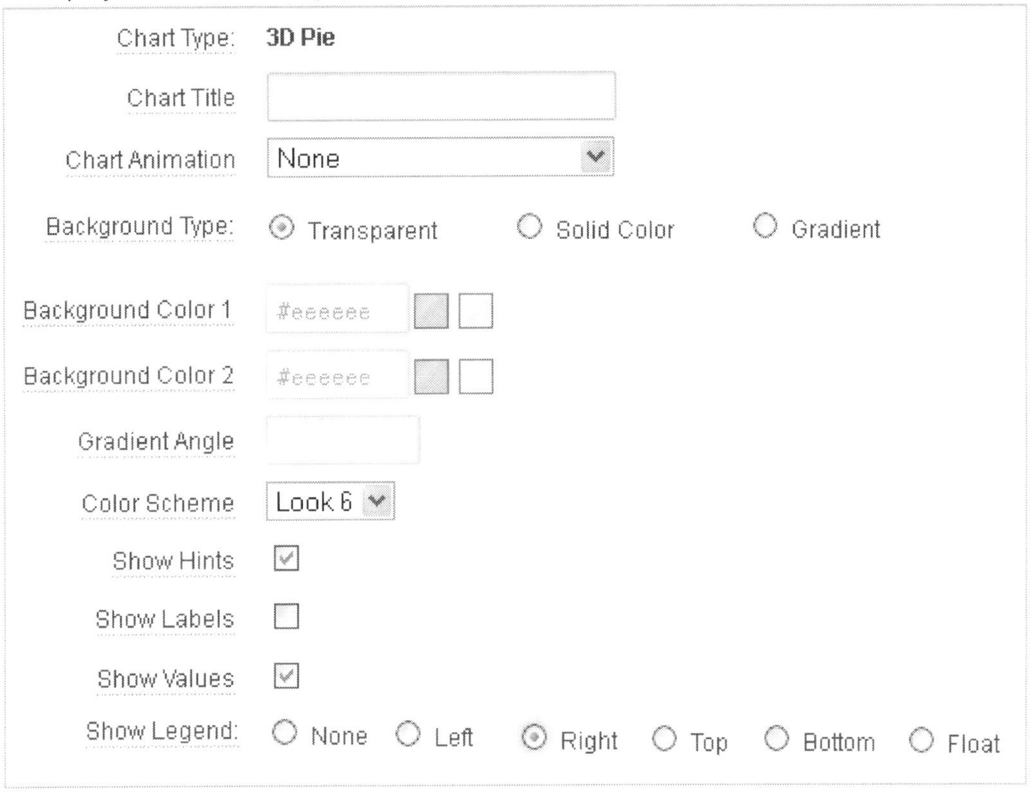

Figure 8-7

7. In Enter SQL Query, write the following statement:

    select null, p.category label, sum(o.order_total)
    from demo_orders o, demo_order_items oi, demo_product_info p
    where o.order_id = oi.order_id
    and oi.product_id = p.product_id
    group by category order by 3 desc

8. Click **Create Region**.

9. Modify the region and set the following values for the **Grid Layout**:

    Start New Row: **No**

    Column: **4**

    Column Span: **6**

10. Click the **Chart Attributes** tab.

11. Set Chart Width to **400** and Chart Height to **200**.

12. Scroll down to Legend Settings, enter **Categories** in Legend.

13. Click **Apply Changes**.

> **NOTE:** In the SQL SELECT statement the link column is replaced with a null to follow the APEX chart syntax rule. The syntax is:
> *SELECT link, label, value FROM ...*

Chapter 8 – Graphical Reports

8.4.2 Create Region – Sales by Product

This is the second region on the page to display sales by product.

1. Create region.
2. Click **Chart**.
3. Select **Flash Chart** and click on **Horizontal Bar**.
4. Click on **3D Bar Chart**.
5. Enter **Sales by Product** in Title, select **Standard Region** for Region Template, select **Page Template Body (3)** for Display Point, and click **Next**.
6. Set values in Display Attributes as shown below:

Figure 8-8

7. In Enter SQL Query, add the following statement:

    select apex_util.prepare_url(
    'f?p=&APP_ID.:6:'||:app_session||':::6:P6_PRODUCT_ID,P6_BRANCH:'||p.product_id||',16:') link,
    p.product_name||' [$'||p.list_price||']' product,
    SUM(oi.quantity * oi.unit_price) sales
    from demo_order_items oi, demo_product_info p
    where oi.product_id = p.product_id
    group by p.product_id, p.product_name, p.list_price
    order by p.product_name

8. Click **Create Region**.
9. Modify the region and set the following values for the Grid Layout:
    Start New Row: **No**
    Column: **4**
    Column Span: **6**
10. Click the **Chart Attributes** tab.
11. Set Chart Width to **400** and Chart Height to **300**.
12. Click **Apply Changes**.
13. Click **Run**.

The chart should look like Figure 8-9. The page has two regions displaying graphical data for category and product sales. Move the mouse cursor over each bar and see respective sales figures. Click on the bar representing Bag's data, the system will drill you down to the products page to show you product's details.

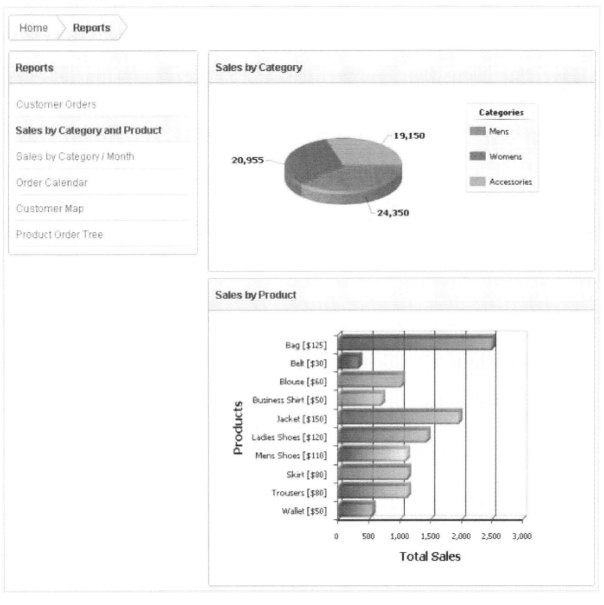

Figure 8-9

Chapter 8 – Graphical Reports

8.5 Sales by Category / Month Report - Page 5

This chart presents category sales in each month.

1. Create a **Blank Page** numbered 5.
2. Complete the next page as shown in Figure 8-10 and click **Next**.

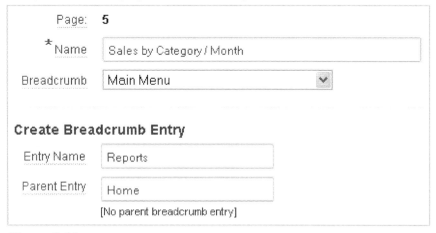

Figure 8-10

3. Select **Use an existing tab set and reuse an existing tab within that tab set**, select **TS1** for Tab Set, **T_REPORTS** for Use Tab, and click **Next**.
4. Click **Finish**.
5. Click **Edit Page** icon.
6. Change the page template to **One Level Tabs – No Sidebar**.

8.5.1 Create Region – Sales by Category/ Month

1. Create a region for the chart.
2. Click on **Chart**.
3. Select **Flash Chart** and pick the first option **Column**.
4. Click on **3D Column**.
5. Enter **Sales by Category / Month** in Title, select **No Template** for Region Template, select **Page Template Body (3)** for Display Point, and click **Next**.
6. Set values in Display Attributes as follows:

Chart Type:	**3D Column**
Chart Title	Sales by Category/Month
Y Axis Title	Total Sales
Color Scheme	Look 6
Show Hints	☑
Show Labels	☑
Show Values	☐
Show Grid:	○ None ○ X-Axis ● Y-Axis ○ Both
Show Scrollbar:	● None ○ X-Axis ○ Y-Axis ○ Both
Show Legend:	○ None ○ Left ● Right ○ Top ○ Bottom ○ Float

Figure 8-11

7. In Enter SQL Query write the following statement:

   select null,
      to_char(o.order_timestamp, 'MON RRRR') label,
      sum (decode(p.category,'Accessories',oi.quantity * oi.unit_price,0)) "Accessories",
      sum (decode(p.category,'Mens',oi.quantity * oi.unit_price,0)) "Mens",
      sum (decode(p.category,'Womens',oi.quantity * oi.unit_price,0)) "Womens"
   from demo_product_info p, demo_order_items oi, demo_orders o
   where oi.product_id = p.product_id and o.order_id = oi.order_id
   group by to_char(o.order_timestamp, 'MON RRRR'), to_char(o.order_timestamp, 'RRRR MM')
   order by to_char(o.order_timestamp, 'RRRR MM')

8. Click **Create Region**.

9. Modify the region and set the following values for the Grid Layout:

   Start New Row: **No**
   Column: **4**
   Column Span: **6**

10. Modify the region and click the **Chart Attributes** tab.

11. Scroll down to Legend Settings section and enter **Categories** in Legend Title.

12. Click **Apply Changes**.

13. Click **Run**.

The output of this graphical report is illustrated below. The chart displays comparative sales figures for each category during a month.

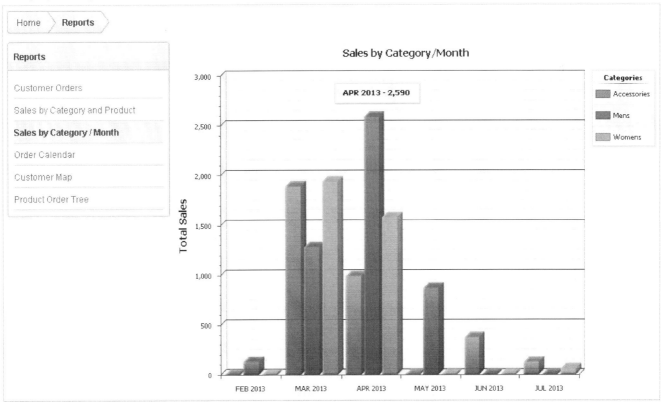

Figure 8-12

8.6 Order Calendar Report - Page 10

In this report, orders will be displayed in a calendar. Application Builder includes a built-in wizard for generating a calendar with monthly, weekly, daily, and list views. Once you specify the table on which the calendar is based, you can create drill-down links to information stored in specific columns and enable drag and drop capability to move a calendar entry to another date. If you choose to enable drag and drop capability in an Easy Calendar, the calendar generation process automatically creates a On Demand process to implement this functionality for you. However, when you create a SQL Calendar on a new page, the Enable Drag and Drop option does not appear. To enable this functionality, create a SQL Calendar page and then edit the page to enable drag and drop.

You can create two types of calendars in APEX:

Easy Calendar – It creates a calendar based on schema, table, and columns you specify. The wizard prompts you to select a date column and display column.

SQL Calendar – This option creates a calendar based on a SQL query you provide. When creating a SQL Calendar, you must select the date and display columns. Also since you are using a SQL source, you must explicitly specify the primary key.

Calendars include the following buttons:

- Monthly – Displays a monthly view of all orders.
- Weekly – Displays orders by week.
- Daily – Displays orders by day.
- List – Displays a list of all orders.
- Previous – Navigates to the previous view.
- Today – Displays the current day.
- Next – Navigates to the next view.

Execute the following steps to create a SQL Calendar.

1. Create a new page.
2. Click **Calendar** icon.
3. Click on **SQL Calendar**.
4. Fill in the next entries as shown in Figure 8-13 and click **Next**.

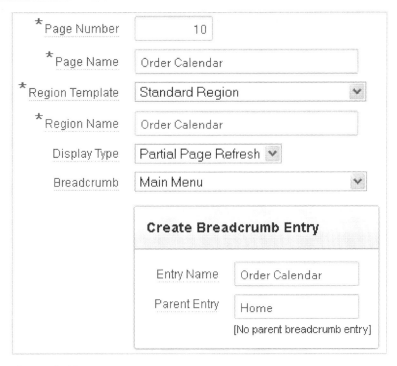

Figure 8-13

5. Select **Use an existing tab set and reuse an existing tab within that tab set**, select **TS1** for Tab Set, **T_REPORTS** for Use Tab, and click **Next**.

6. In Enter SQL Query, type the following statement:

    select order_id, (select cust_first_name||' '||cust_last_name from demo_customers c
          where c.customer_id = o.customer_id) ||'
    ['||to_char(order_total,'FML999G999G999G999G990D00')||']' customer,
        order_timestamp
    from demo_orders o

7. Set the attributes in the next screen as follows. The Date Column attribute specifies which column is used as the date to place an entry on the calendar while the Display Column specifies the column to be displayed on the calendar.

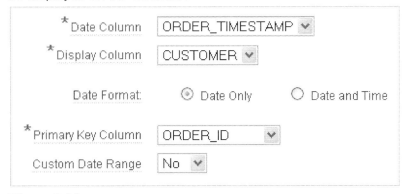

Figure 8-14

Chapter 8 – Graphical Reports

8. Fill in the Link Details page as follows. The link will drill-down to the Order Details (Page 29) to show details of the selected order.

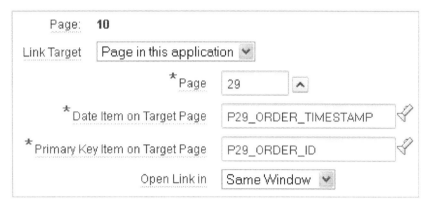

Figure 8-15

9. Click **Create** to finish the calendar generation process.
10. Click **Edit Page** to modify some attributes.
11. Click **Order Calendar** link in the Regions section and set the Grid Layout as shown below:

    Start New Row: **No**
    Column: **4**
    Column Span: **9**

Apply changes and run the page which should look like the following figure. Use the provided buttons to switch back and forth, if you can't see orders in the calendar. Click Eugene Bradley's name link in the calendar report to drill-down and browse his order details. Click the browser's back button. Try and test Weekly, Daily, Previous, Today, Next, and List buttons to see respective functionalities.

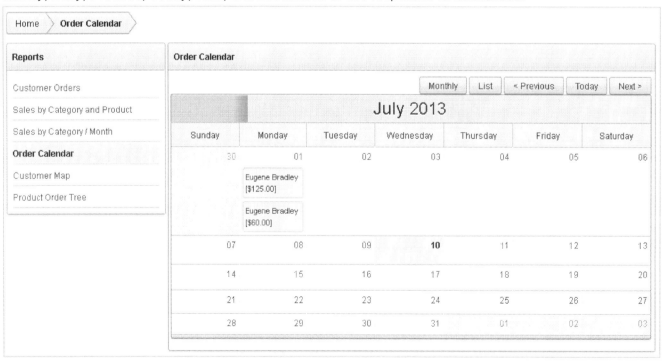

Figure 8-16

8.7 Customer Map Report - Page 15

In this exercise you'll create a map report which shows number of customers in any particular state. Clicking any state link will take you to the customers' main page (Page 2) to display records of that state's customers.

You define a map in Application Builder using a wizard. For most chart wizards, you select a map type, map source, and provide a SQL query using the following syntax:

SELECT link, label, value
FROM ...

Where:
- link is an URL.
- label is the text that identifies the point on the map with which you want to associate data. The Region ID or Region Name of the map will be used as the label.
- value is the numeric column that defines the data to be associated with a point on the map.

Map support in Oracle Application Express is based on the AnyChart AnyMap Interactive Maps Component. AnyMap is a flexible Macromedia Flash-based solution that enables developers to visualize geographical related data. Flash maps are rendered by a browser and require Flash Player 9 or later. AnyChart stores map data in files with a *.amap extension, and supports 300 map files for the United States of America, Europe, Asia, Europe, Africa, Oceania, North America, and South America. To render a desired map, you select the map source in the wizard (for example, Germany) and the map XML automatically references the desired map source .amap file, germany.amap.

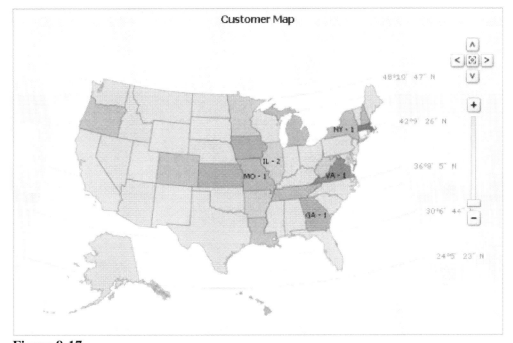

Figure 8-17

Chapter 8 – Graphical Reports

Follow the instruction below to create a map report.

1. Create a new page.
2. Select the **Map** option.
3. For Map Type, select **United States of America**.

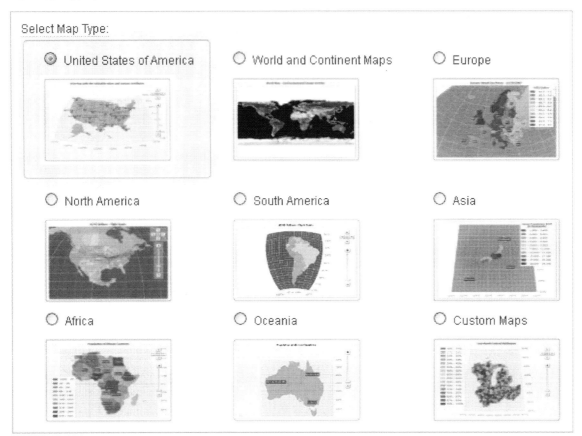

Figure 8-18

4. Expand the Country Maps folder and click on the **States** node to proceed.

Figure 8-19

5. Fill in the next screen as shown in Figure 8-20 and click **Next**.

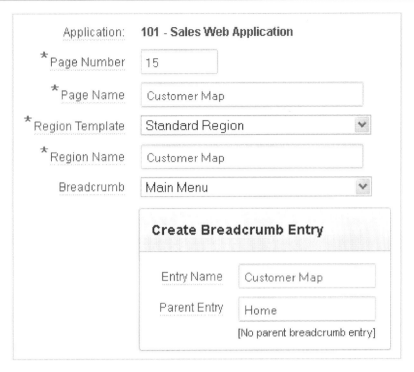

Figure 8-20

6. Select **Use an existing tab set and reuse an existing tab within that tab set**, select **TS1** for Tab Set, **T_REPORTS** for Use Tab, and click **Next**.

7. Enter **Customer Map** in Map Title and click **Next**.

8. In Enter SQL Query, enter the following statement and click **Next**:

   Select
   apex_util.prepare_url('f?p='||:APP_ID||':2:'||:app_session||':::2,RIR:IR_CUST_STATE:'|| cust_state) click_link, cust_state region_id, count(*) count_of_customers
   from demo_customers
   group by cust_state

9. Click **Create**.

10. Click **Edit Page**.

11. Click the **Customer Map** link in the Regions section and set the Grid Layout as show below and apply changes:
    Start New Row: **No**
    Column: **4**
    Column Span: **Automatic**

12. Click the **Map** link in the Regions section. Scroll down to Display Settings section and set Map Region Column to **REGION_ID** and apply changes. This attribute sets the map region column for the selected map. By default, Map Region Column is set to REGION_NAME. This is the AnyChart Map Reference column holding the data that corresponds with the information returned via the LABEL parameter of the map series query. Selecting the REGION_ID column will highlight corresponding states with number of customers, as illustrated in Figure 8-17.

13. Click **Run**. Click the Illinois state marked as IL-2, the page will show a list carrying two customers in the state.

Chapter 8 – Graphical Reports

8.8 Product Order Tree - Page 19

Application Builder includes a built-in wizard for generating a tree. Trees use jsTree, a JavaScript-based, cross browser tree component. You can create a Tree from a query that specifies a hierarchical relationship by identifying an ID and parent ID column in a table or view. The tree query utilizes a **START WITH .. CONNECT BY** clause to generate the hierarchical query.

In this exercise you'll be guided to create a tree view of orders. The root node will show the three product categories, you've been dealing with throughout this book. Level 1 node will be populated with individual categories and each category will have corresponding products at Level 2. The final node (Level 3), will hold names of all customers who placed some orders for the selected product, along with quantity.

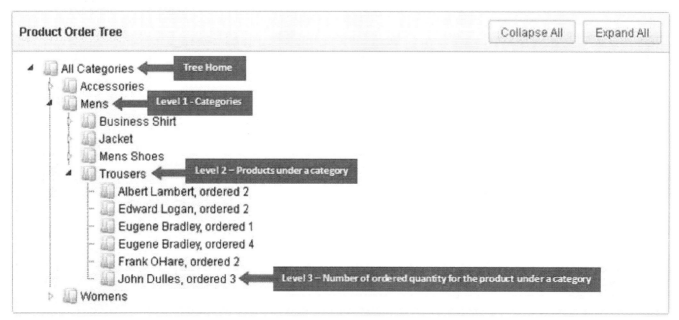

Figure 8-21

Here are the steps to create the tree view.

1. Create a new page.
2. Select the **Tree** option.
3. Complete the next screen as shown in Figure 8-22 and click **Next**.

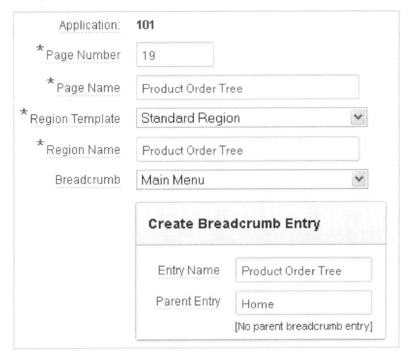

Figure 8-22

4. Select **Use an existing tab set and reuse an existing tab within that tab set**, select **TS1**, select **T_REPORTS**, click **Next**.
5. In Tree Template select the **Default** option.
6. Accept **ASA** as the Table/View Owner and select **DEMO_PRODUCT_INFO** for Table and click **Next**.

7. Click **Next** to accept the default entries in the Query page as shown below. A tree is based on a query and returns data that can be represented in a hierarchy. A *start with .. connect by* clause will be used to generate the hierarchical query for your tree. Use this page to identify the column you want to use as the ID, the Parent ID, and text that should appear on the nodes. The **Start With** column will be used to specify the root of the hierarchical query, and its value can be based on an existing item, static value or SQL query returning a single value.

Figure 8-23

8. Click **Next** again to skip the Where Clause.
9. In the final form, put checks on **Collapse All** and **Expand All** to include these buttons. Set Tooltip to **Static Assignment (value equals Tooltip Source attribute)** and enter **View** in Tooltip Source, click **Next**.
10. Click **Create** to finish the wizard.
11. Click **Edit Page**.
12. Click the **Product Order Tree** link under Regions and set the Grid Layout as shown below and apply changes:

    Start New Row: **No**

    Column: **4**

    Column Span: **Automatic**

13. Click the **Tree** link under Regions.
14. Replace the existing statement in **Tree Query** with the one shown on the next page.
15. Apply changes and **Run** the page.

```sql
with data as (
select 'R' as link_type, null as parent, 'All Categories' as id, 'All Categories' as name, null as sub_id
from demo_product_info
union
select distinct('C') as link_type, 'All Categories' as parent, category as id, category as name, null as
sub_id  from demo_product_info
union
select 'P' as link_type, category parent, to_char(product_id) id, product_name as name, product_id
as sub_id from demo_product_info
union
select 'O' as link_type, to_char(product_id) as parent, null as id, (select c.cust_first_name || ' ' ||
c.cust_last_name from demo_customers c,  demo_orders o where c.customer_id = o.customer_id
and o.order_id = oi.order_id ) || ',  ordered '|| to_char(oi.quantity) as name, order_id as sub_id
from demo_order_items oi
)

select case
        when connect_by_isleaf = 1 then 0
        when level = 1 then 1
        else -1
        end as status, level, name as title, null as icon, id as value, 'View' as tooltip,
    case
      when link_type = 'R'
        then apex_util.prepare_url('f?p='||:APP_ID||':3:'||:APP_SESSION||'::NO:RIR')
      when link_type = 'C'
        then apex_util.prepare_url('f?p='||:APP_ID||':3:'||:APP_SESSION||'::NO:CIR
                        :IR_CATEGORY:' || name)
      when link_type = 'P'
        then apex_util.prepare_url('f?p='||:APP_ID||':6:'||:APP_SESSION||'::NO::
                        P6_PRODUCT_ID, P6_BRANCH:'||sub_id||',19')
      when link_type = 'O'
        then apex_util.prepare_url('f?p='||:APP_ID||':29:'||:APP_SESSION||'::NO::
                        P29_ORDER_ID:' || sub_id)
        else null
        end as link
from data
start with parent is null
connect by prior id = parent
order siblings by name
```

This above custom query is used to form the tree in the following format:
    SELECT status, level, name, icon, id, tooltip, link
    FROM ...
    WHERE ...
    START WITH...
    CONNECT BY PRIOR id = pid
    ORDER SIBLINGS BY ...

Chapter 8 – Graphical Reports

Line #	Tree Query Code
1	WITH data AS (
2	select 'R' as link_type, null as parent, 'All Categories' as id, 'All Categories' as name, null as sub_id from demo_product_info
3	UNION
4	select distinct('C') as link_type, 'All Categories' as parent, category as id, category as name, null as sub_id from demo_product_info
5	UNION
6	select 'P' as link_type, category parent, to_char(product_id) id, product_name as name, product_id as sub_id from demo_product_info
7	UNION
8	select 'O' as link_type, to_char(product_id) as parent, null as id, (select c.cust_first_name || ' ' || c.cust_last_name from demo_customers c, demo_orders o where c.customer_id = o.customer_id and o.order_id = oi.order_id) || ', ordered '|| to_char(oi.quantity) as name, order_id as sub_id from demo_order_items oi
	)

The **WITH query_name AS** clause lets you assign a name to a subquery block. This statement creates the query name "data" with multiple SELECT statements containing UNION set operators. UNION is used to combine the result from multiple SELECT statements into a single result set as illustrated in Figure 8-24.

LINK_TYPE	PARENT	ID	NAME	SUB_ID
R		All Categories	All Categories	
C	All Categories	Accessories	Accessories	
C	All Categories	Mens	Mens	
C	All Categories	Womens	Womens	
P	Accessories	10	Wallet	10
P	Accessories	7	Belt	7
P	Accessories	8	Bag	8
P	Mens	1	Business Shirt	1
P	Mens	2	Trousers	2
P	Mens	3	Jacket	3
P	Mens	9	Mens Shoes	9
P	Womens	4	Blouse	4
P	Womens	5	Skirt	5
P	Womens	6	Ladies Shoes	6
O	1		Albert Lambert, ordered 3	5
O	10		Edward Logan, ordered 3	7
O	2		Albert Lambert, ordered 2	5
O	3		Albert Lambert, ordered 2	5
O	4		Albert Lambert, ordered 3	5
O	5		Albert Lambert, ordered 2	5
O	6		Edward Logan, ordered 3	6
O	7		Edward Logan, ordered 3	7
O	8		Edward Logan, ordered 1	7
O	9		Edward Logan, ordered 3	6

Figure 8-24

Line #	Tree Query Code
1	select case
2	when connect_by_isleaf = 1 then 0
3	when level = 1 then 1
4	else -1
5	end as status, level, name as title, null as icon, id as value, 'View' as tooltip,
6	case
7	when link_type = 'R'
8	then apex_util.prepare_url('f?p='||:APP_ID||':3:'||:APP_SESSION||'::NO:RIR')
9	when link_type = 'C'
10	then apex_util.prepare_url('f?p='||:APP_ID||':3:'||:APP_SESSION||'::NO:CIR :IR_CATEGORY:' || name)
11	when link_type = 'P'
12	then apex_util.prepare_url('f?p='||:APP_ID||':6:'||:APP_SESSION||'::NO:: P6_PRODUCT_ID, P6_BRANCH:'||sub_id||',19')
13	when link_type = 'O'
14	then apex_util.prepare_url('f?p='||:APP_ID||':29:'||:APP_SESSION||'::NO:: P29_ORDER_ID:' || sub_id)
15	else null
16	end as link
17	from data

The CASE statement within the SQL statement is used to evaluate the four link types (R=root,C=categories,P=products, and O=orders). It has the functionality of an IF-THEN-ELSE statement. Lines 8,10,12,14 make the node text a link. The R link type leads you to the main Products page (Page 3). The C link type also leads to Page 3 but, applies a filter on category name. The P link type calls Product Details page (Page 6) to display details of the selected product. The last parameter (19) in the link, defined on line 12, represents the current page to control the application flow. The final O link type displays details of the selected order in the Order Details page (Page 29).

The CONNECT_BY_ISLEAF pseudocolumn, in the first CASE statement, returns 1 if the current row is a leaf of the tree. Otherwise, it returns 0. This information indicates whether a given row can be further expanded to show more of the hierarchy.

If no condition is found to be true, then the CASE statement will return the null value defined in the ELSE clause on line 15.

8.9 Summary

Report is the most significant component of any application. It allows digging information from the data mine for making decisions. This chapter not only demonstrated the power of Oracle Application Express to graphically present the information but also exhibited how to drill-down to a deeper level to obtain detailed information. Here is a short list of reporting features, demonstrated in this chapter.

- Global Page creation and utilization
- Graphical presentation of data
- Use of different types of charts
- Drill-down to browse details
- Usage of calendar, map, and tree views

Chapter 9
Advanced Reporting

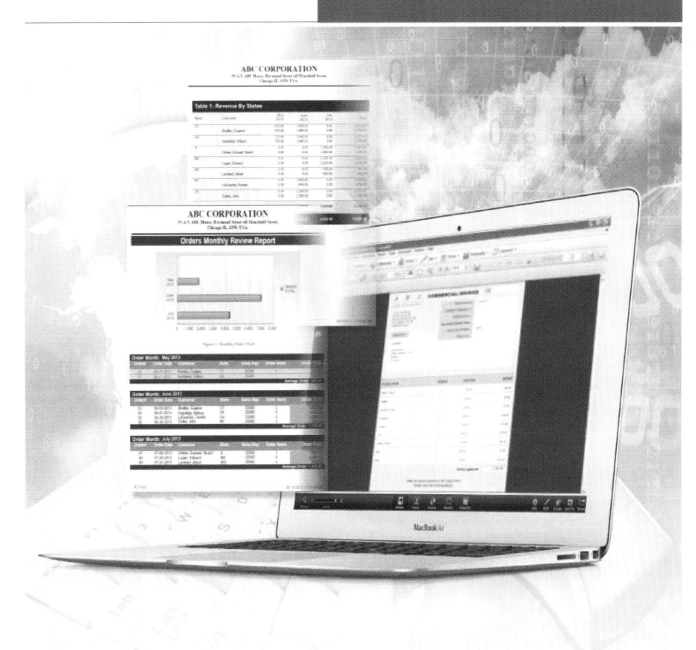

Chapter 9 – Advanced Reporting

9.1 About Advanced Reporting

You have seen the use of interactive reporting feature in APEX to create professional looking on-screen reports. Interactive reports also have the ability to export to PDF, RTF, Microsoft Excel and Comma Separated Values (CSV). Note that for interactive reports, it is not possible to define a custom report layout. If you download the PDF version of these reports to have a hard copy, what you get is a generic report in simple row-column format. For example, if you download the Monthly Review report, created in chapter 7 section 7.3.3; the output is presented without any control breaks and conditional formatting. For serious printing, you have to define an external reporting server to present data in the desired format.

You can use OC4J with Apache FOP, another XSL-FO processing engine, or Oracle BI Publisher as your print server. In this exercise, you will use Oracle BI Publisher to enjoy high level formatting.

Oracle Application Express provides the following two printing options:

Standard: Apache FOP or another XSL-FO processing engine is supported under the standard configuration. Oracle Application Express already includes support for Apache FOP, that allows declarative formatting of report region and queries with basic control over page attributes such as column heading format, orientation, page size, header and footer.

Advanced: This option required Oracle BI Publisher to be configured as your print server. Besides standard configuration, Oracle BI Publisher has Word Template Plug-in to create RTF based report layouts, that provide greater control over every aspect of your report and allows you to add complex control breaks, logos, charts, and pagination control. The following list contains few reports that can be created using the advanced option:

- Tax and Government Forms
- Invoices
- Ledgers
- Financial Statements
- Bill of Lading, using tables and barcode fonts
- Operational Reports with re-grouping, conditional highlighting, summary calculations, and running totals
- Management Reports having Chart with summary functions and table with detail records
- Check Print, using conditional formatting and MICR fonts
- Dunning Letters

To print these professional reports, you have to pay for a valid Oracle BI Publisher license that is worth the price considering the following advantages:

- Multiple Output Formats: In addition to PDF, the other supported output formats include Word, Excel and HTML.
- Included in Export/Import: Being part of the application, RTF based layout are exported and imported along with the application.
- Robust Report Layout: Add complex breaks, pagination control, logos, header-footer, charts, and print data on pre-printed forms.
- Report Scheduling: This unique feature enables you to setup a schedule and deliver the report to the desired destinations including email, fax etc.

The following section will guide you to download and install the limited license version to use the program only for the development purpose.

Oracle BI Publisher required Windows Server Operating System 2000 or later. I completed the exercises in this chapter with the following hardware and software combination.

Server:
- Windows Server 2000 having IP 10.10.1.5
- Downloaded and installed Oracle BI Publisher 10.1.3.4.2 using bipublisher_windows_x86_101342.zip file. See the following section to download and install BI Publisher

Client:
- Windows XP Service Pack 3 having IP 10.1.1.12
- Oracle XE database and Sales Web Application
- Microsoft Word 2007
- Oracle BI Publisher Desktop
- Dot Net Framework 2 and JRE 1.6 or above may be required during BI Publisher Desktop installation.

Steps to Produce Advance Reports

- Install BI Publisher
- Configure APEX to use BI Publisher as a Print Server
- Enabling Network Services in Oracle Database 11g
- Testing the Print Server
- Install BI Publisher Desktop
- Create report query in APEX
- Create report layout in MS Word
- Upload report layout to APEX
- Add button to a page and run the report

Chapter 9 – Advanced Reporting

9.2 Install BI Publisher

Execute instructions in this section on a Windows Server machine.

1. Download BI Publisher from:

    http://www.oracle.com/technetwork/middleware/bi-publisher/downloads/index.html

2. Click the link **BI Publisher 10.1.3.4.2 for Windows (32/64 bit) (1 GB)**.
3. Extract the file **bipublisher_windows_x86_101342.zip**.
4. Start installation by executing **Setup.exe** file from the extracted folder.
5. Click **Next** on the Welcome Screen.
6. In Specify File Location screen **accept the default Source and Destination** and click **Next**.
7. For Installation Type, select **Basic** and click **Next**.
8. Enter and confirm a **strong password** in OC4J Administrator Password screen. Click **Next**.
9. Click the **Install** button to start the installation.
10. After successful installation, the following informative text will be displayed. Write down **Username**, **Password**, and **URL address** to access the BI Publisher interface.

    The installation of Oracle BI Publisher 10.1.3.4.2 was successful.
    These instructions are located in:
    E:\OraHome_1\BI_Publisher_readme.txt
    At the end of this installation BI Publisher will be started.
    You may access it at the following URL:
    http://localhost:9704/xmlpserver
    as
    Username: Administrator
    Password: Administrator
    ...

11. Click the **Exit** button and confirm.
12. In Windows, click **Start | All Programs | Oracle BIPHome > Start BI Publisher**.
13. Open your browser and enter http://localhost:9704/xmlpserver.
14. Enter **Administrator** and **Administrator** in Username and Password as indicated in the above text. Note that the password is case sensitive, so you should use capital A as the initial alphabet in the password.
15. You will be logged in to Oracle BI Publisher as its administrator.

9.3 Configure APEX to use BI Publisher as a Print Server

1. On your client (Windows XP machine), open a browser and enter the following URL to access APEX administrator interface: http://localhost:8080/apex/apex_admin
2. Enter **Admin** and **Gemini_2013** in Username and Password, respectively. These credentials were set in chapter 2 section 2.34 step 2.
3. Click the **Manage Instance** icon.
4. Click the **Instance Settings** link, appearing in the first region to your left.
5. Scroll down to the **Report Printing** section.
6. Select the option **Oracle BI Publisher** for the Print Server.
7. Keep the default **HTTP** protocol in the Print Server Protocol attribute.
8. Enter **name or IP** of your BI Publisher server in the Print Server Host Address. In our example it is 10.10.1.5.
9. Enter **9704** in Print Server Port or another port as indicated in the above installation text.
10. Enter **/xmlpserver/convert** in Print Server Script. This setting defines the script; that is, the print server engine. The default setting is: /xmlpserver/convert
11. Click **Apply Changes**.
12. Click the **Logout** link.

9.4 Enable Network Services in Oracle Database

By default, the ability to interact with network services is disabled in Oracle Database 11g release 1 (11.1). Therefore, if you are running Oracle Application Express with Oracle Database 11g release 1 (11.1), you must use the new DBMS_NETWORK_ACL_ADMIN package to grant connect privileges to any host for the APEX_040200 database user. Failing to grant these privileges results in issues with:

- Sending outbound mail in Oracle Application Express.
- Users can call methods from the APEX_MAIL package, but issues arise when sending outbound email.
- Using Web services in Oracle Application Express.
- PDF/report printing.
- Searching for content in online Help (that is, using the Find link).

9.4.1 Granting Connect Privileges

The following example is a less privileged demonstration of how to access resources on a local PC and a host. This example would enable indexing of Oracle Application Express Online Help and could possibly enable email and PDF printing. Perform the following steps on your Oracle XE database machine, in my scenario it is Windows XP client.

Chapter 9 – Advanced Reporting

1. Create the following two script files APEXprintPDFLocal.SQL and APEXprintPDFHost.SQL in Notepad and save the files on your C drive:

```
-- APEXprintPDFLocal.SQL - Granting Connect Privileges to a Local Host
DECLARE
  ACL_PATH VARCHAR2(4000);
BEGIN
-- Look for the ACL currently assigned to 'localhost' and give APEX_040200 the "connect" privilege -
- if APEX_040200 does not have the privilege yet.
SELECT ACL INTO ACL_PATH FROM DBA_NETWORK_ACLS
WHERE HOST = 'localhost' AND LOWER_PORT IS NULL AND UPPER_PORT IS NULL;
IF DBMS_NETWORK_ACL_ADMIN.CHECK_PRIVILEGE(ACL_PATH, 'APEX_040200','connect') IS NULL
THEN
DBMS_NETWORK_ACL_ADMIN.ADD_PRIVILEGE(ACL_PATH,
'APEX_040200', TRUE, 'connect');
END IF;
EXCEPTION
-- When no ACL has been assigned to 'localhost'.
WHEN NO_DATA_FOUND THEN
DBMS_NETWORK_ACL_ADMIN.CREATE_ACL('local-access-users.xml',
'ACL that lets users to connect to localhost',
'APEX_040200', TRUE, 'connect');
DBMS_NETWORK_ACL_ADMIN.ASSIGN_ACL('local-access-users.xml','localhost');
END;
/
COMMIT;


-- APEXprintPDFHost.SQL  - Granting Connect Privileges to any Host
DECLARE
ACL_PATH VARCHAR2(4000);
BEGIN
-- Look for the ACL currently assigned to '*' and give APEX_040200 the "connect" privilege if
--APEX_040200 does not have the privilege yet.
SELECT ACL INTO ACL_PATH FROM DBA_NETWORK_ACLS
WHERE HOST = '*' AND LOWER_PORT IS NULL AND UPPER_PORT IS NULL;
IF DBMS_NETWORK_ACL_ADMIN.CHECK_PRIVILEGE(ACL_PATH, 'APEX_040200','connect') IS NULL
THEN
DBMS_NETWORK_ACL_ADMIN.ADD_PRIVILEGE(ACL_PATH,
'APEX_040200', TRUE, 'connect');
END IF;
EXCEPTION
-- When no ACL has been assigned to '*'.
WHEN NO_DATA_FOUND THEN
DBMS_NETWORK_ACL_ADMIN.CREATE_ACL('power_users.xml',
'ACL that lets power users to connect to everywhere',
'APEX_040200', TRUE, 'connect');
DBMS_NETWORK_ACL_ADMIN.ASSIGN_ACL('power_users.xml','*');
END;
/
COMMIT;
```

2. Click **Start | All Programs | Oracle Database 11g Express Edition | Run SQL Command Line**.
3. On the SQL prompt enter, **connect sys as sysdba** and enter the **manager** for password.
4. Type **@c:\apexprintpdflocal.sql** and press **Enter** to execute the first script.
5. Type **@c:\apexprintpdfhost.sql** and press **Enter** to execute the second script.
6. A message **PL/SQL procedure successfully completed** should appear for both scripts.
7. Type **Exit** and press **Enter** to quit the SQL prompt.

9.5 Test the Print Server

1. Open a browser on your client machine, type http://localhost:8080/apex and connect to your workspace.
2. Run the **Sales Web Application**.
3. Click the **Customers** tab.
4. Click the button **Edit Page 2** in the Developers Toolbar.
5. Click the **Interactive Report** link under Regions section.
6. Scroll down to the Download section and **put a check on PDF** and **apply changes**.
7. **Run** the page.
8. Click the **Actions** menu and select the **Download** option.
9. Click on the **PDF** option.
10. Click the **Open** button to view the report in Adobe Reader. The report will be displayed. Alternatively, you can save it to your hard disk using the Save File option.

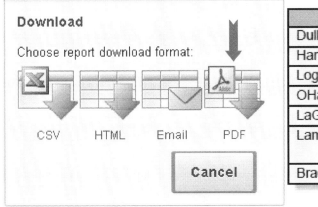

Figure 9-1

Chapter 9 – Advanced Reporting

9.6 Install BI Publisher Desktop

To avoid version conflicts, we will download BI Publisher Desktop from our BI Publisher Sever. Perform the following steps after installing MS Word 2000 or later on your client machine.

1. On Windows XP client type http://10.10.1.5:9704/xmlpserver in a new browser session.

2. Enter **Administrator** and **Administrator** for the username and password and click **Sign In**.

Figure 9-2

3. Click the **MY Folders** link.

4. Click the **Template Builder** download link ![Template Builder] under Developer Tools section.

5. Click the **Save File** button to save **BIPublisherDesktop.exe**.

6. Switch to the download location and launch the exe file.

7. Select your language and accept the default installation path.

8. Once the installation completes, **invoke MS Word.**

9. Click on **BI Publisher** menu. If you are using Word 2007, the BI Publisher plug-in should look like Figure 9-3.

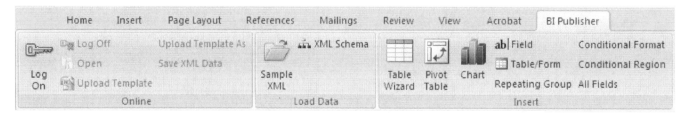

Figure 9-3

9.7 Create Monthly Order Review Report

A report query is a printable document, which can be integrated with an application using buttons, list items, branches or any other navigational components that allow for using URLs as targets. A report query is based on a standard SQL query. It can be downloaded as a PDF document, a Word document (RTF based), an Excel Spreadsheet (HTML based) or as an HTML file. The layout of a report query is customizable using RTF templates. In chapter 7 section 7.3.3, you created an on-screen alternative report named Monthly Review to see details of monthly orders. In this exercise, you will create a PDF version of that report. It is assumed that Oracle BI Publisher is up and running on your host (in our example it is 10.10.1.5). Log in to APEX workspace ASA and open the Sales Web Application.

9.7.1 Create the Report Query

1. Click the **Shared Components** icon.
2. Click **Report Queries** link under the Reports Section.
3. Click **Create**.
4. Type **Monthly_Review** in Report Query Name, set Output Format to **PDF**, View File As to **Attachment**, and click **Next**.
5. Enter the following statement in SQL Query and click Next:

   select
     o.order_id,
     to_char(o.order_timestamp,'Month yyyy') order_month, o.order_timestamp order_date,
     c.cust_last_name || ', ' || c.cust_first_name customer_name, c.cust_state,
     u.user_name sales_rep,
     (select count(*) from demo_order_items oi where oi.order_id = o.order_id) order_items,
     o.order_total
   from demo_orders o, demo_customers c, demo_users u
   where o.customer_id = c.customer_id and o.user_name = u.user_name

6. Select **XML Data** in Data Source for Report Layout to export your report definition as an XML file. This file contains the data (fetched using the above SELECT statement) to populate the report. Click the **Download** button, select **Save File**, and click OK. A file named **Monthly_Review.xml** will be saved to your disk.
7. Click the **Create Report Query** button.
8. Click the **Test Report** button. If the BI Publisher server is down, you will see the error **ORA-29273: HTTP request failed ORA-06512: at "SYS.UTL_HTTP", line 1324 ORA-12570: TNS:packet reader failure**. Start the server and try again. In the popup dialog box, select **Open** with Adobe Acrobat and click **OK**. A generic PDF output similar to Figure 9-4 appears. Click the **Create** button to finish the process.

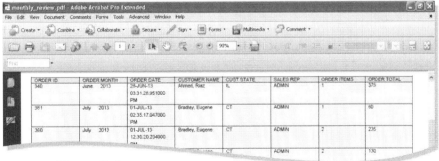

Figure 9-4

9.7.2 Create Report Template in MS Word

1. In **Microsoft Word** click on the BI Publisher menu option.
2. Click on **Sample XML** icon in the Load Data ribbon. Open **Monthly_Review.xml** file that we created in the previous section. Data Loaded Successfully message is displayed.
3. Click on the **Table Wizard** icon. Select **Table** in Report Format and click **Next**.
4. Click **Next** to accept DOCUMENT/ROWSET/ROW for Data Set.
5. Add all the fields to the report by moving them to the right pane using the double arrow button and click **Next**.
6. Select **Order Month** in the first drop down list under Group By and click **Next**.
7. Select **Order Date** in the first Sort By list and select **Order ID** in the first Then By list. Click **Finish**.
8. In the report layout, change Cust State label to **State**.
9. An output similar to Figure 9-5 will be displayed.

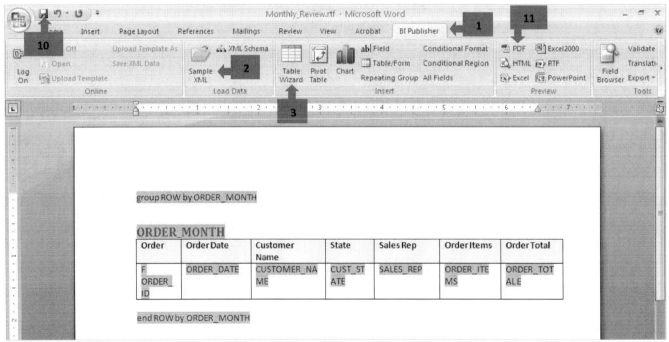

Figure 9-5

10. Press ctrl+s (or click the Save icon) to save the template, enter **Monthly_Review** in the File name, select **Rich Text Format** as the Save as type and click **Save**.
11. In the Preview ribbon, click the **PDF** icon. The output as show in Figure 9-6 will displayed.
12. **Close the PDF** and switch back to MS Word.

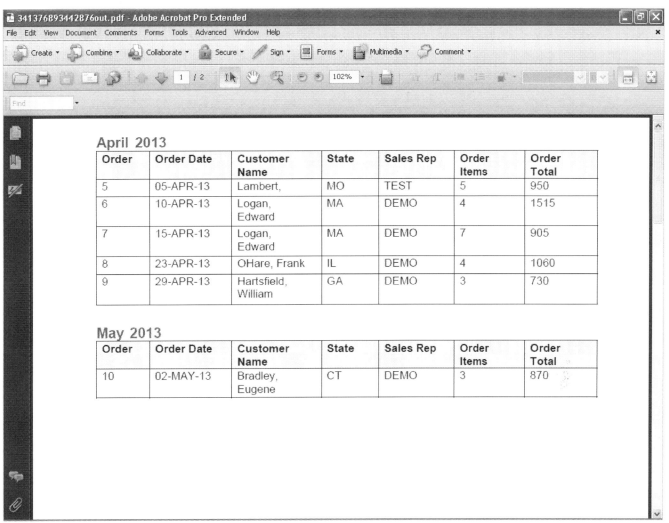

Figure 9-6

9.7.3 Format Report

1. Place the cursor before the **ORDER_MONTH** text and type **Order Month:** to act as a label. Use MS Word standard tools to change font, color and size. Drag the column width to the desired size.

2. Click the **ORDER_TOTAL** field and right-align it. Double click it to call its properties. Select **Number** for Type and **#,##0.00** for Format and click **OK**.

3. Insert a blank line above **group ROW by Order_Month** text to add a title to the report. Type **ABC CORPORATION** and then **Monthly Orders Review Report** on the subsequent line. You can also add logo and page number using the Header and Footer options in MS Word.

Chapter 9 – Advanced Reporting

9.7.4 Conditional Formatting

In these steps we are going to change font and background color of orders for which the amount is less than or equal to 900, as we did in the on-screen report version in chapter 7.

1. Select the **Order Total** field by clicking its name.
2. Click on the **BI Publisher** menu.
3. Select **Conditional Format** from the Insert ribbon.
4. Select field ORDER_TOTAL for Data field, select **Number** in the adjacent list, put a check on **Apply to Entire Table Row**, select **Less than or equal to** in the Data field, enter **900** in the box next to the Data field, click the **Format button**, check the **Background Color**, click the **Select** button to choose different Font and Background colors, and click **OK**.
5. Preview your work and see the application of conditional formatting to all the rows having Order Total less than or equal to 900.

Use the same procedure and change font and background color for orders greater than 2000. Select Greater than for the condition and enter 2000 in the value. This time, do not check the *Apply to Entire Table Row* option to highlight specific cells only. After completion, preview the report to check your work.

9.7.5 Summary Calculation

In this section you will add a summary to reveal average orders for the month.

1. Place your cursor on the blank line before the text **end ROW by ORDER_MONTH**.
2. Click on the **Field** option in the Insert ribbon.
3. In the Field dialog box, select the **Order Total** field, select **average** for Calculation, put a check mark on **On Grouping** and click the **Insert** button. A summary field, *average ORDER_TOTAL* will be added. Close the dialog box.
4. Add a label **Monthly Average:** before the field. Double click the calculated field and set Type property to **Number** and Format to **#,##0.00**. Align the whole expression to the right under the Order Total field.

9.7.6 Add a Summary Chart

1. Insert a blank row above **group ROW by ORDER_MONTH**.
2. Select **Chart** from the Insert ribbon.
3. From the Data tree, drag field **ORDER_TOTAL** to the Values box, set Aggregation to **Sum**, drag **ORDER_MONTH** to Labels, put a check on **Group Data**, select **Bar Graph – Horizontal** for Type, **April** in Style and click **OK**. The completed screen should look like Figure 9-7.
4. Right click the chart in MS Word and select Insert Caption. Type **Monthly Orders Chart** in Caption.

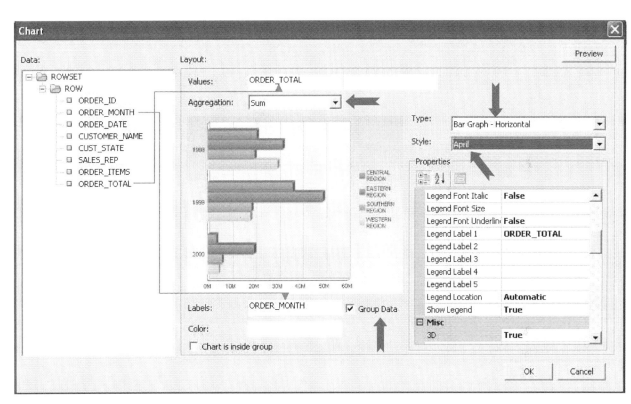

Figure 9-7

Chapter 9 – Advanced Reporting

9.7.7 Add a Pivot Table

1. In MS Word click on the line just after the text **end ROW by ORDER_MONTH**.
2. Select **Pivot Table** from the Insert ribbon.
3. Drag fields **CUST_STATE, CUSTOMER_NAME, ORDER_MONTH,** and **ORDER_TOTAL** to the layout section as shown in Figure 9-8. Click the **Preview** button to see the output within the dialog box. Click the **OK** button. Format the table using MS Word toolbar so that it matches the output shown in Figure 9-9. Browse the report in PDF. Close the preview. **Save the template** and close MS Word.

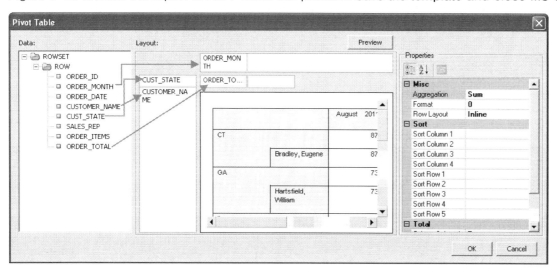

Figure 9-8

Table 1: Revenue By States

State	Customer	May 2013	June 2013	July 2013	Total
CT		870.00	1,890.00	0.00	2,760.00
	Bradley, Eugene	870.00	1,890.00	0.00	2,760.00
GA		730.00	1,640.00	0.00	2,370.00
	Hartsfield, William	730.00	1,640.00	0.00	2,370.00
IL		0.00	0.00	1,060.00	1,060.00
	OHare, Edward "Butch"	0.00	0.00	1,060.00	1,060.00
MA		0.00	0.00	2,420.00	2,420.00
	Logan, Edward	0.00	0.00	2,420.00	2,420.00
MO		0.00	0.00	950.00	950.00
	Lambert, Albert	0.00	0.00	950.00	950.00
NY		0.00	1,090.00	0.00	1,090.00
	LaGuardia, Fiorello	0.00	1,090.00	0.00	1,090.00
VA		0.00	2,380.00	0.00	2,380.00
	Dulles, John	0.00	2,380.00	0.00	2,380.00
	TOTAL	1,600.00	7,000.00	4,430.00	13,030.00

Figure 9-9

9.8 Upload Report Template to APEX

Report Layouts are used in conjunction with a report region or report query to render data in a printer-friendly format, such as PDF, Word or Excel. You can print a report region by defining a report query as a Shared Component. A report query identifies the data to be extracted. Unlike SQL statements contained in regions, report queries contain SQL statements that are validated when you save the query. You can associate a report query with a report layout and download it as a formatted document. If no report layout is selected, a generic layout is used. The generic layout is intended to be used to test and verify a report query. To make these reports available to end users, you then integrate them with an application. For example, you can associate a report query with a button, list item, branch, or other navigational component that enables you to use URLs as targets. Selecting that item then initiates the printing process.

A report layout has been designed using the Template Builder Word plug-in and will now be uploaded to APEX as an RTF file type.

1. Call the **Shared Components** interface.
2. Click **Report Layouts** under Reports.
3. Click **Create**.
4. Select the option **Named Columns (RTF)** and click **Next**. A named column report layout is a query-specific report layout designed to work with a defined list of columns in the query result set. This type of layout is used for custom-designed layouts when precise control of the positioning of page items and query columns is required. This layout is uploaded as an RTF file.
5. In Layout Name enter **Monthly_Review**, click the **Browse** button and select the MS Word template file **Monthly_Review.rtf**, which was created in the previous section.
6. Click the **Create Layout** button.
7. Click the **Shared Components** breadcrumb to apply the report layout.
8. Click the **Report Queries** link under the Reports section.
9. Click the **Monthly Review** icon.
10. In Report Query Attributes, change Report Layout from Use Generic Report Layout to **Monthly_Review**, the layout we created in steps 2 through 6 above.
11. Click **Apply Changes**.

You have created the Report Layout in APEX by uploading the MS Word Template and linked it to your Report Query. In the next section, you will create a button on the Orders page to run the Monthly Orders Review report.

Chapter 9 – Advanced Reporting

9.9 Run the Report

In this section you will add a Print button and a branch to the Orders page to run the report.

1. Click **Application 101** breadcrumb.
2. Open the **Orders** page (Page 4).
3. Click **Create** under Buttons.
4. Select the **Orders** region to place the button in. Click **Next**.
5. Select the option **Create a button in a region position** and click **Next**.
6. Enter **PRINT** in Button Name and **Orders Report** in Label. Set Button Style to **Template Based Button**, Button Template to **Button**, Button Type to **Normal**, and click **Next**.
7. Select **Right of Interactive Report Search Bar** for Position and click **Next**.
8. Keep the default Submit Page value for Action and Yes for Execute Validations. Click **Create Button**.
9. Create a new **Branch**.
10. Accept the default values for Branch Point (On Submit: After Processing (After Computation, Validation, and Processing) and Branch Type (Branch to Page or URL). Click **Next**.
11. Select **Page in this Application** for Branch Target, enter **0** in Page, enter **PRINT_REPORT=Monthly_Review** in Request and click **Next**. For branches implemented as URL, the Request attribute redirects to Application Express pages, resulting in the request value being passed in the URL. The provided value will be appended to the URL as an argument, passing the name of the report query you would like to see like this:

    http://localhost:8080/apex/f?p=108:0:7983587274407:PRINT_REPORT=Monthly_Review:NO:::

12. Select **PRINT (Monthly Review Report)** for When Button Pressed, to associate the branch with the Print button.
13. Click **Create Branch**.
14. Click **Application 101** breadcrumb and **run** the application.
15. Click the **Orders** Tab. You will see the button Orders Report next to the Enter New Order button. Click the button and open the report with Adobe Acrobat which should look something like Figure 9-10 and Figure 9-11. I formatted the layout using the standard MS Word tools, including header-footer, tables, page number, font etc.

Congratulations! You have successfully created a professional looking report that not only matches the on-screen report of chapter 7 but also adds more value to it by incorporating a pivot table, to display the same data from a different perspective. Add a new order through the application and see the automatic reflection in the report.

ABC CORPORATION

35-A/3, ABC House, Raymond Street off Mansfield Street,
Chicago-IL, 6350, USA.

Orders Monthly Review Report

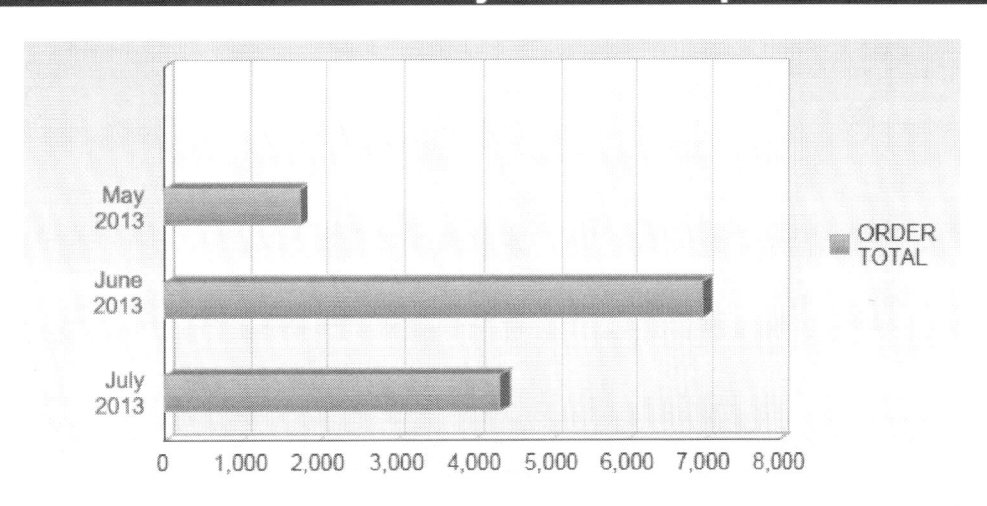

Figure 1: Monthly Order Chart

Order Month: May 2013

Order#	Order Date	Customer	State	Sales Rep	Order Items	Order Total
15	05-15-2013	Bradley, Eugene	CT	DEMO	3	870.00
23	05-21-2013	Hartsfield, William	GA	DEMO	2	730.00
						Average Order: 800.00

Order Month: June 2013

Order#	Order Date	Customer	State	Sales Rep	Order Items	Order Total
33	06-03-2013	Bradley, Eugene	CT	DEMO	3	1,890.00
34	06-07-2013	Hartsfield, William	VA	DEMO	9	1,640.00
35	06-16-2013	LaGuardia, Fiorello	GA	DEMO	4	1,090.00
36	06-30-2013	Dulles, John	NY	DEMO	5	2,380.00
						Average Order: 1,750.00

Order Month: July 2013

Order#	Order Date	Customer	State	Sales Rep	Order Items	Order Total
47	07-05-2013	OHare, Edward "Butch"	IL	DEMO	3	1,060.00
48	07-25-2013	Logan, Edward	MA	DEMO	9	2,240.00
49	07-31-2013	Lambert, Albert	MO	DEMO	4	950.00
						Average Order: 1,416.67

1 | Page   08/19/2013 11:55:45 AM

Figure 9-10

ABC CORPORATION
35-A/3, ABC House, Raymond Street off Mansfield Street, Chicago-IL, 6350, USA.

Table 1: Revenue By States

State	Customer	May 2013	June 2013	July 2013	Total
CT		870.00	1,890.00	0.00	2,760.00
	Bradley, Eugene	870.00	1,890.00	0.00	2,760.00
GA		730.00	1,640.00	0.00	2,370.00
	Hartsfield, William	730.00	1,640.00	0.00	2,370.00
IL		0.00	0.00	1,060.00	1,060.00
	OHare, Edward "Butch"	0.00	0.00	1,060.00	1,060.00
MA		0.00	0.00	2,420.00	2,420.00
	Logan, Edward	0.00	0.00	2,420.00	2,420.00
MO		0.00	0.00	950.00	950.00
	Lambert, Albert	0.00	0.00	950.00	950.00
NY		0.00	1,090.00	0.00	1,090.00
	LaGuardia, Fiorello	0.00	1,090.00	0.00	1,090.00
VA		0.00	2,380.00	0.00	2,380.00
	Dulles, John	0.00	2,380.00	0.00	2,380.00
	TOTAL	**1,600.00**	**7,000.00**	**4,430.00**	**13,030.00**
	TOTAL	**1,600.00**	**7,000.00**	**4,430.00**	**13,030.00**

08/19/2013 11:55:45 AM

Figure 9-11

9.10 Create a Commercial Invoice

In this exercise, you will generate commercial invoice for the placed Orders. You are going to use the same techniques as used in the previous section. This time you will utilize session state to pass master data from the Order form to the Invoice report.

9.10.1 Create Query for the Invoice

1. Go to **Shared Components**.
2. Click the **Report Queries** link.
3. Click **Create**.
4. Enter **Invoice** in the Report Query Name box, select **PDF** for Output Format, select **Attachment** for View File As and check the **Session State**. Click the **List of Values** button, select P29_CUSTOMER_ID and click the **Add** button to add this field to the selected items list. Using the same procedure, add fields from Page 29 as shown in the following figure, and proceed to the next page.

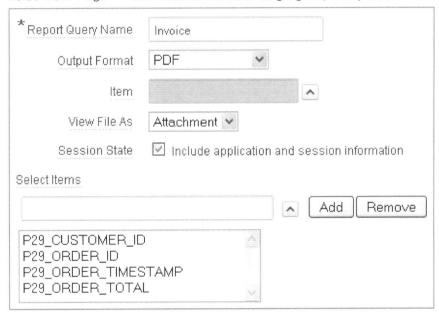

NOTE: You can include session state of your current application in your report. Select this when you want to show additional data with your report. For example, you might want to include order header information along with order details in an order form.

Figure 9-12

5. In SQL Query enter the following statement and click Next:

   select oi.ORDER_ITEM_ID, pi.PRODUCT_NAME, oi.UNIT_PRICE, oi.QUANTITY, oi.Unit_Price * oi.Quantity as Amount, c.cust_first_name || ' ' || c.cust_last_name as customer, c.cust_street_address1, c.cust_street_address2, c.cust_city, c.cust_state, c.cust_postal_code, u.user_name
   from DEMO_ORDER_ITEMS oi, DEMO_PRODUCT_INFO pi, DEMO_CUSTOMERS c, DEMO_USERS u
   where pi.PRODUCT_ID=oi.PRODUCT_ID and ORDER_id = :P29_ORDER_ID and customer_id = :P29_CUSTOMER_ID and user_name = :P29_USER_NAME

6. Select **XML Data** for Report Layout Data Source, click the **Download** button and save the file Invoice.xml to your hard drive.

7. Click **Create Report Query**. Test the report and click **Create**.

Chapter 9 – Advanced Reporting

9.10.2 Create Invoice Template in MS Word

You have the option to create the template yourself or use one from the templates provided in MS Word.

1. Open MS Word.
2. Click the Office button and select the **New** option.
3. From the Templates pane select **Invoices**, select **Sales Invoices** from the middle pane, select an invoice template, and click the **Download** button. The invoice template will appear in MS Word.
4. In the BI Publisher menu, click on **Sample XML** icon. Select **Invoice.xml** file and click the **Open** button to load data from this file. A message Data Successfully Loaded will be displayed.
5. Click on the **Field** option in the Insert ribbon. Drag **P29_Order_Id** field and drop it in the box labeled INVOICE # in the invoice template. Drop **Order_Timestamp, User Name, Customer ID, Customer, Address1, Address2, City, State and Postal Code** fields in their respective boxes.
6. Select fields **Product Name, Quantity, Unit Price, and Amount** and drop them in respective columns in the invoice details section. See Figure 9-13 for reference.
7. Drop the field **Order Total** in the summary section next to Total Amount. Close the dialog box.
8. Format the template fields and save it as **Invoice.rtf**.

9.10.3 Upload the Template to APEX

1. Go to **Shared Components**.
2. Click **Report Layout**.
3. Click **Create**.
4. Select **Named Columns (RTF)**.
5. Type **Invoice** in Layout Name.
6. Click the **Browse** button and select **Invoice.rft** file.
7. Click the **Create Layout** button.
8. Click the **Shared Components** breadcrumb.
9. Click **Report Queries**.
10. Click on the **Invoice** query.
11. Select **Invoice** for Report Layout.
12. Click **Apply Changes**.

9.10.4 Call the Report from a Page

In this section you will add a button, named Print Invoice, and a branch to the Order Detail page to run the invoice.

1. Click **Application 101** breadcrumb.
2. Open the **Order Details** page (Page 29).
3. Click **Create** under Buttons.
4. Select the **Order #** region for button placement and click **Next**.
5. Select the option **Create a button in a region position** and click **Next**.
6. Enter **PRINT** in Button Name and **Print Invoice** in Label. Set Button Style to **Template Based Button**, Button Template to **Button**, Button Type to **Normal**, and click **Next**.
7. Select **Region Template Position #CREATE#** for Position and click **Next**.
8. Keep the default value Submit Page for Action and Yes for Execute Validations and click **Create Button**.
9. Create a new **Branch**.
10. Accept the default values for Branch Point (On Submit: After Processing (After Computation, Validation, and Processing) and Branch Type (Branch to Page or URL) and click **Next**.
11. Select **Page in this Application** for Branch Target, enter **0** in Page, enter **PRINT_REPORT=Invoice** in Request, click **Next**.
12. Select **PRINT (Print Invoice)** for When Button Pressed. In Condition Type select **Value of Item/Column in Expression 1 is NOT NULL** and enter **P29_ORDER_ID** in Expression 1.
13. Click **Create Branch**.

9.10.5 Test Your Work

1. Run **Application 101**.
2. Click the **Orders** Tab.
3. Click an order to call its details.
4. The Print Invoice button should appear on the right hand side. Click it and Open the report with Adobe Acrobat. I created my own invoice template which looked like Figure 9-13.

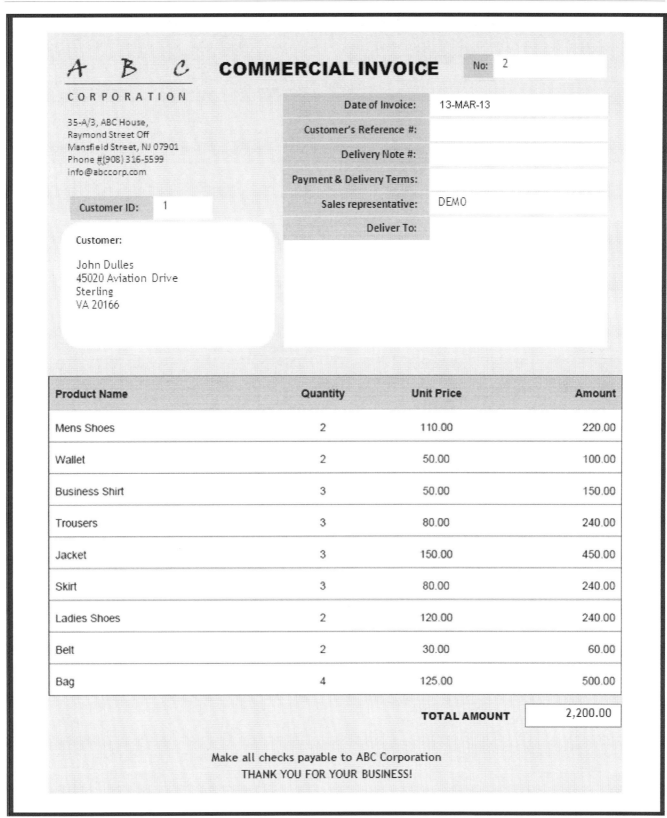

Figure 9-13

Chapter 9 – Advanced Reporting

9.11 Summary

Complex printing is the essence of modern applications that lacked in initial APEX versions. The introduction of print server has bridged this gap to create any kind of report to monitor your business activities in real time. This chapter provided you the following essential information to fulfill your reporting needs:

- Download, install and use Oracle BI Publisher as your print server
- Configure APEX to use BI Publisher as a print server
- How to enable networking services
- Install BI Publisher Desktop and create report templates in MS Word
- Created PDF version of an interactive report
- Used Pivot Table
- Created a Commercial Invoice

Chapter 10
Users Management

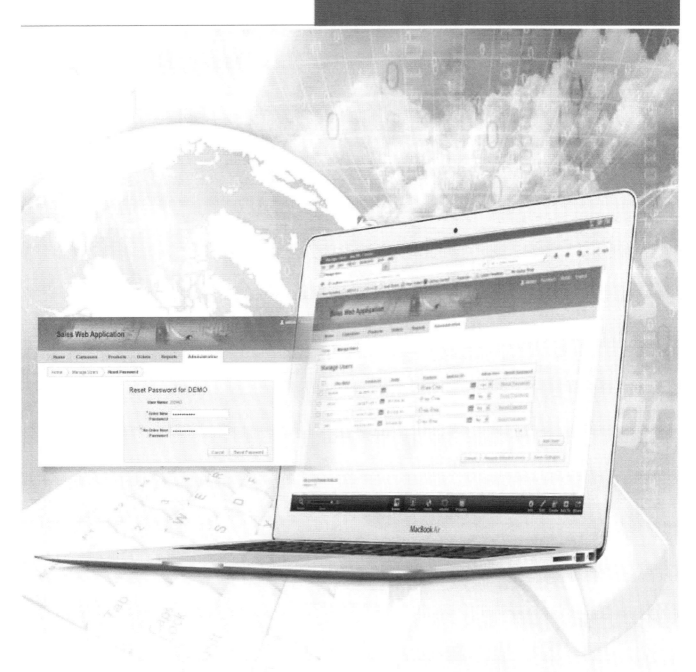

Chapter 10 – Users Management

10.1 About Users Management

Those of you working under client-server atmosphere know that this architecture supports multi-user environment where many users concurrently access the same application on the same server with different privileges. Oracle Application Express allows you to develop similar departmental applications. In such applications you need a mechanism to control users access.

You can control access to an application, individual pages, or page components by using a built-in feature of APEX that creates an access-control framework with three roles: Administrator, Edit, and View. This feature is based on a wizard and provides basic security for an application. However, to avoid the downsides of the built-in access control mechanism, you should consider creating a more robust custom mechanism, as you'll do in this chapter.

In this chapter you will develop a module to create application users and will grant them appropriate rights to access different aspects of the Sales Web Application. In addition to these tasks, you'll work on the most crucial password field to make the application more secure. In this module, you are going to implement the custom authentication scheme, created in chapter 3 section 3.6, and will create two pages under the Administration tab to manage users. These two pages will be displayed only to the users with admin privileges and will allow them to:

- Add a new user
- Remove selected users
- Change users passwords

The custom authentication scheme uses CUSTOM_AUTH and CUSTOM_HASH database functions (created in chapter 2 section 2.37), to handle obfuscated passwords in a table (DEMO_USERS). The Manage Users page (Page 8 – Figure 10-4) will enable you to create additional users and remove selected users, while Page 9 (Figure 10-5) will allow you to change passwords. Let's create this module to learn some more techniques.

10.2 The Manage Users Page - Page 8

1. Click the **Create Page** button.
2. Select the **Form** option.
3. Select **Tabular Form**.
4. Select **ASA** in Table/View Owner, select **DEMO_USERS** table from Table/View Name list. In Select Column list, select all the columns except Password. Keep the default values (Update, Insert, and Delete) in Allowed Operations and click **Next**. The password column is excluded because this field will be handled through Page 9.

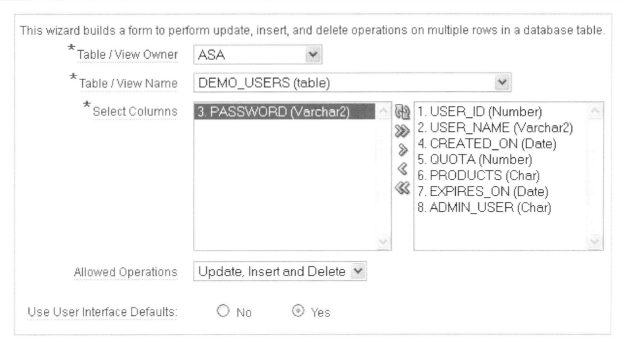

Figure 10-1

5. On the next page, select the second option **Select Primary Key Column** for Primary Key Type, select column **USER_ID** in Primary Key Column 1, and click **Next**.
6. Click **Existing Sequence** icon, select **DEMO_USERS_SEQ** for Sequence and click **Next**.
7. Accept all the columns on the Updatable Columns page and click **Next**.
8. Enter **8** in Page, **Manage Users** in Page Name and Region Title, set Region Template to **Alert Region**, Report Template to **template: Standard**, Breadcrumb to **Main Menu**, click the **Home link** to select it as Parent Entry and click **Next**.
9. Click on **Use an existing tab set and reuse an existing tab within that tab set**, select Tab Set **TS1**, **T_ADMINISTRATION** for Use Tab, and click **Next**.
10. Set attributes in Buttons and Branching page as shown below and click **Next**.

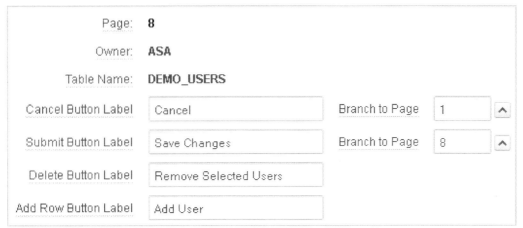

Figure 10-2

11. Click **Create**.
12. Click **Edit Page**.

Chapter 10 – Users Management

10.2.1 Modify Page Attributes

Integrate the Admin Users scheme, created in chapter 3 section 3.7.1, with this page to allow its access to admin users.

1. Click **Edit** under Page section, scroll down to the Security Seciton and set Authorization Scheme to **Admin Users**.
2. Click **Apply Changes**.

10.2.2 Modify Region Attributes

1. Click **Manage Users** link under Regions.
2. Replace existing SQL statement in Region Source with the following:

   Select "USER_ID", "USER_NAME", "CREATED_ON", "QUOTA", decode(password, null, 'Set Password', 'Reset Password') rp, products, expires_on, admin_user from "#OWNER#"."DEMO_USERS"

3. Click **Apply Changes**.
4. Click the **Report** link beside Manage Users.
5. Edit the **RP** (Reset Password) column. Scroll down to the **Column Link** section, set the following attributes and **apply changes**. These setting will display the RP column as a link. Each link will call Page 9 to reset password of the selected user.

Attribute	Value
Link Text	#RP#
Page	9
Clear Cache	9
Item 1	P9_USER_ID
Value	#USER_ID#
Item 1	P9_USER_NAME
Value	#USER_NAME#

NOTE: A Y value in the Products column (in the DEMO_USERS table) allows users to handle the products setup module (chapter 6), while a Y in the ADMIN_USER column specifies that the user is the application administrator.

6. Edit **QUOTA** column. Set Number/Date Format to **$5,234.10** and **apply changes**.
7. Edit **PRODUCTS** column. In Column Attributes, set Display As to **Radio Group (named LOV)**, remove values from Element Width to clear it, and enter **2** in Number of Columns. In List of Values section, set Named LOV to **Y OR N**, Display Extra Values to **No**. In Tabular Form Attributes section enter **Y** in Default. Click **Apply Changes**. This step will display the Product column as a radio group with two static values (Yes/No), by attaching the Y OR N LOV created in chapter 3 section 3.8.4.
8. Edit **ADMIN_USER** column. In Column Attributes, set Display As to **Select List (named LOV)**, remove values from Element Width to clear it. In List of Values section, set Named LOV to **Y OR N**, Display Extra Values to **No**. In Tabular Form Attributes section enter **N** in Default and **apply changes**.

9. Set column headings, alignments and other attributes as show in Figure 10-3 and apply changes:

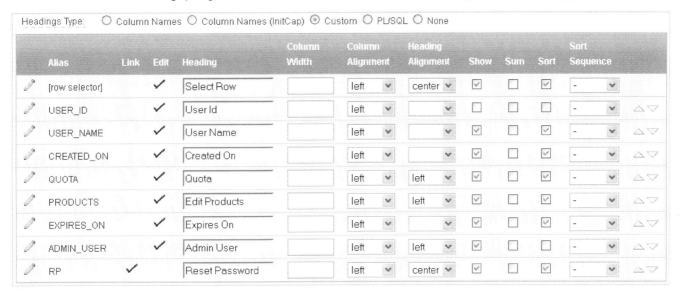

Figure 10-3

10.2.3 Modify Button Attributes

1. Click the **Add User** link under Buttons section. Scroll down to Action When Button Clicked section, set Action to **Submit Page**, Execute Validation to **Yes**, and **Apply Changes**. This button will be associated to a process (Add Row – section 10.2.7) to add a blank row in the tabular form for a new user record.

10.2.4 Create Validation – User Name Not Null

This validation is created to make the User Name field mandatory. At runtime, if you populate all the form fields except this one, you'll be prompted to fill it with as message, like this:

1. Click **Create** in Validation section.
2. Select **Manage Users** from the Tabular Form list. Select **Column** for the Validation Level and click **Next**.
3. Select **USER_NAME** for the column that is to be validated. Click **Next**.
4. Enter **10** in Sequence and **USER NAME NOT NULL** in Validation Name, click **Next**.
5. Select **Not Null** for Validation Type and click **Next**.
6. Type **#COLUMN_HEADER# must have a value** in Error Message.
7. Click the button **Create Validation**.

Chapter 10 – Users Management

10.2.5 Create Validation – Products Not Null

1. Click **Create** in Validation section.
2. Select **Manage Users** from the Tabular Form list. Select **Column** for the Validation Level and click **Next**.
3. Select **PRODUCTS** for the column that is to be validated. Click **Next**.
4. Enter **20** in Sequence and **PRODUCT NOT NULL** in Validation Name, click **Next**.
5. Select **Not Null** for Validation Type and click **Next**.
6. Type **#COLUMN_HEADER# must have a value** in Error Message.
7. Click the button **Create Validation**.

10.2.6 Update Process – ApplyMRU

1. Click **ApplyMRU** link in Processes under Page Processing section.
2. Scroll down to Messages section. Type **Unable to process request** in Process Error Message.
3. Select **Submit (Save Changes)** for When Button Pressed and apply changes. The specified message will be displayed when the process is not able to insert records. See *How Tabular Forms work* under section 7.5 in chapter 7.

10.2.7 Create Process – Add Row

This process will append a blank row to the tabular form to create a new user account.

1. **Create** a process under Page Processing section.
2. In Tabular Form list select **Manage Users**. And click on **Data Manipulation**.
3. Select **Add rows to tabular form** and click **Next**.
4. Enter **AddRows** in Name, **30** in Sequence, and click **Next**.
5. Enter **1** in Number of Rows and click **Next**. This attribute specifies how many rows to add to the tabular form.
6. In Error Message type **Unable to add row** and click **Next**.
7. Select **ADD (Add User)** for When Button Pressed. One row will be added to the tabular form when the Add User button is clicked.
8. Click **Create Process**.

10.3 The Reset Password Page - Page 9

When the Reset Password link (configured in section 10.2.2) is clicked, a new page (Page 9) comes up as illustrated in Figure 10-5, to change a user's password.

1. **Create** a new page.
2. Select the **Form** option.
3. Click **Form on a Table or View**.
4. Select **ASA** in Table/View Owner, select **DEMO_USERS** in Table/View Name, and click **Next**.
5. Enter **9** in Page Number, **Reset Password** in Page Name and Region Title. Set **Alert Region** in Region Template, set Breadcrumb to **Main Menu**, click the **Manage Users link** to select it as Parent Entry and click **Next**.
6. Click on **Use an existing tab set and reuse an existing tab within that tab set**, select **TS1** for Tab Set, **T_ADMINISTRATION** for Use Tab, and click **Next**.
7. In the Primary Key step, select the second option **Select Primary Key Column** for Primary Key Type, select column **USER_ID** in Primary Key Column 1, and click **Next**.
8. Select the option **Existing Sequence**, select **DEMO_USERS_SEQ** for Sequence and click **Next**. Being the mandatory wizard input, you selected values in steps 7 and 8. These selections have no significance for the current form, which will be used to only update a single record.
9. In the next screen, select only two columns: **USER_NAME** and **PASSWORD**. Using the left arrow icon, move the remaining columns to the left pane. Click **Next**.
10. Select **No** for Show Create Button and Show Delete Button, set **Yes** for Show Save Button and enter **Reset Password** in the corresponding label. Click **Next**.
11. Enter **8**, both in **After Page Submit and Processing Branch to Page** and **When Cancel Button Pressed Branch to this Page** to switch back to the Manage Users page. Click **Next**.
12. Click **Create**.
13. Click **Edit Page**.

10.3.1 Modify Page Attributes

1. Click **Edit** under Page section, scroll down to Security Seciton and set Authorization Scheme to **Admin Users** to grant the page access to administrators.
2. Click **Apply Changes**.

Chapter 10 – Users Management

10.3.2 Modify Region Attributes

1. Click on the **Reset Password** region link.
2. Enter **Reset Password for &P9_USER_NAME.** in Title (with the terminating period).
3. Set Template to **Alert Region**.
4. In Grid Layout, set Start New Row to **Yes**, Column to **4**, and Column Span to **6**. This will bring the region in the center of the page.
5. Scroll down to the Conditions section and set Condition Type to **Value of Item/Column in Expression 1 Is NOT NULL** and enter **P9_USER_NAME** in Expression 1. The item P9_USER_NAME must have some value in order for this region to be rendered or processed.
6. Click **Apply Changes**.

10.3.3 Create Region – Error!

The message specified in this region will be displayed when you directly try to access the reset password page. In this situation, the item P9_USER_NAME remains blank which is required to process this page.

1. Click **Create** in Regions.
2. Click on **HTML** to select it as the type of region.
3. Select **HTML** as the type of HTML region container.
4. Enter **Error!** in Title, set Region Template to **Alert Region**, Display Point to **Page Template Body (3)**, Sequence to **20**, and click **Next**.
5. In HTML Text Region Source enter **You cannot reset the password. Please select a user from the Manage Users page**. Click **Next**.
6. In Condition Type select **Value of Item/Column in Expression 1 Is Null** and enter **P9_USER_NAME** in Expression 1
7. Click **Create Region**.

10.3.4 Modify Button Attributes

1. Edit the **Reset Password** button.
2. Enter **RESET_PW** in Button Name.
3. In Action When Button Clicked section, set Database Action to **No Database Action**. Make sure the Action is set to Submit Page and Execute Validation to Yes. By setting the No Database Action value, database processing will execute based on the button name. The button name determines the value of the built-in attribute REQUEST. The Submit Page action calls the sole Update Password process (section 10.3.9) to perform the requested database process.
4. Set Condition Type to **Button NOT Conditional**. The default values for Condition Type and Expression 1 set by the wizard were Value of Item/Column in Expression 1 Is NOT NULL and P9_USER_ID respectively, to activate the button only when the page item P9_USER_ID had some value. You'll control the behavior of this button first by making password items mandatory and then by creating a process to match the two passwords, in subsequent sections.
5. Click **Apply Changes**.

10.3.5 Modify Items Attributes

1. Edit item **P9_USER_ID**.
2. Set Value Protected to **No**.
3. Set Source Used to **Only when current value in session state is null**.
4. Set Source Type to **Static Assignment (value equals source attribute)**.
5. Remove the word **USER_ID** from Source value or expression to make it null.
6. Click **Apply Changes**.
7. Edit item **P9_USER_NAME**.
8. Set Display As to **Display Only**.
9. Enter **User Name** in Label.
10. Set Show Line Breaks to **No**.
11. Set Source Used to **Only when current value in session state is null**.
12. Set Source Type to **Static Assignment (value equals source attribute)**.
13. Remove the word **USER_NAME** from Source value or expression box to make it null.
14. Set Escape Special Characters to **No**.
15. Click **Apply Changes**.
16. Edit item **P9_PASSWORD**.
17. Enter **P9_NEW_PW** in Name.
18. Set Display As to **Password**.
19. In User Interface section, set Template to **Required (Horizontal – Right Aligned)**.
20. Type **Enter New Password** in Label.
21. Set Submit when Enter pressed to **No**.
22. Set Does not save state to **Yes**. This attribute instructs APEX to not write passwords into session state. For security reasons this should always be set to Yes.
23. Enter **30** in Width and **2000** in Maximum Width.
24. Set Source Used to **Only when current value in session state is null**.
25. Set Source Type to **Static Assignment (value equals source attribute)**.
26. Remove the word **PASSWORD** from Source value or expression to make it null.
27. Click **Apply Changes**.

Chapter 10 – Users Management

10.3.6 Create Item

Applications usually ask users to confirm the provided password. For this purpose, and additional password box is provided on the page and this is what you'll be doing in this section.

1. Click **Create** in the Items section.
2. Click on **Password**.
3. Enter **P9_NEW_PW_2** in Item Name, set Sequence to **40**, Region to **Reset Password for &P9_USER_NAME.**, and click **Next**.
4. Type **Re-Enter New Password** in Label, Field Width to 30, Template to **Required (Horizontal – Right Aligned)**, and click **Next**.
5. On the Settings page, set Value Required to **Yes**, Submit when Enter pressed to **No** and Does not save state to **No**. Click **Next**.
6. Click **Create Item**.

10.3.7 Create Validation – Passwords Must Match

1. Click **Create** in Validations.
2. Select the **Page** option for the validation level. You've been using the item level validation throughout this book. Here, you selected the page level validation because you need to validate multiple items on the current page.
3. Enter **Passwords must match** in Validation Name and click **Next**.
4. Click on **PL/SQL**.
5. Select **Function Returning Boolean** and click **Next**.
6. In Validation code enter the following PL/SQL code:

   ```
   begin
   if :P9_NEW_PW = :P9_NEW_PW_2 then
     return true;
   else
     return false;
   end if;
   end;
   ```

7. In Error Message, type **Your passwords must be the same. Please re-enter.**
8. Click **Next**.
9. Click **Create Validation**.
10. **Edit** the newly created validation.
11. Scroll down to Error Message section and set Associate Item to **P9_NEW_PW_2** and apply changes. The message is associated to the second password item. If the value in this item doesn't match with the first one, the user will get the message defined in point 7.

10.3.8 Delete Processes

1. Click **Process Row of DEMO_USERS** in Processes under Page Processing.
2. Click the **Delete** button and confirm deletion.
3. Click **reset page** process and delete it as well. These processes are removed because you are handling the database update operation manually, using the following section.

10.3.9 Create Process – Update Password

1. Click **Create** in Processes.
2. Click **PL/SQL**.
3. Enter **Update Password** in Name. Make sure the Point attribute is set to On Submit – After Computations and Validations. Click **Next**.
4. In Enter PL/SQL Page Process, type the following SQL UPDATE statement. The statement calls the CUSTOM_HASH function to encrypt the provided password prior to updating the database.

   update demo_users set password = custom_hash(:P9_USER_NAME, :P9_NEW_PW) where user_name = upper(:P9_USER_NAME);

5. Click **Next**.
6. In Success Message, type **Password for &P9_USER_NAME. Updated.**
7. Click **Create Process**.

10.3.10 Modify Branch

1. Click Go To Page under Branches.
2. Set **On Submit: Before computation (Before Computation, Validation, and Processing)** for Branch Point. The branch will switch the application flow back to Page 8, without performing any validation and processing.
3. Select **CANCEL (Cancel)** for When Button pressed and **Apply Changes**.

10.3.11 Create Branch

1. Click **Create** in Branches.
2. Accept the default settings for Branch Point – On Submit: After Processing (After Computation, Validation, and Processing and Branch Type – Branch to Page or URL. Click **Next**.
3. Enter **8** in Page, **put a check** on include process success message and click **Next**.
4. Select **RESET_PW (Reset Password)** button for When Button Pressed.
5. Click **Create Branch**.

Chapter 10 – Users Management

10.4 Test Your Work

1. Click the **Run** button.
2. Login as Admin/asa. Click the **Home** tab and then the **Administration** Tab. The screen should look like Figure 10-4.

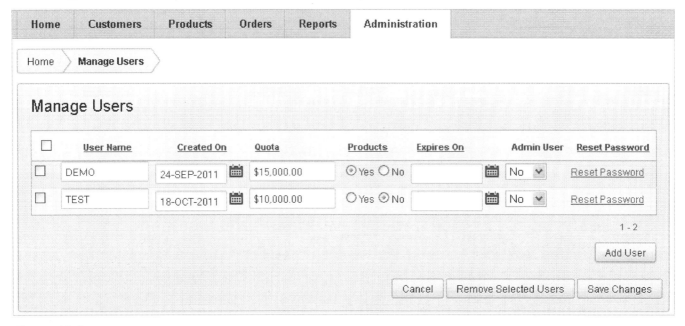

Figure 10-4

3. Click the **Reset Password link** for the TEST user. The password reset page should be displayed as shown below.

Figure 10-5

4. Enter **test123** in Enter New Password, re-enter it in the next box, and click the **Reset Password** button. A message will appear showing: *Password for TEST updated*. Please note that the passwords are case sensitive. Try the new password which used to be test. Login to the application using test/test123. Click on the Administration tab. You'll be prevented from accessing this page because of the Admin User authorization scheme, implemented in section 10.2.1 above. Login again as Admin/asa and click the Administration tab.

5. Click the **Add User** button. A blank row will be added to the tabular form.

6. Enter the following values and click the **Save Changes** button:

Column	Value
User Name	ABC
Created On	Select the current date using the Date Picker
Quota	20000
Products	No
Admin User	No

7. A message will appear indicating 1 row inserted. Note that the Reset Password column value for the newly created user (ABC) is set to SET PASSWORD indicating a new user. This evaluation is based on the SQL SELECT query set in section 10.2.2 – step 2. Click the **SET PASSWORD** link to set password for the new user.

8. Enter **xyz123** in Enter New Password and **xyz** in Re-Enter New Password box. Click the **Reset Password** button. An error message displaying password mismatch should appear. Now, enter the same password in both boxes and click the Reset Password button. This time, you'll see a successful update message with the value Reset Password in the last column.

9. Click the **logout** link in the navigation bar.

10. Enter **abc** and **xyz123** in username and password, respectively.

11. Click the **Administration** Tab.

12. You will get a message: **Access denied by Page security check. You need to be an Admin User in order to view this page.** Click the OK button to move back.

13. Click the **Products** tab. Note that the Add Product button is not visible because we set NO for the Products column for the new user to prevent him from manipulating products data.

Chapter 10 – Users Management

10.5 Hide the Administration Tab

As you saw in the previous exercise, a non-admin user received Access Denied message when he/she clicked on the administration tab. In this exercise you will hide this tab altogether from unauthorized users.

1. Click **Application 101** in the Developers Toolbar.
2. Click the big **Shared Components** icon.
3. In the Navigation section, click **Tabs**.
4. Click **Manage Tabs**.
5. Scroll down and click the **Administration** link.
6. Click the **Authorization** tab, set Authorization Scheme to **Admin Users** and click **Apply Changes**.
7. Click **Application 101** breadcrumb.
8. Click **Run Application**. If you are logged in as either DEMO or ABC, the Administration tab will not be displayed.
9. Click the **Logout** link in the Navigation bar.
10. Enter **admin** and **asa** in username and password, respectively.
11. The Administration tab will now be visible. Click on it and check other functionalities.

10.6 Summary

This chapter concludes our effort to build a professional looking desktop web application in Oracle Application Express. It's the right time to give it a complete test run prior to deploying it to a production machine. In the final part of this book, you will learn how to move this application from your computer to another environment and how to access the application remotely. But prior to that, you'll create the mobile version of this application in the next chapter to experience the new feature provided in APEX 4.2 to develop applications for smartphones and other mobile devices. Here are some main techniques you applied to this module:

- Implement custom authentication scheme.
- Add and Remove users and change their Passwords.
- Apply Products authorization scheme through database.
- Usage of Tabular Form.
- Hiding tab from unauthorized users.

Chapter 11
Smartphone and Mobile Development

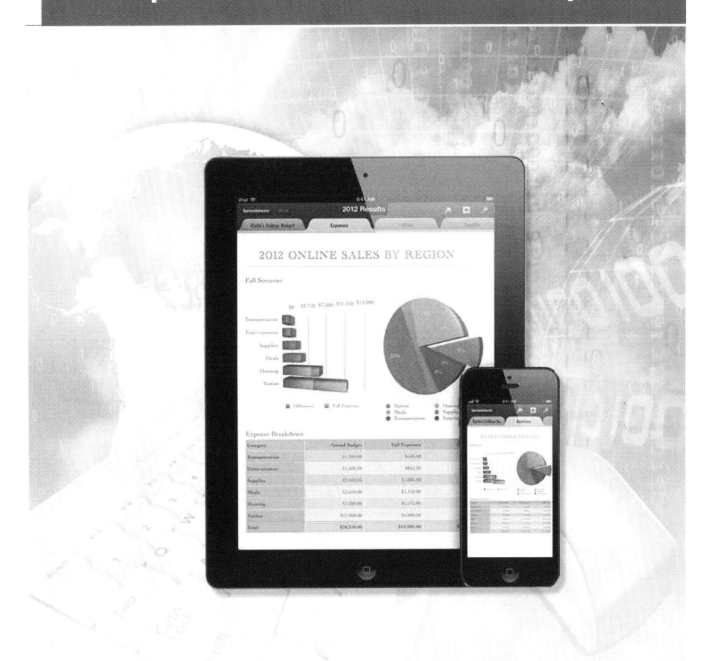

Chapter 11 – Smartphone and Mobile Development

11.1 About Mobile Development

In the last few years there has been an eruption in the market for smartphones and mobile devices demand. As the sales are touching new heights every day, smartphone vendors are trying their level best to provide the excellent product with latest technology. Things that used to be done traditionally by people on their laptops are now being done increasingly on mobile devices. Feeling the heat, application development companies are under pressure to quickly deliver web applications for smartphone and mobile platforms. For this, they need tools and frameworks to roll out new mobile enabled applications and adapt existing applications to mobile devices. The good news is that just like traditional web applications, mobile web applications are also developed using the same core technologies – HTML, CSS, and JavaScript.

With mobile web usage incrementing every year, there is a huge demand in the market for applications supported on smartphones and tablets. To help develop new applications and extend existing web applications for mobile use, the APEX development team has enhanced the product with mobile development features. Probably the most significant new feature incorporated in APEX 4.2 is the ability to build applications specifically aimed at mobile devices. Now you can easily build applications for modern smartphones and tablets, such as iPhone, iPad, Android, and BlackBerry using Oracle APEX. The jQuery Mobile framework is integrated to render an application for the vast majority of mobile devices. Besides, a new mobile-specific theme is incorporated to support touch input and gestures such as swipe, tap, and orientation change. Another theme takes care of responsive design, to automatically adjust the interface according to different screen dimensions, which aids in using the same interface on desktop, tablet, and smartphone devices.

Types of Mobile Applications

Mobile Applications are split into two broad categories:

Web-Based: The application you'll be creating in this chapter is known as a web-based application or simply a mobile web application. These types of applications are accessed using browsers in mobile devices. In this chapter, you'll declaratively build a mobile web application. APEX 4.2 allows you to rapidly build application that can be accessed on the desktop, a mobile device, or both. The mobile development interface uses a collection of templates based on the jQuery Mobile framework. This framework is designed to seamlessly run and correctly deliver mobile web application on varied mobile devices with different operating systems. For you, as a developer, the good news is that you develop such applications with the tools you're already familiar with. To build a mobile application, you use the same application builder, the same SQL and PL/SQL code, and with similar methods that you applied while developing the desktop version. Because of a single codebase, a mobile web application can be accessed from any mobile device, irrespective of operating system. The process of accessing such applications is very simple. All that is needed is to have the correct URL, that you put into the mobile browser, and respective id with password. The application code is not stored on the device but is delivered by the application server. This way you can easily handle application updates. You only need to update the application on the server, allowing potentially thousands of users to enjoy the latest version. The second advantage to this approach is that you are not required to send updates to every client (as required in native applications), which ensures that the accessed application is current with all provided features. Here are some pros and cons to web-based applications:

Pros:
- Updates are uploaded only to the application server and become instantly available for all platforms and devices.
- Same application code for all browser-enabled mobile device.
- Use of same application building procedures and core web technologies.
- Doesn't need app store approval.

Cons:
- To access these applications you need a reasonable Internet connection.
- Slower than native applications because these applications are based on interpreted code rather than compiled code.
- Not available in the app stores.
- Cannot interact with device hardware such as camera, microphone, compass, file uploading etc.

Native (On-Device): These applications are on the other side and are built for specific mobile operating system, such as Windows Mobile, Android, iOS, or BlackBerry. Native mobile applications are written for a specific target operating system in its own supported language. For instance, to develop an application for Windows device, you'll use C# (C Sharp), for iOS devices it is Objective-C, and for Android, you need to be a master of Java. This means that your app is tied to a specific platform and won't run on another. Native applications are downloaded and stored locally on the device. Because of this capability, these applications are considered better performers. Additionally, these applications have the biggest advantage to interact with different device hardware (camera, compass, accelerometer, and more). Using a local data store (SQL Lite), these applications can even work when disconnected from the Internet. As a developer you have to handle version discrepancies because updates of these applications are downloaded manually. Let's see what pros and cons this category has:

Pros:
- Being native, it performs better than its counterpart.
- Offline availability.
- Complete access to device's hardware.
- Can be added to and searched in an app store.

Cons:
- Expensive to develop.
- Single platform support. Need to build a separate app for a different OS, which means additional time and cost.
- To get space on the device's app store, your app is required to undergo an approval process.

Chapter 11 – Smartphone and Mobile Development

11.2 Create the Mobile Application Interface

Oracle APEX allows you to create two types of interfaces: Desktop and jQuery Mobile Smartphone. Each page in an application is associated with one user interface. If a user logs into the application with a mobile device, the pages created with jQuery Mobile Smartphone interface will be rendered; if a desktop is used, the desktop user interface is delivered. You created and used the desktop interface in previous chapters. Here, you'll use jQuery Mobile interface for your mobile application.

1. Click the button **Edit Application Properties** in the main Sales Web Application interface.
2. Click on the **User Interface** tab.
3. Click the button **Add New User Interface**, located at the bottom of the page.
4. On the User Interface Page, set the attributes as follows and click **Next**.

    Type: jQuery Mobile Smartphone
    Selected a user interface type for the application. Select Desktop for applications primarily designed for desktop use. For mobile devices, such as smartphones or tablets, select the jQuery Mobile Smartphone interface.

    Display Name: jQuery Mobile Smartphone
    Specified a display name for the user interface. The display names is shown in wizards.

    Auto Detect: Yes
    Select whether the appropriate user interface should be automatically detected. If auto-detection is enabled, the user will be redirected to the corresponding login page or home page.

    Home URL: f?p=&APP_ID.:HOME_JQM_SMARTPHONE:&SESSION.
    Specifies the home page of the application for the current user interface.

    Login URL: f?p=&APP_ID.:LOGIN_JQM_SMARTPHONE:&SESSION.
    Points towards the login page of the application for the current user interface.

5. In Identify Theme, select **Standard Themes** as Theme Type and **jQuery Mobile Smartphone (Theme 50)** as the mobile application theme. Click **Next**.
6. Click **Create**.

Recall that when you initially created the desktop application, the application wizard created two pages for you (Home and Login). The mobile interface too, creates two default pages: Home (Page 13 in my scenario) and Login (Page 1001). In addition to these pages, the wizard creates a third one: Global Page – jQuery Mobile Smartphone (Page 0). Recall that this page was created manually for the desktop application in chapter 8 section 8.2. The Global page of your application functions as a master page. You can add a separate Global page for each user interface. The Application Express engine renders all components you add to a Global page on every page within your application. Default definitions of all three pages are illustrated on subsequent pages.

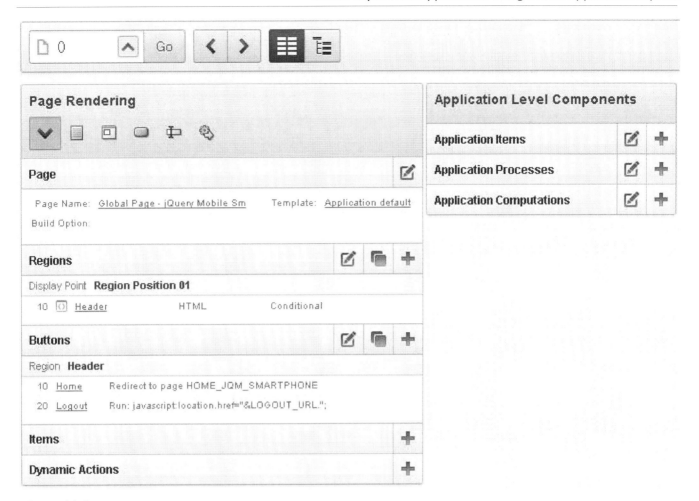

Figure 11-1

Chapter 11 – Smartphone and Mobile Development

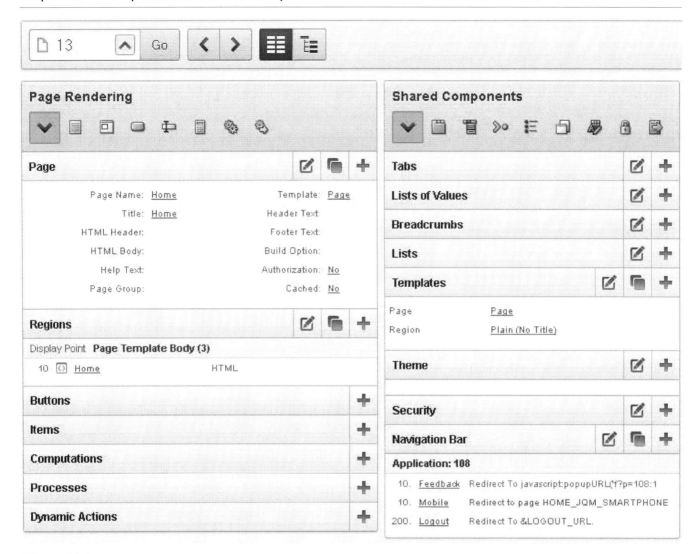

Figure 11-2

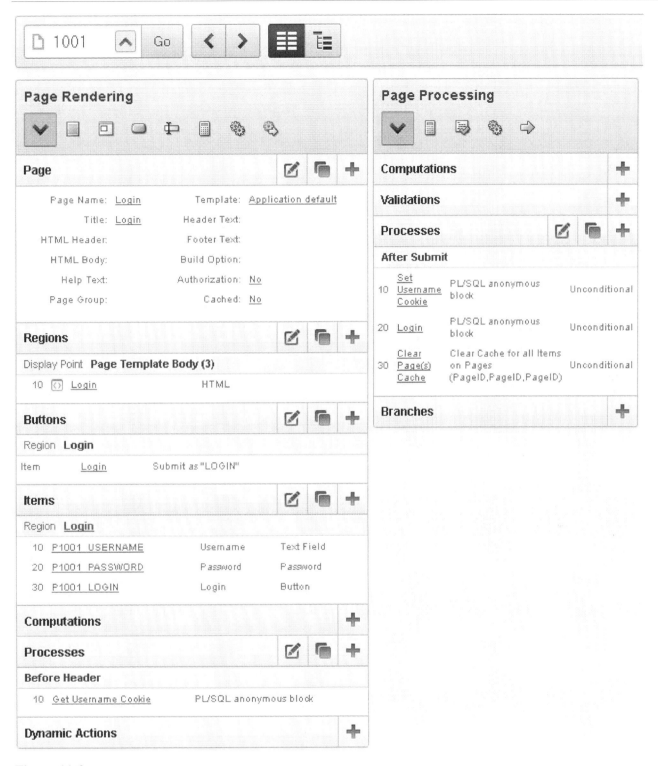

Figure 11-3

Chapter 11 – Smartphone and Mobile Development

Run the Login Page 1001 that will look like the following figure:

Figure 11-4

Enter the usual credentials (admin/asa), you've been using so far, and hit the Login button. A blank mobile home page will appear resembling the one illustrated below.

Figure 11-5

Click the Logout link. You'll be landed to the desktop login page, which is not correct. Call definitions of the Global Page. Click the Logout link in the Buttons section. Scroll down to **Action When Button Clicked** section. Set Action to Redirect to Page in this Application and enter 1001 in Page. Click Apply Changes. These two settings inform APEX where to land user when he clicks the Logout button. Call and run the Home page again, login using the same admin account, and click the Logout button. This time you'll see the correct login page i.e. Page 1001. Use your browser's back button to move back to the development environment.

Let's move on to fine tune the auto-generated pages by changing some attributes, starting with the Global Page.

11.3 Modify the Global Page - Page 0

11.3.1 Modify Region - Header

1. Click on the **Global Page** to call its definitions.
2. Click the **Header** link in the Regions section.
3. Set Display Point to **Page Template Body (3)**.
4. **Apply Changes**.

> **NOTE:** The region is created with a default condition (Current Page Is NOT in Expression 1) and corresponding value (1001). This condition evaluates the login page, to suppress the region display.

11.3.2 Create List - Footer Control

This static list carries two options (Full Site and Logout) and will be displayed at the bottom in the Footer Controls region. The first option will take you to the Home page of the desktop version, while the second one will log you out of the mobile application and will show the mobile login page.

1. Go to **Shared Components**.
2. In the Navigation section, click the **List** link.
3. Click the **Create** Button to create a new list.
4. Select the option **From Scratch**.
5. Enter **Footer Controls** in Name and select **Static** as Type.
6. Fill in the Static Values as shown below:

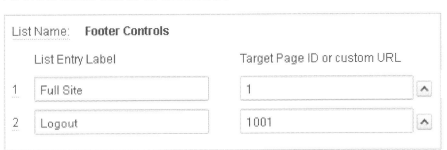

Figure 11-6

7. Click **Create List**.

Chapter 11 – Smartphone and Mobile Development

11.3.3 Create Region - Footer Controls

The list, created in the previous section, will be displayed in this region.

1. Call the Global Page again.
2. Click the **Create** button in the Regions section.
3. Select the **List** option.
4. In Display Attributes page, enter **Footer Controls** in Title, select **Footer Toolbar (Fixed)** for Region Template, **Page Template Body (3)** for Display Point, and enter **30** in Sequence. Click **Next**.
5. In the Source page, select **Footer Controls** as List and **Button Control Group** as List Template.
6. For Condition Type, select **Current Page Is Not in Expression 1** and enter **1001** in Expression 1 to suppress the appearance of footer controls on the login page.
7. Click **Create Region**.
8. Edit this region. Scroll down to the Attributes section and enter **style="text-align:center"** for Region Attributes box. This style will bring the list (being shown as button control group) in the center of the page.
9. **Apply Changes**.

11.3.4 Create Region - Mobile Styles

1. **Create** another region.
2. Select **HTML** as the type of region.
3. Select **HTML** as region container.
4. In Display Attributes page, enter **Mobile Styles** in Title, select **No Template** for Region Template, **Page Template Body (3)** for Display Point, and enter **40** in Sequence. Click **Next**.
5. In Region Source, enter the style sheet defined on the next page and create the region. Note that these rules were created and described earlier in the desktop version to style the *Select Items* page (Page 12), and were defined in the inline page attribute. Here, you added it to the global page to test another approach to style Select Items page (Page 217) of the mobile version. Since the classes defined in these rules are referenced only by Page 217, other pages in the application will not be affected.

```
<style>
  div.CustomerInfo strong{font:bold 12px/16px Arial,sans-serif;display:block;width:120px;}
  div.CustomerInfo p{display:block;margin:0; font: normal 12px/16px Arial, sans-serif;}
  div.Products{clear:both;margin:16px 0 0 0;padding:0 8px 0 0;}
  div.Products table{border:1px solid #CCC;border-bottom:none;}
  div.Products table th{background-color:#DDD;color:#000;font:bold 12px/16px Arial,sans-serif;padding:4px 10px;text-align:right;border-bottom:1px solid #CCC;}
  div.Products table td{border-bottom:1px solid #CCC;font:normal 12px/16px Arial,sans-serif;padding:4px 10px;text-align:right;}
  div.Products table td a{color:#000;}
  div.Products .left{text-align:left;}
  div.CartItem{padding:8px 8px 0 8px;font:normal 11px/14px Arial,sans-serif;}
  div.CartItem a{color:#000;}
  div.CartItem span{display:block;text-align:right;padding:8px 0 0 0;}
  div.CartItem span.subtotal{font-weight:bold;}
  div.CartTotal{border-top:1px solid #FFF;margin-top:8px;padding:8px;border-top:1px dotted #AAA;}
  div.CartTotal span{display:block;text-align:right;font:normal 11px/14px Arial,sans-serif;padding:0 0 4px 0;}
  div.CartTotal p{padding:0;margin:0;font:normal 11px/14px Arial,sans-serif;position:relative;}
  div.CartTotal p.CartTotal{font:bold 12px/14px Arial,sans-serif;padding:8px 0 0 0;}
  div.CartTotal p.CartTotal span{font:bold 12px/14px Arial,sans-serif;padding:8px 0 0 0;}
  div.CartTotal p span{padding:0;position:absolute;right:0;top:0;}
</style>
```

Chapter 11 – Smartphone and Mobile Development

11.4 Modify the Mobile Home Page

11.4.1 Modify the Page attributes

1. Call the mobile **Home** page. On my PC it was numbered 13.
2. Click on the **Edit** link in the Page section.
3. Set the Name of this page to **Mobile Home Page**. Make sure that Page Alias shows HOME_JQM_SMARTPHONE. An alias is a nick name. You can enter an alphanumeric alias for a page. It is used to reference a page instead of a page number. For example, if you were working on page 1 of application 100, you could create an alias called "home" which could then be accessed from other pages using the syntax: f?p=100:home
4. Enter **Sales Web Application** in Title.
5. Apply Changes.

11.4.2 Create List - Mobile Menu

This is the main mobile application menu that will appear after a successful login attempt and is displayed as a list. A list region will also be created on the home page, providing navigation to other application pages.

1. Go to **Shared Components**.
2. In the Navigation section, click the **List** link.
3. Click the **Create** Button to create a new list.
4. Select the option **From Scratch**.
5. Enter **Mobile Menu** in Name and select **Static** as Type.
6. Fill in the Static Values as shown below:
7. Click **Create List**.

List Name:	Mobile Menu	
	List Entry Label	Target Page ID or custom URL
1	Customers	201
2	Products	203
3	Orders	205
4	Reports	208

Figure 11-7

11.4.3 Create Region - Mobile Menu

In mobile applications, some common constructs (such as report linking to a form) are replaced by list linking to forms. In this exercise, you'll apply this approach by presenting the Mobile Menu list as the main linking source.

1. Call the definitions of the Mobile Home page.
2. Click **Create** in the Regions section.
3. Select the **List** option.
4. Enter **Mobile Menu** in Title, select **No Template** for Region Template, **Page Template Body (3)** for Display Point, and enter **20** in Sequence. Click **Next**.
5. In the Source page, select **Mobile Menu** as List and **List View (Inset)** as List Template.
6. Click **Create Region**.

11.5 Test Your Work

The three default mobile pages created by APEX wizard are ready to launch now. You might have noticed that we didn't work on the mobile login page 1001 (we didn't work on the desktop login page either). Application Express is smart enough to create these pages with basic functionalities, suffice to cope with our needs.

Assuming that you're looking at the definitions of the mobile home page, click the Run button. The login page as presented in Figure 11-4 comes up. Enter admin/asa (or demo/demo) in username and password respectively, and click the Login button. Here is the mobile home page that you'll see. Test the page by click all the available options. The Full Site button will take you back to the desktop version, from where you can switch back to the development environment.

Figure 11-8

Chapter 11 – Smartphone and Mobile Development

11.6 Create Customers Page - Page 201

1. As usual, click on the **Create Page** button to create the first mobile application page yourself.
2. Note that for User Interface you now have two options: Desktop and jQuery Mobile Smartphone. Select the second option: **jQuery Mobile Smartphone**. Click on the **Report** icon to move ahead.
3. Select the **List View** option. One of the main differences between an APEX desktop application and a mobile application is the presence of the List View in the mobile world. Due to non-availability of interactive report for the mobile platform, you'll use this option instead.
4. Type **201** in Page Number and **Customers** in Page Name and Region Name. Do not use the breadcrumb.
5. In Region Source type:

   select a.ROWID as "PK_ROWID", a.* from "#OWNER#"."DEMO_CUSTOMERS" a

   For each row in the database the ROWID pseudocolumn returns the address of the row. Oracle Database rowid values contain information necessary to locate a row. If you run the above statement in SQL Commands utility, you'll get the following output:

PK_ROWID	CUSTOMER_ID	CUST_FIRST_NAME	CUST_LAST_NAME
AAAF3ZAAEAAAAQ2AAA	1	John	Dulles
AAAF3ZAAEAAAAQ2AAB	2	William	Hartsfield
AAAF3ZAAEAAAAQ2AAC	3	Edward	Logan
AAAF3ZAAEAAAAQ2AAD	4	Frank	OHare
AAAF3ZAAEAAAAQ2AAE	5	Fiorello	LaGuardia
AAAF3ZAAEAAAAQ2AAF	6	Albert	Lambert
AAAF3ZAAEAAAAQ2AAG	7	Eugene	Bradley
AAAF3ZAAEAAAAQ3AAA	162	Riaz	Ahmed

Figure 11-9

> **NOTE:** Mobile pages created in Oracle APEX do not support constructs such as interactive reports, tabular forms, and master-detail pages.

6. In the Settings page, put a check on **Advanced Formatting** and **Inset List** features. If lists are embedded in a page with other types of content, an inset list packages the list into a block that sits inside the content area with a bit of margin and rounded corners (as shown in Figure 1-10). Fill in the other setting attributes as shown in the following table:

Attribute	Settings
Text Formatting	`<h3>&CUST_FIRST_NAME. &CUST_LAST_NAME.</h3>` `<p>&PHONE_NUMBER1.</p>`
Supplemental Informational Formatting	`<strong>Credit Limit ` `$&CREDIT_LIMIT.</strong>`
Link Target	`f?p=&APP_ID.:202:&APP_SESSION.::&DEBUG.:RP,202:P202_ROWID:&PK_ROWID.`

Clicking the *Advanced Formatting* option brings up four more options that enable you to style your list even further. The first option, *List Attributes*, is used to style the list by overriding the standard list or divider theme. The *List Entry Attributes* can be set to pick an icon other than the standard right arrow (you'll test these two options in the Product module). The mandatory option, *Text Formatting*, gives you the opportunity to show more in the list than just the Customer Name. In this example, you wrapped customer's first and last names in an HTML `<h3>` heading element and added the Phone Number to the list. Besides, you can add more stuff to the list with the help of *Supplemental Information* as you did here by presenting customer's credit limit. The Supplemental Information appears on the right side of the list item. Each customer record will become a link through the *Link Target* attribute. To display record of the selected customer (on Page 202), the link forwards two parameters. The first one, P202_ROWID, is an item on Page 202 that will receive a primary key value from the second one that is based on PK_ROWID selected in step 5.

7. Click the **Create** button and then the **Edit Page** button. Note that rather than creating a blank page and adding main region to it later, we created the page, added a region with its source, and set attributes to display the required information, all at once.

Chapter 11 – Smartphone and Mobile Development

11.6.1 Add Button - Create

1. Click **Create** in the Buttons section.
2. Select the region **Customers** for this button.
3. Select the option **Create a button in a region position**.
4. Enter **CREATE** in Button Name and **Create Customer** in Label. Set Button Style to **Template Based Button**, Button Template to **Inline Button**, Button Type to **Hot**.
5. Set Position to **Bottom of Region** and Alignment to **Right**.
6. On Action When Clicked page, set Action to **Redirect to Page in this Application**. Enter **202** in Page and Clear Cache. Put a check on reset pagination for this page.
7. Click **Create Button**.
8. Click **Run** to test the page. Click the **Home** link to test the menu item which will bring you to this page. In the mobile menu, click **Customers**. You'll see the page, illustrated in Figure 11-10.

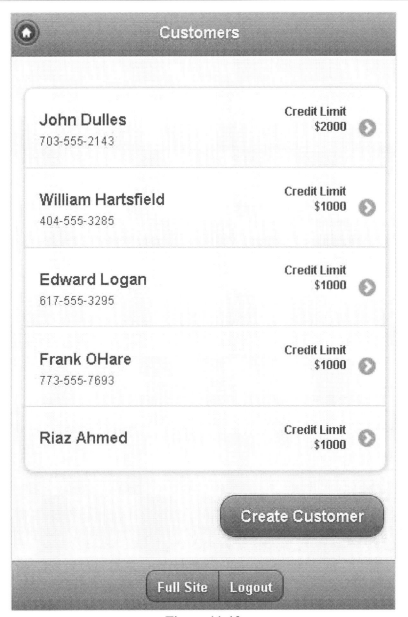

Figure 11-10

Chapter 11 — Smartphone and Mobile Development

11.7 Create Maintain Customer Page - Page 202

1. **Create** a new page.
2. Once again, select the second option – **jQuery Mobile Smartphone**. Click on the **Form** icon to move forward.
3. Select the option – **Form on a Table or View**.
4. Select the schema **ASA** for Table/View Owner and **DEMO_CUSTOMERS** table from Table/View Name.
5. Enter **202** in Page Number, **Maintain Customer** in Page Name and Region Title, and leave Region Template to the default value Plain (No Title). Do not add breadcrumb and click **Next**.
6. For Primary Key Type, select **Managed by Database (ROWID)** option. You've been using the second option (Select Primary Key Column) in the desktop application exercises to select a primary key for the selected table. This time, you're using the alternate method, which is usually selected for tables with multiple primary key columns (more than two).
7. Select **all** columns from the table and click **Next**.
8. Keep **all** the default options on the Buttons page and move on.
9. On the Branching page, enter **201** for both After Page Submit and When Cancel Button Pressed to move back to the main customers page.
10. Click **Create** on the Confirm page.
11. Click **Edit Page**.

11.7.1 Modify Items

Modify attributes of the page items as shown in the following table:

ITEM	ATTRIBUTE:VALUE	ATTRIBUTE:VALUE	ATTRIBUTE:VALUE
P202_CUSTOMER_ID	Display As : Hidden		
P202_CUST_FIRST_NAME	Label : First Name		
P202_CUST_LAST_NAME	Label : Last Name		
P202_CUST_STREET_ADDRESS1	Label : Street Address		
P202_CUST_STREET_ADDRESS2	Label : Line 2		
P202_CUST_CITY	Label : City		
P202_CUST_POSTAL_CODE	Label : Postal Code	Template : Required	Value Required : Yes
P202_CUST_EMAIL	Label : Email		
P202_PHONE_NUMBER1	Label : Phone Number		
P202_PHONE_NUMBER2	Label : Alternate Number		
P202_URL	Label : URL		
P202_CREDIT_LIMIT	–	Template : Required	Value Required : Yes
P202_TAGS	Display As : Text Field		

Call **P202_CUST_STATES** attributes. Change Display As from Text Field to **Select List**, set Template to **Required**, Label to **State**, Value Required to **Yes**, Named LOV to **STATES** and Apply Changes.

11.8 Test Your Work

In Page Definition, click the Run button. Click the Home icon. Select Customers from the mobile menu. Click on any customer's record. Your screen should resemble the following output. Click the Cancel button which will take you back to the main customers page. Click the Create Customer button, located at the bottom of your screen. A new form will be presented with two button: Cancel and Create. Create a new customer record and click the Create button to store it in DEMO_CUSTOMERS table. Call the new record and try to modify and save some information. Finally, delete this record. Using the steps mentioned for Page 7 (Customer Details) in chapter 5, add the two validations: check credit limit and prevent customer's record deletion having orders. Similarly, create another validation for phone number format, as mentioned in chapter 7.

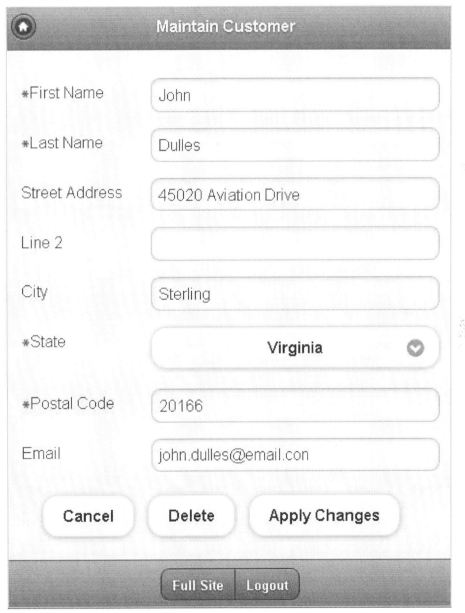

Figure 11-11

11.9 Create Main Products Page - Page 203

1. Create a new page by clicking on the **Create Page** button.
2. Select **jQuery Mobile Smartphone**. Click on the **Report** icon to move ahead.
3. Select the **List View** option.
4. Type **203** in Page Number and **Products** in Page Name and Region Name. Do not use the breadcrumb.
5. In Region Source, input the following SQL statement which is similar to the one you used to fetch customers records on Page 201.

    select a.ROWID as "PK_ROWID", a.*

    from "#OWNER#"."DEMO_PRODUCT_INFO" a

    order by a.product_name
6. Set the attributes in the Settings page as shown in Figure 11-12.
7. Click the **Create** button and then the **Edit Page** button.

Features	☐ Advanced Formatting ☑ Show Image ☐ Show List Divider ☐ Has Split Button ☑ Enable Search ☐ Is Nested List View ☑ Inset List
Text Column	PRODUCT_NAME
Supplemental Information Column	- select -
Counter Column	- select -
Image Type	Image stored in BLOB
Image BLOB Column	PRODUCT_IMAGE
Image Primary Key Column 1	ROWID
Image Primary Key Column 2	- select -
Link Target	f?p=&APP_ID.:204:&APP_SESSION.::&DEBUG.:RP,204:P204_ROWID:&PK_ROWID.
Search Type	Server: Like & Ignore Case
Search Column	PRODUCT_DESCRIPTION
Search Box Placeholder	Search Product Description

Figure 11-12

When you click the option *Show Image*, some more relevant attributes appear on your screen. The same behavior applies to the *Enable Search* option. We used the first option because we need to display products images, while the second option is checked to add search functionality. The selected text column PRODUCT_NAME will appear next to the image at runtime. The *Image Type* attribute specifies what kind of image is displayed and where it is read from. The displayed image can be an icon with a size of 16x16 or a thumbnail with a size of 80x80. The source for the image can be a database BLOB column or a URL to a static file. After setting the *Image Type* attribute, you're required to provide the *Image BLOB Column* which, in our case, is PRODUCT_IMAGE. The *Image Primary Key* attribute specifies the primary key or a unique database column that is used to lookup the image. The value for this attribute (ROWID) is selected by the wizard. We discussed the *Link Target* attribute in the previous module. The *Search Type* attribute defines how a search will be performed. The selected option, *Server: Like & Ignore Case*, will use Oracle's LIKE operator (LIKE %UPPER([search value])%) to query the result. The *Search Column* specifies an alternative database column used for the search. If nothing is specified, then the *Text Column* is used. The text added to the *Search Box Placeholder* will appear in the search box at runtime.

Chapter 11 – Smartphone and Mobile Development

11.9.1 Add Button - Create

1. Click **Create** in the Buttons section.
2. Select the region **Products** where this button will be placed in.
3. Select the option **Create a button in a region position**.
4. Enter **CREATE** in Button Name and **Create** in Label. Set Button Style to **Template Based Button**, Button Template to **Inline Button**, and Button Type to **Hot**.
5. Set Position to **Bottom of Region** and Alignment to **Left**.
6. On *Action When Clicked* page, set Action to **Redirect to Page in this Application**. Enter **204** in Page and Clear Cache. Put a check on reset pagination for this page.
7. Click **Create Button**.
8. Click **Run** to test the page. Click the **Home** link and then the **Products** link in the main mobile menu. You'll see the following Products page. Enter the word **shoes** in the search box and hit enter. Two shoe products (Ladies Shoes and Men Shoes) should appear. Enter **low heel** in the search box. The browser will refresh with one record, displaying Ladies Shoes. This is because the word low heel exists in the description for this product. Type **lower lace** in the search box. This time the Men Shoes will be displayed. Click the Clear Text icon in the search box. All the products will re-appear.

Make this page more meaningful by performing the following steps:

1. In Page Definition, click the **Products** List View link under Regions.
2. Click on the **Region Attributes** tab.
3. Put a check on **Advanced Formatting**.
4. In List Attributes, type: **data-divider-theme="b"**. The theme for list dividers can be set by adding the data-divider-theme to the list and specifying a swatch letter. We set swatch "b" on the dividers.
5. Enter **data-icon="plus"** in List Entry Attributes, to change the default right arrow icon with a plus icon.
6. In Text Formatting, type: **<h3>&PRODUCT_NAME.</h3><p>&PRODUCT_DESCRIPTION.</p>**
7. In Supplemental Information, type: **Price:$&LIST_PRICE.**
8. Put a check on **Show List Divider** and select the **CATEGORY** column in List Divider Column to group products under their relevant categories. Apply changes and run the page to see an output similar to Figure 11-13.

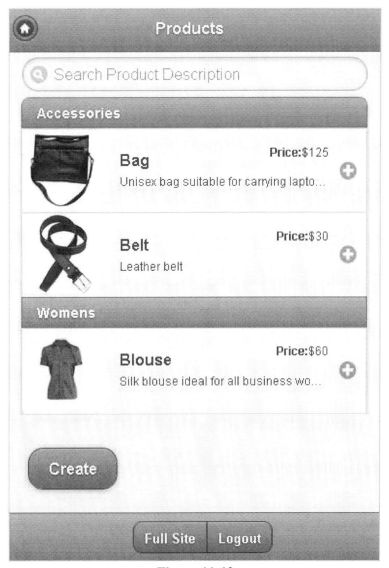

Figure 11-13

Chapter 11 – Smartphone and Mobile Development

11.10 Create Maintain Product Page - Page 204

1. In Application 101 interface, click on **Create Page** button.
2. Select the second option – **jQuery Mobile Smartphone**. Click on the **Form** icon to move forward.
3. Select the option – **Form on a Table or View**.
4. Select the schema **ASA** for Table/View Owner and **DEMO_PRODUCT_INFO** table from Table/View Name.
5. Enter **204** in Page Number, **Maintain Product** in Page Name and Region Title, and leave Region Template to the default value Plain (No Title). Also, do not add breadcrumb and click **Next**.
6. For Primary Key Type, select **Managed by Database (ROWID)** option.
7. Select **all** columns from the table except MIMETYPE, FILENAME, IMAGE_LAST_UPDATE, and PRODUCT_IMAGE. Click **Next**.
8. Keep **all** the default options on the Buttons page and move on.
9. On the Branching page, enter **203** for both After Page Submit and When Cancel Button Pressed.
10. Click **Create** on the Confirm page.
11. Click **Edit Page**.

11.10.1 Modify Items

Modify attributes of the page items as shown in the following table:

ITEM	ATTRIBUTE:VALUE	ATTRIBUTE:VALUE	ATTRIBUTE:VALUE
P204_PRODUCT_ID	Display As : Hidden		
P204_PRODUCT_NAME	Label : Product	Template : Required	Value Required : Yes
P204_LIST_PRICE	Label : List Price	Template : Required	Value Required : Yes
P204_PRODUCT_DESCRIPTION	Sequence : 130		
P204_TAGS	Display As : Text Field		

Call **P204_CATEGORY** item's attributes. Change Display As from Text Field to **Select List**, set Template to **Required**, Label to **Category**, Value Required to **Yes**, Named LOV to **CATEGORIES** and Apply Changes.

Call **P204_PRODUCT_AVAIL** attributes. Change Display As from Text Field to **Yes/No**, Label to **Product Available**, Value Required to **Yes**, and Apply Changes. Recall that in chapter 6 section 6.4.4, we attached the Y or N LOV to the Product Available item in the desktop application. This time, we have used the built-in alternate.

11.11 Test Your Work

Run the module using the Products link in the main mobile menu. Click on the Business Shirt link. What you'll see will be similar to the following output.

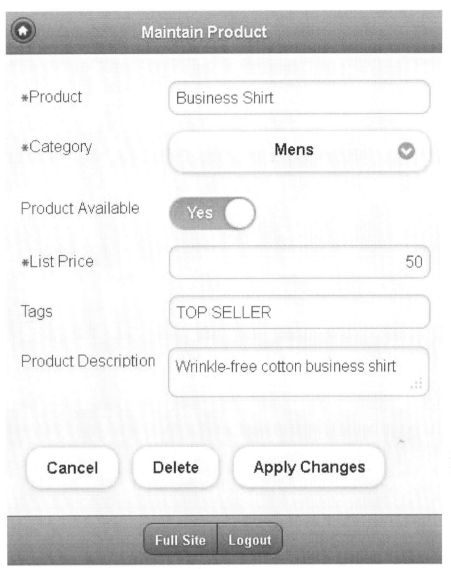

Figure 11-14

11.12 Create Orders and Order Detail Pages 205/206

For desktop version you used Master Detail Form option to simultaneously create Orders (Page 4) and Order Details (Page 29) pages. Since Master-Detail option is not available for mobile platform, you'll use another option provided for this platform: Form on a Table with Report. Just like the desktop version, this option will also create a main report with a corresponding form to show details of the selected order. Let's give it a try.

1. Click on **Create Page** button.
2. Select the option – **jQuery Mobile Smartphone** and click on the **Form** icon.
3. Click on the option: **Form on a Table with Report**.
4. Fill in the Report Page as shown below:

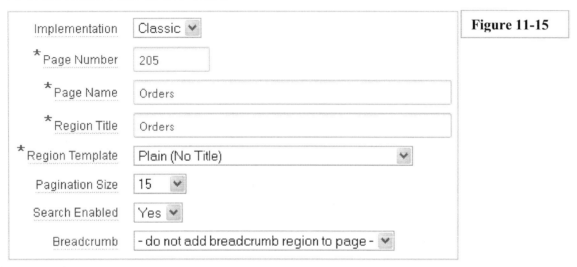

Figure 11-15

5. Select **DEMO_ORDERS** table in Data Source.
6. In Report Columns, select all columns and click **Next**.
7. Click **Next** to accept the default Edit Link Image.
8. Complete the Form page as below:

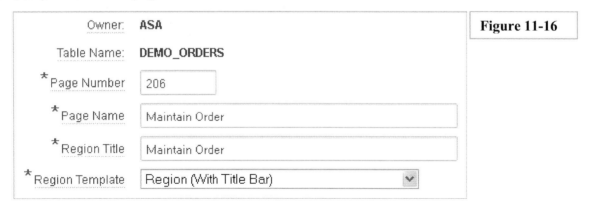

Figure 11-16

9. On the next page select **Managed by Database (ROWID)** for Primary Key Type.
10. Select all the columns from the DEMO_ORDERS table to include in the form page.
11. Set Yes for Insert, Update, and Delete processes.
12. Click the **Create** and then the **Edit Page** button to call Page 205 definitions.

11.12.1 Modify Region - Orders (Page 205)

1. Click on the **Orders** link in the Regions section.
2. In Region Source replace the existing SQL Query with the following one and apply changes:

   select o.rowid,
          o.order_id,
          TO_CHAR(o.order_timestamp,'Mon') order_date,
          o.order_total,
          c.cust_last_name || ', ' || c.cust_first_name customer_name,
          (select count(*) from demo_order_items oi where oi.order_id = o.order_id) order_items
   from   demo_orders o, demo_customers c
   where o.customer_id = c.customer_id

3. Click the **Report** link in the Regions section.
4. Edit the **ORDER_ID** column.
5. Scroll down to the Column Link section. Enter **#ORDER_ID#** in Link Text. Set Target to **Page in this Application**, enter **206** in Page, **P206_ROWID** in Item 1 and **#ROWID#** in Value and Apply Changes. Set meaningful column headings, alignment, Show, and Sort attributes so that the output of the page looks similar to Figure 11-17 below. The ORDER_ID column will be rendered as a link to call Order Details page (Page 208).

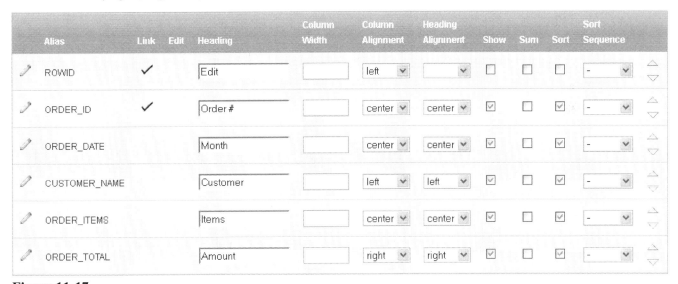

Figure 11-17

11.12.2 Modify Button - Create (Page 205)

1. Modify the sole button (Create) on this page by clicking its link, to set the following attributes. Page 216 is the first page in the order wizard – to be created in section 11.14.

    Text Label: **Enter New Order**

    Button Position: **Bottom of Region**

    Button Alignment: **Left**

    Button Type: **Hot**

    Action: **Redirect to Page in this Application**

    Page: **216**

    Clear Cache: **216**

Run this page to see the following output:

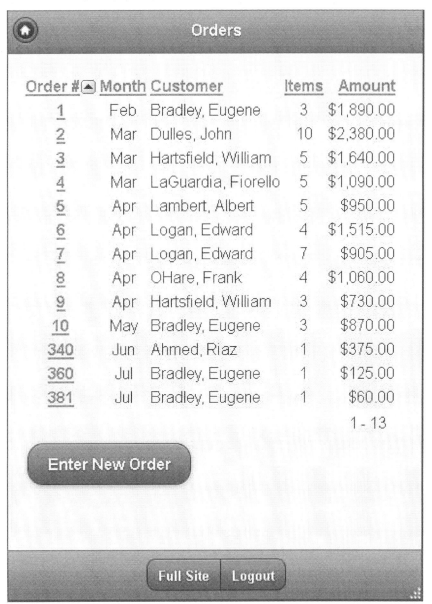

Figure 11-18

11.12.3 Modify/Create Region - Maintain Order (Page 206)

1. Modify the **Maintain Order** region and enter Order #&P206_ORDER_ID. in Title.
2. Click **Create** in the Regions section to add a new region. This region is created to display line item details.
3. Select **Report**.
4. Select **List View**.
5. Set the following values in Display Attributes:

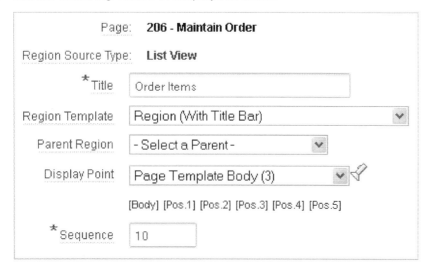

Figure 11-19

6. In Region Source, enter the following query. Also add **P206_ORDER_ID** to Page Items to Submit. This attribute is used to enter a comma separated list of page items on the current page to be set into session state.

```
select oi.order_item_id,
       pi.product_name,
       oi.unit_price,
       oi.quantity,
       to_char((oi.unit_price * oi.quantity), 'FML999G999G999G999G990D00') extended_price,
       pi.product_id,
       pi.product_image product_image
  from DEMO_ORDER_ITEMS oi, DEMO_PRODUCT_INFO pi
 where oi.ORDER_ID = :P206_ORDER_ID
   and oi.product_id = pi.product_id
```

7. Set values in the Settings page as shown in Figure 11-20. In Link Target, enter:

   f?p=&APP_ID.:207:&APP_SESSION.::&DEBUG.:RP,207:P207_ORDER_ITEM_ID:&ORDER_ITEM_ID.

8. Click the **Create Region** button.

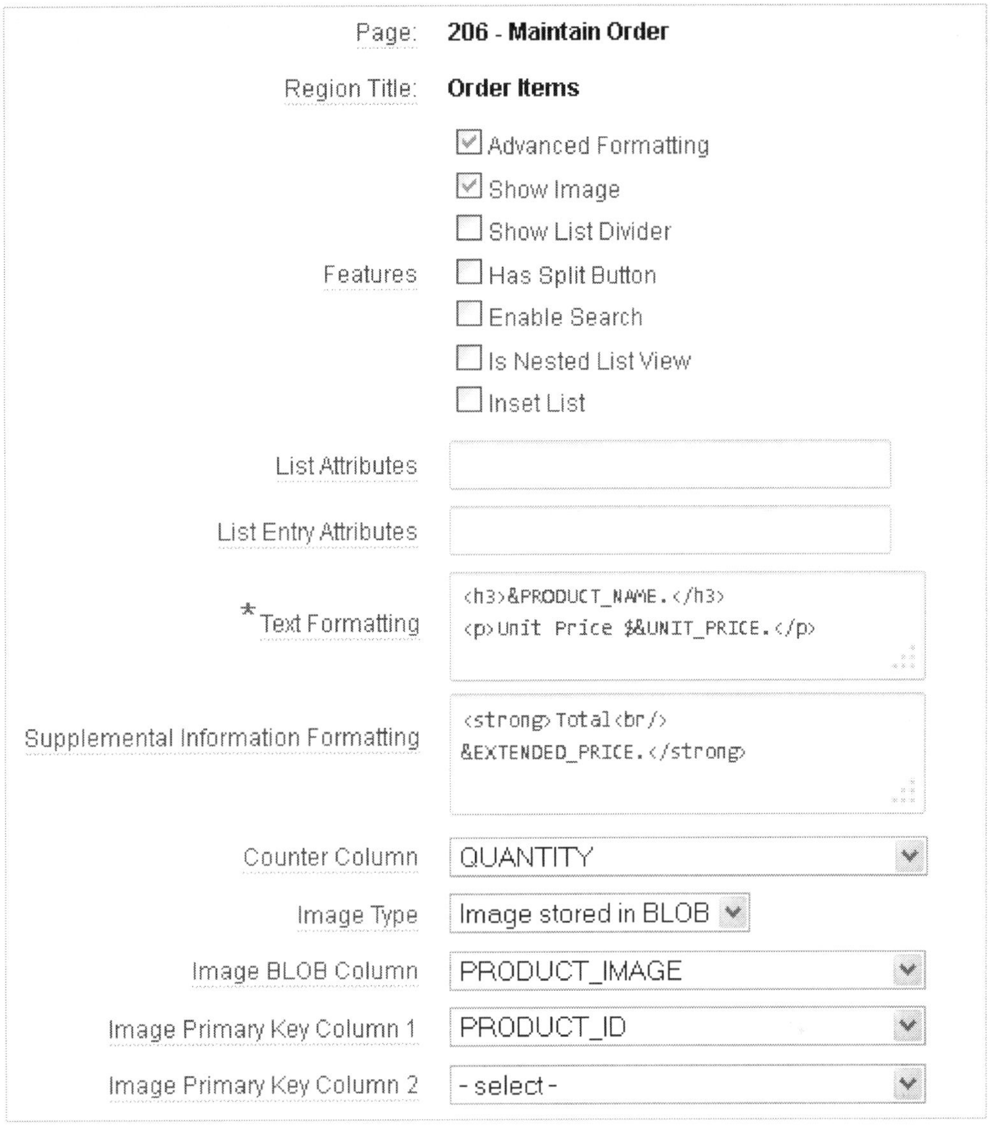

Page:	**206 - Maintain Order**
Region Title:	**Order Items**
Features	☑ Advanced Formatting ☑ Show Image ☐ Show List Divider ☐ Has Split Button ☐ Enable Search ☐ Is Nested List View ☐ Inset List
List Attributes	
List Entry Attributes	
*Text Formatting	`<h3>&PRODUCT_NAME.</h3>` `<p>Unit Price $&UNIT_PRICE.</p>`
Supplemental Information Formatting	`<strong>Total ` `&EXTENDED_PRICE.</strong>`
Counter Column	QUANTITY
Image Type	Image stored in BLOB
Image BLOB Column	PRODUCT_IMAGE
Image Primary Key Column 1	PRODUCT_ID
Image Primary Key Column 2	- select -

Figure 11-20

NOTE: The Counter Column specifies the database column that contains the value to be displayed in the count bubble as shown in Figure 11-21. In that figure quantity for each item is displayed in a count bubble.

Chapter 11 – Smartphone and Mobile Development

11.12.4 Modify/Add Buttons

1. Modify the **Apply Changes** Button, and set the following attributes. When this button is clicked, the page is submitted with a database SQL Update action. This record insert process is executed only when the item P206_ORDER_ID is not null.

   Button Type: **Hot**

   Condition Type: **Value of Item/Column in Expression 1 Is NOT NULL**

   Expression 1: **P206_ORDER_ID**

2. Add a new button with the following attributes. This button will call a separate page (Page 207) to add a line item to an existing order. A different approach is adopted here because Tabular Forms are not supported in mobile applications.

   Region: **Order Items**

   Position: **Create a button in a region position**

   Button Name: **ADD_ITEM**

   Label: **Add Item**

   Button Style: **Template Based Button**

   Button Template: **Inline Button**

   Button Type: **Normal**

   Position: **Bottom of Region**

   Alignment: **Left**

   Action: **Redirect to Page in this Application**

   Page: **207**

   Clear Cache: **207**

   Set these items: **P207_ORDER_ID**

   With these values: **&P206_ORDER_ID.**

11.12.5 Modify/Add Items

1. Modify the following page items:
    - P206_ORDER_ID – Value Protected: **Yes**
    - P206_CUSTOMER_ID – Display As: **Hidden**
    - P206_ORDER_TOTAL – Display As: **Display Only**, Sequence: **50**
    - P206_ORDER_TIMESTAMP – Display As: **Display Only**, Sequence: **60**, Label: **Order Date**, Format Mask: **MM-DD-YYYY**
    - P206_USER_NAME – Display As: **Select List**, Sequence: **70**, Label: **User**, Display Extra Values: **No**. In List of Values Definitions, enter the following SQL statement. You created LOVs in the Shared Component chapter with static Display and Return values. To remind you, values defined as Display are shown in page items e.g. a Select List, and are displayed in the order entered. A Return Value doesn't display, but is the values that is returned as a user selection to the Application Express engine. If you do not specify a Return Value then it is equal to the Display Value. In this step, you have applied another technique to attach values to a Select List item without first creating it in the Shared Component interface. The first SELECT statement gets user names from the DEMO_ORDERS table to show only the users who added records to the table. The second SELECT statement fetches user name from the current session to add this name to the select list. It is done because the current user might me new, and may not have an entry recorded in his/her name in the DEMO_ORDERS table. In a nutshell, this technique demonstrates how to merge table and session state data for display.

        select distinct user_name d, user_name r from demo_orders
        union
        select upper(:APP_USER) d, upper(:APP_USER) r from dual
        order by 1
    - P206_TAGS – Display As: **Text Field**, Sequence: **80**

2. Add a new item. This item will hold complete customer information (name and address), and will be displayed in the Order #&P206_ORDER_ID region, as illustrated in Figure 11-21.

    Item Type: **Display Only**
    Item Name: **P206_CUSTOMER_INFO**
    Sequence: **40**
    Region: **Order #&P206_ORDER_ID.**
    Label: **Customer**
    Source Type: **SQL Query (return single value)**
    Item Source Value:
    select htf.escape_sc(cust_first_name) || ' ' || htf.escape_sc(cust_last_name) || ' : ' ||
    htf.escape_sc(cust_street_address1) || decode(cust_street_address2, null, null, ' ' ||
    htf.escape_sc(cust_street_address2)) || ', ' || htf.escape_sc(cust_city) || ', ' ||
    htf.escape_sc(cust_state) || ' ' || htf.escape_sc(cust_postal_code) from demo_customers where
    customer_id = :P206_CUSTOMER_ID

Chapter 11 – Smartphone and Mobile Development

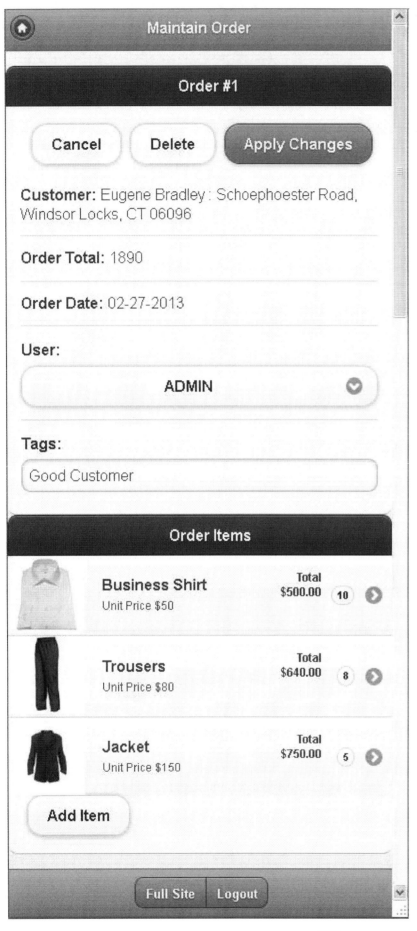

Test the order detail page you just created. In the main orders page, click any order number to call this page. I clicked Order # 1 and here is my output. If you try to add a new item, you can't. Because, the target page (Page 207) that is being called isn't ready to perform the operation. The next section will help you create this page.

Figure 11-21

11.13 Create Maintain Order Item Page 207

The wizard-generated Page 29 in the desktop version comprised a Tabular Form and was created to modify details of an order. That page helped you to:

- Delete an order
- Remove specific items from an order
- Add more items
- Change a product
- Change quantity of a product

In the mobile version, you can perform the first task (delete an order) through Page 206 and can change couple of master information such as User and Tags as well. But to perform the remaining operations, you need to create a separate page. The following section guides you how to create that page.

1. Click **Create Page** in Application Builder.
2. Select the option – **jQuery Mobile Smartphone** and click on the **Form** icon.
3. Click on the option: **Form on a Table or View** and add the following values:

   Table/View Name: DEMO_ORDER_ITEMS

   Page Number: 207

   Page Name: Maintain Order Item

   Region Title: Maintain Order Item

   Region Template: Region (With Title)

   Primary Key Type: Select Primary Key Column(s)

   Primary Key Column 1: ORDER_ITEM_ID

   Source Type: Existing sequence

   Sequence: DEMO_ORDER_ITEMS_SEQ

   Select Column(s): Select all columns

   Buttons Page: Select all default values

   After Page Submit: 206

   When Cancel Button: 206

4. Modify region *Maintain Order Item* and set its Title to **Order #&P207_ORDER_ID.** (with the terminating period).

Chapter 11 – Smartphone and Mobile Development

11.13.1 Modify Buttons

1. Modify **Cancel** button as follows:

    Button Position: **Bottom of Region**
    Button Alignment: **Left**

2. Modify **Delete** button as follows:

    Button Position: **Bottom of Region**
    Button Alignment: **Left**

3. Click the **Apply Changes** Button link and set the following attributes:

    Button Position: **Bottom of Region**
    Button Alignment: **Left**
    Button Type: **Hot**

11.13.2 Modify Items

1. Modify **P207_ORDER_ID** item as follows:

    Display As: **Hidden**

2. Modify **P207_PRODUCT_ID** and set values as follows:

    Display As: **Select List**
    Label: **Product**
    Display Extra Value: **No**
    Display Null Value: **– Select –**
    Cascading LOV Parent Item(s): **P207_ORDER_ID,P207_ORDER_ITEM_ID**
    List of values definition:

    >   select product_name d, product_id r
    >   from demo_product_info pi
    >   where pi.product_avail = 'Y'
    >   and   pi.product_id not in (select oi.product_id from demo_order_items oi
    >   where oi.order_id = :P207_ORDER_ID and
    >   oi.order_item_id <> nvl(:P207_ORDER_ITEM_ID,0)
    >   )
    >   order by 1

    In this step you're using a technique to eliminate inclusion of products to the list that are already on the order. A cascading LOV means that the current item's list of values should be refreshed if the value of another item on this page gets changed. It receives a comma separated list of page items to trigger the refresh. You then used these page items in the where clause of "List of Values" SQL statement. Suppose you have page items for Car Make and Model, Model would identify Car Make as the Cascading LOV Parent Item so that whenever Car Make is changed, the LOV for Model would be refreshed. In the current scenario, the ORDER_ID item represents Car Make while, ORDER_ITEM_ID acts as Car Model which gets refreshed with each order.

3. Modify **P207_QUANTITY** item as follows. It shows how to declare static display;return values (from 1 to 10, where each pair is separated by a comma), to get ordered quantity. This technique shows how to apply minimum/maximum input limit.

    Display As: **Select List**
    Display Extra Values: **No**
    List of values definition: **STATIC2:1;1,2;2,3;3,4;4,5;5,6;6,7;7,8;8,9;9,10;10**

> **NOTE:** The static list of values on the previous page was defined using the following syntax:
> *STATIC[2]:Display Value[;Return Value],Display Value[;Return Value]*
> Where:
> - The first keyword may be STATIC or STATIC2. STATIC results in the values being sorted alphabetically by display value. STATIC2 results in the values being displayed in the order they are entered in the list.
> - A semicolon separates the display value from the return value in each entry.
> - Return Value is optional. If a Return Value is not included, the return value equals the display value.

11.13.3 Create Dynamic Action - Get List Price

At this stage, if the page is run, you'll notice that after selecting a product the Unit Price column doesn't show anything. To automatically populate this field with the corresponding price, you need to create a dynamic action as described in the following step.

1. Click **Create** in the Dynamic Actions section and set the following values:
   Name: **Get List Price**
   Event: **Change**
   Selection Type: **Item(s)**
   Item(s): **P207_PRODUCT_ID**
   Action: **Set Value**
   Fire On Page Load: **Uncheck**
   Set Type: **SQL Statement**
   SQL Statement: **select list_price from demo_product_info where product_id = :P207_PRODUCT_ID**
   Page Items to Submit: **P207_PRODUCT_ID**
   Selection Type: **Item(s)**
   Item(s): **P207_UNIT_PRICE** – You'll have to move the item P207_UNIT_PRICE from the left pane to the right. This page element is the one you would like the dynamic action to control. After moving the item, click the **Create Dynamic Action** button to finish the wizard.

Run the page to see the output similar to the Figure 11-22. Play around with the pages created so far and check the five functionalities mentioned at the start of this section.

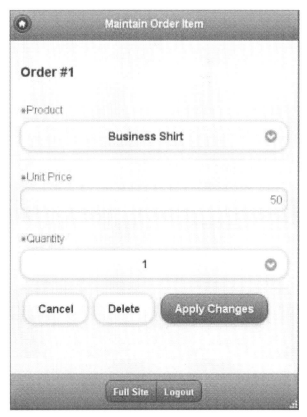

Figure 11-22

11.14 Create Order Page 216

In the desktop version we created a wizard to record customer orders. Here too, you'll adopt the same process to enter an order sequentially. In the desktop module, the first page that appeared after clicking the Enter New Order button was Page 11, where you allowed users to select an existing customer, or to create a new one. To save some time, you'll copy that page for the mobile module. Let's see how it is done.

1. In Application 101 interface, click the link **Enter New Order** representing Page11.
2. Click the **Create** menu button to your right and select **New page as a copy**. Recall that you used this technique earlier to create Page 11 from Page 7.
3. Select the option **Page in this application**.
4. In Page to Copy, set the following attributes. Note that this time we are using the jQuery Mobile Smartphone option for the User Interface.

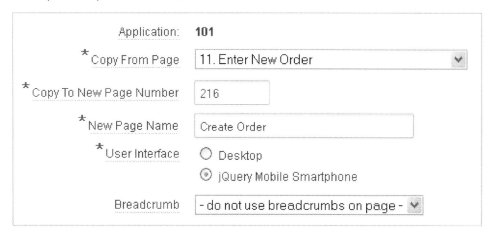

Figure 11-23

5. Accept the default values in the New Names page and click **Next**.
6. Click **Finish** to create the page.
7. Click the **Edit Page** button.

If you run the page at this stage, you'll notice that it looks awkward and slinked to the right side of your screen. Modify different sections of the page as mentioned below, to make it appropriate for smartphone devices.

11.14.1 Modify Regions

1. Click the region **Identify Customer**.
2. In Grid Layout, set Start New Grid and Start New Row to **No**. Set Column to **1**. This setting will start the content from column 1, which was formerly set to 4.
3. **Apply Changes**.
4. Delete the **Breadcrumb** and **Order Progress** regions.
5. Modify the **Button** region. Set the attributes as follows and apply changes.

   Display Point: **Page Template Region Position 1**
   Template : No **Template**
   Start New Grid: **Yes**
   Column: **Automatic**

11.14.2 Modify Buttons

1. Click the **Cancel** Button link and set the following attributes:

   Button Position: **Bottom of Region**
   Button Alignment: **Left**
   Button Template: **Inline Button**
   Action: **Redirect to Page in this Application**
   Page: **205**

2. Click the **Next** Button link and set the following attributes:

   Button Position: **Bottom of Region**
   Button Alignment: **Right**
   Button Template: **Inline Button**
   Button Type: **Hot**

11.14.3 Modify Items

1. Modify the first item P216_CUSTOMER_OPTIONS and set the following attributes:

   Template: **Required**
   Start New Grid: **Yes**
   Column: **Automatic**
   Value Required: **Yes**
   Display Extra Values: **No**

2. Modify P216_CUSTOMER_ID and set these attributes:

   Display As: **Select List**
   Template: **Required**
   Display Extra Values: **No**
   Display Null Value: Yes
   Null Display Value: – **Select a Customer** –

3. Set Template to **Required** for the following five items:

   P216_CUST_FIRST_NAME, P216_CUST_LAST_NAME, P216_CUST_STATE,

   P216_CUST_POSTAL_CODE and P216_CREDIT_LIMIT.

4. Set Template to **Optional** for:

   P216_CUST_STREET_ADDRESS1, P216_CUST_STREET_ADDRESS2, P216_CUST_CITY,
   P216_CUST_EMAIL, P216_URL and P216_TAGS.

5. Modify P216_PHONE_NUMBER1 and P216_PHONE_NUMBER2 as follows:

   Display As: **Text Field**
   Template: **Optional**
   Subtype: **Phone Number**
   Submit when Enter pressed: **No**
   Disabled: **No**

6. Delete item P216_BRANCH.

Chapter 11 – Smartphone and Mobile Development

11.14.4 Modify Branch

Modify the sole branch under Page Processing like this:

Name: **Next**
Target Type: **Page in this Application**
Page: **217** (Also, clear values from Clear Cache, Set these items, and With these values)
When Button Pressed: **Next (Next)**

Apply changes and run the page using the main mobile menu route. After clicking the Enter New Order button, you'll see Figure 11-24. Click the second option, New Customer, to see the output shown in Figure 11-25.

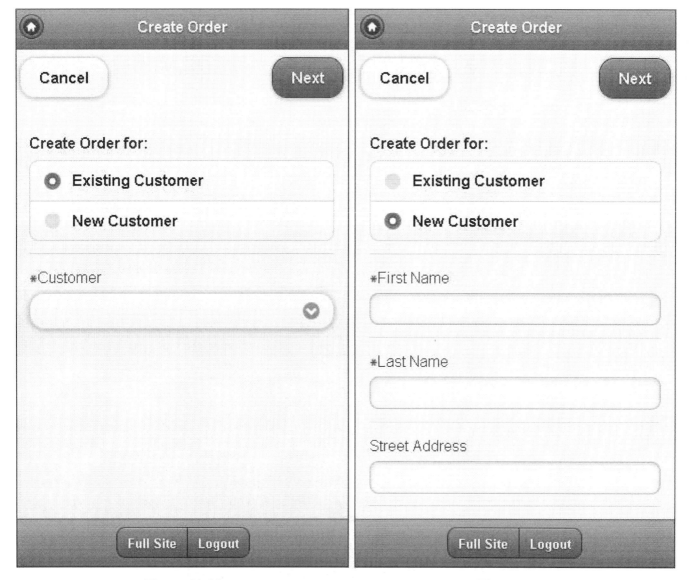

Figure 11-24   Figure 11-25

11.15 Create Select Order Items Page 217

Using the same copy utility, you'll create this page as well, to select order items. In the desktop version you created Page 12 for this purpose and this is the page you'll use as the source for your mobile application. The copied page will inherit all items and processes from the source.

1. In Application 101 interface, click the link **Select Order Items** representing Page12.
2. Click the **Create** menu button to your right and select **New page as a copy**.
3. Select the option **Page in this application**.
4. In Page to Copy, set the following attributes.

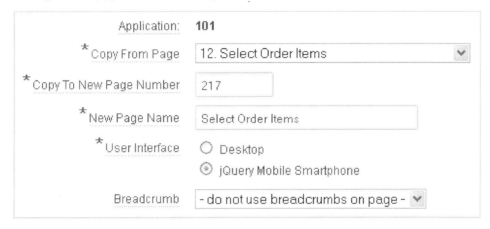

Figure 11-26

5. Accept the default values in the New Names page and click **Next**.
6. Click **Finish** to create the page.
7. Click the **Edit Page** button to modify different sections of the page, as directed hereunder.

11.15.1 Modify Regions

1. Click the region **Select Items** and set the following attributes:

   Template: **Region (With Title)**
   Start New Grid: **No**
   Start New Row: **No**
   Column: **Automatic**
   New Column: **No**

2. Modify region **Maximum Product Quantity** and apply the following settings:
   Start New Grid: **Yes**
   Column: **Automatic**

3. Delete the **Breadcrumb** and **Order Progress** regions.

4. Modify the **Button** region. Set the attributes as follows and apply changes.

   Display Point: **Page Template Region Position 1**
   Template : **No Template**
   Start New Grid: **Yes**
   Column: **Automatic**

333

Chapter 11 – Smartphone and Mobile Development

Enter the following code in the Region Source. Note that this code is similar to the desktop version (section 7.8.2) except for the items marked in bold, modified to represent current page items.

```
declare
  l_customer_id varchar2(30) := :P216_CUSTOMER_ID;
begin
-- display customer information
sys.htp.p('<div class="CustomerInfo">');
if :P216_CUSTOMER_OPTIONS = 'EXISTING' then
  for x in (select * from demo_customers where customer_id = l_customer_id) loop
    sys.htp.p('<div class="CustomerInfo">');
    sys.htp.p('<strong>Customer:</strong>');
    sys.htp.p('<p>');
    sys.htp.p(sys.htf.escape_sc(x.cust_first_name)||' '||sys.htf.escape_sc(x.cust_last_name)||'<br/>');
    sys.htp.p(sys.htf.escape_sc(x.cust_street_address1) || '<br />');
    if x.cust_street_address2 is not null then
      sys.htp.p(sys.htf.escape_sc(x.cust_street_address2) || '<br />');
    end if;
    sys.htp.p(sys.htf.escape_sc(x.cust_city) || ', ' || sys.htf.escape_sc(x.cust_state) || ' ' ||
    sys.htf.escape_sc(x.cust_postal_code));
    sys.htp.p('</p>');
  end loop;
else
  sys.htp.p('<strong>Customer:</strong>');
  sys.htp.p('<p>');
  sys.htp.p(sys.htf.escape_sc(:P216_CUST_FIRST_NAME)||' '||sys.htf.escape_sc(:P216_CUST_LAST_NAME)
  || '<br />');
  sys.htp.p(sys.htf.escape_sc(:P216_CUST_STREET_ADDRESS1) || '<br />');
  if :P216_CUST_STREET_ADDRESS2 is not null then
    sys.htp.p(sys.htf.escape_sc(:P216_CUST_STREET_ADDRESS2) || '<br />');
  end if;
  sys.htp.p(sys.htf.escape_sc(:P216_CUST_CITY) || ', ' ||
  sys.htf.escape_sc(:P216_CUST_STATE) || ' ' ||
  sys.htf.escape_sc(:P216_CUST_POSTAL_CODE));
  sys.htp.p('</p>');
end if;
sys.htp.p('</div>');
-- display products
sys.htp.p('<div class="Products" >');
sys.htp.p('<table width="100%" cellspacing="0" cellpadding="0" border="0">
<thead>
<tr><th class="left">Product</th><th>Price</th><th></th></tr>
</thead>
<tbody>');
for c1 in (select product_id, product_name, list_price, 'Add to Cart' add_to_order
from demo_product_info
where product_avail = 'Y'
order by product_name) loop
sys.htp.p('<tr><td class="left">' ||
sys.htf.escape_sc(c1.product_name)||'</td><td>'||trim(to_char(c1.list_price,'999G999G990D00'))||
  '</td><td><a
            href="'||apex_util.prepare_url('f?p=&APP_ID.:217:'||:app_session
```

```
                    ||':ADD:::P217_PRODUCT_ID:'||c1.product_id)||'"
                class="uButton"><span>Add</span></a></td></tr>');
end loop;
sys.htp.p('</tbody></table>');
sys.htp.p('</div>');
-- display current order
sys.htp.p('<div class="Products" >');
sys.htp.p('<table width="100%" cellspacing="0" cellpadding="0" border="0">
<thead>
<tr><th class="left">Current Order</th></tr>
</thead>
</table>
<table width="100%" cellspacing="0" cellpadding="0" border="0">
<tbody>');
declare
    c number := 0; t number := 0;
begin
-- loop over cart values
for c1 in (select c001 pid, c002 i, to_number(c003) p, count(c002) q, sum(c003) ep, 'Remove' remove
from apex_collections
where collection_name = 'ORDER'
group by c001, c002, c003
order by c002)
loop
sys.htp.p('<div class="CartItem"><a href="'||
apex_util.prepare_url('f?p=&APP_ID.:217:&SESSION.:REMOVE:::P217_PRODUCT_ID:'||sys.htf.escape_sc(c1.pid))||'"><img src="#IMAGE_PREFIX#delete.gif" alt="Remove from cart" title="Remove from cart" /></a>  
'||sys.htf.escape_sc(c1.i)||'
<span>'||trim(to_char(c1.p,'$999G999G999D00'))||'</span>
<span>Quantity: '||c1.q||'</span>
<span class="subtotal">Subtotal: '||trim(to_char(c1.ep,'$999G999G999D00'))||'</span>
</div>');
   c := c + 1;
   t := t + c1.ep;
end loop;
sys.htp.p('</tbody></table>');
if c > 0 then
    sys.htp.p('<div class="CartTotal">
    <p>Items: <span>'||c||'</span></p>
    <p class="CartTotal">Total: <span>'||trim(to_char(t,'$999G999G999D00'))||'</span></p>
</div>');
else
    sys.htp.p('<p class="CartTotal">You have no items in your current order.</p>');
end if;
end;
sys.htp.p('</div>');
end;
```

Chapter 11 – Smartphone and Mobile Development

11.15.2 Modify Buttons

1. Click the **Cancel** Button link and set the following attributes:

    Button Position: **Bottom of Region**
    Button Alignment: **Left**
    Button Template: **Inline Button**
    Action: **Redirect to Page in this Application**
    Page: **205**

2. Click the **Previous** Button link and set the following attributes:

    Button Position: **Bottom of Region**
    Button Alignment: **Left**
    Button Template: **Inline Button**
    Action: **Redirect to Page in this Application**
    Page: **205**
    Clear Cache: **217**

3. Click the **Place Order** Button link and set the following attributes:

    Button Name: **NEXT**
    Button Position: **Bottom of Region**
    Button Alignment: **Right**
    Button Template: **Inline Button**
    Button Type: **Hot**

11.15.3 Modify Items

1. Modify the first item **P217_CUSTOMER_NAME** and set the following attributes:

    Region: **Select Items**

2. Delete item **P217_BRANCH**.

11.15.4 After Submit Process

Modify Process Source in the Place Order process using the code provided below. This is the same PL/SQL procedure used in section 7.8.9 in the desktop module. Items marked in bold are modified in the code to reflect current page elements.

```
declare
    l_order_id    number;
    l_customer_id varchar2(30) := :P216_CUSTOMER_ID;
begin
    -- Create New Customer
    if :P216_CUSTOMER_OPTIONS = 'NEW' then
        insert into DEMO_CUSTOMERS (
            CUST_FIRST_NAME, CUST_LAST_NAME, CUST_STREET_ADDRESS1,
            CUST_STREET_ADDRESS2, CUST_CITY, CUST_STATE, CUST_POSTAL_CODE,
            CUST_EMAIL, PHONE_NUMBER1, PHONE_NUMBER2, URL, CREDIT_LIMIT, TAGS)
        values (
            :P216_CUST_FIRST_NAME, :P216_CUST_LAST_NAME, :P216_CUST_STREET_ADDRESS1,
            :P216_CUST_STREET_ADDRESS2, :P216_CUST_CITY, :P216_CUST_STATE,
            :P216_CUST_POSTAL_CODE, :P216_CUST_EMAIL, :P216_PHONE_NUMBER1,
            :P216_PHONE_NUMBER2, :P216_URL, :P216_CREDIT_LIMIT, :P216_TAGS)
        returning customer_id into l_customer_id;
        :P216_CUSTOMER_ID := l_customer_id;
    end if;
    -- Insert a row into the Order Header table
    insert into demo_orders(customer_id, order_total, order_timestamp, user_name)
    values(l_customer_id, null, systimestamp, upper(:APP_USER)) returning order_id into l_order_id;
    commit;
    -- Loop through the ORDER collection and insert rows into the Order Line Item table
    for x in (select c001, c003, sum(c004) c004 from apex_collections
              where collection_name = 'ORDER' group by c001, c003)
    loop
        insert into demo_order_items(order_item_id, order_id, product_id, unit_price, quantity)
        values (null, l_order_id, to_number(x.c001), to_number(x.c003),to_number(x.c004));
    end loop;
    commit;
    -- Set the item P218_ORDER_ID to the order which was just placed
    :P218_ORDER_ID := l_order_id;
    -- Truncate the collection after the order has been placed
    apex_collection.truncate_collection(p_collection_name => 'ORDER');
end;
```

11.15.5 Modify Branch

1. Modify the first branch represented by Sequence number 10 like this:
   Name: **Next**
   Target Type: **Page in this Application**
   Page: **218**
   When Button Pressed: **Next (Place Order)**
2. Remove branches **Go To Page 4** and **Branch To Page Identified By Item**.

Chapter 11 – Smartphone and Mobile Development

11.16 Create Order Summary Page 218

Again, use the page copy utility to create Order Summary page from Page 14 of the desktop application.

1. In Application 101 interface, click the link **Order Summary** representing Page14.
2. Click the **Create** menu button and select **New page as a copy**.
3. Select the option **Page in this application**.
4. In Page to Copy, set the following attributes.

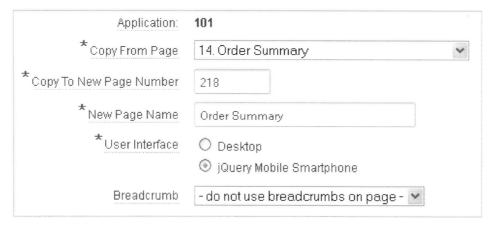

Figure 11-27

5. Accept the default values in the New Names page and click **Next**.
6. Click **Finish** to create the page.
7. Click the **Edit Page** button to modify different sections of the page to fine-tune it for the mobile platform.

11.16.1 Modify Regions

1. Click the **Order Summary** region and set the following attributes:

   Template: **Region (With Title)**
   Start New Grid: **No**
   Start New Row: **No**
   Column: **1**

2. Click the **Order Header** region.

   Template: **No Template**
   Start New Grid: **No**
   Start New Row: **No**
   Column: **1**

3. Modify the **Order Lines** region as follows:

   Start New Grid: **No**
   Start New Row: **No**
   Column: **1**

4. Delete the **Breadcrumb** and **Order Progress** regions.

5. Modify the **Button** region. Set the attributes as follows and apply changes.

   Display Point: **Page Template Region Position 1**
   Template: **No Template**
   Start New Grid: **Yes**
   Column: **Automatic**

11.16.2 Modify Button

1. Click the **View Orders** Button link and set the following attributes:

   Button Position: **Bottom of Region**
   Button Alignment: **Left**
   Button Template: **Inline Button**
   Button Type: **Hot**
   Action: **Redirect to Page in this Application**
   Page: **205**

11.16.3 Modify Item

1. Modify the sole page item **P218_ORDER_ID** and set the following attributes:

   Region: **Order Summary**

Chapter 11 – Smartphone and Mobile Development

11.17 Test Your Work

Run the module using the Orders link in the main mobile menu. Click the button Enter New Order. Select an existing customer and click Next. Select some items using the Add link and click the Place Order button. The Order Summary page as illustrated in Figure 11-28 should come up displaying summary of the most recent order. Click the View Orders button to move back to the main orders listing where you'll see this order added to the list. Create another order using the New Customer option.

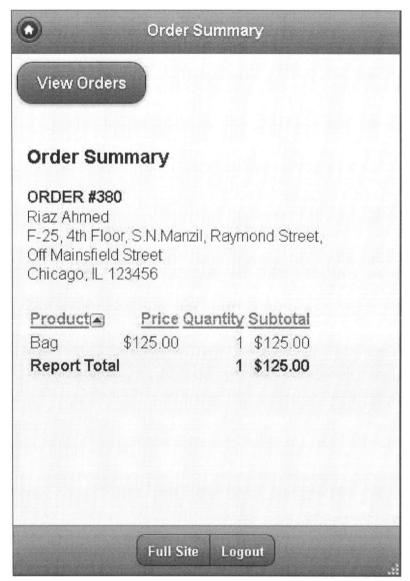

Figure 11-28

Display Reports on Smartphones

11.18 List of Reports Page 208

This is the main reports navigation page for smartphone platform carrying a list of available reports. It is almost similar to the one you went through in the desktop version.

1. Click **Create Page** in Application Builder.
2. Select the option **jQuery Mobile Smartphone** and click on the **Blank Page** icon.
3. Enter **208** in Page Number and click **Next**.
4. Enter **Reports** in Name, click **Next** and then the **Finish** button.
5. Click on **Edit Page**.
6. Create a new Region.
7. Select the **List** option.
8. Enter **Charts** in Title and click Next.
9. For List, select **Mobile Reports List** and for List Template, select **List View (Inset)**. Click **Next** and then **Create Region**.

11.19 Customer Orders Report - Page 209

The reports you'll be creating in this section are the same you created earlier in chapter 8. Starting with the Customer Orders Report, let's see how graphical reports are created for smartphones.

1. Create a new page.
2. Select **jQuery Mobile Smartphone** and then click on the **Blank Page** icon.
3. Enter **209** in Page Number, click **Next**.
4. Enter **Customer Orders** in the name box and click **Next**.
5. Click **Finish**.
6. Click **Edit Page** icon.

11.19.1 Create Region - Customer Orders

1. Click the **Create** button in the Regions section.
2. Click **Chart**.
3. Select the **Horizontal Bar** option.
4. Click on **2D Stacked Bar Chart**.

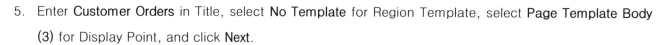

5. Enter **Customer Orders** in Title, select **No Template** for Region Template, select **Page Template Body (3)** for Display Point, and click **Next**.
6. In Display Attributes, enter axis titles and mark other options as shown below and click **Next**.

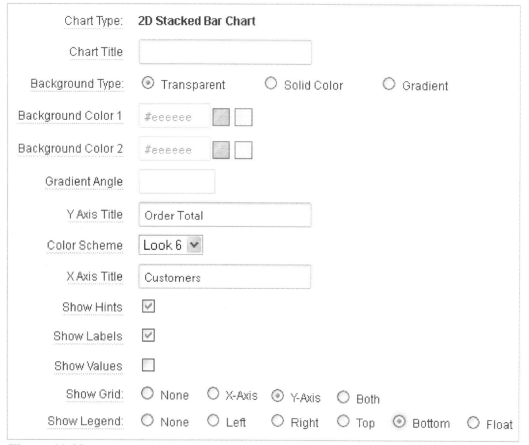

Figure 11-29

7. In Enter SQL Query type the following statement:

```
select c.rowid link,
    c.cust_last_name||', '||c.cust_first_name Customer_Name,
    sum (decode(p.category,'Accessories',oi.quantity * oi.unit_price,0)) "Accessories",
    sum (decode(p.category,'Mens',oi.quantity * oi.unit_price,0)) "Mens",
    sum (decode(p.category,'Womens',oi.quantity * oi.unit_price,0)) "Womens"
from demo_customers c, demo_orders o, demo_order_items oi, demo_product_info p
where c.customer_id = o.customer_id
and   o.order_id = oi.order_id
and   oi.product_id = p.product_id
group by c.rowid, c.customer_id, c.cust_last_name, c.cust_first_name
order by c.cust_last_name
```

8. Click **Create Region**.
9. Click **Customer Orders** link in Regions to modify couple of attributes.
10. Click the **Chart Attributes** tab.
11. Click the edit link ✏ in the Chart Series section. Scroll Down to the Action Link section, set the following attribute values and Apply Changes. After creating the report, when you click on any customer's link, Page 202 – Maintain Customer is called that lets you see and modify record of the selected customer.
    Action Link: **Link to Custom Target**
    Target: **Page in this Application**
    Page: **202**
    Clear Cache: **202**
    Item 1: **P202_ROWID**
    Value: **#LINK#**
12. On the Chart Attributes tab, scroll down to Legend Settings, enter **Categories** in Legend Title and select **Horizontal** for Legend Element Layout.
13. Click **Apply Changes** and **Run** the page see the output similar to Figure 11-30.

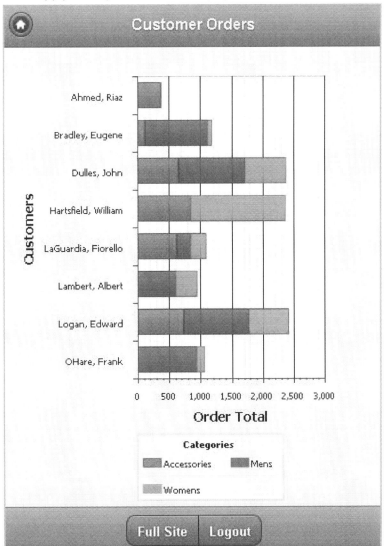

Figure 11-30

NOTE: The #LINK# value in the Value attribute, references the first column named link in the SELECT statement. This chart is created with drill-down functionality. Clicking a bar takes you to Maintain Customer page (Page 202), as defined in step 11.

Chapter 11 – Smartphone and Mobile Development

11.20 Sales by Category and Product - Page 210

This report was created earlier in the desktop application in chapter 8 section 8.4.

1. Create a new page.
2. Select **jQuery Mobile Smartphone** and then click on the **Blank Page** icon.
3. Enter **210** in Page Number. Click **Next**.
4. Enter **Sales by Category and Product** in the name box and click **Next**.
5. Click **Finish**.
6. Click **Edit Page** icon.

11.20.1 Create Region - Sales by Category

1. Click the **Create** button in the Regions section.
2. Click **Chart**.
3. Select the option **Pie and Doughnut**.
4. Click on **3D Pie**.
5. Enter **Sales by Category** in Title, select **Region (With Title Bar)** for Region Template, select **Page Template Body (3)** for Display Point, and click **Next**.

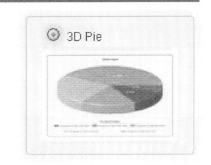

6. In Display Attributes, select chart options as shown in Figure 11-31 and click **Next**.

Figure 11-31

7. In Enter SQL Query, type the following statement:
   ```
   select null, p.category label, sum(o.order_total)
   from demo_orders o, demo_order_items oi, demo_product_info p
   where o.order_id = oi.order_id
   and oi.product_id = p.product_id
   group by category order by 3 desc
   ```

8. Click **Create Region**.
9. Modify the region. Click the **Chart Attributes** tab.
10. Set Chart Width to **400** and Height to **200** and Apply Changes.

11.20.2 Create Region - Sales by Product

1. Create a second region on the same page.
2. Click Chart.
3. Select the option Horizontal Bar.
4. Click on 2D Bar Chart.
5. Enter Sales by Product in Title, select Region (With Title Bar) for Region Template, select Page Template Body (3) for Display Point, and click Next.

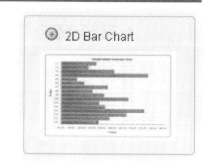

6. In Display Attributes, set the following values and click Next.

Figure 11-32

7. In Enter SQL Query type the following statement:
   ```
   select p.rowid link,
          p.product_name||' [$'||p.list_price||']' product, SUM(oi.quantity * oi.unit_price) sales
   from demo_order_items oi,   demo_product_info p
   where oi.product_id = p.product_id
   group by p.rowid, p.product_id, p.product_name, p.list_price
   order by p.product_name
   ```
8. Click Create Region.
9. Modify the region. Click the Chart Attributes tab.
10. Set Chart Width to 400, Height to 300, and Apply Changes.
11. Click the edit link in the Chart Series section. Scroll Down to the Action Link section, set the following attribute values and Apply Changes. At runtime, when you click any product's link, Page 204 – Maintain Product comes up, where you can see details of the selected product and can even modify that record.
    Action Link: Link to Custom Target
    Target: Page in this Application
    Page: 204
    Clear Cache: 204
    Item 1: P204_ROWID
    Value: #LINK#

12. Run the page to see the output as illustrated in Figure 11-33.

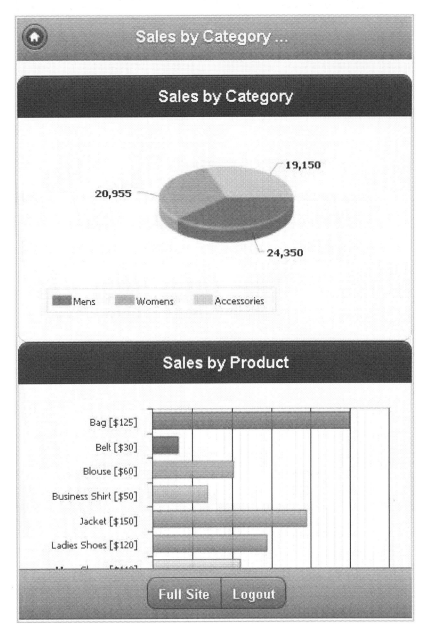

Figure 11-33

Chapter 11 – Smartphone and Mobile Development

11.21 Sales by Category / Month - Page 211

The desktop version of this report was created in chapter 8 section 8.5.
1. Create a new page.
2. Select **jQuery Mobile Smartphone** and then click on the **Blank Page** icon.
3. Enter **211** in Page Number and click **Next**.
4. Enter **Sales by Category / Month** in the name box and click **Next**.
5. Click **Finish**.
6. Click **Edit Page** icon.

11.21.1 Create Region - Sales by Category / Month

1. Click **Create** in the Regions section.
2. Click **Chart**.
3. Select the **Column** option.
4. Click on **2D Stacked Column**.
5. Enter **Sales by Category / Month** in Title, select **Region (With Title Bar)** for Region Template, select **Page Template Body (3)** for Display Point, and click **Next**.

6. In Display Attributes, enter titles and select options as shown below and click **Next**.

Figure 11-34

7. In Enter SQL Query type the following statement:
   select null, to_char(o.order_timestamp, 'MON RRRR') label,
       sum (decode(p.category,'Accessories',oi.quantity * oi.unit_price,0)) "Accessories",
       sum (decode(p.category,'Mens',oi.quantity * oi.unit_price,0)) "Mens",
       sum (decode(p.category,'Womens',oi.quantity * oi.unit_price,0)) "Womens"
   from demo_product_info p, demo_order_items oi, demo_orders o
   where oi.product_id = p.product_id
   and o.order_id = oi.order_id
   group by to_char(o.order_timestamp, 'MON RRRR'), to_char(o.order_timestamp, 'RRRR MM')
   order by to_char(o.order_timestamp, 'RRRR MM')
8. Click **Create Region**.
9. Modify the region. Click the **Chart Attributes** tab.
10. Set Chart Width to **400**, Height to **200**, and Apply Changes.
11. Run the page to see the report illustrated in Figure 11-35.

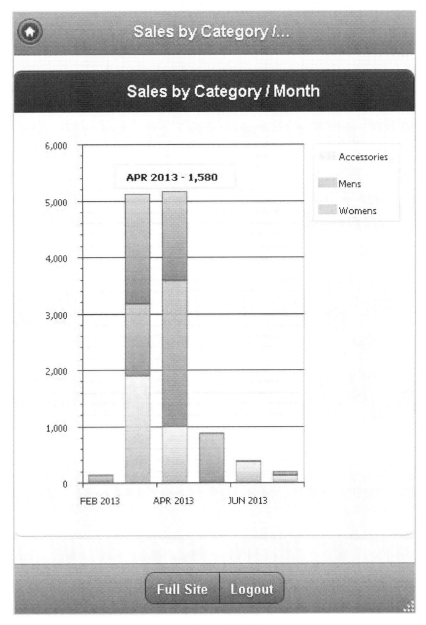

Figure 11-35

11.22 Order Calendar - Page 212

You created the desktop version of Order Calendar in chapter 8 section 8.6.

1. Create a new page.
2. Select **jQuery Mobile Smartphone** and then click on the **Calendar** icon.
3. Select **SQL Calendar**.
4. Enter **212** in Page Number, **Order Calendar** in Page and Region Names, keep region template to the default value *Plain (No Title)*, and click **Next**.
5. Enter the following SQL SELECT statement:

   select o.rowid, order_id, (select cust_first_name||' '||cust_last_name from demo_customers c where c.customer_id = o.customer_id) ||'
   ['||to_char(order_total,'FML999G999G999G999G990D00')||']' customer, order_timestamp
   from demo_orders o

6. Fill in the Calendar Attributes page as follows:

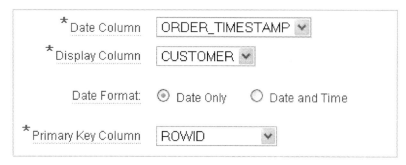

Figure 11-36

7. Set Link Details as shown below:

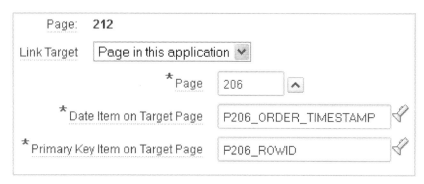

Figure 11-37

8. Click **Create** to finish the wizard.

Run the page to see the following output. The small blue circle in the second column in row number one indicates some orders on 1st July 2013. Click this column to show the two orders of Bradley Eugene. Click any of these orders to call Page 206 (Maintain Order), where you can perform all DML operations.

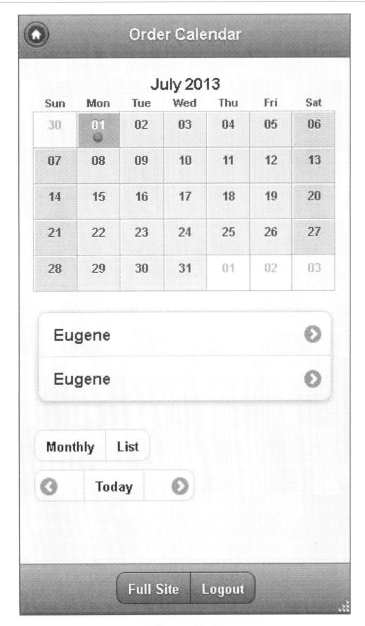

Figure 11-38

11.23 Summary

This concludes our efforts to create a web-based mobile application. As you saw, development of web applications for mobile platform is almost similar to creating one for the desktop. A unique thing that is worth mentioning at this stage is the use of copy page utility. You did use this utility in the desktop version to utilize metadata of existing application pages but, converting a desktop page for mobile use is icing on the cake.

This chapter opened an exciting door for you to create data-centric mobile applications for your organization with minimal coding. You can access both flavors of the application that were created in this book at the following URLs:

- Desktop Application URL: http://apex.oracle.com/pls/apex/f?p=1267
- Mobile Application URL: http://apex.oracle.com/pls/apex/f?p=1267:HOME_JQM_SMARTPHONE

Chapter 12
Deploy Application

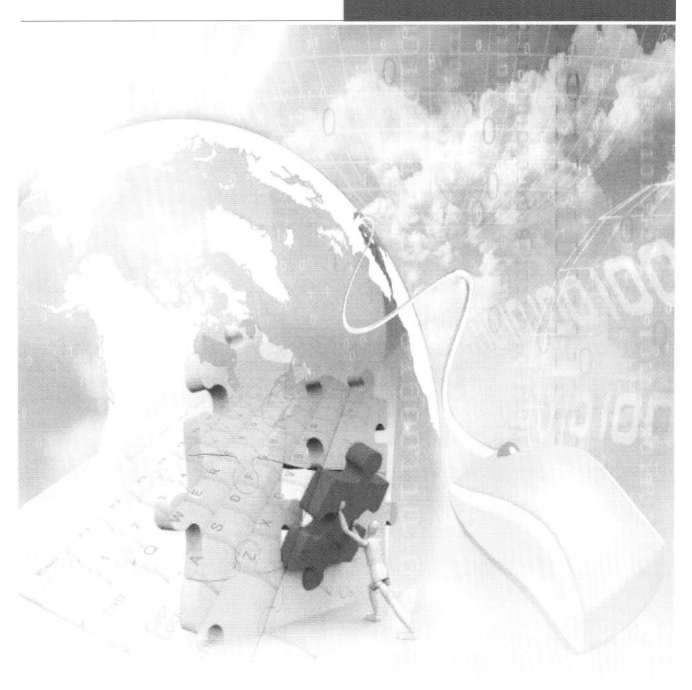

Chapter 12 – Deploy Application

12.1 About Application Deployment

APEX application deployment consists of two steps. Export the desired components to a script file, and import the script file into your production environment. Till now, you were running the application on your computer. Having completed the development phase, you will definitely run the application in a production environment. For this, you have to decide where and how the application will run. The following section provides you some deployment options to choose from.

No Deployment: The development environment becomes the production environment and nothing is moved to another computer. In this option users are provided just the URL to access application.

Application: You will use this option if the target computer is already running a production Oracle database with all underlying objects. You only need to export the application and import it into the target database.

Application and Table Structures: In this deployment option you have to create two scripts, one for your application and another for the database table structures using Generate DDL utility in SQL Workshop.

Application, Database Objects with Data: We are going to use this option to deploy our application along with all database objects and will utilize oracle's data pump utility to export data from the development machine to the production environment.

Individual Components: With the development phase going on, you can supplement your deployment plan with the export of selective components. We will see how this option can be used when we will export our application logo.

For simplicity, we will deploy the application on the same development computer using another schema and workspace to understand the deployment concept. The same technique is applicable to the production environment.

In this exercise the following tasks will be performed:

- Export application from the existing workspace (ASA).
- Export data from the existing Oracle schema (ASA) using Oracle's data pump utility.
- Export application logo to demonstrate selective component export.
- Create a new Workspace (ASACLONE) in the production environment to hold the application.
- Create a new Oracle schema (ASACLONE) to hold the application database objects (backed up in point 2).
- Access the application in LAN and through the Internet.

12.2 Export Application

The first step is to export the application that will be imported into a new workspace.

1. Login to the application and click the **Application Builder** icon.
2. Click the **Edit** button under **Sales Web Application**.
3. Click on the **Export/Import** icon as show in Figure 12-1.
4. On the ensuing page, click on the **Export** icon.
5. Set Application to **Sales Web Application**, File Format to **DOS**, Export Supporting Object Definitions to **No**, and click the **Export Application** button.
6. Select the **Save File** option and click the **OK** button. A file named **f101.sql** will be saved in the Download folder under My Documents.

Figure 12-1

File Format - Select how rows in the export file are formatted:
- Choose UNIX to have the resulting file contain rows delimited by line feeds.
- Choose DOS to have the resulting file contain rows delimited by carriage returns and line feeds.

Supporting Object Definitions include all configuration options and scripts and enable an application export to include database object definitions, image definitions, and seed data SQL statements encapsulated in a single file. The No option is selected because you will export and import all application definitions individually.

Chapter 12 – Deploy Application

12.3 Export Data

During the application development phase, we entered some seed data to test our work. Here we are going to export that data and other database objects to utilize them in our production environment. We will be using Oracle's export and import data pump utilities to achieve the task. Oracle Data Pump technology enables very high-speed movement of data and metadata from one database to another. It includes expdp and impdp utilities that enable the exporting and importing of data and metadata for a complete database or subsets of a database. In order to use this technology, you must first create a directory object it can access (step 4). The directory object is only a pointer to a physical directory, creating it does not actually create the physical directory on the file system of the database server. The physical directory is created in step 1 to store the generated physical files.

1. Using the OS utilities, create a folder named datapump under the database folder so that the path to this folder look like this: **C:\OracleXE\datapump**.

2. **Run the SQL Command Line** utility using Start | All Program | Oracle Database 11g Express Edition route.

3. On the SQL prompt type **connect system/manager** and press Enter. The connected message appears.

4. On the SQL prompt type **create directory datapump as 'c:\oraclexe\datapump';** and press Enter. Directory Created message will be displayed.

5. Open a command prompt using Start | Run. Type cmd in the Open box and click OK.

6. Type **cd c:\oraclexe\datapump** and press Enter. The prompt should look like **C:\OracleXE\datapump>**.

7. On this prompt, type **ExpDP system/manager schemas=ASA directory=datapump dumpfile=ASA.dmp logfile=ASAExp.log** and press Enter. The export process and the final success message are depicted in the following screen shot. The ExpDP utility exports all database object to ASA.DMP file that you can see under c:\oraclexe\datapump directory after the completion of this process. The second file ASAExp.log is a log file carrying export log information and holds similar information as shown in Figure 12-2.

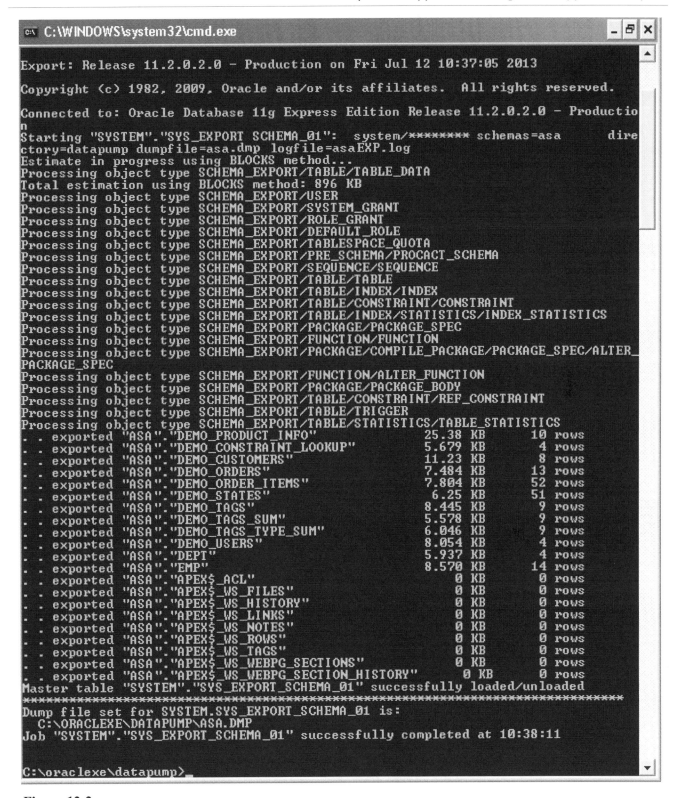

Figure 12-2

Chapter 12 – Deploy Application

12.4 Export Selective Component

In the following steps, you will export the application's logo to demonstrate how individual components can be exported in APEX.

1. On the main page of the application, click on the **Export/Import** icon again.
2. Select the **Export** option.
3. Click on the **Files** tab and then on the **Image** sub tab.
4. For *Export Images in Application*, select **Sales Web Application**. Set export File Format to **DOS**, and click the **Export Images** button. A dialog box comes up asking either to open or to save the file. Select the **Save File** option and click the **OK** button. A file **f101_img.sql** will be saved to your download folder.

12.5 Lock and Unlock Application

After finishing the development task, and applying patches received through users' feedback, it's a good practice to lock down your application to prevent users from accessing the development environment. In this exercise we are going to make the application unavailable for further modifications on the development computer by changing its *Build Status*. When an application's Build Status is set to Run and Build Application, developers in the application's workspace may use the Application Builder to edit and alter the application definition. When an application's Build Status is set to Run Application Only, the Application Builder can see that the application exists but the details cannot be viewed or edited in any way. It can be run by end users.

1. Click the **Application Builder** icon.
2. Select **Sales Web Application**.
3. Click on **Shared Components**.
4. Click **Edit Definition** link under the Application section in the right sidebar.
5. Click on **Availability** tab.
6. Change Build Status to **Run Application Only**.
7. Click **Apply Changes**.

If required in future, the following steps will be performed to unlock the locked application.

1. Enter **http://localhost:8080/apex/apex_admin** in the browser.
2. Provide Admin username and password.
3. Click the **Manage Workspace** icon as indicated in Figure 12-3.

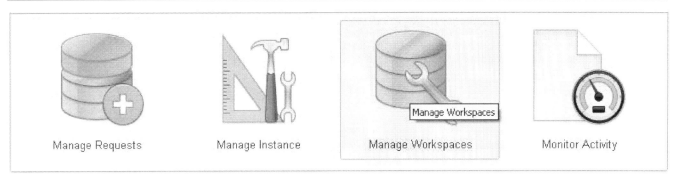

Figure 12-3

4. In Manage Applications section, click **Build Status**.
5. Click the application's **Edit** link (see Figure 12-4) to unlock. Set Build Status to **Run and Build Application**.
6. Click **Apply Changes**.
7. **Logout** from the APEX admin interface.
8. Enter **http://localhost:8080/apex/** in your browser.
9. Login to the workspace (ASA).
10. Click **Application Builder**. The application icon is changed and now you can modify the application.

Edit	Workspace	Application	Application Name	Parsing Schema	Build Status
✏	ASA	101	Sales Web Application	ASA	Run and Build Application

Figure 12-4

12.6 Create a New Workspace

In the production environment, you need a new workspace to import the application.

1. Enter **http://localhost:8080/apex/apex_admin** in your browser to access the administration page.
2. Enter administrative credentials.
3. Select the **Manage Workspaces** option.
4. Click the link **Create Workspace** under Workspace Actions.
5. Enter **ASACLONE** in Workspace Name and click **Next**.
6. Select **No** for Re-use existing schema, enter **ASACLONE** in Schema Name, enter **asaclone** in Schema Password, and click **Next**. This will create a new Oracle schema.
7. In Administrator Username type **ADMIN**, enter **123** in Administrator Password, **abc@abc.com** in email, and click **Next**.
8. Click **Create Workspace** button.
9. The next screen indicates successful provision of the workspace. Click **Done**.
10. Click the **Logout** link.

Chapter 12 – Deploy Application

12.7 Import Application

We have successfully created the workspace. Now it's time to import the application into the newly created workspace.

1. Enter **http://localhost:8080/apex** in your browser.
2. Enter **ASACLONE, Admin, 123** for Workspace, Username and Password respectively and click the Login button.
3. Change Password form appears. Enter **123** in Enter Current Password and **asaclone** both in New Password and Confirmation boxes. Click **Apply Changes**.
4. Click the **Return** button to move back to the main login page to enter the workspace using the current password.
5. Enter **ASACLONE, Admin,** and **asaclone** and click the **Login** button.
6. Click the **Application Builder** icon.
7. Select the **Export/Import** utility.
8. Click the **Browse** button and select **f101.sql** file (created in section 12.2), leave File Type to the default **Database Application, Page or Component Export** and click **Next**.
9. A message, The export file has been imported successfully appears. Click **Next**.
10. Select **ASACLONE** for Parsing Schema, select **Auto Assign New Application ID** for Install As Application.
11. Click the **Install** button.
12. In the next screen, click on **Run Application** icon.
13. Enter **DEMO** in Username, **asaclone** in Password, and click login.

At first glance you will notice:

- No Logo.
- Existence of Developer Toolbar, which should not appear in a deployed application.
- Data that we entered in the source application does not exist.

In the next sections you will address the above shortfalls.

12.8 Import the Application Logo

You have successfully imported the application but without the logo. Remember that we exported the logo to a separate file f101_img.sql in section 12.4. Here you will import that file to display the logo.

1. Click on the **Export/Import** icon and select the **Import** option.
2. Using the Browse button, select **f101_img.sql** file.
3. Select the option **Image Export** and click **Next**.
4. Click **Next**.
5. In Install Image select **Sales Web Application**.
6. Click **Install Image** button.
7. Click the **Application Builder** tab.
8. Click **Sales Web Application**.
9. Click **Run Application**. The logo appears.

12.9 Remove Developers Toolbar

We used the Developers Toolbar throughout this book to access the application source. In this exercise we are going to prevent users from modifying the application by suppressing the toolbar.

1. Click the **Application101** button in the Developers Toolbar.
2. Click on **Shared Components**.
3. Click **Globalization Attributes** link.
4. Click the **Definition** tab.
5. Scroll down to **Availability section**, set Build Status to **Run Application Only**.
6. Click **Apply Changes**.
7. Open another session of your browser and type **http://localhost:8080/apex/f?p=101**. The Developer Toolbar is disappeared and users cannot access the application source.
8. Close all browser windows.

12.10 Import Data

While creating the workspace ASACLONE we created a database schema with the same name to hold database objects (section 12.6 step 6). APEX not only created the schema but also created the default tables. Right now, the deployed application is using the default data. In section 12.3 of this chapter we exported data from the development environment. Our last task is to retrieve that data to complete our deployment task.

1. Open the **SQL Command Line** utility and type **connect system/manager**, press **Enter**.
2. Type **drop user ASACLONE cascade;** and press **Enter**.
3. Type **create user ASACLONE identified by clone default tablespace users;** and press **Enter**. User Created message appears.
4. Type **grant connect, resource to ASACLONE;** and press **Enter**. Grant Succeeded message is displayed.
5. Open a **Windows command prompt**.
6. Type **cd c:\oraclexe\datapump** and press **Enter**. While importing data on a production server, the datapump directory must be created as described in section 12.3 and must have the .dmp file.
7. Type **ImpDP system/manager remap_schema=ASA:ASAclone remap_tablespace=ASA:Users directory=datapump dumpfile=ASA.dmp logfile=ASAimport.log** and press **Enter**. All the objects will be imported.
8. Open a new browser session and type **http://localhost:8080/apex/f?p=101**
9. In Username type **demo** and **asaclone** in the password. The Invalid Login Credentials message appears, indicating that the default tables have been replaced by those imported from the development environment. Type **demo** in the password. You'll be logged in. Move within the application and see the data you entered in your development computer.

That's it. We have successfully deployed our application on the same computer but in a different workspace and schema. You can apply the same procedure to deploy the application in another environment. In the next section, you will try to connect this application in a LAN environment as well as from the Internet. It is assumed that you have deployed the application on a computer having two network interface cards with static IPs. One connected to the local area network, and the other connected to a DSL modem.

12.11 Accessing the Application

The following figure depicts a scenario to access the application in an office LAN and through the Internet. This scenario assumes that you have a computer to act as the application server, with the following components:

- Windows XP or higher OS
- Oracle Express Edition (XE) 11g
- Sales Web Application deployed and running locally
- Two network interface cards, with static IP, connected to local area network and the Internet

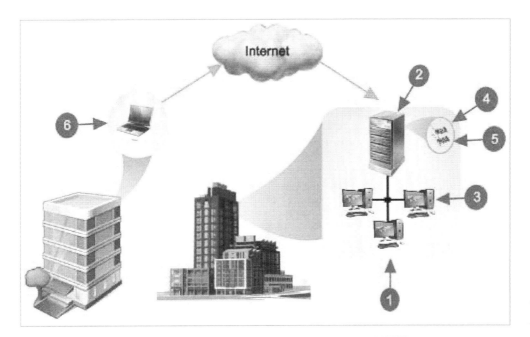

Figure 12-5 Local and remote clients connected to Oracle APEX server

1. Office LAN
2. Database Server
3. LAN Clients
4. NIC-1 with static local IP 10.1.1.12
5. NIC-2 with static external IP 255.266.204.231
6. Remote Client

> **Be Careful:** The scenario presented in this section is intended for demonstration purpose only and should not be used in a production environment. You are currently running the application under the EPG architecture, which is not recommended for Internet applications. Using the procedure defined in earlier sections, you can test your work in a more secured environment. Follow the link to open a free trial account on Oracle Database Cloud Service:
> https://cloud.oracle.com/mycloud/f?p=service:home:0

Chapter 12 – Deploy Application

Perform the following steps to get the IP addresses of the server computer. In this scenario, we will be using 10.1.1.12 for the LAN and 255.266.204.231 for the Internet.

1. Right-click the **LAN connection** in the task bar and click **Open Network Connections**.

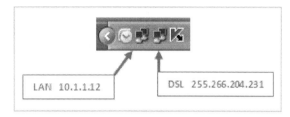

Figure 12-6

2. Right-click the Local Area Network connection and click **Properties**.
3. Select **Internet Protocol (TCP/IP)** in the list and click the **Properties** button.
4. Note down the IP address.
5. Repeat the same process and write down the external IP address for the Internet.

12.11.1 Connect to application in Local Area Network (LAN)

From a client computer in your LAN:

1. Open a browser session and type http://10.1.1.12:8080/apex/f?p=117 (replace 117 with your application ID)
2. Type **demo, demo** for the Username and Password, respectively

You may get an error message at this stage as show in Figure 12-5, indicating your computer or network is protected by a firewall. If so, you need to create an exception in the Windows Firewall to accept incoming connection on the APEX port, that is 8080 in our scenario.

The connection has timed out

The server at 10.1.1.12 is taking too long to respond.

- The site could be temporarily unavailable or too busy. Try again in a few moments.
- If you are unable to load any pages, check your computer's network connection.
- If your computer or network is protected by a firewall or proxy, make sure that Firefox is permitted to access the Web.

Try Again

Figure 12-7

1. In Windows, click **Start**, click on **Control Panel**, and double click the **Windows Firewall** icon.
2. Click on the **Exceptions** tab.
3. Click the **Add Port** button.
4. Type **APEX Port** in Name, **8080** in Number, select **TCP** and click **OK**.
5. Click **OK** to close the Windows Firewall dialog box. APEX Port exception is added to the Program and Services section which will now allow you to access the application.

12.11.2 Connect to application through the Internet

Perform the following steps on a computer connected to the Internet and **NOT** connected to your LAN:

1. Open a browser session and type **http:// 255.266.204.231:8080/apex/f?p=117** (replace 117 with your application ID).
2. Type **demo, demo** for the Username and Password, respectively. This time you will connect to the same application server, over the Internet.

12.11.3 Dealing with Firewalls

If your application server is behind a firewall such as ISA, you will have to create a protocol for APEX port 8080 with an allow rule to grant remote access to the APEX application. Follow the instructions to create the rule:

1. Open **ISA Server Management**.
2. On the right side, click **Toolbox | Protocols** and then **User-Defined**.
3. With User-Defined selected, click **New > Protocol**.
4. In Protocol definition name type **APEX PROTOCOL** and click **Next**.
5. Select **TCP** for Protocol type, **Outbound** for Direction and enter **8080** in From and To boxes.
6. Click **OK**.
7. Click **Next**.
8. Accept the default value **No** for Do you want to use secondary connections?
9. Click **Next** and then the **Finish** button.
10. On the left side, **right-click Firewall Policy** and select **New | Access Rule**.
11. In Access rule name type **APEX ALLOW RULE** and click **Next**.
12. Select **Allow** and click **Next**.
13. Set This rule applies to: to **Selected protocols**, click the **Add** button, expand the User-Defined node and select **APEX PROTOCOL**, click **Next**.
14. Click the **Add** button in Access Rule Sources, open the Networks node, select **External** and click **Next**.
15. Click the **Add** button in Access Rule Destinations, open the Networks node, select **Local Host** and click **Next**.
16. Click **Next** to accept All Users.
17. Click **Finish**.

If you followed the instructions correctly, you will definitely access the application internally as well as remotely. This chapter taught you the implementation process of your application. You saw how easy it was to take the application from your development PC to the production environment. Besides application access scenario, we also resolved the firewall issues that might prevent you from accessing the application internally, as well as from a remote location.

12.12 Conclusion

Oracle Application Express has come a long way from its simple beginning. With the addition of new features in every release it provides so much possibilities and promises for today and for the days to come. I hope this book has provided you a solid foundation of Oracle Application Express and set a firm ground to develop robust application systems to fulfill the information requirements of your organization. The sky is the limit, you are limited by your imagination. Be creative, and put the power of APEX to your work. Good luck!

ABOUT THE AUTHOR

Riaz Ahmed is an IT professional with over twenty years of hard-earned experience. He started his career as a programmer in early 90's and is currently working as the head of IT with a reputed group of companies. His areas of interest include web-based development technologies. Prior to this book, he wrote "Create Rapid Web Applications Using Oracle Application Express" (1st Edition), "Implement Oracle Business Intelligence (Volume I)", and "The Web Book - Build Static and Dynamic Websites". You can reach him at:

E-mail: realtech@cyber.net.pk
Website: www.creating-website.com
Blog: http://Oracle-Tutorial-Books.blogspot.com
Errata: http://oracle-apex-book.blogspot.com/2013/09/errata-create-rapid-web-applications.html

Implement Oracle
Business Intelligence

**Analyze the Past
Streamline the Present
Control the Future**

http://www.amazon.com/Implement-Oracle-Business-Intelligence-Volume/dp/1475122012

The Web Book -
Build Static and Dynamic Websites

The ultimate resource to build static and dynamic websites

http://www.creating-website.com

Download Book Code → http://www.creating-website.com/ApexBookCode.rar

INDEX

Symbols
\# input mask placeholder 126
\# special substitution string 140
: bind variable 144,201
|| concatenation operator 118
< less than operator 161
> greater than operator 160

-A-

Accept Page process 29
Access Control (page) 27
Actions menu 6,8,119,137
add order 3
advanced reporting 13
After Row attribute 140
aggregation 27
Alternative Report *see Interactive Reports*
Android 295
APEX_UTIL package 136,196,234
    defined 205
application
    access (local/remote) 363
    control access 27,52
    convert 23
    create 23,63
    deployment 59,354
    export 23,354-355
    import 23,354,360
    lock/unlock 358-359
    migrate 23
    repository 23
    translating in other languages 36
    Websheet 23
Application Builder 23,26-27
Application Express (APEX)
    application components and controls 49
    application deployment 59,354
    application types 26
    architecture 54
    authentication scheme 83
    collections 186,197,205-206,214-215
    core development languages 2
    database support 57
    engine 25,29
    environment 25,58
    introduction and concepts 20,22
    migrate 24
    port 60,364-365
    send email 52
    upgrade 61
    URL 95
    URL syntax 40

Application Globalization 36
audit trail 24
authentication
    create Custom Scheme 83
    APEX engine task 25
authorization
    {NOT} scheme 84
    Admin Users scheme 84,112,282,285,292
    Allow Product Modification scheme 85,142-143
    APEX engine task 25
    Verify Order Ownership scheme 85,172
Average (Interactive Report function) 164,166

-B-

backup 24
Bar Chart 5
Before Rows attribute 139
bind variable 44,144
BlackBerry 295
BLOB columns 133,147,313,323
Boolean 144
branch 22
    create 128,149,170,218
    defined 32
    process 171
    utilize 108
breadcrumb 4,26,81
    defined 33
break
    column 121,123
    report 27
browser 2,25
    Apple Safari 25
    Google Chrome 25
    Microsoft Internet Explorer 25
    Mozilla Firefox 25
bugs 23
built-in features 2
business logic 22

INDEX

buttons 4,26
    Add Customer 108
    Add/View Orders 110
    Add/View Products 109
    defined 30
    run report 270,275
    View Customers 5,107
    View Order for this Month 106

- C -

C# (C-Sharp) 295
calendar 12,26-27
    create 242
    defined 50
    types 242
Cascading Style Sheet (CSS) 2,22,25,139,172,302
    apexir 139
    built-in classes 106-110,198
    defined 191-192
Categories 5
chart 5,12,22,26-27,163
    color scheme 97-98
    defined 51
    MS Word plug-in 267
    syntax 99
Chart View 163,166
checkbox 22,26
Classic Reports
    created 100,102,121,141,221,225
    defined 39
    mobile platform 318
clear cache 41,46-47
client 22
    devices 2
    software 24
    technologies 2
code generation 22
Collection (APEX)
    Add Product to Order Collection process 214
    add_member() function 205,214
    create or truncate 186
    defined 206
    delete_member() function 208,215
    fetch values 197
    Remove Product from Order Collection process 215
column
    arrange in desired order 137
    BLOB 133,147
    hide 103,119
    ROWID 156
    set headings 158,174,221,225,283,319
Column Link 101,103,122,282,319
Component View 28
computation 27
    defined 32
    perform 164,266

Condition Type attribute 75
Control Break 160,165
convert application 23
Count (Interactive Report function) 164
count() function 86
Counter Column 323
create
    application 23
    table 70
Create Application Wizard 26
CUSTOM_HASH/CUSTOM_AUTH functions 68-69,83
customers management 3,114
    create new 5
    view and edit 6

- D -

dashboard (create) 112
data
    export 356
    grid 26
    import 362
    present graphically 112,230,341
    structured/unstructured 26
data entry forms 22
data manipulation 22
Data Manipulation process types 177
Data Workshop 23
database 2,5,22
    application objects 68
    browse objects 23
    functions 68
database application 26
datapump 354,356
date picker 22,26,157
dbms_lob (database package) 136,144,173,220
debug 41
decisions 3
declarative development 2,20,22
decode() function 118,136,173
delete (declarative process) 117,135,280,318
departmental database applications 22
deploy data-centric web application 2,59,354
desktop application 2
Detail View 138
developer toolbar 4,120,360
    remove 361
development environment 25
devices 2-3
Dial Chart 5
Display Extra Values (attribute) 125
Display Null Value (attribute) 125
Display Point 30
drill-down 12,20,22,112
    in charts 99

INDEX

Dynamic Actions
    create 186,329
    defined 31
dynamic data-driven web applications 23
Dynamic List 34
dynamic list of values (LOV) 88
multi-user desktop database applications 22

- E -

e-mail 52
Embedded PL/SQL Gateway (EPG) 56
escape_sc function 88,175,195-199
export
    application 23,354-355
    repository 23
    selective components 358

- F -

feedback 27
filters (report) 27
Find 53
firewall 36,364-365
Flash chart 5,27,51,98-99,233
For Each Row attribute 140
FOR loop 144,196
    defined 200
form 26
    controls 22
    definition and types 49
    handlers 2
    Master/Detail 154,156,318
Format Mask attribute 173
    Date 325
format numbers 204
framework 22
function (database object) 23,68
function (custom) 8

- G -

Generate DDL 23
get_blog_file_src function 136,220
getlength() function 136,144,173,220
Global Page 28
graphical
    mobile reports 19-20
    presentation 5
    reports 12,230,341
grid layout 97-100,102,104,137,144,330
Group By View 164,167

- H -

hidden item 111,126
highlight (in report) 27,160-161,266
HTML 5 chart 27,51,97
HTP/HTF packages 88,175,195-198,199
HTTP 36
Hyper Text Markup Language (HTML) 2,13,22,25
    <a> 140,196
    <b/> 175,195-198
    <b> 175
    <div> 202
    <h1> 140
    <img> 136,173
    <p> 195-198
    <span> 196
    <strong> 140,195-198
    <style> 139
    <table> 139
    <tbody> 196
    <td> 140,172,196
    <th> 196-198
    <thead> 196
    <title> 96
    <tr> 140,196-198
    using in PL/SQL code 198
hypertext links 26

- I -

Icon View 138
IF-THEN-ELSE statement 86,119,144,198,209
images 8,35,91
    delete 145,149
    display 148,220
    export 358
    import 361
    show in mobile application 313,323
import
    application 23,354,360
initcap() function 88
input mask 126
insert (declarative process) 117,135,280,318
interactive report 6,27,115
    Alternative 38,160,164
    defined 37
    format 122
    operators and filters 105
    Primary 10,38,138,159
    Private 38
    Public 38,159,165
interactive web applications 2
Internet 2,354,363-365
Intranet 2

INDEX

iOS 295
IP address 364
IR string 104-105
Item
    defined 31
    hidden 111,126
    hide and show 186
itemNames/itemValues 41

-J-
Java 295
JavaScript 2,22,25,31,52,196,209
jQuery Mobile 3,27,294

-L-
Link Target attribute 322
links
    column 101,103
    hypertext 26
    icon 136
    mobile reports 343
    to additional details 5,112
list of values (LOV) 26
    Cascading LOV 328
    Categories LOV 87,146,316
    defined 33
    New or Existing Customer LOV 89,185
    Products with Price LOV 88,173
    States LOV 88,125,310
    Static 328-329
    Y or N LOV 89,146,282,316
List View 322
Listener (Apex Listener) 55
lists 26
    defined 33
    Desktop Reports List 77,231
    Mobile Reports List 78,341
    Order Wizard List 79,183,211,225
    static 301,304
Local Area Network (LAN) 354,363-364
login 27,71
logo 4,91,360-361

-M-
Manage Users and Groups 23
map 12,26-27
    create 245
    defined 50
    SQL syntax 245
markup language 2
Master/Detail form 154,156,318
max() function 136

message 127,286
metadata 2,22
Microsoft Access 23
Microsoft Excel 13,24
Microsoft Word 13,264
migrate 24
mobile application 2-3,52,294
    Advanced Formatting 307
    copy page from desktop application 330,333,338
    create interface 296
    Customers page 16,306-310
    Global page 296,301
    Grid Layout 330
    Home page 304
    languages 295
    link to custom target 343
    link to other page 307
    login page 15,300
    main menu 15,304-305
    Order Calendar 19,350
    Orders page 18,318-340
    Products page 17,312-317
    Reports page 19,341-349
    search 313
    show image 313
    style pages 302-303
    types (Web-Based/Native) 294-295
    URL (Home/Login page) 296
mobile devices 3
mobile operating systems 295
mobile page transitions 3
mobile-based interface 3
mod_plsql 55
Multi Row Delete (MRD) process 178
Multi Row Update (MRU) process 178,284

-N-
Native (On-Device) mobile applications 295
    pros and cons 295
navigation 22
    bar 4,26,34
    control 2,26
    create 81
network services in Oracle Database 259
Number/Date Format 123,159
nvl() function 100,136,144

INDEX

-O-

Object Browser 23
Objective-C 295
Oracle BI Publisher 39
    BI Publisher Desktop 262
    configure as a print server 259
    download and install 258
Oracle Forms 23
Oracle HTTP Server 55
Oracle XE Database 56
    download and install 60

-P-

package (database object) 23,88,136
Packaged Applications 53
Page (desktop application)
    access control 27
    alias 42,81
    area utilization 8
    blank 27,190,219
    copy 181
    Customers Page 5-6
    form 27
    Global 28,231
    Home Page 4,94
    login 27
    Manage Users 280
    Map report 245
    Order Calendar 242
    Order Summary 223
    Order Tree 248
    Orders Page 5,10,154
    Product Info 219
    Products Setup 8,132
    report 27
    Reset Password 285
    what is a page? 27
Page Definition 2,28
page processing 25,28,32
page rendering 22,25,28-29
    Add Product to Order Collection process 214
    Place Order process 216
password
    obfuscated 14
    reset 14,285
PDF 13,39,261,263-265
PHP: Hypertext Preprocessor (PHP) 2
Pie Chart 5
pivot table 268
PL/SQL 2,22-23,86,127,144
    code explanation 201
    defined 194
    using with HTML 198

plug-ins 26-27,36
    CSS Bar Chart plug-in 90,104
    Masked Field plug-in 90,126
prepare_url() function 196-197,234
    defined 205
Primary Interactive Report 38,159
primary key 117,119,318
Private Interactive Report 38
Processes (defined) 31-32
production environment 25
productivity 3
products 3
    create new 5
    view and edit 8
programming language 2
property sheets 22
Public Interactive Report 38
Public/Private Cloud 58

-Q-

Query Builder 23

-R-

radio group 22,26,146,185
Rapid Application Development (RAD) 2
regions 4-5,26,29
    control positioning 30
    hide and show 121,187
    multiple regions 8,20,112
    Sales by Category 5,99
    Sales by Product 5,98
    set condition 122
    This Month's Sales 5,96
    Top Customers 5,100
    Top Orders by Date 5,104
    Top Products 5,102
Report Layouts 269
Report Queries 263,269,273
Report View 160,165
reports 2,12-13,22,26
    advanced 256
    commercial invoice 273
    custom layout 39
    defined 37
    graphical (desktop) 230
    graphical (mobile) 341
    Monthly Order Review 263
    upload template to APEX 269,274
REQUEST 31,40
    ADD (item to cart) 197,205,214
    REMOVE (item from cart) 197,208,215
    report 270,275

INDEX

Required (template) 125
RESTful Services 23,35
Rich Text Format (RTF) 39,264,269,274
RIR string 104-105
ROWID pseudo column 156
runtime environment 25

- S -

Sales Web Application 59
schema 22,354
    comparison 23
    defined 62
screen dimensions 3
scripting language 2,22
search
    capability 26
security
    defined 34
Select List 22,325
SELECT SQL statement 84,85,86,88,97-100,102,104,111,118,121,319,322
sequence (database object) 117,135,156,281
server 2,22
session state 23,25-26,322
    defined 43
    merge with table data 325
Shared Components 26,28
    create 74
    defined 33
Shortcut 35
    Delete_Confirm_Msg 182
Show Page 29
shuttles 22
smartphones 3,15
SOAP 36
software 2,23
sort
    defined 162
    interactive report 6,10,27,159
SQL based reporting application 22
SQL Command 23,306,356
SQL Lite 295
SQL script file 23
SQL Scripts 23
SQL Update action 324
SQL Workshop 23,354
Static List 34,301
static list of values (LOV) 87,89
Structured Query Language (SQL) 2,5,8,20,22,23
Submit a page 31
substitution string 40
    defined 48
sum() function 97-100,102,104,136
swipe 3
sysdate 97

- T -

tables (database object) 2,23
tablets 3,15
tabs 4,26
    Administration 14,281
    create 75
    Customers 3,116
    defined 33
    hide 292
    Home 3
    Orders 3,157,181,190
    Products 3,134
    Reports 3,12,232
Tabular Form 177-178,280
    add row 177,284
    alternate approach for mobile platform 324
tap 3
Team Development 23
template 30
text editors 22
text field 26
themes 2-3
    defined 34
to_char() function 97,102,104,111,158,196
to_date() function 97,111,158
tree 12,26-27
    create 248
    defined 50
    SQL syntax 251
Tree View 28
trim() function 196
trunc() function 104,158

- U -

UNION set operator 252,325
update (declarative process) 117,135,280,318
Update (SQL) action 324
update order 3
upload
    images 35
    static files 35
upper() function 325
users
    APEX Administrator 71
    Application Administrator 14
    Demo 71
    Test 71
    Workspace Administrator 71
Users Management 14,280

INDEX

- V -
view order 3
validate input 210
validation 25
    Can't Delete Customer with Orders 127
    Check Credit Limit 127
    Customer ID Not Null 187
    defined 32,127
    First Name Not Null 188
    item level 187-188
    page level 127
    Phone Number Format 188
Value Required (attribute) 125
view (database object) 23
views (icon, report, detail) 8,138

- W -
web applications
    add more functionalities 2
    benefits in Oracle APEX 2-3
    core technologies 2
    deploy 2
    popularity and access requirement 2
    update and maintain 2
web page *see page*
Web Services 23,26,35
Web-Based mobile applications 294
    pros and cons 295
Websheet Application 23,26
Windows Mobile 295
wizards (built-in) 2,22
    Create Application 26
    Form on a Table with Report 18
    Report 27
workspace 23,354
    administration 23
    create 62,359

- X -
XML (Extensible Markup Language) 36,39
XML Data 263-264,274
XSS (Cross Site Scripting) attack 88,199

66553621R00217

Made in the USA
San Bernardino, CA
13 January 2018